THE RECOVERY OF FAMILY LIFE

THE RECOVERY OF FAMILY LIFE

Exposing the Limits of Modern Ideologies

SCOTT YENOR

BAYLOR UNIVERSITY PRESS

Cover and book design by Kasey McBeath, Baylor University Press

Library of Congress Cataloging-in-Publication Data
Names: Yenor, Scott, 1970- author.
Title: The recovery of family life : exposing the limits of modern
  ideologies / Scott Yenor.
Description: Waco : Baylor University Press, 2020. | Includes
  bibliographical references and index. | Summary: "Argues that the
  "rolling revolution" of contemporary liberalism undermines family life
  and marriage with a false vision of the human condition"-- Provided by
  publisher.
Identifiers: LCCN 2020020290 (print) | LCCN 2020020291 (ebook) | ISBN
  9781481312820 (hardcover) | ISBN 9781481313292 | ISBN 9781481313285
  (mobi) | ISBN 9781481312844 (epub)
Subjects: LCSH: Families--Psychological aspects. | Families. | Marriage. |
  Family policy.
Classification: LCC HQ519 .Y35 2020 (print) | LCC HQ519 (ebook) | DDC
  306.85--dc23
LC record available at https://lccn.loc.gov/2020020290
LC ebook record available at https://lccn.loc.gov/2020020291

NATIONAL
ENDOWMENT
FOR THE
HUMANITIES

The Recovery of Family Life has been made possible in part by a major grant from the National Endowment for the Humanities: Exploring the human endeavor. Any views, findings, conclusions, or recommendations expressed in this book do not necessarily represent those of the National Endowment for the Humanities.

Printed in the United States of America on acid-free paper with a minimum of thirty percent recycled content.

To Amy

CONTENTS

PREFACE AND ACKNOWLEDGMENTS

Near the onset of his *Democracy in America*, Tocqueville recognizes the rise of democracy as a "providential fact," in that it is nearly universal (especially in the Western, modern world), enduring, and seems to escape human control. Tocqueville praises the Americans for containing that democratic revolution within bounds so that the equality that democracy brings is consistent with genuine human flourishing. He especially praises the American family, supported through a relatively moralistic public opinion and a healthy respect for the differences between men and women, as promoting satisfying, communal lives in an otherwise quite individualistic world.

The Sexual Revolution, afoot since the 1950s, at least, shows that Tocqueville may have been too optimistic about the good sense of the Americans. Public opinion is no longer as family and marriage friendly. A healthy respect for sex difference can hardly be mentioned in polite company among the nation's elite. The mores surrounding sound marital practices have been upset in a concerted effort to promote greater individualism and liberty, among other things. In fact, this Sexual Revolution appears to be the culmination of the democratic revolution that filled Tocqueville with a sort of religious dread. The Sexual Revolution seems, like the democratic revolution, to be universal and almost providential as its revolution rolls on and on. We are still only in the infancy of this Sexual Revolution. We proceed without a frame of reference or adequate knowledge of what Sexual Revolution is, and we often lament or praise what the revolution has accomplished without turning our eyes to what remains to be done in its name.

This book is an attempt to show where the Sexual Revolution is heading—which is onward toward an abolition of marriage and the family. This is an extreme statement, and few today express such a goal. I hope to show that the incremental reforms of the revolutionaries point toward the abolition of marriage and the family and, further, that the revolutionaries entertain no principle that could restrain that abolition. Their principles and premises point to a never-ending revolution in marriage and family life—I call it a rolling revolution. This seemingly irresistible revolution continues to advance amidst the ruins of what it has destroyed.

This book also attempts to show where this revolution falls short of understanding the human condition and hence to identify the limits to its rolling revolution. In any event, some account of this revolution from outside its dogmas is indispensable for understanding our times. Perhaps ours is a time when the interests of philosophy and politics meet—when the attempt to step outside our cave and pursue the truth about the human condition is also politically necessary. I seek to appeal to all who would understand the human situation instead of those who would simply apply the "modern" or pursue the revolution. I also hope that revolutionaries who have forgotten or never knew their principles or reject the destination of the radical revolution may find reason for pause in what follows. Today's lukewarm reformers may not recognize the revolution as their own: my analysis encourages them to ask about the grounds of their seeming moderation.

I cannot guarantee that I have sympathetically understood all aspects of the Sexual Revolution. There are genuine questions of evidence on this. The testimony of later thinkers is rarely as deep or penetrating as the founders of these movements. It may appear that I have smeared today's moderate advocates for the Sexual Revolution with the principles and arguments of yesterday's unseemly, radical thinkers. That is far from my intention. Several insights inform my approach. Seemingly moderate advocates have real interests in hiding all the implications of their policies and thoughts, for fear that today's somewhat popular aspirations will betray the larger, less popular project. Sexual revolutionaries have every interest in misunderstanding and misrepresenting thoughts and ways inconsistent with their goals. I take every care to present the thinkers of what I call the rolling revolution as they would understand themselves and to identify the kernels and more than kernels of truth in their modes of thinking. It has been a painful undertaking to get underneath the Old Wisdom that the rolling revolution would displace. I have sought to understand this Old Wisdom just as sympathetically as I approach the new.

Nothing will be easier to criticize than this book. It treats a great diversity of objects. Future readers may be able to cite isolated facts that contradict specific arguments. They will be able to point to omissions and a lack of learning or social science in various parts. They will be able to accuse me of a lack of charity in my attempt to articulate a particular point of view. Vantage points may differ. I try to maintain a "civilizational" perspective while others are more concerned with recent obstacles and advances. I hope readers will judge the general thrust of this work and its general thesis and be willing to forgive what might appear to be sins of omission or commission in the particular parts.

No work of this scope can be completed without many conversations and arguments, mostly among sympathetic friends but also with those who disagree. Several institutions helped. Boise State University and my then-Chairman, Brian Wampler, provided a sabbatical during the 2015–2016 academic year. I spent that year at the Heritage Foundation, where David Azerrad and Arthur Milikh, my bosses in the Simon Center for Principles and Politics, pushed me to sharpen my thinking and clarify my writing on the family. Some chapters in this book began as First Principles essays I wrote for Heritage. More importantly, the time at Heritage allowed me to think this book's framework into being. Since my time there these friends have pushed me to see more and further. Baylor University Press, first under the directorship of Carey Newman and now under the leadership of David Aycock and my handler, Cade Jarrell, has provided thorough reader reports and allowed me the space I needed to pursue this argument. Speaking engagements at several universities and other places have also helped me to sharpen my ways of thinking.

Many others have prodded me to think through my argument and its application to our present condition or have helped me bring this manuscript to completion. I hesitate to mention any by name, in part for fear of omitting anyone and in part to protect the names of the innocent. I alone am responsible for the analysis that follows. To my friends, teachers, students, and interlocutors—continue to enjoy the gift of life, to use our precious freedoms, and please know that I am grateful.

I am most grateful to my family. As I completed my first book, my young daughter Sarah had just survived cancer; she is now nearing twenty as I publish this book. Four of my children—Jackson, Travis, Sarah, and Paul—have grown up to honorable adulthood, and Jackson has married a wonderful young woman, Leah. One more child—Mark—sits on the cusp of being a teenager. Having and raising these five children with Amy, my wife of over twenty-five years, has been a singularly enriching experience and a great adventure. Sarah's illness was the trial of our lives (so far!). We have both come to realize that human beings are never really freed from trial and that there is no garden of perfect peace and contentment in this life. The trip together is beautiful, but the destination lies beyond. Take this book, Amy, as an emblem of my love for you and ours and my vow to honor and cherish you until death does us part.

1

OUR NEW FAMILY REGIME?

A sexual revolution is taking place among us; all see it, but all do not judge it in the same way. Some celebrate this revolution as the fulfillment of the democratic and modern promise, and seek more ways to deepen and extend it. For these advocates the revolution represents being on the "right side of history." They judge all proposals for change by whether they keep the revolution rolling. Others think or affect to think that the great revolution is a product of happy accidents ("the '60s" or "the pill"), but sinister forces could rally to reverse it in a backlash so it is crucial to be forward in defense of yesterday's gains. Others see the sexual revolution as an element of an irreversible democratic revolution, and they despair of all efforts to limit the revolution; they retreat or plan a retreat from this new world. Others see the *seemingly* irresistible march of the sexual revolution as part of the democratic revolution, but see how that revolution ignores many human goods and undermines human thriving and political prosperity.

This last perspective animates this book. To arrive at this perspective is difficult, since few pursue philosophic knowledge about the nature of marriage and family life. People are mostly concerned with *today's* controversies, finding little time and energy to invest in deeper understanding about what political communities should seek to accomplish with marriage and family life and what marriage and family life are. Those claiming philosophic knowledge spend their energy working out the principles of our *public* philosophy, where human things are susceptible to remaking according to our arbitrary

1

human wills. These pretended philosophers of family life conjure ways to establish greater human liberation or autonomy—and leave behind the old marriage and family life.

A better philosophy recognizes that the human world is not infinitely plastic. Human nature, marriage, and family life cannot be made, unmade, and remade according to any reformer's fancy, to achieve the goods that reformer would like. All ways of organizing marriage and family life involve costs and compromises. We may not always be able to see those costs and compromises and we may not always look, but the logic of nature is there, in what we do and what we leave undone. The beginning of wisdom about marriage and the family involves knowing what challenges of nature they respond to. The irreducible core of marriage and family life centers on sex, procreation, education of children, and an adult dyad (at least) who bear common responsibilities. There is also a predictable structure to how the goods of marriage and family relate, though there is not perfect support in nature for how goods are structured. The logic of nature limits how marriage and family life are lived in a particular time and place.

The way marriage and family life are lived reflects a way of understanding and ranking goods such as love, independence, equality, justice, and community. Consider a few examples. Emphasis on extended family and intergenerational responsibility, characteristic of aristocratic families, comes at the price of individual freedom, emotional attachment, public justice, and choice. Emphasis on independence within marriage, more characteristic of modern democracy, comes at the expense of community within marriage and responsibility to one's grandchildren or one's grandparents. Emphasis on romantic love within marriage comes with some cost to stability and endurance and to concern for "external goods" such as children or property.

Different political communities tend to have different family structures and different rankings of goods, or different *family regimes*. By *family regime* I mean a manner of distinguishing the valuable from the non-valuable concerns of family life, of attaching shame or honor, of connecting pride and unconcern to actions within marriage and family life, and of imagining how the various concerns of marriage and family life relate one to another in a particular time and place. Just as, per Aristotle, there seem to be a limited number of political regimes, there are a limited number of family regimes. The great changes in marriage and family life, underway throughout the Western world and beyond since the 1950s or 1960s, mark, in the final analysis, a displacement of an older, dependency-making marriage and family regime with one centered on autonomy (more on this in a moment). Marriage and family life are complex interplays of nature and political regime, or culture and law (as we say today). Marriage and family regimes follow the logic of nature—revealing the power and durability of nature. There are different family regimes—revealing the power and durability of political regimes—but there are not an infinite number of marriage and family forms, which would undermine our ability to study and talk about these human things.

Family Regimes within the "Fatal Circle" of a Political Regime

Marriage and family life are embedded in political communities, which transform them to an extent. To use Aristotle's frame, forms of human association like the household and village, concerned with meeting daily and non-daily needs, do not force inhabitants to ask what it means to live well, but citizens in political communities are free to think about what it means to live well. As a result political communities organize themselves around commonly held ideas, arrived at through speech, about "the advantageous and the harmful, and hence also the just and unjust."[1] While families and villages are temporally prior to the emergence of the city, the political community is "prior to the household and to each of us," for Aristotle, since citizens and households take their character from the political community in which they dwell. Placing the household within a particular political community gives the household a particular hue consistent with the principles of advantage and justice embodied in a political community's *regime*—its way of life or its common understanding of the advantageous, good, and just. Democratic regimes manifest more egalitarian relations between parents and children or husbands and wives, while oligarchies have more oligarchic or hierarchical relations between parents and children or husbands and wives.[2] All political communities are partial in their understanding of living well, emphasizing some idea of justice and some particular understanding of the good and advantageous at the expense of others. All aim at part of the truth, but none grasps the whole truth when it comes to governing a city. All regimes "fasten on a certain sort of justice, but proceed only to a certain point, and do not speak of the whole of justice in the authoritative sense."[3]

Recognizing the partial character of each political community is no more than saying that political communities are founded on contested and contestable opinions about the good, true, and beautiful. It is to say, with St. Augustine, that a political community or a people "is an assemblage of reasonable beings bound together by a common agreement as to the objects of their love,"[4] though none of their loves encompasses all lovable things. It is to imagine, with Plato's Socrates, that the education of citizens is like living as prisoners in a cave, where poets cast shadows on the wall that harden into citizens' opinions about the advantageous, good, beautiful, and just,[5] though none of those opinions is complete as an *idea* of good and beautiful things. It is to say, with Alexis de Tocqueville, that "there is a society only when men consider a great number of objects under the same aspect; when on a great number of

subjects they have the same opinions; when, finally, the same facts give rise in
them to the same impressions and the same thoughts," and to follow him in
recognizing that "the social and political constitution of a people disposes it
to certain beliefs and tastes which then become abundant without difficulty;
whereas these same causes turn it away from certain opinions and penchants
without working at it and so to speak without suspecting it."[6]

Study of political things reveals that regimes tend to become purer, more
one-sided, and hence more exclusive and extreme as time goes on; they
become more and more *like themselves.*[7] A predominant good, virtue, or characteristic, perhaps important at the onset of a regime, becomes of ever-greater
and eventually of overweening importance as the regime's life proceeds. Tocqueville, for instance, shows equality of condition is the "generative fact" in
modern democracy, which, as his *Democracy in America* shows, "modifies
everything that it does not produce."[8] For Aristotle democracy (justice as
equality or the rule of the poor) and oligarchy (justice as inequality or the rule
of the rich) were the most prevalent regimes. Democracies decline when the
parts of the city that used to restrain the love of equality or the poor's thirst
to rule erode.[9] Oligarchies at first are broadly based and have low property
requirements, but the oligarchs "tighten" the requirements and concentrate
more power in fewer, wealthier hands.[10] Aristotle never writes that regimes
necessarily have a gravitational pull to become purer, though his treatment of
democracy in book 6 of *The Politics*, among other places, makes this seem the
likely scenario for political life.[11] As regimes *tighten*, they ignore elements of
the human good that a partisan political community no longer sees.

For Aristotle a regime can resist its own gravitational pull toward extremism, blindness, and purity through *mixing* its predominant goods with other
less dominant human goods. Thus his famed mixed regime. Elements of
democracy and oligarchy may be blended—all can vote but juries have property qualifications or vice versa, for instance—or the mean between democracy and oligarchy can be established.[12] The great difficulty of establishing a
mixed regime lies in the fact that the "voice" of one side is easier to hear in
a particular regime than the voices outside of it. The gravitational pull of a
democracy, for instance, makes it difficult to recognize virtues that result from
natural inequality, difference, inequalities in property or wealth, and human
excellence. No constituency for nondemocratic goods exists in a democracy,
and a big constituency arises for exposing nondemocratic goods as elitist, sinister, and tyrannical, and democratic politicians win power by attacking such
inequalities mercilessly.

Education "relative to the regimes" preserves regimes, for Aristotle. Such
education counters the manifest tendency of a regime, through appreciating
the other side.[13] This educational variant of political mixing is much easier
said than done. Tocqueville suspects that such political mixtures do not work,

just as Aristotle sees how difficult securing mixtures can be. "The government called mixed," Tocqueville writes, "has always seemed to me to be a chimera . . . because in each society one discovers in the end one principle of action that dominates all the others."[14] Time reveals a gravitational pull in politics, though conflicts and events can obscure its direction for a time. Tocqueville recommends using a species of the political mixing chimera to combat the gravitational pull. The "whole art of the legislator" consists, he writes, "in discerning well and in advance these natural inclinations of human societies in order to know when one must aid their efforts and when it would rather be necessary to slow them down." In Tocqueville's immediate examples, aristocratic times focused on the next world may require a legislator inducing citizens to focus on the goods of this world and even to encourage "new desires" of the body and physical studies bordering on materialism. Democracies, inclined to focus on material well-being, demand statesmen "relentlessly raising up souls and keeping them turned toward Heaven," spreading a "sentiment of greatness, and a love of immaterial pleasures," and turning their minds to the long term.[15] Democratic statesmen would find ways to "sell" nondemocratic virtues on more or less democratic grounds. Tocqueville is skeptical that democratic people will have ears to hear and hearts to love what does not strictly reflect equality of condition, but human beings will best thrive in a democracy only with an appreciation for such nondemocratic ways.

Marriage and family life can be leading edges for the purification of a political regime as it becomes more extreme. As a regime becomes purer, marriage and family life are very likely to mirror the new extremism. Oligarchic families become *more* oligarchic as political oligarchy tightens. Oligarchic families may emphasize the transmission of property above all else in family life, or emphasize the rule of the man within the family to the detriment of familial love and companionship. Marriage and family life can also be vehicles for mixing a regime or obstacles to the purification of a regime. There may come a point when married couples or families themselves in an extreme oligarchy buck the regime within which they live and from which they receive some of their ideas. Think, perhaps, of a Christian family in a narrow oligarchy—one that refuses to reduce the marriage bond to an economic relationship or one where a father willingly lays down his life for his children or wife, even though he has the power to rule the family with an iron fist. Such experiences cannot be understood in terms of oligarchy.

Much the same is true of families in democratic regimes. Families tend to become more democratic as democracies become purer or more extreme. The Roman or aristocratic family (where the father had absolute, arbitrary power over children and a wife), Tocqueville writes, in the strict sense did "not exist" in nineteenth-century America. One found only "vestiges of it in the first years" after the birth of a child.[16] Americans of Tocqueville's day had a special way of understanding sexual equality as well, one that dignified the sexual division of labor or the idea of public man, private woman. Vestiges of inequality and difference remain even in our late republic: some parental authority over children exists, many people still marry and live together, and men and women still think of themselves as somewhat different. Yet our late modern regime eliminates many inequalities and seeks, in a manner of speaking, to promote the independence of all. Our democratic family regime has become ever purer as the political order has become ever purer; changes in marriage and family life also abet the making of a more democratic political order. As the family regime purifies, democracy comes up against its own limits. Are elements of marriage and family life so rooted in nature, necessity, and morality that an extreme or purified democratic family would cease to be a family in any recognizable sense?

An image from Tocqueville, the very last words of *Democracy in America*, illustrates the fate of marriage and the family within our modern regime. Some people, Tocqueville writes, entertain "false, and cowardly doctrines" that unmanageable forces control human affairs—like many of our advocates today, they trace social change to fate or the "right side of history." It is not history, however, that moves, but the drama of a political regime. We live in a "fatal circle," which we cannot leave but within which we are "powerful and free." Modernity is the "fatal circle" of today's politics and today's family regime. All actions concerning the family take place in a regime committed to equality of conditions (among other things), but it depends on us whether this equality leads us "to servitude or freedom, to enlightenment or barbarism, to prosperity or misery."[17]

Statesmen must understand the nature of marriage and family life *and* the fatal circle within which they can operate. There have been tremendous changes in marriage and family life since the advent of modernity. As politics separated from the Church, so also did marriage move from covenant to contract. As political communities opened the vote to more citizens and accepted women to full citizenship, women's independence loosened marital and familial bonds. The welfare state became more interested in household issues such as education, health, and income support. As families became less concerned with economic production to meet their daily needs, they had fewer children. Generally, as modern principles shape peoples, marriage and family life have sunk in importance compared to goods such as individual freedom and career achievement; marriage and family life have become more temporary; old marital forms have been undercut with greater acceptance of divorce, living together outside of marriage, having children outside of marriage, and same-sex marriage; sex outside of marriage is more prevalent; the culture that seems necessary to cultivate character conducive to marriage dissipates.

The difficulties of educating relative to the family regime are manifest in marriage and family life—there may not be ears sufficiently willing to hear or strong enough countervailing opinions with which to mix. Countervailing opinions and experiences exist in marriage and family life, however. Marriage and family life can correct political regimes, since an irreducible core related to the permanent issues of love, procreation, sex, and education makes marriage and family life more necessary than institutions of political justice. A family can be a "haven in a heartless world" (in Christopher Lasch's phrase),[18] supplying individuals with attention and demanding the loyalty of individuals as few other institutions do. It is private to an extent and hence escapes the shaping effects of the political regime somewhat.

The Modern Family Regime of Autonomy, Properly Understood

Our modern world has a family regime, a way of imagining marriage and family life and love. I explored the rise of this purer, more extreme family regime in *Family Politics: The Idea of Marriage in Modern Political Thought* (2011). Two ideas especially transformed marriage and family life in modernity. First, the idea of marriage as a contract slowly displaced the idea of marriage either as a sacrament or as a moment creating a community transcending the individualistic standpoint of contract. Individuals now mostly think of themselves as free to determine the terms of the marriage contract—its duration, its form, its purposes, its depth and breadth. In early modernity, individuals conformed to an idea of marriage that society made; society inhibited divorce, for instance. In late modernity, individuals seem to decide for themselves the nature and duration of marriage; society's role has receded. Once society upheld marriage as important to the perpetuation of society through its role in the procreation and education of children, but today marriage is seen to be, in the words of *Obergefell v. Hodges* (the Supreme Court decision mandating same-sex marriage), about an adult's "expression, intimacy, spirituality" centered on choice.[19] With the triumph of contract, marriage and family life are more made for the individual and less able to take on public purposes or reflect publicly approved forms.

The second powerful modern idea is that human beings should seek to bring nature under rational human control. Many of the things that appear as "givens" of the human condition—for instance, the birth process, procreation, the differences between the sexes, the fact that children are taken care of mostly by their birth parents, our dependence on others—might be remediable parts of the human condition if we but created new institutions to deal with them. The greater our control over the "givens" of life, the greater our freedom and power. Perhaps single parents can replace the two-parent family. Perhaps other ways of engineering children will replace the genetic lottery of sexual reproduction. Perhaps state institutions could replace the family as primary vehicles for education. Perhaps society can overcome sex differences. As modernity proceeds, human beings, in a sense, exercise their will more over their condition and create a new moral and physical continent for future generations.

The ideas of contract and of conquering nature merge in the contemporary concept of autonomy. Autonomy demands more than consent. Truly autonomous choices must, on an ever more radical understanding, be made without the influence of imposed habits, human reason, education, social pressure, legal pressure, cultural expectations, previous decisions, our sex or bodies, or any other external demand. Autonomous choices spring from an individual's will alone, lest they be traceable to something alien to the individual. This affords individuals a chance to make themselves what they, for whatever reason, want themselves to be. Autonomous people may still forge bonds with others, but autonomous bonds must be continually re-willed and renewed. If bonds were "natural," "corporeal," "habitual," or "divine," our liberty would not proceed from our will alone and individuals would be less than autonomous. People must be free to form relationships and to exit relationships when they stop serving their life plans. This means close, intimate relations must be open as to the form and number of partners and the extent of their commitment.

With the rise of autonomy, contemporary liberalism, which makes autonomy its chief concern, appears as the goal of modern political thought as such. Before the twentieth century, the concept of autonomy hardly appeared in political discourse. Each thinker and most laws had good reasons to embrace ideas of contract or movements toward conquering nature, but also to mix the embrace of such modern principles with other principles that restrained, limited, and regulated them. When early modern thinkers embraced ideas of contract or recommended the conquest of nature, they may have been offering, in the spirit of Aristotelian mixing, principles that balanced the patriarchal and otherworldly nature of the previous feudal or aristocratic regime. Marriage was a contract (acknowledging individual freedom), but for necessary purposes involving the procreation and education of children (acknowledging the limit on the contractual mode of thinking), for instance. Parents had rights and power to oversee the education of their children toward independence, without thinking that children were either consigned forever to live within the extended family or that they were already independent.

The situation appears different now and the mixing history has given way to a view that all thinkers sought autonomy, but had only just begun to work out its meaning.[20] Changes in family practice and "family law are fully in accord with the rise of a modern, secular, individualistic state."[21] All aspects of marriage and family life are being reconceived in terms of liberal autonomy as contemporary liberals march across marital and familial institutions. This march is what I call the *rolling revolution* in marriage and family life. By *rolling revolution* I mean the seemingly unfinishable series of changes in marriage and family life toward the realization of individual autonomy. Virtually all changes in law, practice, and opinion in this area have had the effect of stripping away the Christian or traditional aspects of marriage. Cohabitation, fornication, and adultery are not only no longer crimes, but are more and more accepted as matters of course and perhaps even as highly recommended practices. Contraception and abortion are legal, widely available, used, and honored. People have fewer children. Marriage is no longer limited to heterosexual couples, and hence less related to the needs of the body or the state's interest in the procreation and education of a future generation. Gender identity is, in decisive respects and ever more, seen as the product of choice or assertion. The gravitational pull of regime-level politics makes these developments appear as "living up to our ideals" or applying modern principles to all facets of life. What from the perspective of political philosophy appears as purity and tightness, and hence as destructive of the regime, appears as progress and the realization of justice to our rolling revolutionaries inside the regime.

A new balancing effort is required in a world that itself seems new. Political and familial health require education against autonomy that points to and appreciates human limits. These human limits are grounded in the body. They also implicate crucial moral goods that attract human beings—including most prominently the goods of love and human happiness. This new balancing ethic, integrated into a public philosophy, emphasizes responsibility and duty, not rights; the long term over the short term; the body and its necessities, not autonomy; the goods associated with human dependence such as love, not the glorification of autonomy and independence; and the virtues associated with sexual difference, not gender neutrality.

Perhaps the most striking feature of today's marriage and family landscape—where one finds little public support for marital roles or for marital stability, and where people can live together and drift apart at will—is that marriage is as strong as it is today. Call me an optimist, but things could be much worse! Still a majority of children in America are raised in intact marriages by their biological parents. Still more than half of marriages last until death. Still most women have children and manifest no little desire to care for them. Still men and women, by and large, act differently within marriage, though they may be embarrassed about that. Luckily the goods to which family life appeals are still grounded in practice, though our regime of autonomy makes it difficult to see these sources of marital and familial health and the public benefits that accrue from that health. Those who would defend marriage and family life lack the vocabulary to do it and have a hard time showing that the rise of autonomy is hardly an unmixed blessing.

The fact that things could be worse does not make a defense of a mixed family regime any easier. One must divine, as Tocqueville suggests, when to aid the efforts of reformers and balancers, when to slow them down, and, I would add, when to resist further rolls in the revolution. One must seek resources and arguments suited for the hearing of today's ears, though there may not be enough ears to hear and the ears have been trained not to hear. Any defense of marriage and family life in our situation must expose the hidden assumptions and blind spots of those who advocate for the rolling revolution. This often means defending Old Wisdom, on topics that touch on people's identity, pride, and passions. In any event the demands of statesmanship coincide with a philosophic respect for truth, and it is almost impossible to be a statesman at our late date without possessing philosophic or at least genuine wisdom.

Plan of the Book

Today's rolling revolution structures our vision of marriage, family life, love, sex, and gender. It does so through deconstructing Old Wisdom about marriage, family life, love, sex, and gender and offering new autonomy-centered ideas.

Part 1 of this book lays bare how our rolling revolution reflects the aspiration of the modern regime to achieve autonomy. It brings the conclusions of my *Family Politics* into our time, and shows how autonomy advocates seek to restructure and reimagine crucial aspects of human experience, marriage, and family life. The desire to achieve autonomy sets forth a rolling revolution in several areas of family life. Efforts of feminists (treated in chapter 2), contemporary liberals (chapter 3), and sexual liberationists (chapter 4), in their own ways, follow from the modern aspiration for autonomy in its most radical form. Each presents a great challenge to marriage and family life. All three interacting in the world roil marriage and family life.

Feminism, we shall see, points to the abolition of gender; as gender has some relationship to sex, it requires the forgetting of the body and the minimizing of a sexual difference that has its roots in the human body and closely related psychological traits; as those bodily roots can point to marriage and family life, a successful feminism aims to abolish marriage and family life. Contemporary liberalism seeks to reengineer the family as a state-created unit for the giving of care so that the public takes no notice of and does not favor any particular brand of human relationship. Sexual liberationists seek a sexuality freed from procreation, from relationships such as marriage, and from morality as such: for them sexual desire is a building block that everyone should be able to integrate into their chosen life plan as they see fit, so long as it is, for some reason, consistent with the equal ability of others to choose their life plans. They seek a world beyond repression.

Part 2 provides a critique of each movement within the rolling revolution. Chapter 5 presents an account of what feminism ignores—and hence of the limits of feminism. The world that feminism would like to see runs up against some tough nuts to crack, including most prominently the persistence of sex differences traceable to the body and the goods these differences serve. Its approach to these differences—namely, that they are really gender differences—is hardly a half-truth. Sex provides persistent grooves within which gender is always imagined and understood, and these grooves support the ways people pursue happiness and meaning in life. Chapter 6 presents the limits of contemporary liberalism. All laws peddle some kind of morality, and the contemporary liberal approach emphasizes what is known as the "pure relationship," one where all aspects of the relationship are chosen or determined by the autonomous will of the individuals. Furthermore, that liberal aspiration cannot account for inescapable parts of the human situation that it must acknowledge. Liberal theories assume that those who give birth to children should, in some fashion, be parents of those children, but liberal theory cannot on its own terms justify that assumption.

Chapter 7 presents what is problematical about sexuality in sexual liberation theories. The sexual desire that liberationists affect to favor is always more civilized than natural sexual desire is prone to be. Sexual desire and expression are not simply "repressed"; human beings govern and subordinate sexual desire. Those having sex are not often concerned solely with gratification and release: personal considerations—questions about whether one has done right for oneself or for the others—are part of sexual relations, as are the shame and modesty that accompany and protect sexual relations. Sex is different from other animal desires in human beings—and the efforts among the sexual liberationists to make it consistent with animal desire leaves out the relational element and the special significance of sex to personal identity. The liberationist's effort to make sex about pleasure and gratification also runs up against male and female differences in sexual relations on these and other matters.

Together parts 1 and 2 of the book show the partisan character of our late modern family regime. Part 1 is an act of prognosis about what the fully built-out feminist, liberal, and liberationist projects require, as their own advocates say; part 2 is an act of recovery of the Old Wisdom that must be ignored or suppressed for the rolling revolution to continue apace. The rudiments of part 2 ground the project for those who would reestablish or continue defending a mixed family regime amidst the rolling revolution.

Part 3 applies the Old Wisdom in part 2 to our contemporary situation. This is the statesmanlike portion of the book, where I seek to identify the vulnerabilities in the rolling revolution and to recommend ways where those who would maintain the mixed character of our family regime can accomplish something. Sometimes this means returning to the Old Wisdom on particular policies and seeking ways to vindicate it in new circumstances. Sometimes it involves anticipating and defending against the rolling revolution's upcoming advances. Sometimes it means violating widely held new norms deriving from the rolling revolution. Sometimes it means asking questions that are uncomfortable or indecent. I have tried to adopt few temporizing expedients, but to probe the defects in the rolling revolution to the bottom and sometimes to suggest radical cures. This conduct, I hope, will stamp wisdom and dignity on what I have written, and, I hope, what I have written will be looked to as a luminary, which sooner or later will spread its influence.[22]

This task happens on many fronts. I lay out the principles family advocates should adopt and how to apply those principles, knowing that no book can cover all of the circumstances where the rolling revolution challenges the Old Wisdom.[23] Chapter 8 lays out the general framework for how a modern society must understand marriage and family policy. There are natural passions out of which a sound marital culture can be built, but none or few of these passions point unambiguously to marriage and family life. Governments can take actions indirectly, through favoring a particular form of marriage so as to shape and civilize those passions, and through shaping the environment within which human beings make dutiful decisions about their lives.

Chapter 9 on the new sexual regime begins to treat how societies can come to privilege procreative, marital sex within this general framework. Nature provides more than a few incentives in this direction, but the family regime and broader culture can either aid or deflect nature. Sometimes elements of our contemporary culture must be challenged directly. What I will call our reigning civil rights ideology, which imagines that every disparity or inequality is traceable to an act of unjust oppression, condemns the broad culture as both homophobic and misogynist. This mode of thinking cannot endure if we are to discover and defend a healthy marriage or family culture. There will be disparities traceable to sex differences—and disparities reveal much about the ways of men, the ways of women, and the ways of those who have sex with those of the same sex.

Chapter 10 concerns the theoretical question "What is consent?" as it relates to consent to sex, the age of consent, and divorce. The tendency in the rolling revolution is to see consent as overcoming circumstances, biology, and the givens of life, but going all the way in this direction would lead modern societies to inhumane conclusions.

Chapter 11 forms an interlude of sorts, where I name the new "problem with no name," the decline of marital character. It addresses the question of how men and women have changed since the advent of the rolling revolution and how those changes compromise marriage and family life. Changes in our world affect people at a personal level. Everything combines to affect such character—the predominant mode of thinking affects what individuals value and the way of life that they would lead.

Chapter 12 concerns two of the main dilemmas of promoting marriage and family life in a liberal society. First, how might parental rights and duties be conceived of in a liberal society? The predominant approach, good enough in the main, emphasizes parental rights, but it also opens the parent–child relation up to much regulation from the state because the state is allowed to intervene "in the best interests of the child." The state's idea of the child's "best interests" often clashes with the parents' idea, and under modern circumstances the state is increasingly likely to win this conflict where it deems the conflict important. A deeper investigation of the genuine conflict between the family and the political community—a conflict as old as politics—reveals the dangers each poses to the other, and points to a more family-friendly manner of policing the boundary between the two. Second, how might a culture more suited to marital and familial values be promoted? I answer this through an investigation of the deregulation of obscenity and pornography. Much modern law and culture abets the proliferation of pornography. The proliferation of pornography on the internet is both an effect and a cause of declines in marital responsibility. Those interested in maintaining the compromised family culture of today must start with knowing why they should oppose public nudity, public fornication, child pornography, and other innovations. Opposition to these things points toward the need to roll back laws that have deregulated pornography. I outline a series of steps whereby this could be accomplished.

This book, like the rolling revolution it criticizes, could be endless. The rolling revolution affects marriage and family life in many untold ways. The conclusion in chapter 13 consolidates as much practical guidance and theoretical wisdom in a few words as possible. Proponents of the rolling revolution have put forward much wisdom that has become our old clichés. We need new clichés! I provide these, as well as my theoretical basis for thinking that my new clichés are superior.

Part I
The Rolling Revolution

A vast change, amounting to a revolution, has taken place in marriage and family life since the 1950s. A person transported from today back to the early 1900s or before would notice above all, perhaps, that the place and character of marriage and family life are diminished. This is not simply a matter of the rise in some factors (children born out of wedlock, women in college, access to pornography, divorce, cohabitation, and all of the others) and a decline in others (birth rates, marriage rates, marriage ages). There is a palpable difference in the qualities of married and family lives, affecting how people dress, how they walk, what they live their daily lives. What is this revolution? Where is it heading? How would we know when it has been completely successful?

This revolution is a "sexual revolution" in the large and proper sense. I call it the rolling revolution because its principles are such that they will only with great difficulty, if ever, be achieved and they call for a continuous transformation of marriage and family life. Kate Millett imagines "a fully realized sexual revolution" with three main facets in her 1970 book *Sexual Politics*. First and principally, this revolution would abolish "the ideology of male supremacy and the traditional socialization by which it is upheld in matters of status, role, and temperament" leading to the "integration of the separate sexual subcultures, an assimilation of both sides of previously segregated human experience."[1] Roles in child-rearing, for instance, would also fade and eventually disappear, it seems, as maternal and paternal roles are less gender-defined and more androgynous and parental. Disparities in the workplace and sex differences in career aspirations would vanish. Anything leading to the unequal power between the sexes and their different statuses, roles, and characters would have to be eliminated in law and culture so that an androgynous future could be secured.

Second, drastic change in the "patriarchal propriety family" is necessary for women to secure "complete economic independence." Women must obviously secure fulfilling employment outside of the home. An "important corollary" to this goal is "the end of the present chattel status and denial of right to minors."[2] The dependence of children is an invention of patriarchy, designed to make women feel as if they were needed to raise their children and hence dependent on their husbands. Complete economic independence and the freeing of women (and men as well, it seems) from the burdens of parenthood would lead to greater emancipation from unchosen duties. This second plank of the rolling revolution calls for a neutral public philosophy, informed by a desire for independence and autonomy for each; contemporary liberalism, as practiced since the 1990s, is the public philosophy whereby this plank is accomplished.

Lastly, this rolling revolution requires "an end to traditional sexual inhibitions and taboos, particularly those that most threaten patriarchal monogamous marriage: homosexuality, 'illegitimacy,' adolescent, and pre- and extra-marital sexuality." The sexual revolution in the broadest sense requires a sexual revolution in this narrower sense. Restrictions on sexual activity have had the effect of reinforcing ideas of romantic love, monogamous love, parental responsibility, sexual self-control, economic dependence, and other cultural attributes that define traditional family life. Emancipating sexuality from such restrictions would open up marriage at the same time, divorcing marriage from sexuality and allowing individuals to express primal human drives without inhibition and to achieve greater happiness or satisfaction. Sex has been repressed and channeled toward responsible reproduction, but under conditions of sexual freedom all sexual outlets would be greeted with equal public approval.[3]

Millett's three facets of revolution correspond, roughly, to the aspirations of modern feminists, contemporary liberals, and those advocating for sexual liberation. The aspirations of these advocates overlap to no little extent. None of these facets can be accomplished easily: there may always be another, previously unnoticed obstacle representing patriarchy or economic dependence to be removed or another sexual taboo to be debunked. The evolution in marriage and family life thus appears to be a *rolling revolution*—which, like a snowball rolling down an endless hill, picks up new material and gains speed with each roll. Its path is not always straight or predictable, but its momentum is clear. This rolling revolution is the way I understand that the family regime is becoming purer in our late modern time. The next three chapters treat each facet of the rolling revolution so as to illuminate the predominant tendency in modern marriage and family life and the trajectory of the modern American family regime and perhaps the American regime as such.

2

FEMINISM AND THE ABOLITION OF GENDER

Contemporary, second-wave, or radical feminism stands for the proposition that the subordinate status, roles, and temperament of women are products of patriarchal socialization, not nature. No essential difference between the sexes exists; the sex differences we observe are products of society. The male-dominated world, or patriarchy, has made women into the "second sex" (in Simone de Beauvoir's phrase), or feminine and subordinate. Patriarchy is deeply embedded in our moral teachings, expectations, political ideals, and founding myths, and a woman's idea of her body and her choices. As a result of this indoctrination, according to this diagnosis, women live destinies as mothers and wives or work in the caring professions instead of arenas of manly competition.

The task of identifying all sources of patriarchal socialization makes feminism a prominent feature of the rolling revolution. Second-wave feminists would deconstruct the patriarchal structures through feminist analysis and build a new society through feminist activism. This activism would bring change, akin to a religious conversion, moving women and society generally toward a future beyond gender, or where sex is divorced from gender. With this new society would come a new woman—an independent woman.

This abstract, radical feminism does not sound like the run-of-the-mill retail feminism, which today is concerned with equal pay or more women becoming chief executive officers (CEOs), or a woman becoming president of the United States. Retail feminists like Hillary Clinton just want the next reform. They encourage women to become law partners, orthopedic sur-geons, or engineers. Retail feminists just want women to feel safer than they do now. No retail feminist talks about achieving a world beyond gender or deconstructing patriarchy. They just want a world with less gender, in partic-ular areas. They appear moderate, measured, realistic.

This is often a pretense. Retail feminists may be genuinely moderate feminists (more on this term and concept later), but only if they reject the principles and goals of radical feminism. Press most retail feminists, however, and they will either move directly to the numerical parity standard (i.e., the abolition of gender) or suggest ever more moves toward it. Numerical parity and the abolition of gender is guiding the standard. The quintessential retail feminist, Sheryl Sandberg, for instance, cannot stomach the idea that the same number of women do not want to be CEOs or politicians as men, and that an equal number of men and women do not want to be household managers.[1] Retail feminism, when pressed, merges with radical feminism in rejecting all disparities between men and women as the product of patriarchal socializa-tion. Their moderate talk fits in perfectly with the long-term aspirations of radical feminism.

From First-Wave to Second-Wave Feminism

Feminist thinkers of all stripes define themselves against biological essential-ism and its political and cultural patriarchy. Biological essentialists think the different characters and roles of men and women have a permanent basis in sex or biology and in psychological proclivities originating in sex.

The first wave of feminist reformers (1850–1920) arose to criticize the subordinate *legal* condition of women. These feminist thinkers, finding inspiration in Mary Wollstonecraft (1759–1797) and their greatest advocate in John Stuart Mill (1806–1873), operated within a classically liberal intellec-tual framework and hoped, as the title of Wollstonecraft's book's implied, for the "vindication of the rights of women" (1792). First-wave thinkers hoped to vindicate the legal right to own property, the right to divorce, and the right to vote. Perhaps women had appeared uninterested in exercising such rights previously, but, these early feminists argued, women's apolitical appearance was traceable to society's failure to acknowledge and protect their political rights. *Of course* women paid them little heed: the exercise of those rights was fruitless without securing legal protection for them first. Early feminists were concerned that, as Mill argued in *Subjection of Women* (1869), no society could yet know what *woman* actually was because the laws and "the whole force of education . . . enslaves [women's] minds" to the sacrificial duties of wife and mother.[2] The old system of coverture, where women lost their legal identity within marriage, *underestimated* women's capacity for citizenship.

Women and men might still choose differently from one another, for these first-wave thinkers.[3] The legal framework that they wished for was established, throughout the most of the Western world, during the first third of the twentieth century after a "century of struggle" (borrowing from the title of Eleanor Flexner's history of women winning the right to vote).

Winning rights is not enough for second-wave feminists. Beginning with Beauvoir, the founding mother of second-wave feminism, around 1950, feminists have expressed disappointment at the choices women have made since they have won rights and protections.[4] Many women still gave priority to vocations as mothers instead of careers. Women continued to value their loving relationships within marriage over their market relations outside the home; togetherness over independence; fidelity over adventure; and sexual passivity and modesty over sexual liberation and conquest. When women chose careers, they were more likely to enter the caring professions like nurses or grade school teachers instead of aspiring to be CEOs, bohemian poets, or academics. Women failed to sink more of their identities into their careers, splitting time between their family and their work. Generally women lived more passively and dependently than these early second-wave feminists thought appropriate for dignified, independent creatures. "Encouraged by the mystique . . . women once again are living with their feet bound in the old image of glorified femininity. And it is the same old image, despite its shiny new clothes, that trapped women for centuries and made feminists rebel," Betty Friedan writes in her *Feminine Mystique* (1963).[5] Legal freedom had not led to *substantive* equality for women, nor had it been sufficient for gaining the even greater goal of independence or autonomy.

The deeply entrenched cultural patriarchy, in which men and women continue to indulge beliefs consistent with biological essentialism, prevents further progress, second-wave feminists argue. Getting women to choose independence would require a *cultural* reformation centered on encouraging women to shed their previous maternal, wifely personalities, educate themselves, embrace their sexuality, enter the workforce, and shun dependence on any particular man. Beauvoir and her disciples have spent much intellectual energy identifying the assumptions and opinions that enslave women to their old, dependent character, hoping to deepen this great revolution in human affairs.[6]

Second-wave feminists aim to free women from inherited ideas of specifically womanly thriving, which later feminists call *gender* or *gender roles*. Gender roles are society's way of imagining what it means to be a woman. They build on what seems an obvious interpretation of the female body. Linking gender to body means that a woman's character or gender is as unchangeable as her body or sex, and also that bodies stunt women's progress in achieving substantive equality or independence. Second-wave feminists aim to liberate women's characters from their bodies, and to take women beyond the socially constructed gender supposedly grounded in the sexed human body.

Beauvoir provides intellectual justification for divorcing sex from gender and for holding that culture determines the meaning of sex, the body, and gender. This critical manner defines *The Second Sex*, which she begins by asking, "What is a woman?" She answers,

> One is not born, but rather becomes, a woman. No biological, psychological, or economic fate determines the figure that the human female presents in society; it is civilization as a whole that produces this creature, intermediate between male and eunuch, which is described as feminine.[7]

Biological and cultural situations have long defined women. Women seem satisfied with the artificial roles of dependent wives and sacrificing mothers, and with working in the caring professions, because the cultural teaching (or "civilization") bends women toward this gender role. Women are less than human beings, for Beauvoir, because they accept "fate" and allow themselves to be defined by their biology and culture, falsely swallowing the myth that culture reflects nature. Women manifest an almost subhuman "immanence," in Beauvoir's word, because they accept their identity from pervasive social indoctrination or socialization.

Immanence is taught and reinforced in a thousand different ways, all conspiring to keep women the second sex. No one could identify all sources of subordination, not even Beauvoir in her seven-hundred-page tome. Her *Second Sex* set the pattern and parameters for subsequent feminists, who have spent their lives or careers criticizing and deconstructing what previously seemed to be natural or unchangeable distinctions in life. Beauvoir emphasizes sexual relations as a main source of subordination throughout *The Second Sex*. Society prepares women to be passive, modest, and tender, and to favor intimacy over adventure and experimentation, while it prepares men to take the initiative in sex and to love sexual variety. Male initiative in sex is "an essential element" in patriarchy's "general frame":

> Everything helps to confirm this hierarchy in the eyes of the little girl. The historical and literary culture to which she belongs, the songs and legends with which she is lulled to sleep, are one long exaltation of man. . . . Children's books, mythology, stories, tales, all reflect the myths born of the pride and the desires of men; thus it is that through the eyes of men the little girl discovers the world and reads therein her destiny.[8]

Girls are taught to be mothers and wives and to value a dependency-making love. Society teaches girls to love being wooed, while it teaches boys to woo. It teaches girls that they are the weaker sex, so it invents womanly indirection to cultivate male attachment and harness male initiative. It teaches that marriage is the locus of committed love—and that women should use their wiles to get the supposedly stronger sex to commit.

Patriarchal indoctrination toward these social constructs starts early. Society creates and baptizes male promiscuity and sexual desire, while women receive male overtures in "the posture of defeat" (i.e., on their backs). Such passivity makes women sex objects for men, a reality that makes women think of themselves as objects of erotic desire and to concern themselves overly with how they look. Men are to take women or possess them; women to dream of being taken or possessed. Girls are taught sexual shame, chastity, and modesty, while boys are taught boldness, confidence, and eroticism.[9] Thus there is the universal acceptance of the sexual double standard, where rakes are given a pass for sexual promiscuity while women are punished, and where men and women feel differently about sex.[10] Trained to be passive sexually, women accept their seemingly subordinate roles as mothers and housewives. Women could be as promiscuous, sexually adventurous, and sexually aggressive as men if we recreated society.

Sports and athleticism are other venues where myths of female inferiority abound. Men are made faster, stronger, more competitive, and more aggressive than girls, not by nature, but because of our belief that sports are "good for boys"; girls are weaker because they are encouraged to be meek, caring, timid, feminine, and maternal instead of risking injury.[11] Latter-day followers of Beauvoir bemoan the "frailty myth," used either to discourage women's aggressiveness in sports or to encourage women to accept something less than their best in athletic performance. Women are taught to be weaker, slower, and less athletic than men. Women enter professions consistent with this meeker character, becoming teachers of youth or nurses or sundry other things. Fit to be mothers, they enter mothering careers until a husband comes along.

In Beauvoir's view *everything* confirms the hierarchy run by males. Beauvoir's under-laborers in academia try to give an account of how women are oppressed and distorted under conditions of patriarchy. Differences between the sexes, perhaps even *all* differences between the sexes, and the importance of monogamous, enduring, exclusive marriage are especially pernicious myths.

Beauvoir's ideal society is one where all individuals are independent and face a largely open, indefinable future. Against socialization or immanence, Beauvoir encourages what she calls "transcendence," the idea that human beings must ever struggle to free themselves from the social or natural influence in a "continual reaching out toward other liberties" and in an effort "to engage in freely chosen projects."[12] Human beings will either be made passive by their situation (immanence) or define and make themselves (transcendence). "Man [i.e., a human being] is defined as a being who is not fixed, who makes himself what he is," Beauvoir writes. "Man is not a natural species: he is a historical idea."[13] As historical beings without fixed boundaries or natures, women are not bound to be governed by the customs, psychological traits, economic considerations, moral virtues, bodies, cultural attributes, or other limits that have relegated them to being the "second sex." Men have been transcendent; women have been stuck in a world of immanence. If women would transcend their subordinate fate, they would enjoy an "indefinitely open future" as they strive for autonomy and independence.[14] Nothing can be denied women in this endlessly open future; everything must be permitted them: they will lean in and just do it. No limits!

As Beauvoir and her followers see it, the traps of motherhood and marriage can be sprung and a transcendent future glimpsed with sexual revolution and independent careers in a genuinely liberated workplace. These initial steps make reaching higher liberties possible. Many myths persist about how certain feminine traits are natural (e.g., women are not as good at math, likelier to laugh, smile more, less funny, less interested in engineering, better talkers, gossipy, more emotional and vain, etc.); all sex differences, seemingly natural, intractable, and universal, must be exposed, for these feminists, as mutable *gender* differences. Gender can be otherwise than it is.

Sexual revolutionaries must shun domesticity and adopt independent careers, for instance, and develop the qualities of character to pursue them. Contraception and abortion were crucial at Beauvoir's stage for reform. Birth control, she argues, helps women to be more sexually adventurous and promiscuous and less dependent on one man for sex; with it, women can integrate sex however they choose into more meaningful lives. Untroubled about the consequences of sex, women might take initiative in sex, perhaps becoming the controlling partners and escaping the posture of defeat.[15] To help this along, Beauvoir follows Freud, arguing that passive women have been sexually "frigid," repressed, narcissistic, and nervous.[16] Beauvoir would first persuade passive, clingy women that they are uninteresting lovers, unable to keep the interest of their man by objectifying themselves with good looks and makeup and a passive role in sex. This is a step toward greater sexual assertiveness, where women aspire to sexual independence in open adultery or borderless marriages.

Available birth control and abortion are mere points "of departure for the liberation of women,"[17] because women must think using contraception and getting abortions make honorable, key contributions to the good life. Sex lives must express womanly independence; women must not be dependent on any particular man or person for satisfaction, much less experience an unwanted pregnancy. The woman who achieves virile independence has the great privilege of carrying on her sexual life with individuals who are themselves autonomous and effective in action, who—as a rule—will not play a parasitic role in her life, who will not enchain her through their weakness and the exigency of their needs.[18]

Beauvoir appeals beyond making contraception and abortion legal and providing public provision for each. Since unprotected sex could lead to motherhood, the best way to encourage the use of birth control is leveling a powerful critique of motherhood and family life, calling into question not only their naturalness but also their nobility, their relation to human happiness, and our need for them. Women must want to use contraception for contraception to make a new kind of woman. As she says in her reflection on *The Second Sex* (and with the assistance of Shulamith Firestone's powerful elaboration of her thought), "I think that the family must be abolished," and women who agree are much more likely to use contraception (if not forgo sexual relations) and to institutionalize their children from an early age, if they have children.[19]

The relegation of women to the second sex includes the sexual division of labor, where men have interesting careers outside the household (or produce for the family) while women mind the home. Leaving her stuck at home performing Sisyphean, boring, limitless, "tiresome, empty, monotonous" household tasks, marriage "mutilates" and "annihilates" the wife. In marriage "her life is virtually finished forever."[20] Marriage provides little solace too, since no man doing creative work outside the home could, in Beauvoir's eyes, respect a woman who is just a housewife. No wonder marriage marks a boring, "slow assassination" of life for husbands and wives.[21] Women who imbibe Beauvoir's thoughts on motherhood and marriage use contraception to avoid the slow death of life as mothers and wives. Use contraception—that could be a moderate goal. Balance career and family—that could be moderate too. Achieve independence and liberation—that is radical feminism. For Beauvoir contraception makes possible subsequent reforms that can accelerate gender deconstruction and promote independence and liberation.

In leveling this critique, Beauvoir suggests that all (or most) elements of feminine identity that have been regarded as sex or permanent (e.g., motherhood, sexual passivity, minding the home) are *really* socially constructed or gender and hence changeable.[22] For those who would argue that the differences between the bodies of men and women place limits on how much social experimentation could be undertaken, Beauvoir answers emphatically, "The situation does not depend on the body; the reverse is true."[23] How we conceive of the body matters, not the body itself: the body is open to great, perhaps limitless reinterpretation. No limits!

If biological essentialists collapsed gender into sex, Beauvoir does the opposite: There is no sex, no natural woman or man, no stable, meaningful biology underlying an "Absolute" man or woman. Women and men are social construction or "gender" all the way down; sex and the body are as much gender as are career focuses for women.[24] Human ingenuity, manipulating our material situation, sometimes with technology and at other times with creative moral reform, can manufacture this new independent woman and, perhaps, a new man to suit her. Transcendent individuals make themselves, freed from society's gender roles, nature, or sex. Beauvoir collapses sex and gender into a new more comprehensive "gender," which includes both culture and what had been called nature. The fact that so many people today use "gender" to refer to "sex" testifies to the success of Beauvoir's revolution. What was thought to be permanent "sex" is now changeable "gender"—and the expectations of society have been shaped accordingly. Even her enemies often adopt her language and hence her metaphysic.

The End of the Feminist Project

Second-wave feminists are debunkers or myth-busters. They find an alleged sex difference (for instance, men are more aggressive and violent than women). That sex difference, the debunkers show, is thought to reflect a permanent difference between the two sexes, or thought to be sex. Further research shows, however, that that difference is traceable to the cultural context, or what Beauvoir calls "the situation." No difference is natural or permanent. Change the situation intelligently and we can erase the difference, bringing about more equality or sameness between men and women. Making contraception legal and honorable changes the situation. Reforming education changes the situation. Anti-discrimination laws change the situation. Such changes are the object of the Women's Movement, initiated during the late 1960s in America and ongoing.

Feminist thinkers have reproduced themselves academically since Beauvoir's book (a process that has been accelerating rapidly since the early 1970s). Try an experiment. Go to a university library and seek out the section on feminist thought and social science (the HQ section between 1075 and 1410 or so). Boise State University, my home institution, has about 330 linear feet of books in this section as of summer 2017. Nearly all these books have been published since 1980. My judgment, after sampling many such books, is that a vast majority accept Beauvoir's frame of reference, her method, and her aspiration to abolish the patriarchal manner of constructing gender. Most hands agree with the aspiration to root out patriarchal images of femininity. Most hands agree that these deconstructed concepts help to establish a society beyond gender that can situate human beings for the undefined experience of liberation. Most imagine a world beyond gender and would find a way to get there. Most find much the same way there.

The most impressive second-wave feminists are Beauvoir's under-laborers. They reduce Beauvoir's highly abstract and existential philosophy to a more workable research and political agenda (e.g., Friedan, Millett), or explain its radicalism with even greater ambition (e.g., Shulamith Firestone). Since these pathbreaking thinkers from the 1960s and early 1970s, most feminist academics and activists have spent their careers in retail feminism filling in the interstices of the broad agenda or focusing their attention on the next great reform in the feminist project. They may oppose (or, at least, do not endorse) movements that are two or three steps ahead of public opinion at any particular time, but usually on strategic grounds. As time has gone on, the big picture of feminist ambition has receded into the background, as feminists take its broad ambitions for granted or find it inconvenient to articulate them. Feminists just muddle through pragmatically and make change happen through exposing *another* patriarchal assumption, and then another. It is also easier to sell particular reforms to those who do not buy the whole feminist project, so feminists learn to couch their arguments in terms of other, nonfeminist goods like "the children." National day care is not about abolishing the family (Beauvoir's ultimate ambition and how she sees government-provided day care), but about achieving a better work–family balance (for now!). Establish a new balance and then that new balance can be rebalanced later, but only after a particular point is won.[25]

Beauvoir's under-laborers themselves have under-laborers. Millett distinguishes sex and gender in her *Sexual Politics* and then shows, through short sketches, how academic disciplines have confused sex with gender.[26] That's *the* problem. Subsequent "big think" books then support Millett's findings in various academic disciplines. The field of political philosophy, for instance, has "big think" books applying feminist categories to the history of political philosophy. Susan Moller Okin's *Women in Western Political Thought* (1979) purports to show how the great Western thinkers from Plato and Aristotle to Rousseau and Mill presumed and perpetuated the inequality of the sexes.[27] Formal equality for women has been won through liberal reform, but substantive equality requires an overturning of patriarchy in the Western tradition at least. Carole Pateman's *Sexual Contract* (1988) shows how the idea of man has been confused with the idea of the human in social contract theory, and hence that contracts social, marital, and otherwise have presumed the "power that men exercise over women."[28] Okin's *Justice, Gender, and the Family* (1989) focuses on how contemporary liberal and communitarian thinkers have stopped their reform efforts at the kitchen door, failing to take into account the deep-seated assumptions about gender that must be upended through genuine efforts at social reform.[29]

Subsequent feminist scholars (under-laborers to under-laborers like Pateman, who are under-laborers to Millet and Friedan, who are under-laborers to Beauvoir) have taken a narrower view, focusing on the patriarchal assumptions of one thinker or another or one particular time or another.[30] All of these results, when taken as a whole, further Beauvoir's project and Millett's distillation of it in the field of political philosophy. Eventually every thinker and every era is passed through the patriarchal wringer: their hidden assumptions about gender are exposed so that their authority on these matters dissipates. Only thoughts consistent with second-wave feminism survive, and hence their ideology pervades disciplines ever more. Someday, perhaps in the not-so-distant future, thoughts inconsistent with feminism will not be thought.

Political philosophy is just one field of inquiry. To get an idea of how the project of academic, second-wave feminism works, multiply the feminist project as it arises in political philosophy by all fields of inquiry and human experience (works on literature, sex, sociology, psychology, pornography, working conditions, household tasks, motherhood, the scientific method, medical testing, etc.) and what emerges is the second-wave feminist project to move beyond gender as it manifests in thought and activism. Disciplines have pathbreaking books on the ways gender shapes literature, history, psychology, sociology, or whatever. Within the theoretical frameworks of these pathbreaking books appear smaller books, with more limited ambitions, suited to less impressive brains, to show how gender bent history in East Asia, or in East Asia between 1782 and 1794, or in Thailand. The books of the 1980s think bigger than the books of the next generation, and so on. Entire academic careers and departments are dedicated to furthering this sacred project, and the project gets narrower and covers more ground at the same time. The feminist project has never been more pervasive and influential, and it has never been weaker as its biggest claims have receded quietly into the background.

This project of academic feminism is present in Friedan's *Feminine Mystique*:

> I think the experts in a great many fields have been holding pieces of [the] truth [that the feminine mystique stunts the development of individual independence] under their microscopes for a long time without realizing it. I found pieces of it in certain new research and theoretical developments in psychological social and biological science whose implications for women seem never to have been examined....
> I became aware of a growing body of evidence, much of which has not been reported publicly because it does not fit the current modes of thought about women—evidence which throws into question the standards of feminine normality, feminine adjustment, feminine fulfillment, and feminine maturity.[31]

Change the modes of thought and then the findings will be recognized. Most, if not all, later feminists walk in these footsteps. Consider Carol Tavris' *The*

Mismeasure of Woman: Why Women Are Not the Better Sex, the Inferior Sex, or the Opposite Sex (1992), a classic in the genre of debunking alleged sex differences. "There is," Tavris asserts, "no underlying sexual nature apart from those veneers, and . . . trying to find one is as impossible as trying to find a 'true self' unaffected by the world in which it develops."³² Generally, Tavris seeks to show that differences in sexual desire, sexual capacity, reasoning ability, cooperation and competition, mental health, moral reasoning, and a slew of other areas are traceable to context and situation and education, though she remains open, as a matter of principle, maybe, to the idea that some natural differences exist. Or consider Cordelia Fine's *Delusions of Gender: How Our Minds, Society, and Neurosexism Create Difference* (2010). "Pick a gender difference, any difference. Now watch very closely and—poof!—it's gone."³³ The mind emerges from Fine's analysis as dependent on its context and hence changeable with changes in context, not an independent cause of sex differences.

Each feminist under-laborer focuses on a small part of the big picture. All *appear* to be small, retail feminists. All the sisters work toward that big picture of a world beyond sex and gender as feminists reconceive these concepts. Okin, thinking big, expresses the feminist goal of a world beyond gender with unparalleled clarity:

> A just future would be one without gender. In social structures and practices, one's sex would have no more relevance than one's eye color or the length of one's toes. No assumptions would be made about "male" or "female" roles; childbearing would be so conceptually separated from child rearing and other family responsibilities that it would be a cause for surprise, and no little concern, if men and women were not equally responsible for domestic life or if children were to spend much more time with one parent than the other. It would be a future in which men and women participated in more or less equal numbers in every sphere of life, from infant care to different kinds of paid work to high-level politics.³⁴

All disparities between the sexes testify to the continuation of patriarchy. Okin collapses equality and sameness and expects that a world "without gender" would be one where men and women divide society's roles fifty-fifty. A society of equal opportunity would have equality of result because gender is an imposition. Bodies and minds can be remolded to bring this world beyond gender about, because previous iterations bent bodies and minds toward inequality and difference. The creation of such a world would require, returning to Millett's delicious formulation, adverted to earlier, the dismantling of "the ideology of male supremacy and the traditional socialization by which it is upheld in matters of status, role, and temperament." Thus feminism constitutes a rolling revolution in itself.

What is necessary to create the fifty-fifty society? Herewith Firestone's *Dialectic of Sex: The Case for Feminist Revolution* (1970), a book dedicated to Beauvoir. *Dialectic* takes Beauvoir's thought further toward a world beyond the second sex, as Beauvoir herself recognized.[35] Few exceed Firestone in seeking to ensure that the identity of women is not affected by morality, biology, or culture. Dismantle patriarchy; undermine chastity, modesty, and the morality of patriarchy; make women as promiscuous as men; get society to accept that promiscuity; dishonor the household; undermine motherhood; promote contraception and celebrate abortion; put forth a new, more egalitarian, less needy concept of love—do all that Beauvoir recommends, that is, and society will *still* be patriarchal because of women's role in reproduction. For Firestone reproductive biology accounts for women's "original and continued oppression."[36] Therefore marriage itself must be abolished in law and opinion and the biological family with it. This may require coercive measures, but a feminist culture may require some coercion until the genuine equality of opportunity shown by a genuine equality of result comes into being.

At the center of Firestone's deep critique lie the outer limits of the radical refashioning of sex, love, marriage, and motherhood—fulcrums of the key connections in traditional family life.

Firestone sees love as "the pivot of women's oppression today." Romantic love has in some respects taken the place of biology as the glue of marriage and family life or the "cultural tool of male power to keep women from knowing their conditions." The oppressive, objectifying love is born of a "*political*, i.e., unequal *power* context; the who, why, when, and where of it is what makes it now such a holocaust." Romantic love in particular, and love in general, presumes the image of a clinging dependent woman valued, ostensibly, as wife or mother or for her feminine beauty, but who is really a piece of property and an extension of a man's ego. She is owned under the clever guise of being loved. Eroticism, private monogamous relations, the beauty ideal, and other tools of romantic love "keep sex oppression going strong."[37] Women, concerned with love, tailor their bodies for attractions and relations; their concern with their own appearance is an instrument of patriarchy's oppression—a beauty myth, designed by men to ensure that men would be in a position to evaluate a woman's worth.[38] Romantic love coincides with the "privatization of sex" or monogamy, where a particular woman hitches her destiny to a particular man, while separating herself from her sisters, and each man pretends faithfulness to his lucky woman. Firestone lays the foundation for the idea that all sex, under conditions of patriarchy, is coerced (see chapter 10).

Culture would not suggest the superiority of lifelong partners, enduring commitment, sex within marriage and commitment, and such to a good life in Firestone's world. She follows Beauvoir in seeing sexual liberation as key to creating a world beyond gender or culture. After the feminist revolution, "all forms of sexuality would be allowed and indulged," including especially the "natural polymorphous sexuality" that has been channeled and repressed especially in women *and children*.[39] Equal people experience a freer, truer love as a mutual exchange when individuals share, sexually and otherwise, spontaneously from their plenty, never out of need. True love proceeds only when individuals are free from biological and cultural expectations and are self-sufficient, so that any sharing is the result of a generosity of spirit that adds to the value of their own lives and the lives of others. Anything less than complete sexual liberation compromises autonomous love and represents, for Firestone, patriarchal remnants that foil the revolution. No double standard here; no standards at all.

And children? This captures Firestone's extension of Beauvoir's thought. If love was the pivot of women's oppression, "the heart of woman's oppression is her childbearing and child-rearing role."[40] The feminist revolution must eliminate childbearing and child-rearing because each centers a woman's life on her children and encourages women to be less than fully independent. Before the modern world, Firestone contends, seeming to follow the work of Philippe Aries,[41] children were not thought to be distinct from adults. Children were thought to be adults in apprenticeship more than to be going through a distinct stage in life with its own manners and integrity. Premodern children were not heavily dependent on their parents or segregated from adult experiences or activities: "in every respect the child was integrated into the total community as soon as possible." Later, at the birth of the modern world, the "concept of childhood" as a separate stage—a stage of innocence, dependence, vulnerability, and development—arose as an "adjunct" to the child-centered "modern family."[42] Herewith the myth of femininity, or the "feminine mystique," corresponding to the myth of childhood, arises: women are expected to have characters to dote on, nurture, and please children as a means of preparing those children for the self-control of adulthood. Giving children such care creates physical and economic dependence in children; represses their healthy, pleasure-seeking sexuality toward conventional sexual expressions within marriage and delaying gratification; and pigeonholes children into a way of life determined through school authorities and seemingly voluntary organizations. Within the nuclear family, "children are repressed at every waking minute. Childhood is hell."[43]

It would not be thus in Firestone's future world. Against such repression, Firestone recommends the experience of "ghetto" children, who escape the "supervised nightmare" to be free thinkers, revolutionaries, and sexually free.[44] The child of the future would say that he could not "remember an age when he didn't have sexual intercourse with other kids as a natural thing: everyone was doing it." (Even Firestone had not yet imagined the oppression gendered pronouns cause!) If children are to know self-restraint and especially sexual self-restraint, someone has to supervise them more closely, and mothers might put themselves in that position. Instead, the child-rearing role, such as it is, would be diffused throughout society as a whole, perhaps even with "twenty-four-hour child-care centres staffed by men as well as women," which, though radical, would be "timid if not entirely worthless as a transition."[45] Independent children would probably demand their "fair integration into the labour force," as well as permission and (perhaps) encouragement for children to "do it on the stairs" or wherever, among other things.[46]

National day care appears timid, for Firestone, because genuinely revolutionary change would require severing the cord between mothers and children altogether. Contraception is not enough: "artificial reproduction" of all sorts is necessary to "free women . . . from their biology" and undermine the "*social* unit . . . organized around biological reproduction."[47] Our culture will transcend patriarchy only when it conquers nature through socially directed cloning or artificial reproduction or, perhaps, through not reproducing at all. This would end that seemingly most natural injustice, "family chauvinism," where parents indulge in the pleasing delusion that their own child is worthier of attention than other children. Women would then feel no obligation to any particular child or any particular man (as the father of what used to be considered her child). Women would be sexually free, economically independent, free of marital and maternal duties, and autonomous politically.

Society will move toward feminist revolution—from 1970 onward, Firestone imagines—haltingly but flexibly, as feminists, moderates and radicals, seize opportunities where they present themselves.[48] Initially, Firestone predicts, a woman will be more inclined to lead a "single life" organized around choosing a career that satisfies her "social and emotional needs."[49] Women will also undertake experimental relationships, which will at first "probably be monogamous," but after "several generations of non-family living," Firestone predicts, "our psychological structures would become altered so radically that the monogamous couple . . . would become obsolescent" and replaced by group marriages, trans-sexual group marriages, or a hookup culture. "All cultural incentives" will then gradually be transferred to these new groups. If there is a natural parental instinct, people may continue to procreate during this transition stage. If there is not a natural parental instinct, artificial reproduction will have to arise, or else unnamed "cultural inducements . . . less destructive" than those depending on parental ego will have to arise to produce children.[50] Children will make up a regulated percentage of a household; children will be able to join households unless family chauvinism reemerges; the adults in these groupings will then spontaneously provide what babies need.

"Cybernetic communism" as "an alternative to the family for reproduction of children, combined with every imaginable life style for those who choose to live singly or in non productive units" is the last stage of the revolution. This will be accomplished when the following requirements (at a minimum) are met: technological childbearing and communal child-rearing; the complete integration of children and women into the larger society so that children have full "political, economic, and sexual rights" and their activities are no different from those of adults; and complete sexual freedom for women and children (all can have sex with whomever they want—the "incest taboo . . . age-ist and homosexual sex taboos would disappear").[51] The abolition of gender, the "death of the family," and the disappearance of culture will mark the completed feminist revolution, when humanity can realize the conceivable in the actual and hence assert complete power over its own future and nature.

Firestone's vision is radical. Few feminist under-laborers embrace her goals, her specific proposals, or her project of reform, or even imagine her end point. Few speak of cybernetic communism or ghetto children enjoying sexual rights today. At the same time, I am not aware of any extended criticism of Firestone's feminist revolution among today's feminists. Firestone describes what it would mean to live beyond gender, where feminists aspire to go. Why would they worry about the means or policies necessary to arrive at the Elysian fields beyond gender? What does the silence of feminists mean in this context? Beauvoir realized right away that Firestone had furthered her project, and she lauded Firestone accordingly. Susan Faludi, herself a not insignificant under-laborer in second-wave feminism,[52] writes, in her eulogy to Firestone, that Faludi and other feminists regard Firestone as taking on the "whole ball of wax," while they have only dealt on the retail level with reforming mere parts. Faludi refrains from endorsing Firestone's specific proposals, while praising her for bringing "new thoughts" as grist for the mill. No sustained criticism of Firestone's radical proposals has made its way into the greatest works of subsequent feminist philosophy, as far as I can find (though there are many unexplored shelves in the Boise State library and life is too short). Firestone was "ahead of her time" more than wrong on the merits, it seems. That is what I take to be the position of radical feminism and its willing accomplices in the retail feminist business.

Few, if any, feminist thinkers in the 2010s seek to abolish the incest taboo or the family, or to encourage sexual relations among young children, or to develop human cloning as means of moving beyond gender. Is this reticence a mark of prudence, cowardice, lack of imagination, ignorance, self-contradiction, principle, or some combination of these things? Some feminists, emphasizing strategy, not principle, worry that a world beyond gender now would upset the solidarity necessary for the sisterhood of activists and intellectuals to move the world beyond gender.[53] If feminists oppose such moves on principle (not just opposing them for now),[54] they are seeking to preserve something beneficial and good through that opposition; this would mean that we might have the beginnings of a familial mixture and an approach to sex differences that preserves or protects some of the old womanly character. Radical feminist thought rules out such mixing arguments on principle, however, since mixtures are remnants of patriarchal indoctrination.

The Transgender Turn beyond Gender

Firestone imagines a rolling revolution, where the supposed insights of one generation may be obstacles for the next. Chief among feminists who extend Firestone's already quite extensive thought is Judith Butler, who accepts the feminist divorce of sex from gender and its aspiration to move "beyond gender" or to "undo" gender (in Butler's phrase). Second-wave feminists are not radical enough, for Butler, because they do not reject the binary character of gender and instead just encourage supposedly "immanent" women to perform more like "transcendent" men. What better way to move toward a world beyond gender, Butler, in effect, asks, than by moving beyond the binary through the proliferation of genders and thereby undoing gender as a concept?

Postmodern thinking, afoot in second-wave feminism, laid foundations for this later extension. Thinkers such as Butler rely especially on the French post-structuralist philosophers Michel Foucault and Jacques Lacan, who seek to expose political power as it manifests itself in our structured ideas of truth, reality, and language. According to this view structures reinforce the dominant group's vision of political power and make its way of life implicitly normal. Language spiritualizes violence and shapes what all people think to be possible, imaginable, and desirable. Society exerts this power subtly by constructing "truth" and "reality," and thereby constructing a theory about what counts as human. Many subtle social teachings, for instance, from religious teaching to popular culture, encourage people to expect love relations between men and women. Our pronouns for "he" and "she" construct a binary world. Ideas such as "fireman" or "policeman" tell women that they should look elsewhere for careers.

These expectations must be exposed as artificial so that a more open, "queer" future can arise. Foucault's *History of Sexuality*, to use Butler's technical language, exposes the "mechanism of coercion" behind the modern preference for heterosexual sex and ethic of self-control (and opposition to childhood sexuality and incest) in the hope of releasing a more polymorphous expression of sexual desire and, ultimately, new engenderings.[55] For Butler gender is an imposition, an act of pseudo-violence integrated into our language and expectations. Gender and sexuality are "performances" arising from and constituting common life.

Feminists may once have opposed the inclusion of homosexual ("queer"), drag (men dressed as women), butch (masculine lesbians), femme (feminine lesbians), and transgender persons because such individuals undermined the idea of sisterhood that bound the movement together and they reinforced sexual stereotypes.[56] Some early homosexual activists seemed to accept the idea of homosexual or heterosexual orientation as embedded in a person's genetic makeup or as somehow natural. Butler rejects such stodginess, allying her feminism to developments in queer theory, homosexual advocacy, and transgender rights.[57] Queer theory holds that all expressions of gender and sexuality are socially constructed and hence changeable. Queer theorists hope that celebrating the supposedly queer lifestyles will "problematize" rigid notions of personal identity.[58] Society's way of pigeonholing individuals into binary male and female categories is especially prominent. Queer theory finds liberation beyond the binary and the norm. Among those liberated through a wide acceptance of queer theory are first homosexuals and then transgendered people, whose self-conception transcends supposedly normal binary conceptions of gender but who do not necessarily reconfigure their bodies to accommodate this self-conception.

Leslie Feinberg, whose pamphlet *Transgender Liberation: A Movement Whose Time Has Come* (1992) is likely the first full treatment of transgenderism, considers the discrimination suffered by the transgendered as "an oppression without a name" because it is so engrained in culture as to appear natural.[59] Engendering has been an unseen "violence" that "emerges from a profound desire to make the order of binary gender appear natural or necessary, to make of it a structure, either natural or cultural or both, which no human being can oppose, and still remain human."[60]

Undoing gender requires empowerment of those who fantasize about and perform different gender spectacles, revealing fluid possibilities and new realities. Butler's *Gender Trouble* emphasizes the transgressive nature of drag and cross-dressing,[61] while her *Undoing Gender* adds transgender as the latest new gender performance. "When something [seemingly] unreal," Butler writes, "lays claim to reality . . . something other than a simple assimilation into prevailing norms can and does take place. The norms themselves become rattled, display their instability, and become open to resignification."[62] Accordingly, a better feminism integrates queer theory because "queers . . . struggle to rework the norms" and posit "a different future for the norm itself." They "make us not only question what is real and what 'must' be, but they also show us how the norms that govern contemporary notions of reality can be questioned and how new modes of reality can become instituted," just as second-wave feminists have hoped.[63] With new transgressive possibilities, "a new legitimating lexicon for . . . gender complexity" can develop within "law, psychiatry, social and literary theory."[64] Thus, a recognition for transgenderism is consistent with and moves beyond the philosophical premises of second-wave feminism (i.e., divorcing one's body from one's identity).

Freedom from society's constructions is not enough, however. In a future of transgender liberation, say such theorists, a thousand genders will bloom only if the public recognizes the legitimacy and beauty of all gender performances. "We are not carving out a place for autonomy," Butler writes, "if by autonomy we mean a state of individuation, taken as self-persisting prior to and apart from any relations of dependency on the world of others." Persons "cannot persist without norms of recognition" that support their persistence and build their mental health. One's identity is never fully real or fully one's own until one's fellow citizens recognize it as such. The "very sense of personhood is linked to the desire for recognition, and that desire places us outside ourselves, in a realm of social norms that we do not fully choose."[65] Institutions of society, from administrative agencies at the national and local levels to cake makers or other public businesses to schools and even families, must recognize and affirm new engenderings if those with new genders are to feel at home in the world. This task, demanded under feminism, must continue in this difficult landscape beyond feminism. Dignitary harms matter as much as overt discrimination, and both must be relieved in a world beyond gender. It is difficult to imagine how the work of undoing gender could be completed: it seems to demand continual social transformation not only in the name of liberation from past impositions, but also as a way to secure recognition for tomorrow's desires. What is with Firestone an attempt to abolish culture culminates, with Butler, strangely, in the building of a new one.

Butler's argument leads to a transgressive defense of same-sex marriage. Far from welcoming "virtually normal" couples into a traditional marriage culture, Butler embraces same-sex marriage because it combats essentialism and upsets expected gender norms about heterosexuality within marriage. It introduces new realities such as open marriage, thereby creating new performances that perhaps may point toward dethroning marriage as an important public value and ending the legal recognition of marriage. Shaking the public recognition of man–woman marriage in this way is a step toward creating a more open future and abolishing the family and its roles.[66]

Butler expects that witnessing transgender incidents would produce a disruptive effect much like that produced by observing two men or two women in wedlock. Following the logic, public restrooms and showering facilities are based on a binary conception of gender, serving as instruments of oppression for those who do not conform to society's norms. Support for women's sports also seems to be based on such essentialism, so finding a place for transgender athletes likewise becomes a moral imperative. After all, women's sports are based on the seemingly benighted assumption that there are women. Transgendered persons create "gender trouble" for contemporary notions of reality, and call for affirmation and recognition so that those who formerly were considered "unreal" can be welcomed into the human race. "Men" competing in "women's" sports may seem unjust according to the old way of thinking, but that old way is constructed to maintain power relations: beyond the binary it is both just and fitting to see such diverse gender performances. The more performances, the more upset the norm.

According to Butler the body is neither a given nor a limit: our identity is limited only by our ability to fantasize, which is "an internal film that we project inside the interior theater of the mind."[67] A new politics must "create a world in which those who understand their gender and their desire to be nonnormative can live and thrive not only without the threat of violence from the outside but without the pervasive sense of their own unreality, which can lead to suicide or a suicidal life."[68]

Perhaps few transgendered activists are self-consciously post-structuralist queer theorists, just as few feminists of the 1960s and 1970s understood all of the implications of Beauvoir's radical feminism or Firestone's. Their activism, however, bends in the direction of these theories, and these theories contribute to today's rolling revolution. Transgender activism begins with the help of a science that deconstructs, claims that individuals' health is compromised by society's repressions, and names a psychological syndrome from which such individuals suffer. It is retail transgenderism. The first scientific keystone to this new establishment is the disorder known as "gender dysphoria,"[69] which seems to cause a persistent and consistent unease about one's gender identity or an incongruity between one's biological sex and internal sense of life as either a man or a woman. In this case a scientific name is assigned to an issue that on other occasions might have gone unnamed. From the perspective of queer theory, these reactions are almost charming in their adherence to the traditional relation between sex and gender.[70] For queer theorists those experiencing gender confusion should not be cured; rather, their identities should be affirmed and celebrated. Affirming transgenderism is the cure for gender dysphoria, not transitioning, conversion, or sex reassignment. When a child suffering from "gender dysphoria" arrives at school, it is not simply a question of demanding transitioning measures and hormone treatments. For queer theorists such a child arrives with a demand that the school and its community recognize and affirm the child's questionable gender status as a permanent fact.

The 2015 experience of Minnesota's Nova Classical Academy illustrates this point. A parent enrolled his five-year-old in the charter school. The child, according to the parent, thought of himself as a boy who likes "girl things." The parent demanded that the school support the non-gender-conforming student with changes in curriculum and policies (among other things), and the school complied under legal and public pressure.[71] There are multiple stories of how professionals in some states are prevented from treating "gender dysphoria" as a pathological syndrome requiring counseling and preventive parenting. The ultimate goal is public recognition of queer theory's view of the human landscape.

The World beyond Gender Meets Liberal Choice

An aging Simone de Beauvoir sat down for an interview with pathbreaking American feminist Betty Friedan in 1975. In the interview Friedan suggests that the public should compensate women for the child-rearing housework they perform. Beauvoir memorably demurs, on behalf of radical French feminists:

> No, we don't believe that a woman should have this choice [to be a mother]. No woman should be authorized to stay at home to raise her children. Women should not have that choice, precisely because if there is such a choice, too many women will make that one. It is a way of forcing women in a certain direction.

Friedan seems to object to Beauvoir on prudential grounds, at least: "I follow the argument," she responds, "but politically, at the moment, I don't agree with it," since, she argues, the United States lacks a sufficient number of day care facilities. Plus, she adds, the "tradition of individual freedom" in America is such that she would "never say that every woman must put her child in child-care center."[72] The conversation continues. For Beauvoir women will "be oppressed" as long as "the family and the myth of the family and the myth of maternity and maternal instinct are not destroyed"—a destruction that would require much formal and informal public power. "The family must be abolished," Beauvoir answers, "with absolute assurance." Beauvoir's extremism comes from her dismissal of any notion of natural tenderness, human posterity, natural duties, or the importance of the body in constituting human identity, and from her willingness to use the coercive power of the state to interrupt parental rights and personal choice. Few retail feminists today would admit to thinking these things, but the question is why. Is there a level of disparity that they would accept? On what grounds would they accept it?

Since retail feminists are leery of saying that enough has been achieved, they are always vulnerable to the ratcheting arguments of radical feminism. Much feminism is therefore equally liable to becoming coercive in order to achieve its goals. If pregnancy, breastfeeding, marital monogamy, fidelity, child-rearing, chastity, housework, cultural scripts surrounding romantic love, and binary conceptions of gender are obstacles to the abolition of gender, the coercive powers of government may be needed to remove them when possible, someday. Why not require women to take mandatory pregnancy suppression drugs, à la Huxley's *Brave New World*? Why not establish mandatory public supervision of child-rearing, à la Plato's *Republic*? Why not mandate promiscuity, à la Aristophanes' *Assembly of Women* and Huxley's dystopia? Why not make housework a public concern, as Beauvoir, Engels, and other feminists suggest it should be in a genuinely free society?

Neither second-wave feminists nor their transgressive successors seem to have qualms about using public power to reform the world around them to make it more congenial to feminist liberation. For now they appear to be retail feminists. For sex they want contraception, abortion, and abundant choices to be available. For careers no doors should be closed and anti-discrimination laws should be enforced. For motherhood highly subsidized, if not governmentally provided, day care must be available and the workplace reconfigured to get them in full-time work. For marriage women need a way out and a substitute to maintain their independence. When will enough be enough? Their principles demand a liberated world beyond gender, and use of the state's coercive power is necessary to get there. The only evidence of a world beyond gender is a fifty-fifty world where men and women, if such words can still matter, occupy equal numbers in all of society's roles. If all disparity means tyranny, then the abolition of gender requires the abolition of tyranny—even if that requires not a little coercion and a little tyranny to achieve.

3

CONTEMPORARY LIBERALISM AND THE ABOLITION OF MARRIAGE

Feminists would abolish marriage and the family to create a world beyond gender. Contemporary liberals criticize marriage and family life in the name of moral neutrality or a state that refrains from legislating morality or, more broadly, in the name of autonomy or choice. Feminists speak about an "indefinite future" and the independent woman, while contemporary liberals would secure autonomy and relational diversity. Contemporary liberals provide the justification for a complete independence for women (and children) from marriage. These different frameworks, while analytically separable, have become one, though in a tense amalgamation.

Contemporary liberal aims like autonomy, expressive individualism, and personal independence inform celebratory progressive narratives about the rolling revolution in family life,[1] and they direct conservative laments about family decline.[2] The morality tale is familiar enough. In the beginning covenantal marriage and family life were pretty patriarchal and monogamous. Official divorce was difficult to acquire, though desertion was easy because people were difficult to track. Spouses and children labored together and couples acquired joint property, under the legal ownership of the male head of household who covered his wife's legal identity. Coverture was the legal mechanism suited to securing marital and familial unity: husbands owned property, accepted responsibility for family members before the law, voted, and generally were the public face of a family, while women were "republican mothers" and minded the home. Couples had many children because, on the farm, there was much to do and many of the children died early anyway, so stoical parents needed replacements. Americans jettisoned some English common law (primogeniture and entail, for instance) to accommodate different circumstances as a means of encouraging youth to shift for themselves at an appropriate age, and marriage and family, for the most part, proceeded as contracts at modernity's dawn.

Each of the supposed pillars of marriage and family life has been shaken and reshaped to secure greater autonomy or independence for each spouse. Divorce went from proscribed, to regulated with the assignment of fault, to at-will. Cohabitation outside of wedlock followed a similar trajectory, from proscribed, to almost expected as a "test drive" for marriage, and, increasingly, as a replacement for formalized marriage; even cohabitation may be too long-term in a hookup culture of one-night stands. Women went from supposedly being veritable property of their husbands under coverture, to free from the confines of coverture, but culturally traditional, to more emancipated and potentially independent of the family, to independent of the family in reality. Alternative lifestyles such as homosexuality went from legally proscribed and culturally stigmatized, to legal, to normal, and, perhaps, to celebrated. Perhaps the same will happen with open marriage. Marriage concerns property at first, then finding a suitable helpmate for the purposes of procreation, production, and education, but culminates in love and passion.

In any event, histories present the rolling revolution in family life as a triumph involving the unstoppable realization of modern principles. Steven Mintz and Susan Kellogg, authors of *Domestic Revolutions: A Social History of American Family Life* (1988), see a "new morality" emerging, whose "watchwords" are "'growth,' 'self-realization,' and 'fulfillment,'" and where new "expectations for personal happiness," "sexual fulfillment, intimacy, and companionship" have "risen and collided with more traditional concern (and sacrifice) for the family." This new ethic emphasizes "the separateness and autonomy of family members."[3] Nancy Cott's *Public Vows: A History of Marriage and the Nation* (2000) is more subtle, but sees the same phenomenon: the emergence of a new ethic remaking marriage in the image of "liberty, privacy, consent, and freedom."[4] Hendrik Hartog, whose *Man and Wife in America: A History* (2000) charts the fall of coverture, completes his analysis before the changes in the late twentieth century, but sees marriage as a field marking "freedom to create a union—a private sphere—that would express creatively our individuality, our shared identity, and our changing commitments, our love."[5] Mark Brandon provides a legal analysis in *States of Union: Family and Change in the American Constitutional Order* (2013), where the aim of family change is said to be the realization of "associational liberty and choice."[6]

Political theorists of the rolling revolution pick up where historians leave off. Contemporary liberals aspire to purge, control, or limit the elements in married life that contradict or threaten individual freedom; generally, they would bring married life *as far as possible* into line with the fundamental aspirations of equality, individual independence, and autonomy. According to contemporary liberals, public law about marriage cannot support any controversial ideas about marital form, matter, or character. Should marriage be enduring, permanent, or at-will? The law cannot say. Should marriage be for the purposes of procreation and education of children or adult fulfillment? The law cannot say. Should marriage be essentially heterosexual? The law cannot say. Should people living together be married, or is living together without the piece of paper sufficient for public recognition? The law cannot say. Ultimately the question becomes, "Should there be marriage?" and we shall see that the law, under contemporary liberalism, cannot say, "Yes."

One must go further. Neither legal nor social pressures should, according to these advocates of neutrality, inhibit autonomous individuals from pursuing their chosen life plans. Feminist concerns, articulated in the previous chapter, have dogged this liberal aspiration and have led to revisions in contemporary liberal theory that combine liberal neutrality with a smidgen of feminist value promotion. The result of these accommodations is the embrace of "intimacy," "commitment," and "care" as the values that contemporary liberals would, for now, at least, promote. Ultimately, their way of understanding these values leads, we shall see, to the abolition of marriage and to the reconstruction of the family itself. How contemporary liberalism challenges the family changes over time, but its critical stance endures. Its tendency to abolish marriage and family life is woven into its nature.

Libertarians and a Privatized Marriage

Today's liberalism comes in two broad hues: libertarianism and contemporary liberalism.

For libertarians actions that do not physically and directly harm others should be immune from state regulation. Individuals should be free to enter into relationships without official permission or approval. These two ideas are in fact mutually reinforcing: as individuals need no permission ("mind your own business"), they also require no praise or affirmation (no "equal concern and respect").[7] Much more concerned with guarding neutrality than reconstructing public opinion, libertarians seem, on principle, interested in limiting state power and providing space for private decisions without seeking to shape how people act. Getting the state out of marriage helps manage society's conflict about the meaning of marriage: we can all live in peace if we refrain from imposing our views on others. This expands freedom. As freedom expands, libertarians expect more experiments in living and, they believe, more happiness and less social friction as adults follow their passions.[8]

Libertarians would not abolish marriage, but would privatize it. "Marriage contracts," David Boaz writes, "could be as individually tailored as other contracts are in our diverse capitalist world." Debates over marriage would, Boaz continues, be "depoliticized and somewhat defused if we keep them out of the realm of government."[9]

Privatizing marriage would include two moves. First, absent a contract, the state would take no cognizance of adult relationships. Adult marriage-like relationships would not be part of the social contract. They would remain outside the notice of civil government, akin to friendships.[10] Whether they were a couple or throuple, a foursome or a moresome; whether gay or straight; whether its members were faithful or its borders porous; whether they were monogamous parents of six children, swingers, traditional polygamists, or other forms of "complex marriage"—the state would recognize only individuals and would be prohibited from recognizing marital contracts as different from contracts for service, for instance. Second, privatizing marriage would require government to refrain from promoting and supporting marriage and parenthood. While it is difficult to describe all that this would involve, laws that have as their justification the maintenance of mores that support marital relationships would be immediately suspect. Laws prohibiting prostitution, pornography, and public nudity, for instance, might lose their raison d'être under these circumstances, for such laws exist mostly to guide people's actions and ideas concerning proper sexual relations and to point people toward devoted monogamous relations.

The libertarian assumption that human beings are autonomous choosers runs up against serious problems when it must deal with the care of children, who are dependent and incapable of genuine choice. Libertarians such as Murray Rothbard and Wendy McElroy, believing that "libertarianism does not recognize positive legal obligations except as established by agreement," think "there is no positive obligation that legally forces a parent to provide sustenance or shelter" to a child.[11] No duties but those freely chosen. Parents are legally liable for abusing their children, but not for neglecting them. Other libertarians seek to show that their emphasis is on securing parental rights, remaking parental obligations to provide care for children as the product of consent and agreement.[12] Even when they recognize a need for positive obligations to children, libertarians entertain a long-term aspiration to end government involvement in recognizing marriage.

The libertarian position seems theoretically different from the contemporary liberal perspective. In practice, libertarianism clears away the underbrush while contemporary liberalism builds a new world. Once libertarians help to establish a right, contemporary liberals busy themselves with ensuring that society acknowledges and supports the exercise of that right. Libertarians help to establish a right to abortion or contraception, and contemporary liberals translate that into a requirement that abortion and contraception be publicly funded. Libertarians assist in expanding marital freedom to homosexuals, and contemporary liberals then require businesses to provide services to homosexual weddings despite their private opposition on religious grounds. Genuine autonomy, contemporary liberalism holds, requires a formal freedom to engage in an activity and a substantive liberty and support actually to engage in that activity. Example after example of the rolling revolution shows that contemporary liberalism is the effectual truth of libertarianism. (Other problems with libertarian thinking are canvassed in chapter 6.).

Contemporary Liberalism and the Liberal Wringer

Contemporary liberals sound libertarian. They think a just society respects each individual's autonomy, with an official policy of government neutrality on the question of the good.[13] No particular lifestyle can be promoted or forbidden through state action, nor can a lifestyle be burdened or discouraged. Governments cannot favor marriage over non-marriage or favor one form of marriage over others, for instance. The ground shifts more than a little, however, with an emphasis on self-respect. Ronald Dworkin, the paradigm of contemporary liberalism, finds "moralism" is out of bounds: "no self-respecting person who believes that a particular way to live is most valuable for him can accept that this way of life is base or degrading."[14] Laws that disfavor a person's lifestyle choice degrade that person's self-respect, insult that person's choice, and discourage a person from putting that choice into practice. People must be affirmed in their choice if they are to be truly free to make it. Regarding marriage, this would mean that a society recognizing only heterosexual monogamous marriage would deprive those interested in same-sex or open marriage of equal concern and respect and may stigmatize them.

Contemporary liberals have a "mixing" opportunity. State neutrality is commanded, they say, unless there is a "compelling state interest" for the state to take a side in a moral controversy, and unless the state's way of achieving its interest is "narrowly tailored." For instance, individuals may purchase pornography, but a state may have a compelling interest in limiting impressionable children from purchasing it and can narrowly tailor laws to accomplish that goal (no selling pornography to minors). Perhaps compelling interests can limit individual choice when important values are at stake. Perhaps the state could defend the man–woman form of marriage, if that form served the public interest in encouraging procreation. Perhaps the state could limit divorce if limiting divorce encouraged the proper education of children. Perhaps it could limit a marriage to two people if that limiting fostered enduring relations or promoted sexual equality.

While this suggests moderation, contemporary liberals practically rule out restrictive laws. "If someone has a right to something," Dworkin writes, defending the right to obscene speech, "then it would be wrong to deny it to him *even though it would be in the general interest to do so*."[15] Liberals insist that such general interests serve a "compelling state interest" in a "narrowly tailored" way, and that nearly all legislation restricting moral activity fails these tests. Ronald Den Otter's *In Defense of Plural Marriage* (2015), concerned to show that laws proscribing polygamy violate the principles of contemporary liberalism, serves as a model. Den Otter makes four arguments with wide application that constitute what I call the liberal wringer.[16]

First, studies show that polygamy in Islamic countries is often patriarchal, illiberal, and abusive. Perhaps polygamy should be proscribed because it fosters such an ethic. But no. These studies reflect, Den Otter notes, a "statistical generalization" not applicable to the Western world. "Whatever it might be like in Africa or the Middle East," Den Otter writes, "legalized polygyny in this country would differ from what it would be like in a place with a different culture, different levels of wealth, and different political and legal systems."[17] An American polygamy might be a healthier "postmodern" polygamy based on consent and equality. More generally, this aspect of the wringer suggests the bad things associated with proscribed practices are not endemic to the proscribed practice. They are caused by something else (in this case the Islamic context); future conditions will render proscribed practices less bad, innocuous, or positively beneficial, so prohibiting practices does not yield the public benefits it promises.

Second, studies show that polygamists in southern Utah or Northern Arizona are insular, abusive, and inclined toward underage, arranged marriages. Perhaps this means polygamy should be proscribed because it fosters such practices. But no. Those characteristics are not intrinsic to plural marriage. "The criminalization of polygamy . . . is more likely than not to be counterproductive." Plural marriage under conditions of taboo and sanction is bound to manifest illegal practices, hierarchies characteristic of criminal enterprises, unnatural distortions, jealousies, and excessively narrow education. The solution to this problem is to baptize the practice with public acceptance. "Very much like drug use, prostitution, gambling and other human vices, legal prohibitions will not only not solve the problem but will probably also worsen it."[18] Bring plural marriage out of the shadows and liberal culture will transform it into something consensual, egalitarian, open, and liberating. More generally the bad things associated with proscribed practices are caused by the stigma attached to them; removing the stigma tames the practice, so legalizing the practice is the path to normalizing it.

Third, studies show that plural marriages cause problems such as underage marriage or spousal abuse. Perhaps polygamy should be proscribed because it fosters illegal activities. But no. The public can regulate secondary effects rather than banning plural marriage. Punish the crime of statutory rape or spousal abuse, but allow the institution that may cause it to survive. After all, "polygamy will be practiced. The real issue is how the state can best respond to its inevitable existence" and the incidental effects associated with it.[19] Let us improve the plural marriage experience through proper regulation of its occasional nasty effects. In any event we should not judge the whole bushel because of a couple or a few or even a bunch of bad apples. More generally, even if bad things still occur, there are "narrowly tailored" ways of discouraging bad things; it is easier to curtail those bad things if the practice is made legal.

Fourth, if our liberal society were *really* interested in securing gender equality or the well-being of children, it would have to ban many monogamous marriages. Many monogamous marriages are, after all, not as egalitarian as liberals would like; some are downright abusive. Despite this the public does not ban monogamy, which shows that the public is not really serious about those problems, and that our evaluations rely "too heavily on . . . structure" and not enough on function.[20] More generally, bad things may be associated with a particular proscribed practice, but the bad things sometimes happen in other practices that we accept, so seriousness about those bad things would mean going after those accepted practices as well. The fact that we do not go after those other instances suggests that society manifests an irrational animus when it proscribes some practices and not others.

Contemporary liberalism puts a gun to the head of marriage and demands that it provide a kind of scientific account of its public necessity. I say "kind of" scientific because a social science account will not suffice to prove the case against same-sex marriage or plural marriage or any other public teaching on marriage. A practice could not be proscribed or discouraged (or encouraged) even if supporting it were correlated with public benefits, or if the public were proscribing it because it is associated with public vices. "Once the issue is framed in terms of freedom of marital choice and marital equality," Den Otter writes, prohibitions on plural marriage face such heightened scrutiny that "none of the reasons offered against plural marriage" can survive. Perhaps the question is, Is there *any* evidence that an advocate for traditional marriage could marshal that would lead advocates of plural marriage to concede the point? All who opposed "same-sex marriage [found] it nearly impossible to contend that such different treatment of gays and lesbians [could satisfy] the constitutional requirement of equal treatment," Den Otter writes.[21] Those involved in defending anything resembling traditional marriage have seen this movie before on drug legalization, abortion, pornography, and many other cultural issues.[22] No concept of marriage and no legislation of morals can survive the liberal wringer.

Informing the liberal wringer is the liberal demand for neutrality. Any public understanding of marriage violates "the type of neutrality necessary for the state to secure liberty and equality in a diverse polity," according to Tamara Metz. Morals legislation casts the state in "the role of an *ethical authority*, a role for which it neither is nor ought to be suited."[23] For now liberals apply the principle of neutrality to decrease the number of benefits channeled through marriage, and simultaneously to extend marriage to ever more kinds of close personal relationships. They seek, in the words of Elizabeth Brake, to "minimize" marriage.[24] Marriage is not thereby abolished so much as extended (using Brake's list) to "same-sex partners and diverse care networks," which include "urban tribes, best friends, quirkyalones, polyamorists," but also "throuples, foursomes and moresomes."[25] As the breadth of marriage expands, its depth, from the state's point of view, contracts.[26] Greater minimizing of marriage eventually leads to disentangling the cords between marriage and the state. As marriage becomes so thin under the law, "untying the knot" between marriage and the state is possible.[27] Therefore liberals such as Metz, Martha Fineman, and others think neutrality culminates in the abolition of marriage as a legal category.[28]

With apologies to Alexander Pope: whether minimizing marriage amounts to its abolition let fools contest; all arguments in support of marriage fail the test. Thus the rolling revolution manifests itself in contemporary liberalism.

Nor is this all. Not satisfied with being left alone, anxious liberals, affecting to hang their self-worth on how the community judges their life choices, make private choices the community's business. Once people are entitled to "equal concern and respect," the community must provide that concern and respect by teaching citizens what to think and how to act. Communities must regulate opinions so all feel accepted. Private organizations must rethink how they treat what used to be considered alternative lifestyles. Securing "equal concern and respect" requires a revamping of public opinion in the name of securing respect and sensitivity to different, diverse lifestyles,

Contemporary liberalism affects to leave people free to arrange their private, marriage-like relationships how they want. Let a thousand family forms bloom! Yet fears, originating in feminism, linger that traditional women will not choose independence. As second-wave feminists chafe under complacent first-wave feminists, contemporary liberals are not satisfied if patriarchs and the women who love them resurrect patriarchal ways under the contemporary liberal framework (with the sexual division of labor, different jobs, and sexually passive women lying in the posture of defeat). Since feminists think modern society resembles a medieval patriarchy if there are any sexual differences, they appropriate contemporary liberalism to further feminist ends. The result is a contemporary liberalism that promotes the conceptual separation of sex and gender.

Feminism and Contemporary Liberalism

Earlier iterations of classic liberalism (as in John Locke) and contemporary liberalism (as in John Rawls) did not aim to abolish marriage. Was this a mixing prudence or lack of imagination? The decisive argument in contemporary liberal thought, with respect to marriage and family life, is Okin's *Justice, Gender, and the Family*,[29] which exposes blind spots or secret moderation in Rawls' *Theory of Justice* (1971) that had provided the impetus for contemporary liberalism.

For Rawls the family, like the competitive market economy and the political constitution, is a "major social institution" in the "basic structure of society" because "its effects are so profound and present from the start."[30] For Rawls people behind the veil of ignorance, where they do not know important attributes about their identity (e.g., their class, race, creed, or sex), can best determine the roles and rights of those participating in family life. Questions asked from behind such a veil reveal answers unbiased by knowledge of a person's situation and self.

Okin asks whether people (read: women) behind the veil of ignorance would accept economic dependence on another wage earner, a division of labor that denies or limits access to the competitive market, unequal pay in the marketplace, or, broadly, the hierarchical, gendered structure of authority in the family and its ramifications outside the family—in sum, whether women behind the veil of ignorance would accept a patriarchal family with males as heads of household and women as homemakers. People behind the veil would not, Okin insists, want their sex to shape their lives.[31] People would want to be free to pursue lives of fulfillment, regardless of what their bodies or society tell them about the role of women (or men) or about marital love and family life. This feminist move requires the abolition of gender from the "basic structures of society," like the economy and the family.[32]

As Okin relates it, Rawls never places women behind the veil of ignorance before determining their roles and rights. He *assumes* the justice of a fairly traditional family because he assumes that the family is the primary agent of moral development; he does not really dig into the morality that the gendered (and domineering, dependency-making) family peddles.[33] The formal state neutrality of Rawls' theory keeps the gendered family in practice, unless things change.[34] Rawls' theory appears more a remnant of first-wave feminism than of the advancing second wave.

Abolishing gender would require policies regulating workplaces and incentivizing just conduct in family life. Laws would need to proscribe domestic abuse and rape, and allow women to own property and have more freedom to divorce. Workplaces would have to become vehicles for conceptually separating childbearing from child-rearing, treating pregnancy as a "disabling condition like any other." All would need provision for or at least access to reproductive technologies. Caregiving or parenting would have to become gender-neutral, so workplaces would need to offer paid time off for both parents to care. Day care and after-school programs could relieve the burdens of the "second shift" women often work at home by involving public entities in the job of minding children and keeping the home. Hiring practices could no longer reflect gender stereotypes—affirmative action would be required to even out hiring practices and hence support role models so both sexes could dream (males becoming kindergarten teachers and females becoming superintendents and football coaches). These are second-wave demands. More work thinking through the policies to support the principles must be done: Okin provides the framework for proposing new policies.

Making the family gender-neutral and just requires the reshaping of the culture and economy outside the family. Perhaps this requirement initially made Rawls a bit shy: it puts the state in a position where it must visit private, apparently consensual actions of men and women to marry and make families or to burden certain individual choices and hence to compromise choice. Whatever the reason for Rawls' reticence, Okin will have none of it. "A just future would be one without gender," Okin writes (as we saw in chapter 2). People behind the veil would choose a "basic model that would absolutely minimize gender" everywhere.[35] Political representatives would, if the world were just, come, more or less equally, from each sex, as would kindergarten teachers and plumbers. Childcare and housework would be split fifty-fifty between the spouses. Men and women would have equal concepts of self-respect and self-worth and be able to dream the same dreams with the same likelihood that those dreams would come true.

Faced with Okin's objection that he left women enslaved to the traditional family, Rawls conditionally confesses his sin of patriarchal non-neutrality. He praises Okin for generating a "critique of the family and gender-structured social institutions," and produces a theory where the parties in the original position do "not know their sex."[36] Rawls requires "no particular form of the family (monogamous, heterosexual, or otherwise)," so long as it provides effective child-rearing. Effective child-rearing involves (1) the cultivation of "self-esteem" and (2) an appreciation for the contemporary liberal principles of justice (i.e., living according to Rawls' teaching). The family's traditional structure (e.g., the sexual division of labor) is, Rawls writes, "the linchpin of gender injustice" that perpetuates ineffective child-rearing. "If the basic . . . cause of women's inequality is their greater share in the bearing, nurturing, and caring for children in the traditional division of labor within the family," he endorses efforts "to equalize their share, or to compensate them for it."[37] Perhaps other solutions could work. The later, chastened Rawls justifies government's corrective efforts to change how families conduct their business.

Rawls' more conservative-appearing position on the family seems to bespeak appreciation for the different kinds of relationship within the family. The husband–wife relationship can be much more equal than the parent–child (father–child and mother–child) relationship. The adult relationship is more easily imagined in terms of the independence of each, while parent–child relations cannot easily be so conceived. Excessive focus on making adults independent may compromise parenting. Children are dependent on parents for their very being, their bodily needs, their education, and the shaping of their character. Assumptions about age linger behind Rawls' initial veil. Are those behind the veil adults or children? Children behind the veil might ask for individualized attention and unconditional love and support from a mother and a father, while adults may seek independence and sufficient resources to follow a life plan—one that may or may not involve providing attention and love to that child. In the face of these conflicts, the Rawls of *Theory of Justice* maintains the prudent silence of one too embarrassed to choose between two legitimate alternatives.[38]

Rawls' second position eschews such prudence and mixing, and focuses on eliminating male dominance, establishing genuine reproductive freedom, and cultivating individual growth and independence in women. Anything less would be uncivilized, at this late date. This position narrows the responsibility of parents to their children and focuses on establishing *adult* autonomy and equality within marriage. Educating children becomes simpler, limited to having the children learn the principles of justice by watching their parents practice justice (i.e., transcending gender) and to cultivating "self-esteem" independent of any substantive understanding of what is estimable.

The family is thereby revised and reconstituted. The context for family life (i.e., the government, economy, and culture) changes. Central to revising the family is moving the goal of marriage beyond the traditional view that it involves the procreation and education of children, which depend on gender difference. This move beyond children constitutes contemporary liberalism's move "beyond conjugality" toward the equation of marriage with the state recognition of "close personal relationships." Early theorists like John Stuart Mill and later Okin refuse to identify what the purpose of marriage is, thinking that this deemphasis on childbearing and child-rearing will redound to the benefit of woman's independence and equality. Subsequent reforms of family life have led contemporary liberals to identify the purpose of marriage apart from its emphasis on having and raising children, and the attendant suggestion that there might be differences between the sexes. We await, as Martha Fineman writes, a restatement of the "relationships among the state, the market, the family and individuals who are now freed [formally] from their historic family expectations."[39]

None of these reforms has (yet!) finished the job of moving marriage beyond childbearing and child-rearing or abolishing that sexual division of labor. For contemporary liberalism the gender-neutral family is, to borrow a phrase, a standard "familiar to all, and revered by all; constantly looked to, constantly labored for, and even though never perfectly attained, constantly approximated, and thereby constantly spreading and deepening its influence." Contemporary liberalism, pointing to the abolition of marriage, reformed through Okin's courageous complaint, furthers the feminist abolition of gender.[40]

Today's Reduction of the Family

The contemporary liberal effort to disestablish the family is permanent; however, as the revolution rolls through marriage and family life, it aims at different aspects of marriage and family life along the way. What follows concerns how contemporary liberal arguments about the family point to a thinner image of the family today.

The contemporary liberal effort to disestablish marriage began with the effort to erase the procreative purpose in marriage and move toward an emphasis on personal choice of adults in marriage. Marriage is, in the words of Chief Justice Earl Warren in 1967, "one of the 'basic *civil rights* of man,' fundamental to our very existence and survival."[41] Warren's language is cagey, in that he does not say what in marriage concerns "our very existence and survival." Subsequent decisions have revealed a private and adult-centered conception of marriage. Accordingly, the Supreme Court, in its statements about marriage during the 1980s, saw marriage's core not as the "ordering purpose of procreation"; marriage had a new core consisting of "expressions of emotional support and public commitment"; "an exercise of religious faith," in recognition of its spiritual dimension; and "the receipt of government benefits."[42] Marriage concerns the adults joining the marriage; it no longer includes a mention of sexual consummation (which would connect it to procreation). Marriage is, in the words of the celebrated *Goodridge* decision establishing same-sex marriage in Massachusetts, "at once a deeply personal commitment to another human being and a highly public celebration of the ideals of mutuality, companionship, intimacy, fidelity, and family." It encourages, for some reason, "stable relations over transient ones," and "fulfills yearnings for security, safe haven, and connection that express our common humanity."[43]

This change in the core meaning of marriage reflects a dramatic, unprecedented shift toward abolishing marriage as a legal category. Nor should we be distracted by secondary arguments, drawn from the liberal wringer, that have led to the divorce between marriage and procreation. If procreation is central to marriage, why do marriage licenses not require a promise or commitment to procreate? Or why do we allow those heterosexual couples past the age of childbearing to marry? Or why do we continue to acknowledge the marriages of those who are sterile?[44] These objections assume that what is essential to the marriage *must always be fully present in a marriage* for marriage to be marriage. Holding the idea that marriage has a public purpose to an impossibly high standard, these questions presume and establish the formlessness *and purposelessness* of marriage.

This works itself out in the values that contemporary liberals promote in their current understanding of marriage. Three of the most important, oft-repeated values promoted through contemporary marriage are *intimacy*, *commitment*, and *care* (for now!). Consider, for instance, Ralph Wedgwood, who sees marriage involving "sexual intimacy, economic and domestic cooperation, and voluntary mutual commitment to sustaining the relationship."[45] Adrian Wellington similarly envisions the function of marriage to be the recognition of voluntary intimate relationships.[46] These attributes constitute an evolving paradigm that deconstructs previous forms. The evolution points toward less form and vaguer purpose in marriage.

Intimacy

Intimacy points above and below itself. The state might be concerned with *sexual* intimacy because it can lead to children. This old view points above intimacy to connections in marital unions centered on child-making and child-rearing. Liberal feminists, as we have seen, resist this move as overbroad, as unable to take counterexamples into account, and as insufficiently reflective of our diverse practices with respect to intimacy, and also as constitutive of a family with an inescapably biological, "gendered" component.

The new intimacy points below itself in contemporary liberalism's "evolving paradigm" of marriage. If the old view assumed that sexual consummation is connected to marriage and procreation, advocates for same-sex marriage emphasize the sexual, marital intimacy as a bond for two lovers. The same-sex argument apes the old view, with the crucial change that sexual intimacy has become an end in itself. Severed from procreative purpose, *sexual* intimacy loses its privileged status as an intimacy. Today's contemporary liberals refuse to privilege "sexual intimacy" within marriage.[47] A neutral state may favor "intimacy" (so the argument goes), but it must be neutral among ideas of intimacy. Some people value emotional intimacy, while others value social intimacy. Intimacy may know some bounds (one cannot be emotionally or sexually active with all humanity), but its bounds reflect individual difference and cannot be prescribed beforehand. There are questions about whether marital forms can be limited to *exclusive*, intimate relations, much less sexual relations or those having procreative sex. Groups of friends are intimate, as are entire families (emotionally, at least), members of communities, roommates, teachers and students, members of a team, adult care networks, and other groups of people. Brothers or sisters taking care of a nephew may be sufficiently intimate even though they are not sexually intimate. Intimacy can be a general attachment, a willingness to be near someone or some group or to share something with someone or some group.

Advocates of opening up marriage quantitatively and qualitatively see soft bigotry in emphasizing *sexual* intimacy or exclusive attachments, as was done in the excessively moralistic same-sex debate. "Once marriage is understood as a legal framework for intimate or committed or caring adult relationships," writes Brake, "the implications of neutrality and political liberalism are much more far-reaching than has been generally realized." Focusing on intimacy, same-sex marriage advocates' efforts to limit marriage to "a cohabiting, financially entangled, sexual, monogamous, exclusive, romantic relationship . . . depends on a view justifiable only within comprehensive moral doctrines—amatonormativity [i.e., the view that love is between two]."[48] Intimacy severed from procreation points beyond conjugality, beyond monogamy, beyond same-sex marriage, toward open-ended sexually intimate relations (polygamy and polygyny) and toward state recognition for intimate, *non*sexual, nonexclusive relations.

If marriage is about intimacy, and intimacy is what people assert it to be, many intimacies are marriages. Scholar-activists prepared such grounds for actions "beyond same-sex marriage" (the name of a 2006 statement of principles). These hoped to build a coalition for recognizing marriages among "close friends and siblings who live together in long-term, committed, nonconjugal relationships, serving as each other's primary support and caregivers," or "extended families (especially in particular immigrant populations) living under one roof, whose members care for one another."[49] Intimacy severed from procreation ends up in a conception of "marriage" that emphasizes care for dependents,[50] or the replacement of marriage with caretaker(s)–dependent(s) relationship.[51]

Some same-sex marriage advocates affect to reject the move from intimacy severed from procreation to polygamy, or even greater formlessness or "marital freedom." They affect to think there are good reasons for maintaining *exclusive* marriage, though not *heterosexual* marriage.[52] There is a hedging, playful "not-yet" character in claims that the "evolving paradigm" will have reached its final destination with the latest reform. The staid and legalistic Linda McClain, for instance, concedes that "there will be an ongoing debate about the normative, empirical, and regulatory questions raised by polyamory," but she affects not to "believe that recognizing same-sex marriage *compels* an evolution to embrace plural marriage."[53] Perhaps McClain is sincere. Perhaps she is settling for exclusive, same-sex marriage *for now*. Arguments for exclusivity have, after all, already been shredded in the liberal wringer (see Den Otter's *In Defense of Plural Marriage*).

Intimacy presents an instance of the rolling revolution. An intimate marriage begins with moorings in a marriage with procreative and educative purposes; then it is connected to exclusive sexual relations divorced from broader purpose; then it is shorn of sexual relations but maintains the element of closeness, proximity, and agreed-upon shared purposes among a couple, of whatever sex or gender, and then including ever larger groups of people, blood related or not, who assert their intimacy. Intimacy is too thin and amorphous to ground state recognition for marriage

Commitment

Like intimacy, commitment points above itself to traditional marriage and below itself toward greater formlessness. Under the old view, the state encourages commitment between spouses as central to and mirroring the commitment parents have for their children. Marital commitment or fidelity is exclusive and (hopefully) enduring.

Contemporary liberals, disconnecting what seems connected, hold that marriage need not entail commitment; love or sex need not entail commitment; and commitment need not be funneled solely into the marital dyad. Commitment can be exclusive or not, unconditional or not, permanent or not. Personal relations with others can involve commitment, but one "cannot be obligated to have a commitment." Commitments arise from one's emotions, passions, or will, not from one's promises. "Commitment is not only expressed through marriage, and marriage is not necessary to develop committedness; institutions other than permanent and exclusive marriage can express or promote committedness."[54]

Commitment unmoored from its relationship to procreation, parenting, or exclusive marital relations involves more general characteristics. It encompasses a variety of relationships—parental, friendly, political, ideological—in a great variety of forms—a single person committed to a political cause, several people committed to the upbringing of a child, two people committed to their Lenten vows, a group committed to losing weight or exercising regularly or promoting the cause of environmental protection. Friends, roommates, parents, extended families, urban tribes—all can claim to offer "emotional support" buoyed by "public commitment." If states lend dignity to such commitments through state recognition, there will be no end to state activity but that activity will signify nearly nothing. Perhaps it will one day stop.

Care

Neither the staid McClain nor the outrageous Brake recommend the abolition of marriage. They look into the abyss and ask, "Why not abolish marriage?" and, after much deliberation, suggest that marriage must only be fundamentally reconceived (for now!). They seek publicly defensible "primary goods" that support people's needs no matter their life choice.[55] Such defenses of marriage go like this: we need marriage because marriage promotes [blank] and people more or less lack [blank] without marriage. Efforts to fill in the blank with "intimacy" or "commitment" lead to the ever-greater formlessness in marriage—so that marriage ceases to be a meaningful category, needing public support. What can fill in the blank and foster a publicly defensible conception of marriage on contemporary liberal terms and be satisfactory to liberal feminists?

Recognizing this problem, contemporary liberals who do not seek to abolish marriage—and even some who do!—fill in the blank with "care." Care too points either above itself to the traditional family or below itself toward greater formlessness.

The etymology of "care" suggests its relation to the traditional family. Care is a trouble, burden, or worry. Caring spouses bear each other's burdens and bear their children's burdens through "better or worse; in sickness or in health." Caring spouses feel a responsibility about the common life they are forging and seek to work through its unpredictable highs and lows. Spouses bearing each other's burdens attend a good school for parenting. Spouses care for a child because a child is their own and they recognize it: because they helped call a child into existence, almost all couples sense a responsibility concerning everything about their children, though circumstances may teach a more modest mode. They are equipped to heed the peculiarities of each child where more standardized institutions are not. This heavy care limits the autonomy and perhaps even the equality of a spouse and a parent. It may even involve tragic decisions, where a parent's burden is that he or she must navigate between the competing goods of life and sacrifice one to another or to others.

Contemporary liberals reject heavy care as too exclusive, as being associated with unjust inequalities, as calling forth too much parental responsibility, and as unable to account for the arbitrary nature of care's passions. Let me pull out the liberal wringer. Care can be wrung from the traditional family and the procreative prejudice: many people care for children without giving birth to them (e.g., adoptive parents, grandparents, teachers, doctors, babysitters, and stepparents), and many people who give birth to children fail to care for them (e.g., deadbeat dads, careerists). Many couples do not have children, so their care or burden is smaller, but they may still care about the health of the oceans. Most problematical about thick care is its deep conception of a child's dependence on another and of the spouses' dependence on each other, and the related offenses to autonomy and gender neutrality. Parents have too much responsibility for shaping the character and capacities of their children, and what this means in practice (until we have changed things) is that some parents forgo career opportunities and become dependent on their spouse: the public must support more equal and less burdensome ways of caring. Familial independence as a caregiving institution can be bad for children if they have bad parents or if parents lack the resources to give adequate care.

Providing neutral care involves recentering private family arrangements around caring for dependents without reinforcing the gendered familial experience for men, women, and children. Care cannot be limited to heterosexuals or homosexuals, nor by number, nor by other things. Martha Fineman is the best guide to the radical implications of this understanding of care. She takes us back to where we can envision the place of children behind Rawls' veil of ignorance. Dependency is, Fineman notes, a "natural part of the human condition," an "economic, psychological and emotional" reality.[56] The dependence of children is "inevitable," and the dependence of caregivers is "derivative" of inevitable dependence. Liberal feminism has long sought to erase the "derivative" dependency of wives upon husbands that comes from the often-womanly effort to raise children from "inevitable dependency." Fineman would erase all derivative dependences. "We do not need marriage and we should abolish it as a legal category," she writes.[57] State recognition tends to be gendered, couplist (favoring dyads), and amatonormativist, and hence it imposes a form on how the family organizes derivative and inevitable dependencies. Focus on form traps women. Sometimes Fineman suggests that getting the government out of adult relations is a necessary or prudential matter of adjusting to the deinstitutionalizing or liberalizing changes afoot in family practice, but she is really an enthusiastic supporter of liberal and feminist efforts because the traditional form is, she contends, good neither for women nor for the children they raise.[58]

Previous liberals ignored relationships with origins in "inevitable dependency" (as Rawls' original theory seemingly does) or wished them away (as, arguably, Okin's contemporary liberal feminism does). Previous thinkers and advocates hoped to get men to share roles involving "derivative dependency," or to convince women to embrace more opportunities outside the home and to leave the home behind. Policies based on these hopes have *not* led to an elimination of gender scripts, dictated, Fineman thinks, by social conditioning and by the "spouse with superior economic and social power" (i.e., the man). Fineman almost gives up on efforts to further equality among adults. She embraces same-sex marriage, cohabitation, and nontraditional adult relationships, and hopes they break the gendered family down more. She realizes that state promotion of gender neutrality and equality can only be "imposed in a formal manner" and cannot crack the tough nut of individual choice—or, as she conceives of it, "the whim of the person with the most economic and cultural clout" (i.e., the man).[59] Women have secured the right to work, access to contraception, legal abortion, educational opportunities, anti-discrimination laws, a restructured culture that welcomes female careers, easy divorce, and more. Marriage is very open as to form. Girls also achieve more than boys in school and women make up an increasingly large proportion of professional and social elite positions than men.[60] It is quixotic for feminists to think the *next* reform will take marriage beyond gender. Asking for more radical measures to increase women's opportunities or to get men to share in more household work is a "dead end," Fineman thinks.[61]

Feminists have focused on securing independence or even equality, but they have not given a realistic account of motherhood, which is "mired in dependency."[62] Fineman's autonomy myth is the wishing away of dependency and biology, and hence the inability to conceive of a real motherhood. Women have been harmed by that myth since their role is misconceived under the ideology of autonomy. This has the odor of truth.

Fineman embraces every aspect of today's retail feminism, in which reformers focus on building a "more humane workplace and a more responsive state" in the hopes that these changes will minimize the derivative dependencies from which women in need suffer.[63] Paid parental leave, highly subsidized, high-quality day care, more working from home, flexible work weeks, shorter work weeks, and some form of income redistribution from producers to caretakers might ease this conflict.[64] Feminists and liberals support such efforts at cultural reconstruction in principle. These policies are just, they think, since the public benefits, so subsidies and perhaps even direct payments to caregivers are not out of the question.[65] They are necessary for improving the lives of women, since, Fineman admits, despite all the feminist victories, "the societally constructed role of mother continues to exact unique costs for women."[66]

More fundamental, Fineman argues, is inventing a policy that bypasses marriage and abolishes it as a legal category while supporting "the direct relationship of dependent-caretaker."[67] Precisely what this involves is best captured by Teresa Metz, who follows Fineman in hoping to abolish marriage as a legal category and to replace it with Intimate Care-Giving Units (ICGUs).[68] These new units, Metz writes, would "look like [traditional] marriage," but they would be "expressly tailored to protect intimate care." The state-created status would contain "assumptions of longevity" (since caring implies duration) and "resource sharing" (since caring means sharing); ICGUs would receive cash payments from the state, public subsidies for health care and day care. All caregivers and dependents could enter ICGUs—friends caring for one another; brothers and sisters; parents raising children; children caring for an elderly aunt, mother, or friend. The state could regulate or license these units, since it creates them; advocates for this approach affect to shudder at this possibility, since it might tempt some to regulate the inner workings of ICGUs or to prefer some to others. Metz and her allies hope to assert a "limited shield" against state intrusion into ICGUs.[69] The state is thereby invited to ensure that care is delivered properly by whatever unit claims to be giving it.

Others stop short of calling for the abolition of marriage and creating new state units. McClain affects to find the state acknowledgment of commitment and intimate relations important enough to provide meaning to the institution and to facilitate the dependency of adults upon each other. She is willing to settle for a reconstruction of marriage or to move, as she writes, "partly, but not wholly beyond marriage."[70] Marriage would become a public-private contract with a "kinship registration system" at its center. Such a system would allow adults in relationships (whether same-sex or opposite-sex, whether two or many, whether related or not) to "express their commitment to one another, receive public recognition and support to voluntarily assume a range of legal rights and obligations."

McClain's newly reconstituted marriage resembles the minimized marriage of Brake, who would allow consenting units to marry. The state would assume each member of the new body is economically independent. "Minimal marriage would consist only in rights that recognize (e.g., state designation for third parties, burial rights, bereavement leave) and support (e.g., immigration rights, care-taking leave) for *caring relationships*."[71]

There is some debate among liberals and feminists over how the state should get out of adult relationships (for now!) and how far caring justifies support for relationships. Perhaps the intimacy and commitment require a registration system that will replace marriage (McClain). Perhaps supporting adult care justifies a minimal registration system (Brake). Perhaps none of this is worth the state's trouble and it can be handled privately through contract (Fineman). McClain would partly abolish marriage; Brake would minimize it; Fineman would abolish it. Do not let these nuanced variations distract from the deep agreement about the implications of care for children: all embrace nuanced variations on the theme of abolishing marriage and moving beyond what marriage has long been.

The Blinders of Liberalism

Contemporary liberals seek gender neutrality and neutral public values in family policy. This runs up against some daunting challenges. They cannot tell us why the state should recognize or support the axis that marriage once occupied. The result is an ever-thinner, more minimal marriage expanded to more varieties of relationships culminating in the abolition of marriage.

The nuanced, shifting borders between minimizing marriage and abolishing marriage make up the meandering border between mainstream and radical thought among contemporary liberal feminists. It is not a difference in principle, however. Mainstream, retail feminists may not want to abolish marriage (yet!). Much of feminism's intellectual and political energy involves erasing the form of marriage so as to better free women from its perceived abuses, dependencies, and cultural scripts, and to allow them to live lives of freedom and equality.

The contemporary liberal feminist vision of what we used to call marriage and family life would involve two different axes and a changed world. Groups or pairs of adults would come together on a chosen level of intimacy and commitment. Perhaps these groups or pairs would share a common conception of the good. Perhaps these groups or pairs would be related to one another by blood and live together for convenience. Perhaps it would be two husbands with an intense, highly personal relationship. Perhaps the couple would be living together outside of marriage. Perhaps it would be a single parent, struggling to get by. Perhaps it would be a throuple, a threesome, or a moresome. Perhaps it would be a husband and wife, living together and sharing a life. Adults would form relationships based on freely chosen and revocable psychological dependency, a minimum of economic dependency, and a rich measure of equality, with various levels of commitment and intimacy.

Perhaps most of these relationships would be heterosexual with all or most of the trappings of marriage—exclusivity, economic codependence, love, the sharing of a last name, the presence of children, intimacy, commitment, mutual support, a division of labor, a common economic destiny, a shared domicile, an expectation of sexual union. Laws, taking no notice of this norm, would have to be neutral about what relations were in this category, and public opinion would need, insofar as possible, to bless all relations with public approval.

Children are most likely to come from heterosexual couples with all or most of the trappings of marriage, and children need the time, attention, and resources that parents provide. More embarrassment follows from this. Parents assume that they can, should, and must take care of their own children. Parents often, for whatever reason, prefer their own children to the children of others. Women appear better suited biologically and psychologically than men to provide the care and education that children need.

Whatever these norms may be and however natural or useful they may be, none of these norms can be integrated into public policy, according to contemporary liberal feminists. The public can assume no biological connection between caregiver and dependent. It can assume no duty of a parent to a child. It can assume no duty of a child to a parent. Birthing a child is of no importance for assigning these duties. How biological parents become "caregivers," or if they should become caregivers, is something contemporary liberals cannot say. The public cannot assume that the caregiver–dependent relation is between an adult and a child, since many kinds of people, including the disabled and the aged and the addicted, may become dependent.

The ideal liberal feminist arrangement would involve a caregiver, supported through governmental regulation, responsible corporate action, and welfare state redistributions, who would take care of dependents or at least hire trusted, perhaps subsidized people to care for dependents. Caregivers would have adequate resources to spend on dependents, while also having adequate resources to maintain a fulfilling career independent of dependent–caregiver obligations. There might be a tragic conflict if a caregiver wanted fulfilling work as a lawyer (which would take time and training) and found a strange fulfillment in being a caregiver for a friend injured in a polo accident (which would also take time) or for a person who once was a caregiver for the person who would be a caregiver today (i.e., what used to be called a parent, which would also take time), or in being a caregiver for someone's dependent child. When it is a conflict of time and fulfillment, caregivers and careerists cannot have it all.

The workplace reforms of contemporary liberal feminists suggest that they would like to reconceive this conflict. Time would be invested in careers, though flextime and vacation time and parental leave would be available when a caregiver would like to give care. Paid caregivers would be charged with taking care of dependents either by a generous employer or through a subsidized day care. It might require subsidies to be available so one's domicile could be cleaned, dinners prepared, shopping done, the clothes laundered, and other mundane tasks completed. Perhaps these problems could be automated, or done through cheap labor. These day cares would educate dependents in a gender-neutral way. Through this arrangement dependents would become independent with proper care, and without unduly compromising the autonomy of the caregiver. Contemporary liberal feminism, trying to avoid this tension, delays it and expects an answer consistent with the opportunity-for-all ethic, but it cannot afford to say so since that would violate neutrality.

Contemporary liberalism provides the mundane parts of the rolling revolution in marriage and family life. By transferring what used to be private obligations to public entities, it augments the responsibility of the state and provides a venue for greater independence from the family for all. By putting forward a never-ending goal, it ensures that there will always be more work for the state to do and more responsibilities for the family to shed.

4

BEYOND SEXUAL REPRESSION

Feminists embrace sexual liberation to break down the expectation of women having a modest and maternal character, abolish gender, realize greater gender equality, and foster the abolition of the family. Contemporary liberals ally themselves with sexual liberation theorists, but that alliance is, to believe contemporary liberals, an accident. The alliance between contemporary liberals and sexual libertines since the 1950s comes from the fact that our laws have, both think, taken the side of those who would shape public morality toward an ethic of sexual self-control that supports monogamous, enduring love. Just as, for contemporary liberals, the state can favor no particular, gendered vision of the family, so can it favor no particular vision of proper sexual activity. No legislation of sexual morality is permissible. Laws prohibiting adultery, fornication, sodomy, or the purchase of contraception take sides in moral controversies, and therefore disfavor and denigrate the choices of those who indulge such activities. Sexual libertines, in contrast, think such laws harm the good life because they repress natural, healthy sexual urges and instincts. A society of technically free but actually repressed individuals is unhappy, so sexual libertines would cultivate an ethic of liberation and expression in sexual matters. They want to legislate morality. For now the libertine's legislation of morality is consistent with contemporary liberalism's effort to strip legislation of taints of traditional morality. Contemporary liberalism has thus been a delivery system for emancipating people from "traditional sexual inhibitions and taboos" (in Millett's phrase) as they appear in law, but the alliance is, in theory, an accident of history.

Sexual liberation is the third element of the rolling revolution in marriage and family life. Feminists seek to rid the world of patriarchal indoctrination. The work of feminists involves identifying and deconstructing successive layers of hidden socialization, including socialization around sexual morality, so that the new independent woman can arise. Contemporary liberals encourage all to embrace autonomy while seeking to rid society of incentives and public support that encourage people to form monogamous, nuclear families.

Sexual liberation is different. It is based on the assumption that human beings—young and old, men and women—are sexual beings. Repression of sexual desire distorts human character and undermines human happiness. Sexual liberation gives rise to the imperative that legal, cultural, and corporeal obstacles to the expression of human sexuality be removed. To achieve sexual liberation, laws prohibiting certain sexual practices such as sodomy must be repealed; the culture must welcome and encourage diverse expressions of sexuality, from endorsing sexual experimentation outside of marriage, to breaking down notions of sexual fidelity in marriage and the incest taboo, to encouraging masturbation, legalizing pornography, encouraging the use of sex toys, and other sexual experiments now unknown; the impotence problems of old age and the declining sex drive of the middle-aged must be remedied technologically so the sexual character of human life persists throughout human life, just as sex has been (somewhat) liberated from the biological imperatives of pregnancy through easy and cheap contraception; childhood sexuality must be acknowledged and encouraged. There will probably always be new fields to plow for sexual liberation, because human beings, infinitely inventive but often plagued by conscience, will discover new ways to satisfy sexual desire and hence will identify old repressions to remove. Sexual liberation thus constitutes a rolling revolution all in itself.

The Varieties of Sexual Liberation

Today's sexual liberationists ride the second wave of sexual liberation. The first, more moderate wave appeared in the early 1900s, when scientific theoreticians such as Sigmund Freud, intellectuals like Bertrand Russell, in *Marriage and Morals* (1929), and reformers such as Judge Ben Lindsey, who wrote *Companionate Marriage* (1927), advocated for loosening up the obligations of marriage and for greater public acceptance of alternative lifestyles, including sex before marriage. Included among the practical reforms that Russell and Lindsey hoped to see were the legalization of divorce, greater acceptance of sexual experimentation, including sex among the unmarried, and of masturbation, protections for homosexuality, and legalization of contraception.[1]

Later reformers believe these early revolutionaries imagined a sexual revolution too much *within* the marital regime or as a means of changing marriage.[2] These first-wave sexual reformers did not seem to think that marriage itself, or the civilization to which the peculiarly patriarchal modern form had attached itself, was the problem. Earlier reformers thought that the presence of children within a relationship made the need for permanence more acute, and that society must be involved in securing something akin to permanence through marriages.

Second-wave liberationists bless the first wave's sexual reform, but go further by calling marriage and "civilizing" sexual morality itself into question. Later theorists of sexual liberation come in two guises. First there are scientific advocates, somewhat overlapping with the first wave of sexual liberation, who see sexual liberation as the "modernization of sex,"[3] and who use the debunking lights of science to demystify sex and suggest its emancipation from restraints. This scientific approach to sex began in earnest, arguably, with Freud, who thought, among other things, that sexual experience should be freed from extraneous baggage—ideas of sin, shame, or modesty; a relation to procreation or romantic, monogamous love; a longing for another or one's other half; or other stories. The work that began with Lester Ward in the late 1800s continued with Havelock Ellis in the early 1900s, Alfred Kinsey and his colleagues in the 1940s and beyond, William Masters and Virginia Johnson in the late 1960s and beyond, and countless other scientists of sex or sexologists following within their general principles.

By *modernization of sex* I mean the equation of human and animal sex, or the denial that there is something distinctively human or personal in human sexual desire;[4] a belief that shame, modesty, guilt, and reticence compromise rather than reveal the nature of sexual relations; a conception of orgasm as the *real* end of sexual action;[5] agnosticism, permissiveness, and expanding tolerance about how orgasm is reached;[6] the belief that how men and women experience sex and orgasm must be understood in a gender-neutral way;[7] and the critique of Victorian, bourgeois, or traditional morality as repressions inhibiting sexual release or sublimating sexual passion into unhealthy outlets. Lester Ward captures these premises in *Dynamic Sociology* (1883):

> All desires are alike before Nature—equally pure, equally respectable. All are performed with the same freedom, the same publicity, the same disregard for appearances. Nature knows no shame. She affects no modesty. The acts which are necessary to the perpetuation of a species possess no quality which distinguishes them from those necessary to its preservation.[8]

For scientific sexual modernists, Western society has long sanctioned only sexual release as marital, procreative sex supported by love. Second-wave thinkers see love, for instance, as a myth that stands in for sexual need; society's conception of love has gotten in the way of the *real*, underlying concern for orgasm, so love itself must be stripped away. Loveless, nonmarital means of sexual release were seen first as sins and later as signs of mental disorder, according to the old, repressive order. Human beings will be sexually free only when they are liberated from the traditional morality that has repressed and stigmatized nonmarital, nonmonogamous sexual experiences. Homosexuality, premarital relations, extramarital affairs, prostitution, heavy petting, masturbation, group sex, bestiality, open marriages, plural marriages, complex marriages, necrophilia, fetishism, sadomasochism, sex dolls or sex robots (sexbots), and more must be destigmatized to secure human liberation and happiness. These practices, according to sexual modernists, can be as effective as marital heterosexual, procreative sex in securing the orgasmic end of sexual desire. All orgasms are created equal.

This demystified conception boils sex down to an animal desire for orgasm or sexual release. Like animals, human beings eat, drink, digest, copulate, urinate, and perform other bodily functions. Sexual arousal is a localized bodily irritation from which human beings, like animals, find relief and release. Something triggers arousal, which enlarges or softens the sexual glands and leads the aroused to gain sexual release in the most efficient or pleasurable manner. Desire aims at orgasm; another person, if he or she is there, is but an instrument of release or provides an occasion for it. Treating sex as if it is a different kind of desire is the source of sexual and personal ills. For sexual modernizers sex is more central to human happiness than other bodily functions, so securing its ends is crucial to being well-adjusted and to individual growth.[9]

The second group of sexual liberationist thinkers reach the same orgasmic destination through Critical Theory, a mixture of Freud and Karl Marx. From Freud they get the idea that human beings are innately sexual, and that repressing sexuality can cause neuroses and otherwise undermine healthy human life. While abandoning Marx's economic determinism, they get from him the idea that society's contradictions can be finally overcome through a revolution from the bourgeois order that removes the problem of alienation. Modern bourgeois civilization heightens these contradictions and thus prepares its own gravediggers, as people experience genital satisfaction in different ways than they did in the past. Marx, after all, imagined universal sex love would replace the private bourgeois family after the revolution. The deepest and most influential advocates for sexual liberation include Wilhelm Reich, Herbert Marcuse, and Norman O. Brown, all of whom envision an abolition of repression and a healthy, safe, natural sexuality emerging when repression vanishes.

Both the scientist-advocates and the theorists assert that traditional morality obstructs human health and happiness. Both groups question whether their theories have any limits or whether any "repressions" serve the human good. Those adhering to traditional morality must be actively discouraged (perhaps even proscribed) for their own good and for society's—or so the theories imply. Thus, like feminism, sexual liberation theories, ultimately, point to the question of whether people can be forced to be free and happy.

"Scientific" Sexual Liberation against Traditional Morality

Liberation presumes that traditional morality is a repressive jailer. Traditional morality connects and nourishes connections between sexual desire and love or responsibility. Modernized sex isolates sexual desire or the sex act from other aspects of human experience and nourishes that isolation.

Consider the difference between traditional morality and modernized sex through the example of virtual sex. By *virtual sex* I mean sexual experiences with sexbots, perhaps lifelike in their soft skin and sex organs, and also programmed to talk and interact with their users. It may also consist of full-body suits that allow one to be kissed, stimulated, or touched in one's preferred areas and to feel and imagine a virtual other as one's lover, like in the feelies of Huxley's *Brave New World*. Virtual sex separates sex from procreation; it separates sex from human love and even from other human beings, and thus even from the need for consent. What would the use of sexbots for sexual gratification reveal about the user and about sex? A decent person would hesitate to ask this indecent question in more reticent, better times. We live when we live, however, so let us seek the truth.

Take first the lowest sexbot. The crudest sex machine (e.g., a vibrator) might be better at producing orgasms than simple masturbation, which is already an orgasm brought about without the unreliable intervention of another.[10] Orgasm machines focus on the genitalia, reduce sex to sexual arousal or stimulation antecedent to orgasm, and then bring the individual to climax. If we believe sexbot enthusiasts,[11] orgasm machines are as old as machinery itself. Such machines are consistent with the criteria of consent and safety. There is no worry about getting a crude orgasm machine pregnant and not much worry about catching a sexually transmitted disease from one, if it is properly sanitized.

These machines, from the perspective of modernized sexuality, however, may not be reliable in producing orgasms. An orgasmic experience that focuses on the orgasm may not deliver orgasms for long.[12] Most people need a more personal feel, in imagination or in reality, even to secure climax with regularity. The ineffectiveness of crude machines is an important entrée into traditional thinking about human sexuality. Crude machines lack the knowing looks, the lips, the eyes, the colored cheeks, the kissing, the closeness, the idea that your partner is someone different and unique, the touch of the whole body, the excitement or unpredictability of sex with another person; in short, crude, impersonal orgasm machines are without the attraction, mystery, and resistance presented by another.

This suggests that, on traditional grounds, orgasm is only part of the sexual experience. There is much that is the same or nearly the same in all human beings, sex organs or genitalia chief among them: you have seen one vagina, you have seen them all, and the same with the penis. Much is different in each human being, or so we think. Sexual attraction, the beginning of sexual desire, begins not in the look of the genitalia, but in these "unique" traits of the other person, the appearance and personality that ground liking and loving others. People are sexually attracted to others; attraction transcends what is necessary to sexual acts, and sex acts find a place within a larger relation. This notion of sexual attraction provides a window into how human beings in sex are directed toward a particular person they view as good.

Modernized sex sees attraction as a species of stimulus, or a self-centered build-up of tension or expression of a barely governable urge, with orgasm as the response. Passion builds up to a hydraulic release. All surmounting this stimulus–response, including any concern or directedness to another person or any sense of shame, is fakery and fluff. On the traditional view, attraction transcends mere stimulation. Sexual partners get to sex, but usually only after they turn the lights down low as if they are a bit ashamed of the common nature of the mere sexual deed. Human beings do not often have sex in public places, and not only to spare others from looking. Crude orgasm machines de-link orgasm from prior, personal attraction to another, and from the recognition given to another person who is capable of loving back. They reflect an incomplete idea of sex.

A more sophisticated modern female sexbot, one that affects to cure the impersonal nature of the crude orgasm machine, may have lips to kiss, soft skin to touch, a tongue with which to speak or whisper or perhaps do other things, appropriate programmed reactions to a partner's touch, bodily organs to simulate and complete the sex act, and an aim to please. Programmed with artificial intelligence, she converses. She may dance. She may ask for more. She may even manifest simulacra of virtues or modesty and materials of attraction in how she dresses, if she is so programmed. The kiss in her eyes and the touch of her hand makes the man weak, and his heart may grow very dizzy and fall. The sexbot is not asking for an enduring relationship, unless she is programmed to clingy monogamy. The female sexbot can simulate a genuine relationship with a real human being focused on sexual completion. Perhaps a male sexbot can be produced to satisfy customers interested in such pleasures.

This sophisticated sexbot experience, in a sop to traditional morality, seeks to establish the link between sexual attraction and the act of sex and to make it *seem* as if the sex fits into a larger, loving relationship. The man is attracted to the "person" of the sexbot, the little things that make for a unique relation; this attraction leads to desire and ultimately to sex and orgasm. Sophisticated sexbots encourage us "to like and to love them" because of their "appearance and personality."[13] From the man's perspective, they may resemble a prostitute (and prostitutes should worry that sexbots will leave them unemployed!).[14] Sexbots are prostitution without the alienation of labor or threats from the vice squad.

Sophisticated sexbots, too, fail to provide loving relations on the traditional view. They are immature expressions of human sexuality built upon a fear of rejection or resistance. Sexbots resemble programmed masturbation through the aid of a manufactured product. Sexbots reflect "realistic representations of the human body,"[15] without any of the troubles brought about by human difference or by the psychology or demands of another person. There is sexual attraction, sexual desire, and a simulacrum of a desire to join one's life to another's without sacrificing one's independence, without taking risks, and with each trait of the robot emanating from one's own will. The "lover" designs what is attractive in the "beloved." The common life is appearance and delusion.

Even enthusiastic defenders of sexbots recognize the immature sexuality in a sexbot's love. One of the "principal reasons" people will be attracted to sexbots, an advocate writes, "will be the certainty that one's robot friend will behave in ways that one finds empathetic, always being loyal and having a combination of social, emotional and intellectual skills." Again: Sexbots are "perfect because they're always ready and available, because they provide all the benefits of a female partner without any of the complications involved with human relationships, and because they make no demands of their owners, with no conversation and no foreplay required."[16] Sexbots make life and love easy, secure, and enclosed within the self. Sexbot "relations" make a sexual experience that maintains individual *independence*. This *independence*, *self-centeredness*, and *focus on pleasure* are central to modernized sexuality. Sexbots are edgy and bring with them the sexual experiences of Nietzsche's last man, who invents happiness and secures his little pleasures for the night.

From the traditional point of view, sophisticated sexbots preclude genuine sexual drama, the wooing and resistance, the uncertainty, the "getting-to-know-you," and the adventure that reveal the somewhat chaotic or unpredictable nature of attraction, sexual desire, and love. Sexbot relations deprive human relations of the soil within which they usually grow, and stunt the growth of human aspirations that may have their grounding in erotic desire. Boring "traditional morality" is more chaotic, mysterious, and unpredictable than "edgy," modern sexual practices such as those involving sexbots. Having sex with another, loving that other, and living with that other means, to some extent, that individuals, not yet last men, have chaos in their souls.

Traditional morality sees sexuality as a mysterious, risky endeavor, and sexual desire as something that must be tamed and channeled toward love and another. The growth of attraction is fraught with risk, difficulties, and misjudgments. A person attracted to another can misunderstand that person, or find out later that "she is not for me" or "he is not interested." Attractive women can prove vicious, and attractive men can disappoint. Sexual attraction may lead people to think that the other is good for them. Attraction, which may lead to sex, arises from insights and actions not involving the sex organs. Each has a unique perspective on the actions of the other, and each has a distinctive experience of attraction and desire. Mutual attraction is grounded in the individual features and may find mutual expression. When it does, attraction can transcend the sex act and sexual union toward sharing love and a common life with the other. Attraction goes through the body to seek a broader unity that is good for each, a better, more complete life that is shared with another. Perhaps an excessive concern with the body halts at sexual attraction and inhibits the couple from growing together in a common life. Perhaps the commonalities between the partners are less complete than each had thought, and the life together is unhappy or will not work. It is much easier to find someone sexually than to find someone who is concerned deep down for one's good and who will act for that good. Risk plagues attraction. Rejection does not simply mean that one is not going to have a timely orgasm; it means one has been rejected, body and soul, by another. Love hurts.

Attraction does not always hit its mark. The culmination of attraction is a mystery that participates in the problem of human embodiment. Sex may fool us temporarily into thinking that the pursuer seeks to join a body with the pursued. A moment's reflection on sexual experience teaches us the impossibility of a bodily union lasting. That the union seems to aim beyond the body should not fool us into thinking that union is simply spiritual, on the level of a friendship that shares common goals and goods but does not involve physical intimacy. The body is not uninvolved, for it provides some of the nourishment from which attraction and union spring. The soul peers through the body and cannot escape. Partners spiritualize their separate embodiment and they embody their separate spirits; they can each recognize their inescapably complex nature in the very bodily sex act. Sex is different from eating and urinating.

Traditional morality connects sexual desire to love, children, and marriage. Sex stays at the level of a particular mystery because it is not clear what human beings want or get from it, or that their aim or their means are virtuous. The aim of sexual desire can be a broader, deeper union with another, but its means are, partly, the commonplace, physical act. Sexual desire is intensified through the partner who shares attraction and desire, and it still involves each aiming beyond this. Children often lie beyond the sex act, though they are not necessarily what sexual partners aim at.

The traditional proscription against sexbots and other abnormal sex acts (i.e., perversions) keeps all sides of this mystery alive and in their place, without reducing them to one thing or another. Translating sex into mutual dependence is not automatic and the proscriptions guide. Sex acts that trap us in our own body, that simplify the complex character of what we want, or that prevent the movement from attraction to sex to common goods are problematic. They appear to hold the same ground as heresy holds against divine mysteries in resolving, and hence simplifying, the mysteries of the faith.[17] Disfavored sex acts or perversions reduce sex to one side of its nature, and cut off a human being from confronting another person in that person's complexity. Sexbots are the paradigmatic case of this, reducing the sexual union to a self-referential orgasm.

Following Roger Scruton's pathbreaking work on perversity, we could identify more. In bestiality a person sees only the bodily expression of desire and removes the possibility of entering into another's perspective. Necrophiliacs abjure genuine human contact, emotion, and perspective from the sex act, though with imagination it seems closer to human sex than bestiality. Pedophiliacs seek a child's body and another's perspective, but only in diminished, presumably controllable form. Incest may lack the perspective of the other and hence approaches perversity; more fundamentally it corrupts the ties in the household where open, spontaneous cooperation relating to common goods should transpire. Fetishes find attraction in items that cannot be objects of sexual union and with which a common life cannot be lived. Masturbation traps one in one's own bodily hungers without risking involvement with another's perspective.[18] Voyeurism objectifies and focuses on the body and maintains distance, without joining or uniting with the unique person of the other; victims of voyeurism often feel violated even though they have not been touched, because the voyeur reduced his victim to a body.[19] Evaluation of these actions provides entrée into the complex world of human being.

Pornography is another perversity. It depicts, above all, the sex organs and the excitement found in the moment of orgasm. As sex is modernized, pornography is more readily available, consumed more, and less easily resisted. From a meticulous study of *Swank* and other skin magazines, Harry M. Clor sees pornography reducing sex to the physical act:

> The purpose—to arouse an elemental passion for other people's bodies independently of any affection or regard for a particular person—virtually guarantees that human beings will be represented as instruments. And

the intention to violate, maximally, those conventional proprieties or delicacies that guard the privacy of the erotic act leads to the graphic focus upon bodily functions, parts, and reactions. Pornography caters to the craving for sexual excitation per se and to the voyeuristic interest in viewing people's intimacies. The inevitable consequence of catering to these two inclinations is the phenomenon [of] objectification: a heavy emphasis on the observable externals, hence the animal and mechanical dimensions, of sexuality, and the depiction of its subjects as things to be used for the gratification of the user.[20]

Pornography, so described, separates sex from meaningful loving relation; it focuses on the objects and instruments of sex. It is thus an incomplete manifestation of sexual attraction, sexual desire, and love.

Thus the essential difference between the modern and traditional views: the modernization of sex involves *separating* things that traditional morality joins and *simplifying* things that traditional morality sees as complex. In this separation modern people find autonomy to arrange their lives and their institutions as they choose. The parts of our lives that seem given to us can, on this view, be brought under *our* control and organized according to *our* wills, by *our* logic. On the traditional view, sex—the bodily act, the personal, distinctive attraction—and love are brought together, just as sexual acts involve sexual attraction and sexual desire. Sex is "making love."[21] These connections are not naturally occurring, in the sense that they spontaneously emerge from unregulated relations. These connections must be understood and taught, reinforced and imagined, interpreted by a welcoming culture leading people to a good life.

Why do modernized sexologists dissolve these connections? Start with diversity. Monogamous, exclusive marriage is not the only possible way of connecting the complex features of love, sex, attraction, desire, body, and soul into an ethic that represents (most of) the aspects of the mysteries around sexual desire. Polygamous societies add these features up differently than societies emphasizing monogamy. Some societies frown on premarital sex as a way of reflecting all of these features, while others may be welcoming to it or see it as a matter of indifference. Other societies allow for arranged marriages as a way of keeping subjective feelings in their subordinate place. Homosexual love and sex present a somewhat different way of manifesting these experiences, and they are accepted or not in differing degrees in different societies. One could go on in relating the range of human diversity on these matters, but the range is not limitless.

Proceed second to examples of misfiring. Sexual modernizers question how attraction, arousal, and sex and then love and sex have previously been connected, or whether the high exists, or whether the high depends upon the low. Run the connections through the liberal wringer and nothing remains. First, old connections are seen as vestiges of a Romantic or religious view of how men and women should get along, but those vestiges were really just a way of leaving women in a situation of subordination or trapping men to suppress their wandering ways; they stand for repression, not freedom, love, or self-control. Human beings are, after all, animals, and sex is when our animal nature seems most apparent. Our untutored sexual desires are the "real me," and sexual liberation consists in emancipating the "real me" from civilization's artifices. The high is a myth or a tool of repression. Second, many of those who dwell with pornography or buy sexbots may seem creepy or psychologically unhealthy today, but that comes more from the proscriptions society has imposed upon these actions than from the acts themselves; remove the proscriptions and the "deviants" will be virtually normal. Third, if the higher love exists, it will be able to flourish on its own without artificial moral education to prop it up. If it requires moral education, then it is not human *nature*. Human nature is what exists in the absence of social conventions, and that is the experience of sexual freedom.[22] Fourth, sexual passions are going to find fulfillment no matter what; society might as well accept the deviations and try to regulate whatever problems they may cause (such as broken homes or sex trafficking), or change its unrealistic expectations to accommodate what is really going on so that people do not suffer from pent-up anxiety or frustration.

These arguments point individuals toward the experience of sex in an atmosphere of supposed freedom, untainted by psychological constraints such as shame or modesty, and unimpeded by laws or conventions pointing people toward broader personal attractions or shared lives. Modernizers also promote the use of artificial contraception to bring about sexual freedom and, as Germaine Greer contends, a "demystification" of the human body.[23] Artificial birth control makes natural sexual freedom possible. Divorced from the balderdash of romance or a desire for a more perfect union, from the threat of pregnancy afterwards and from responsibility to other people, sex acts are finally autonomous. The modernization of sex is *the isolation of sex* from any larger context and from the physical consequences that follow from it.

Sexual modernizers, it seems, believe that people can integrate the moment of sexual climax into their life plans however they choose. Sex is a menu item that can be integrated, along with others, à la carte, however an individual imagines and chooses. Nature and culture do not and should not present limits to human construction (and any suggestion that nature and culture present limits is scrutinized with the dissolving reason of the liberal wringer). Human beings have a menu of choices for their lives: exclusivity or open relations; with one, two, or more; with men or women, machines or sexbots; permanent, temporary, or fleeting; sex every hour, daily, weekly, or whatever; pornography or not; masturbation or not; at whatever age, after 80 years old and before 18; whatever position one wants; with contraception or not; with parental responsibilities or not; in public or in private. Individuals build sexual menus without one item necessarily affecting other areas. On the most sophisticated view of modernized sex, human sexuality and human relational life are plastic, and human beings can combine the elements they want in an atmosphere shorn of external constraints. Human nature and the materials of sex and human relations appear as "standing reserve" that can be added up, however people want, according to their free wills.

One must go further. As in the case of traditional morality, human beings must be educated to the tenets of modernized sex. *Everyone* has to be carefully taught! This is accomplished in the supposedly nonjudgmental sex education that people formally receive at school and through laws (oh! How contemporary liberals *should* oppose such public teachings that violate neutrality in peddling a particular form of anti-traditional morality!), as well as through cultural examples, clichés, religious teachings, and the media, at home and elsewhere. This education will eliminate vestiges of the connections that nature and culture foist on people. The old moral education of the affections in the connections of attraction, desire, sex, and love must be countered with a new education, first, erasing the old and second, endorsing creativity for individuals in reconstructing their love lives. The liberationist ethic defines itself against something from which it demands liberation. One must remove guilt, shame, modesty, jealousy, heterosexual norms, exclusivity, and possessiveness, for instance, as remnants of the connections that defined a previous era. In removing shame from voyeurism or public nudity, the liberationist reeducates the human being who used to experience shame and perhaps blush. (Perhaps the traditional ethic could be rebuilt after it has been dissolved, but that would no longer be the *traditional* ethic. Constructors of a neo-traditional ethic would not blush.) Such an education would demand more than the brainwashing and reeducation that Huxley imagines in the Pavlovian education he depicts in *Brave New World.*[24]

The evaluation of sexbots points to the tips of two very large icebergs: one seeing sex within a broader universe of meaning, while the other isolates sex from other areas; one finds sex in a subordinate place with a reciprocal relation with another, while for the other sex can take on whatever meaning that the individual would have it take; one sticking with the given as an accepted good that must be sustained and reinforced through culture, while the other seeks a culture that liberates people from the given; one seeing that the "high does not stand without the low," while the other sees "the low as the real"; one seeking integration, the other isolation and perhaps reconstruction as an exercise of autonomy.

Beyond Repression to Sexual Liberation

Freud's *Civilization and Its Discontents* sets the pattern, if not exactly the substance, for subsequent arguments for sexual liberation: Human sexuality begins at birth, though all of the institutions of civilization (including the family) channel it away from incest, for instance, and toward other, "respectable" things. Sexual desire is repressed and sublimated from the get-go. While Freud and some of his followers thought repression was inseparable from the worthy project of civilization, other Freudians such as Marcuse and Reich gave sexual desire unquestioned priority in its struggle against the repression of an unworthy bourgeois society.

The stakes are in a sense higher for these theorists than they are for the scientists we have examined. Not only is sex about pleasure, for such theorists, but sexual pleasure or orgasm is the model for human happiness. Consider Freud: "what we call happiness in the strictest sense comes from the (preferably sudden) satisfaction of needs which have been dammed up to a high degree, and it is from its nature only possible as an episodic phenomenon." Also: "man's discovery that sexual (genital) love afforded him the strongest experiences of satisfaction and in fact provided him with the prototype of all happiness."[25] Reich agrees: "the core of happiness in life is *sexual* happiness."[26]

For Freud the superego—the socially constructed rules that each individual internalizes—represses or channels sexual pleasure until it must find an outlet. Then it bursts out. Sometimes it bursts out in satisfying sex. Sometimes in artistic creation or scientific discovery. Not all sublimations of sexual desire are healthy, however. We know from Hollywood that many Christian characters, revealing themselves to be repressed hypocrites, are likely to commit rape, or see prostitutes, or commit other outrages against the "normal" decency they profess; this hypocrisy is inevitable given our sexual nature and our repressive society. Freud's followers in the movies build upon these seminal insights about sublimation, without Freud's moderation. Whereas Freud thought repressing sexual desires was essential for the advancement of civilization, his second-wave followers cannot stomach a repressed civilization. A sexually liberated society would bring about "the elimination of sexual repression" (Reich) or "the abolition of repression" (Brown) or, more modestly, would abolish "surplus repression" (Marcuse). The liberated society would manifest the "vision of a non-repressive culture" (Marcuse).[27]

Repression in the bourgeois order causes much personal frustration, unhappiness, crime, sadism, venality, prostitution, frigidity in sex, turning to "perverse" outlets, and so on.[28] Sexual desire must find a way out, and it is not always pretty absent conditions of genuine liberation. Personal misery becomes political. Sexual inhibitions, serving traditional morality, prepare young children and hence human beings generally to submit first to rules announced by fathers and then ultimately to authoritarian political regimes. America has fathers; Nazi Germany had fathers; America has rules about proper sexual behavior; Nazi Germany had rules about proper sexual behavior. This is no coincidence!

In Reich's formulation the repression of youthful sexuality is *"part of the crisis of authoritarian social order itself."*[29] Authoritarians include, for Reich, Nazi Germany, Soviet communism, and American capitalism comprehensively understood. As Reich writes, "Since authoritarian society reproduces itself in the structure of the mass individual by means of the authoritarian family, it follows that political reaction must defend the authoritarian family as the basis of the state, of culture, and of civilization."[30] In Marcuse's formulation the individual has been abolished and the family's power is curtailed: "The repressive organization of the instincts seems to be *collective*, and the ego seems to be prematurely socialized by the whole system of extra-familial agents and agencies." "Contemporary industrial civilization" itself, made secure through distracting individuals with "thoughtless leisure activities" and "the triumph of anti-intellectual ideologies," manipulates consciousness and deflects human sexual desire in the direction of domination, war, exploitation of the environment, and state-managed capitalism.[31] If this repression or surplus repression is intrinsic to the bourgeois order, if repression causes human unhappiness, and if it is linked to authoritarian regimes through authoritarian families, then the future of human happiness and perhaps the survival of the species requires the erosion of the modern order and its props.

After the destruction of the alienating, repressive order, human beings would be free to be themselves, reconciled to the world, free to engage in acts of intercourse, and able to express their innate polymorphous perversity (to use Freud's term, repeated not infrequently among the liberationists). Without sexual liberation, political reform is impossible, nor is sexual liberation possible without political reform. Modern society depends on monogamy and the patriarchal family. Sexual liberation helps transcend the repressive capitalist order that depends on masses who willingly submit to authority. Reich describes a sexually liberated world:

> The girl does not merely need to be free genitally; she also needs privacy, a means of contraception, a sexually potent friend who is capable of love (i.e., not a National Socialist with a negative sexual structure), and a sex-affirmative social atmosphere.[32]

As early as puberty, boys and girls must be counseled against feeling shame, guilt, or modesty about sex or their bodies (through practice);[33] must be counseled in the need for contraception and abortion;[34] must be encouraged to engage in homosexual sexual experiments;[35] must think of sex divorced from any ecclesiastical or moral order;[36] should accept much prepubescent, adolescent masturbation;[37] and must be taught away from fidelity (which damages a sexual relationship) and from fidelity's concomitant, sexual jealousy.[38] The public should supply housing for pubescent children to bed one another, as well as sex education, contraception, and other "social support" or encouragement for sexual escapades.[39] All need a "sex-affirmative social environment"—including the repeal of reticence in art, language, education, and culture—within which to lead lives of genital satisfaction.[40] Perhaps there should be public provision for sexbots. In any event everyone must be carefully taught, and affirmed, in their "natural" desires.

Reich, like Marcuse, wants some limits and regulation. Marcuse differentiates repression from surplus repression, while Reich sees two kinds of morality and propounds the "self-regulated" morality over the repressive one. Reich writes,

> That "morality" which all people affirm to be self-evident (not to rape, not to murder, etc.) can be established only if natural needs are fully gratified. But the other "morality" which we reject (abstinence for children and adolescents, absolute and eternal marital fidelity, compulsory marriage, etc.) is itself pathological and causes the very chaos it feels called upon to master.[41]

Eliminate repression of natural sexual needs and not only will people be happy and free, but they will no longer murder, rape, or invade Poland. Nor will a man pinch a waitress' behind.[42] Sexual liberation leads to easygoing, noncoercive sexual relations. Natural sexual desires will be healthy in themselves if they develop in an atmosphere without repression. Nature presents no problem, if we could just clear out the repressive underbrush so that we could *see* and act according to nature.

Reich would not draw lines. Human beings are sexual at birth and have sexual desires directed toward their mothers and fathers, just as mothers and fathers may them for children. Young children should be encouraged to masturbate instead of having incestuous dreams about parents. How early is too early for sexual activity? Reich seems to think that all who can, should, while those who cannot, cannot, so there are no worries. This rule, such as it is, affects young girls more than it does young boys, but girls shorn of shame need not worry overmuch. Natural sexual desires are, for Reich, harmless and unproblematic. Rape is caused by the morality that aspires to restrain sexual desire, but which really causes a sexual repression that bursts out dangerously. Rape, sexual harassment, and the casting couch will disappear along with repression and sexual frustration in our liberated future.

Marcuse, not as detailed as Reich on these matters, distinguishes "surplus repression" from "basic repression." Basic repression aims at instincts that must be controlled for the survival of society itself or the human race (e.g., norms against murderous desires and the lust to dominate), while surplus repression guards a specific group's domination.[43] What repression is surplus changes over time, so that an institution that performs something basic to human advancement in one time (such as the monogamous family in early modernity) becomes surplus repression in another time (like the monogamous family in later modernity). Marcuse's project involves exposing institutions of surplus repression to prepare for a future liberated from them.

Marcuse sees no limiting principle to his identification of society's surplus repression. He would abolish the family, a formerly basic institution: "The change in the value and scope of libidinal relations would lead to the disintegration of the institutions in which the private interpersonal relations have been organized, particularly the monogamic and patriarchal family." Sex must be freed from subjection to procreative sexual activity. He would "undo . . . the taboo on perversions" and lessen "the taboo on the reification of the body."[44] (As far as I can tell, Marcuse never applies his principles to incest, nor does he supply a list of perversions.)

People may worry that "instinctual liberation can lead only to a society of sex maniacs—that is, to no society," he writes, but the libido is transformed and not just released from repressive rules. This transformed libido leads to the "erotization of the entire personality": the "free development of transformed libido within transformed institutions" would "eroticiz[e] previously tabooed zones, times, and relations." Sex would be satisfying, as would be labor and education and any other activity, since all such activities would be filled with erotic desire that previously had only a few acceptable outlets. Sexual liberation baptizes all human activity with the natural goodness of sexual desire. What begins as some combination of Freud and Marx ends up with the utopian politics of Charles Fourier's "giant socialist utopia," where the possibility of attractive, fulfilling labor is predicated "above all" on "the release of libidinal forces."[45] Sexual reform and political reform complete each other.

Marcuse brings sexual liberation down from the heavens; we must compel it to inquire about human life and customs. The sexual revolution has heroes, just like the American Revolution. These later Washingtons proudly escape repressed morality and celebrate emancipated sexuality. They may cross-dress or express themselves in exotic dancing, feeling no shame about nudity and pole dancing. They show courage in "coming out of the closet." They may practice open marriage and evangelize its liberating potential. They may attend bathhouses and engage in serial sodomy until all their strength is gone. Perhaps they will construct a sexbot and live with it, openly and alluringly. These heroes call into question the norm and hence erode sexual repression. As a matter of moral teaching, heroism conjoins sexual pleasure, each reinforcing the other so long as heroic acts violate previous taboos. Just as transgressive gender performances "undo gender" (Butler), so do transgressive sexual performances move people "beyond repression" (Marcuse).

The ethic of sexual liberation insinuates itself through these heroes. Sex education teaches that the limiting principle for sexual activity is consent and safety (for now!). Other means of sexual expression are perfectly normal and should be safe, so long as people shun repression and judgment. Shame and modesty are remnants of an older, lesser age, when there were many restraints and where there was yet little encouragement to sexual release. Sex release is a crucial human need, sexual satisfaction a human right; sexual experimentation is a crucial aspect of our identities. Our children must be taught what Phillip Larkin writes (reflecting on sexual liberation): "Sexual intercourse began / in nineteen sixty-three . . . / Between the end of the 'Chatterley' ban / And the Beatles' first LP." Ending the "Chatterley ban," as Larkin posits, stands for the end of obscenity and sexual repression in law and opinion. It involves making scantily clad images and more available to young and old alike, so that they will be encouraged to express sexual desire from cradle to grave.[46] The ban marks the end of sexual judgment, for sex outside of marriage and for any other form of sex consistent with consent and safety. The ban is replaced with a "sex-affirmative" environment, as seen in the "Beatles' first LP" (*Please, Please Me* [1963]), and in suggestive youth clothing models, in the pharmaceutical advertisement about how impotent men can still get it on, and in countless ways that a new, pro-sexual experimentation "script" has become a new norm. Even the natural aging process deprives people of the greatest things in life, and, as with contraception, artifice rescues nature so human happiness can be realized. Medicines for erectile dysfunction presuppose Marcuse.

Sexual liberationists provide an independent justification for the rolling revolution. The sexual revolution requires, as Millett writes, "an end to traditional sexual inhibitions and taboos, particularly those that most threaten patriarchal monogamous marriage: homosexuality, 'illegitimacy,' adolescent, and pre- and extra-marital sexuality." Sexual liberationists go at least that far in the name of human liberation and political reform.

The Careful Teaching of Sexual Liberation

It may seem strange to say that sex, among the most private physical experiences, is shaped in decisive ways by a public teaching or a script about what is appropriate and what is out of bounds. Who, at moments of arousal or climax, is thinking about England, the public purposes of procreation, the telos of the penis, the values of their mothers or fathers, or the unjust "B" one received on an Aristotle paper as an undergraduate? The incipient teaching of sexual liberation, in both its scientific and its theoretical guises, is that sexual passions are unproblematic in themselves, concerned with pleasure, and hence are best left alone. The desire for food is dangerous only when food is scarce, and the same holds true for sex: the desire for sex is dangerous only when the availability of sex is kept artificially low through society's repressive norms. A greater supply of sex eases things. Sexual desires are safe, in fact, *only* if they are left alone or untutored. Combining them with extraneous concerns such as love, commitment, children, procreation, moral considerations, eternity, death, marriage, fidelity, jealousy, and so on limits the supply and hence fosters frustration, repression, neuroses, authoritarianism, and worse. If we educate children about sexuality in isolation of these other goods—emphasizing only safety and consent as limiting principles—we teach that sex is isolated from these experiences and concerned mostly with individual gratification.[47]

It is not clear how strong erotic passions for sex are by nature. Erotic passions would be sated, but they do not tell us how often, with whom, when, and why, and human imagination and experience pose diverse answers to these questions. Nor is the direction of erotic passions clear. Passions may aim at one, few, or many; the forbidden or the easy; a person of the opposite sex or one of the same; one's spouse, a stranger, or nobody; frequently, rarely, or much in between. Desire for sexual variety is not new, nor is pornography, nor are (apparently) orgasm machines and the taste for them. Prostitution is called the oldest profession, suggesting that men have always been interested in sex without consequences or attachment. It is not clear what erotic passions culminating in sex signify. They could be about orgasms pure and simple, or possession of another, or domination of another, or being dominated, or "making love," or perpetuating one's genes. As unstable as erotic passion is love itself, which, as so much literature demonstrates, is a "restless and impatient passion, full of caprices and variations; arising in a moment from a feature, from an air, from nothing, and suddenly extinguishing after the same manner."[48]

The modernized effort to separate what traditional morality has joined is, in reality, an effort to presume and foster the most benign manifestation of these passions, as liberals understand benign. Erotic passion, divorced from love, appears as only an animal act, implicating our plumbing and not our being. Sex is significant only if we make it so—or so the sentiment (selectively applied) goes. Sexual passions are natural and healthy. Sexual needs must be met. What matters is *that* one's erotic passions are fulfilled, not *how* they are fulfilled, so long as they are not fulfilled against consent. No one should entertain thoughts of possessing or mastering another, or of being possessed or mastered by another, or perhaps of losing one's independence to another. Such dependence is dangerous and, in any event, it is not humanly important. One should not close oneself to sexual experiences as they come along. Pornography can be as satisfying as vaginal intercourse or masturbation. Women will adapt themselves to pornographic expectations in relationships. Sexual jealousy is beneath the dignity of a rational being, since it would be wrong to think that one owns one's partner and such ownership is the basis of jealousy. If two people should fall out of love as they understood it, no personal obligation or feeling of guilt should get in the way of their happiness or fulfillment: they should part and each partner should be happy for the other, who has found a new happiness.

Modernizers seem to believe that people and children must be taught to this liberationist ethic as long as the integrated, traditional morality lingers. Since there is nothing to be ashamed of in one's sex life, formerly disfavored sex practices can be displayed openly instead of being consigned to back alleys or skid row; the marketplace and internet services can bring people together who formerly would have had a difficult time finding one another. Even shame or modesty about the human body, eroded with clothes that show a lot of skin, can be stripped away as people become comfortable showing their bodies in public. Responsibility may be more optional. Sex, on the modern view, is elevated and denigrated in one swoop—never has there been so much attention to sex and hopes for sexual satisfaction, while sex itself is seen as a low, merely animal act.

If desires are naturally indeterminate, everyone must be carefully taught, even the liberationists: people must be taught to separate them and build their own lives. There are good reasons to think that the integrated morality will linger among at least some people and in many aspects of people's lives, even as this new interpretation of sex becomes widely accepted and believed. There is not a little secret coercion in the move to sexual liberation: the old ways must be gotten rid of, through ridicule if possible, but through force if necessary.

A good measure of success for the sexual liberation movement toward a world without repression is seen in the demise of those who think sex is for procreation and the rise in those who think sex is for pleasure. The uniting descriptive of the sexual liberationists is what Anthony Giddens calls the "plastic sexuality."[49] Plastic sexuality is "fully autonomous." Sexuality has no essence or form but that which human beings ascribe to it; it suffers no connection to anything but what human beings choose to connect it to.[50] Male sexuality does not aim at dominance, nor does female sexuality aim at establishing relations.[51] Sexuality is oriented neither heterosexually nor homosexually. Society has long molded sexuality for individuals; now it is possible for those who would enter genuinely free relations to mold sexuality for themselves. This marks an important element of the "Transformation of Intimacy" and the rise of a purer relationship. Like our bodies for radical feminists (as we saw in chapter 2), sexual desires for liberationists provide no tip-off or meaning for individual acts of creative identity-making.

The persistence of shame, in any event, shows how far we have to go in ending repression. Shame protects delicate, integrated relations from being seen as public things; it counsels people away from perverse practices that are incomplete, immature expressions of sexual desire. Shame protects love and the conditions that make love possible. While people proudly say, "I am an accountant," or, "I read Russian literature," they do not proudly declare, "I masturbate," or, "I am a voyeur," or, "I cheat on my wife," or, "I am a frequent John." People may be scantily clad and leave little to the imagination, but they still cover their privates and mostly abjure public fornication. Such reticence, even in a permissive environment, may be traceable to the fear of being labeled a deviant grounded in a reasonable, perhaps necessary public morality that protects the integrated view of sexual desire. It may also be grounded in natural shame understood as a durable characteristic of human nature.

The same holds for sexual fidelity: Americans, for instance, seem to adopt an ethic of "serial monogamy" or a one-person-at-a-time ethic, but to expect fidelity within relationships.[52] While modern people are quite accepting of sex outside of marriage, they are a bit less enamored of procreation outside of marriage. Women still act quite a bit differently from men in sexual relations—the double standard as concerns expectations, at least, endures. Many people still think that sex is a bedrock of enduring relations or at least faithful relations, and this vision of sex, central to the traditional view, has proven an especially tough nut to crack. The work of ending sexual repression is in its early adolescence. We have taken many steps toward eliminating sexual repression, but we have not yet gone all the way!

Part II
Curbs on the Rolling Revolution

These aspirations of the rolling revolution can never be completed to the satisfaction of its advocates. Each branch runs up against demands and realities of human life and political life, as we shall see in the next three chapters. Feminism runs up against the tough nut of the human body, which suggests sex differences between men and women and hence limits the kinds of equality that feminists dare to expect. Contemporary liberalism runs up against the political reality that there are no neutral laws and hence that every legislative act reflects and imposes a kind of morality. Sexual liberationists run up against the reality that most human beings most of the time seek to subsume sex within a larger horizon of meaning and that sexual desire is essentially different than other kinds of desires and human contact. Every society has a vision of where these limits lead and how these limits should be understood and defined. Every society seeks a mixed regime when it comes to sexual difference, political morality, and sexual desire. Every decent society sees through the radicalism in the rolling revolution and gives a sympathetic account of its limits, or it surrenders to its totalitarian ambitions to remake human nature.

5

SEXUAL DIFFERENCE AND HUMAN LIFE

On the Limits of Feminism

Feminists define success as the abolition of gender, based on the assumption that there is nothing distinctively male or female and the body provides no direction for human life. To wit, Okin, again:

> A just future would be one without gender. In social structures and practices, one's sex would have no more relevance than one's eye color or the length of one's toes. No assumptions would be made about "male" or "female" roles; childbearing would be so conceptually separated from child rearing and other family responsibilities that it would be a cause for surprise, and no little concern, if men and women were not equally responsible for domestic life or if children were to spend much more time with one parent than the other. It would be a future in which men and women participated in more or less equal numbers in every sphere of life, from infant care to different kinds of paid work to high-level politics.[1]

Women are free from cultural patriarchy when they choose no differently than men in any sphere of life. The differences that still persist, feminists insist, disappear once we eliminate cultural patriarchy.

That world beyond gender has proved elusive. Differences between men and women persist, despite feminism's successes. Men and women generally have different chemical bases, brains, susceptibility to diseases, interests or penchants, ways of thinking, psychological traits, and, generally, ways of feeling and acting; they differ in size, strength, and speed. Many more men than women are in prison everywhere and at all times, for instance. I could go on, and will.

Differences between men and women appear changeable *and* persistent. By *sexual difference* I mean differences grounded, directly or indirectly, in the body or physical nature of men and women and in closely related psychological attributes. Gender properly understood is the meaning and importance lent to sex difference in a particular time and place. The concept of gender, unmoored from sex, is waxing as an explanation for difference in the modern world—thanks to feminism; many, including the feminists surveyed in chapter 2, doubt the independent reality of sex.[2]

No one experiences human life or sex in a pure, natural form. All human beings experience "nature" or "pure form" in a cave (to use Plato's image). There is variation in how sex relates to gender in human practice. Cultures differentiate men from women. Women and men dress differently today than they did in the past, for instance. Men and women nevertheless dress differently from each other and emphasize their distinctive bodily characteristics in their dress. Sex differences are partly natural, partly cultural. How natural? How cultural? What difference does it make? Sex differences, generally, provide grooves within which gender operates, and the effectual truth of feminism is not the abolition of gender, once we know this. First, however, we must know this.

Overdetermining and Under-Determining the Relation between Sex and Gender

Before getting to sex differences and their significance, let us consider two intellectual errors: one arising when people think sex determines gender and one when people deny sex has any relationship with gender. The first as it appears in the modern world comes from historical, positivist, and perhaps Darwinian theories of human being. Inquirers trace sex differences to biological differences. Philosophers and scientists began moving from different genitals to difference, and different brain sizes as determined by phrenology to difference. Today scientists emphasize the hormonal and genetic differences between men and women and the different ways their brains are hardwired.

Consider some writings that see an overlap between sex and gender from when women's emancipation advanced during feminism's first wave. Otto Weininger (1903), an Austrian philosopher, writes, in words we could find charming or antiquated if we did not find them so repugnant,

> Emancipation . . . is not a woman's desire for *external* equality with
> a man. The *problem* that I wish to solve . . . in the Woman's Ques-
> tion is that of a woman's *will* to *become internally equal* to a man, to
> attain his intellectual and moral freedom, his interests and creative
> power . . . *Woman has no need and accordingly no capacity for this kind*
> *of emancipation. All those women who really strive for emancipation,*
> *all those women who have some genuine claim to fame and intellectual*
> *eminence, always display some male properties, and the more perceptive*
> *observer will always recognize in them some anatomically male charac-*
> *teristics, an approximation to the physical appearance of a man.*[3]

Weininger committed suicide, perhaps at the behest of the gods of liberal
equality, within a year of the book's publication. Georg Wilhelm Friedrich
Hegel, a greater thinker, sees a similar difference based in the body between
the sexes:

> Women may well be educated, but they are not made for the higher sci-
> ences, for philosophy and certain artistic productions that require the
> universal element. Women may have insights, taste, and delicacy, but
> they do not possess the ideal. The difference between man and woman
> is the difference between animal and plant; the animal is closer in
> character to man, the plant to woman, for the latter is more unity of
> feeling. When women are in charge of government, the state is in dan-
> ger, for their actions are based not on the demands of universality but
> on contingent inclination and opinion.[4]

Such thinkers reify the differences between the sexes currently predominant
into differences true for all time. When traceable to discredited sciences such
as phrenology (as it was in the case of Hegel), the treatment appears ridiculous
to our eyes.

Many defenders of something that resembles traditional sex roles within
marriage and family life have sympathetic recourse to Darwinian theory or
evolutionary psychology as a scientifically valid way of showing that gender
has a stable ground in genes. Current traits and tendencies of the sexes derive
from a moment when our genetic inheritance was set. Men and women have
sex to perpetuate their genes. Men perpetuate genes by sowing their seed in
many different women, who ensure that their brood is nurtured. Men appear
more aggressive, especially against other men. Winners in the competition for
sexual access gain status and resources, which themselves become objects for
contention. The strongest and fastest survive to perpetuate their genes, while
weaklings fare badly. Men like big breasts because they are good for suckling
men's children, and hence they make it easier to perpetuate their genes. Same
for childbearing hips and youthful vitality, which attract for their contribution

to perpetuating the genes. Women perpetuate their genes by attracting strong men who will impregnate them and then have the strength to protect and assist in nourishing children. Nurturing women survive. Men and women who cooperate survive too. Given the long nonage of human children, women need more time to nurture and care, and they are attracted to men with status and strength to provide security. Thus arises something like a marriage bargain.[5] Men perpetuate their genes with some certainty by demanding an exclusive relationship with a woman, while the woman gets the security she needs to perpetuate her genes from the man. The sexual double standard, where men's infidelity is less scorned than women's, arises from men's need to know their children as their own.

Traits in men and women follow from this picture. Men are adventurous, strong, jealous, and status-seeking or aggressive—because their genes are thereby perpetuated. Women are discerning, agreeable, interested in a strong, respectable man, indirect, valued for chastity and hence more chaste, inclined to private life, nurturing, and caring—and genes are thereby perpetuated. Genes drive the mating game.[6] The gene-perpetuating human animal shapes what is moral in a time and place. Through this gene-perpetuating mechanism, the bodily and the sexual limit how gender manifests itself. Thus, while Darwinian evolutionists might not be happy about it, men *just are* more violent, sexually adventurous, jealous, and dangerous, and women *just are* weaker, more nurturing, and more indirect—facts we should either bow to or reform only with wide-eyed realism about the extreme difficulties involved.

These thinkers recognize the import of social conventions such as marriage and family life for procreation and education of children, for the production of moral citizens, and as a satisfying locus of love and human happiness. The sexual division of labor (public man, private woman) is an element of marriage and family life, though it leads to some disparities between men and women. Such difference is to be expected as natural and suited to the abilities and fulfillment of the two sexes. The argument where sex or the body may overdetermine gender thus became connected to some modern defenses of marriage and family life.[7]

Evolutionists seem to have bad news for those who see gender as more a product of culture or choice. Sex and the body limit our ability to construct a world beyond gender or to bring about a new independent woman. They have some good news for gender theorists too, since some expectations related to gender seem less essential to our genetic heritage. Evolutionism strips away our pleasing illusions about love, about the goodness of uniting with another as part of a good life, and about the beauty of a common home. According to evolutionists love and other such good, beautiful things are window dressing that human beings invent, to pile metaphor on metaphor, to grease the wheels of reproduction. Men and women may invest more in their children if they think they are acting out of love, the good, or the beautiful, but their genes, not morality, move them. For instance, face-to-face sex encourages emotional closeness and "respect for persons" more than sex in the manner of dogs, so humans with sex organs conducive to face-to-face sex gained the evolutionary upper hand over those with organs easier to approach from the rear. Pair-bonding works. The decline in estrus in females encouraged men to be always interested in sex instead of just when women were ripe. This encouraged the pair-bonding necessary to keep men around as fathers. None of these institutions demands the monogamous family, however. Other devices may arise to replace outmoded social institutions.

Much can be said and has been said against the evolutionary account generally, and against its conception of sex and gender in particular. One can wonder whether its evolutionary conception of biology and sex provides stable ground for constructing gender in the face of the modern aspiration to control nature.[8] One can worry about the theory's internal consistency, its metaphysical implications, and whether it is a "just-so" story. Generally, evolutionary theory underplays how gender tips off a human reality beyond genetic perpetuation. Gender for evolutionary theory registers biological, sexual reality. Gender construction is a cooperative, imaginative project—people must give reasons, provide vision, justify participation, and gain something akin to consent from others as they construct gender. Gender scripts are political acts broadly. Those scripts cannot be constructed contrary to the demands of the individual or the species, or contrary to the sexual interests and experiences of males and females; through this common effort to make sense of sexual difference, human beings construct rituals, mores, practices, and cultures. No birds or bees or educated fleas do that!

Feminist critics of such schools swing in the opposite direction, divorcing sex from gender or subsuming sex under gender. Gender, as we saw in chapter 2, emerges in feminism as a cultural construct or an individual choice apart from sex and the body. This is the implication of Beauvoir's verse: one becomes a woman, if one chooses, but one can become whatever one wants. An almost endless variety of genders may be discovered or asserted, if gender has no basis in sex.

The case for gender determining sex presupposes a very modern vision of human being that emphasizes our freedom, reason, and autonomy. Whether it is Beauvoir's distinction between "transcendence" and "immanence," Martin Heidegger's recognition of how "technology" appears to give shape to "standing reserve," or Immanuel Kant's broad distinction between freedom and reason on the one hand and nature or necessity and science on the other, the idea that our bodies are stuff to be manipulated infuses the later modern thought that begets second-wave feminism. On this view, our bodies and passions are naturally indeterminate. Human character, including society's view of male and female, are without essence and can be changed according to human will. There are indeed male and female bodies (immanent, standing reserve, nature), but there is only one kind of person (transcendent, free) with equal rights and freedom to make itself what it wills. Personhood is essential; the body or sex is unchosen, an accident, directionless. What has been made can be unmade and remade through concerted public and private actions to achieve genuine equality and freedom. No limits!

No one went further in this direction than Beauvoir. Women's "sexuality is *in no way* determined by any anatomical 'fate,'" she writes.[9] One's culture or one's "situation" determines the meaning and manner of going to the bathroom, sexual relations, talk, morality, communication, athletics, childbirth, sexual desire, political engagement, career, and education. People can transcend their given culture or situation through concerted, intentional action if they can summon the will. No limits!

Or perhaps, I digress, no one went further than Judith Butler. She recognizes how "nature" could limit the feminist project. "Certain formulations of the radical constructivist position," writes Butler, "appear almost compulsively to produce a moment of recurrent exasperation," for "when the constructivist is construed as a linguistic idealist, the constructivist refutes the reality of bodies, the relevance of science, the alleged facts of birth, aging, illness, and death." The critic, she continues, "might also suspect the constructivist of a certain somatophobia [i.e., fear of the body] and seek assurances that this abstracted theorist will admit that there are, minimally, sexually differentiated parts, activities, capacities, hormonal and chromosomal differences that can be conceded without reference to 'construction.'"[10] She is concerned with how "certain formulations" of a radical emphasis on gender "appear" and with how gender is "construed" by a "linguistic idealist." Death, birth, sex, and aging are "alleged facts." Put simply and without jargon, the theorist who thinks that all human experience is a gender performance apart from any foundation in sex or other *realities* must also deal with human experiences such as birth, human aging, death, and sexual difference. Are people just *performing* death? Or do they die? Do they *perform* childhood, or are they young and inexperienced?

Butler offers "absolute reassurance" to critics that she recognizes the reality of underlying reality. She does "'concede'" the "undeniability of 'sex'" and "its 'materiality,'" but she also puts these words in scare quotes. Put these shenanigans to the side. Butler's first position is that "there is no reference to a pure body which is not at the same time a further formation of that body." All experiences with primordial, elemental human experience come through a regime or culture or particular linguistic discourse. Death and aging happen, and how a regime teaches them is the first thing citizens of that regime know about death and aging. Much the same is true of sex differences. If this is Butler's position, her thought is a remarkable *corrective* to radical constructivism, because it would seem open to a dialogue among various images of these natural phenomena as the beginning of a search for wisdom.

Butler goes further, responding to a "moderate critic," who thinks "*some part* of 'sex'" is constructed but not the whole of it. Such moderate critics must, she argues, "draw the line" between what is made and what is natural, and then explain how the natural part is natural. This is problematic, for Butler, because the boundary between natural and constructed elements of sexual identity is constructed in language. Even the natural is constructed. This constructed boundary then acts as a fence that performs "a more or less tacit operation of exclusion" from the human family of those who transcend or transgress those limits. "Performativity," Butler writes, becomes "citationality."[11] Let me illustrate Butler's thought with a syllogism: No good writer uses the word "citationality." Butler uses the word "citationality." Therefore Butler is not a good writer. The first premise is an act of exclusion that writes her out of the family of good writers. Butler's vision assumes that language is an expression of power instead of (also being) a tip-off into the nature of being. From Butler's theory there can be no appeal to nature and hence no real reasoning, because all appeals to nature become convention when they are put into language; human life is a series of power plays if it does not involve the liberation from the power plays of others. It is all cave, all the time. But what appears to be the bad news of relativism is taken to be the good news of liberation. No limits!

This is by the by. Modern society is working out the implications of feminist theory. Anti-discrimination laws emphasizing disparate impact are justified on grounds separating one's person from one's sex, or in seeing that the gender that society constructs may be deconstructed and reconstructed. With a sex change or sex reassignment surgery or puberty-delaying drugs, one's sex is brought into alignment with one's gender. One's real sex is one's gender, not the sex given us by nature or birth or social assignment. In fact, many use the word "gender" to mean "sex." "No more vivid example exists," writes Roger Scruton, "of the human determination to triumph over biological destiny, in the interests of a moral idea" (i.e., human liberation).[12] Sex and bodies are malleable to reconstruction through acts of human will—and, possibly, through deep, reparative medical treatments.

Feminists face a dilemma. If they admit a limit in nature, they seem to concede a reality of sex difference and risk defending some disparities that would make achieving Okin's fifty-fifty world or a world beyond gender impossible. If they do not admit a limit in nature, then they cannot accept anything except the elimination of all disparity between the sexes or a world where everything is undefined. Feminists choose the latter path. All reference to limits makes one a misogynist indistinguishable from Otto Weininger.

A respect for truth demands that we give more than an inch to a feminist critique of essentialism. It is quite another thing to take the whole mile, as feminists do,[13] and to collapse sex into gender. The greatest contribution of feminist thought is the idea that human beings perceive their bodies and sex through a particular and contestable understanding of gender—up to a point. That "up to a point"—pointing to nature and a limit—*corrects* feminism.

Gender is a testament to how human beings are political animals possessed of speech. People speak and deliberate about the just, the advantageous, the necessary, and the good. How political communities conceive gender tells us something about each community's regime and about sex as such. This is not the end of the debate, as it is for Butler and her comrades, who presume the historical and contingent character of thought informing ideas about gender. The observation that political communities are somewhat different on gender is the beginning of wisdom about how different ideas of gender, in different circumstances, satisfy the needs and desires of each sex, comport with sexual experience itself, meet the requirements of the species, accommodate different circumstances, and help or hinder each in an effort to live a good life. Gender lends meaning, for better and worse, to our bodily reality and sexual difference, and connects that meaning to human aspirations. Aspiring to understand those is a higher wisdom.

The Sexual Grooves in Ideas of Gender

The feminist critique of biological essentialism goes with the grain of modern aspirations emphasizing human exertions of autonomy and minimizing the import of the naturally given. In arguing against the feminist position, I argue against views from some of the deepest thinkers of modernity and in the twentieth century (i.e., Heidegger) as they apply to sex and gender. Every word aimed at feminism is aimed also at this deeper stream of thought, but that deeper stream remains, mostly, subterranean. Against this feminist view, I submit that gender is not as malleable or arbitrary as the shadows on the wall. Gender is an attempt to articulate the significance of maleness and femaleness in a time and place. Maleness and femaleness provide grooves within which gender travels. Defending grooves in modernity is difficult, for grooves point to limits on human power and will. Accusations of old-fogeyism are sure to fly. Am I a phrenologist? Am I now or have I ever been a member of the Otto Weininger fan club?

Gender is a reflection of a community's way of explaining sexual differentiation. Sex and sexual difference, like birth and death, are stubborn facts of life important enough to demand attention from all. Feminists tell a story about the prominence of gender—gender is invented and oppressive, but liberation is just around the corner. Against this view, I hold that gender is constructed partly, but not *arbitrarily* or (simply) to satisfy power demands of men and produce the subordination of women. Not just any story of gender can do or will do. Images about gender go with the grooves of sex.

Gender differences across cultures, universal for the most part, display the grooves of sexual difference. By "universal for the most part" I mean traits that, within the realm of complex human affairs, are, for the most part, true and prevalent. Exceptions to for-the-most-part universals exist, but exceptions always arise in human affairs. The art of the scientist lies in sifting the essential from the inessential, the normal from the abnormal.[14] It is conceivable, as contemporary feminists imply, that almost every culture, Western and Eastern, premodern, modern, and postmodern, has manufactured gender in almost the exact same way without any reference to the body or closely related psychological traits. What a coincidence! Perhaps a future revolution will erase disparities. No one can refute the prophecy of the limitless future where neither essences nor biology limit human transcendence. Evidence for feminism awaits a complete revolution in human affairs, and the revolution will be evidence for feminism. But the fact that this revolution has not happened is evidence that it will not happen. Will human beings be happy under these circumstances? Will those beings be human? The silence of these infinite spaces strikes terror in my soul.

Common life and the simple man, confirmed by science,[15] provide for-the-most-part universal patterns of male and female ways as beginning points for such analysis.[16] The more they are cross-cultural, the less likely it is that they are traceable to *arbitrary* socialization. Sex informs how people imagine and lead their lives as men and women. Or, as a scientist might say, "Large, cross-culturally universal sex differences that are impervious to cultural influence may provide compelling evidence for biological causation."[17] None of these differences will shock anyone with eyes to see and the courage to speak:

- Men are physically stronger and faster, jump higher than women, and are more likely to embrace competition than women.
- Men are more physically aggressive and violent; are more likely than women to die of suicide, of workplace accidents, and in war; and are disproportionately perpetrators and victims of crime.[18]
- Women are more nurturing and agreeable and more desirous of personal intimacy than men.[19]
- Men are more sexually adventurous than women and want more sex without connection; women more modest and less satisfied with sex unconnected from enduring relations.[20]

- Men are more attracted to physical beauty—and hence more sensual—than women; women are more attracted to status and resources than men.[21]
- Men are more interested in things, while women are more interested in people and relationships—disparate occupation choices follow.[22]
- For much of early life through adolescence, boys and girls segregate themselves from one another voluntarily, and they keep on doing this throughout their lives (more or less).[23]

Institutions arise in different contexts to manifest, limit, and channel these tendencies. Gender registers sex differences.

What follows is a survey of surveys of four for-the-most-part universal sex differences. The assumptions of the rolling revolution lead, predictably, to an argument for a fifty-fifty world, but the aspirations are dashed each time, with revealing results. Modern efforts to introduce greater flexibility or to make or presume androgyny have an effect on the sexes—sometimes unintended and perhaps unwanted effects. They also run up against sexual grooves. Let us make more women engineers, some say, for instance, never considering that fewer women want to be engineers and hence more will leave the profession upon graduation or change majors; many younger women end up wasting valuable time in their life on aspirations their feminist role models have advised them to take up.[24] Perhaps we are remedying a nonproblem. Nor do optimistic "social role" theories, who trace "gender differences" to "gender roles that have evolved in some societies," get much support, since these differences, if anything, grow in countries with laws protecting and promoting gender equality and economic development.[25] Women may not be mothers, but they are much more likely to be agreeable, sociable, and caring and make choices accordingly. Men may not all be plumbers, but they are more interested in things and occupations that involve physical accomplishment. All men may not be soldiers or sportsmen, but they are generally more competitive, riskier, and less agreeable than women.

The shadows on our wall, cast by rolling revolutionaries, tell citizens in liberal democracies that there is equality and sameness between women and men. In the silent recesses of hearts, citizens glimpse rays that reveal the truth of things; they continue to act upon such truths but in a way shaped by our feminist education. To see the rays is to philosophize, or at least to be free. Philosophy must also reconcile us to the rose in the cross of the not-fifty-fifty present and illumine the truth of the human situation—and maybe its beauty.

Athletic Ability

If we cannot admit sex differences in athletics, we cannot admit them any-where. If sex were to be irrelevant, as Okin hoped, to "every sphere of life," it would be irrelevant in athletics too. Olympic events would not need to be sex-segregated; major sports leagues would have as many women as men play-ers (not because of quotas). Consistent second-wave feminists believe that women would be equal to men in athletic accomplishments if women were encouraged to be "playing with the boys" (as the title of one feminist book on sports suggests).[26] The iron-sharpening-iron character of competition makes men stronger and spurs them on to greater speeds and accomplish-ments, some think; entering competition with men would make women big-ger, stronger, and faster too. Segregation in sports competitions perpetuates patriarchy: men keep women out of "their" sports for fear of losing all of the social advantages that come with athletic excellence.[27]

Also holding women back is a "frailty myth" (the title of another book on women's athletics).[28] According to this myth, men and boys learn to think "they have a right to get their way through aggression," while the same struc-tures hold that women and girls "are not permitted to fight physically with their enemies."[29] Men and boys are *taught* competitiveness, commitment, ded-ication, and the single-minded purposiveness conducive to athletic success, while most women are taught balance, caring, agreeableness, and multitasking, seeing athletics or fitness as a part of a good life—and pushed into gymnastics, cheerleading, figure-skating, and other fields of grace. Young girls are diverted from sports so their strength and aerobic powers are underdeveloped. Girls lose interest in developing the motor skills and physical prowess necessary to achieve athletic excellence. Instead girls must be encouraged early and often to compete in sports, not told that sports are too rough or unladylike for them. With echoes of Beauvoir, advocates for women in sports claim, "Women aren't born less interested in sports. Society conditions them."[30]

Interesting theories. Are they true? Testifying to gender, sex differences in sports performance have narrowed since women were encouraged to concern themselves more with sport and (everyone) started to receive better training. Despite the fact that the gap is narrowed, it persists at the highest levels and in the depths, testifying to the persistence of sex differences.

No respectable American argues against "equality of opportunity" in sports; the question is, How do we know when "equality" or equal opportunity has been achieved in sports or what equality in this venue means? Answers to this question turn on what one expects. If, as feminists contend, no *natural* physical or psychological differences between men and women exist, equal-ity of opportunity and equality of results or sameness are synonymous. Sex differences in the fifty-meter dash would be traceable to social conditioning.

Men and women would have to be as interested in sports as the other, as competitive, and as good as the other. More moderate-seeming retail feminists affect to believe that the time will arise when differences between men and women will be voluntary and hence legitimate. A chosen but less-than-same world would be just fine. However, these feminists cannot explain how, if differences between the sexes are made, anything but a fifty-fifty world could be legitimate.[31] Retail feminists lack a limiting principle—so they become radical.

Despite this inequalities between the sexes persist at the peaks of athletic achievement. World records in swimming and track and field yield apples-to-apples comparisons, and men are faster, stronger, and better. While these records will one day be dated, I prophesy that the trend will continue.

Table 5.1: World Record Holders in Select Swimming and Track Sports

Event	Men (secs.)	Women (secs.)	Performance ratio (%)
100 m freestyle	46.91	52.07	90.1
100 m breast	58.46	64.45	90.7
100 m butterfly	49.82	55.98	89.0
100 m backstroke	51.94	58.12	89.4
200 m medley	114.00	126.15	90.4
400 m medley	243.84	268.43	90.8
1500 m swim	874.14	942.54	92.7
100 m run	9.58	10.49	91.3
400 m run	43.18	47.60	90.7
1500 m run	206.00	230.46	89.4
5 km run	757.35	851.15	89.0
Marathon	7418.00	8125.00	91.3

Elite male and female athletes, I assume, receive comparable comprehensive training in technique, strength, nutrition, and mental focus. As a testament to sexual grooves, the superiority of men to women at the highest levels is enduring and consistent. Women's world record performances appear to be about 90% of male performance in swimming and track. On the other hand, as a testament to gender, the difference between men and women has narrowed.[32] The fastest woman today in many of these sports is as fast as the fastest man was in 1967 (100 m butterfly) or in 1921 (100 m dash). The times of women have improved much more than the times of men since 1900. Perhaps what has narrowed can disappear with the spur of greater competition brought about through integration of women into men's sports. Women need more positive role models and then they will break through athletic glass ceilings.

This investigation of peaks in athletic achievement shows that men's mountain is higher. It does not reveal whether only elite men are better than elite women in these categories, or whether the mean or median women are equal or better. A comparison between women's world record holders as of 2017, men's 2015 NCAA Division III champions, and boys' high school champions in comparable events shows that women's world record holders (beneficiaries of world-class training for a longer time) are comparable to elite teenage male athletes (who presumably receive less elite training for a shorter time).

Table 5.2: Comparison between Women's World Record Holders and College and High School Boys in Select Track Sports

Event	Women's world record holder	2015 men's Division III champion	2015 California boys' high school champion	2015 Louisiana boys' high school champion
100 m run	10.49 secs.	10.24 secs.	10.34 secs.	10.91 secs.
200 m run	21.34 secs.	21.06 secs.	20.30 secs.	22.07 secs.
400 m run	47.60 secs.	47.07 secs.	45.19 secs.	48.98 secs.
800 m run	113.28 secs.	112.57 secs.	111.55 secs.	121.12 secs.
1500 m run	230.46 secs.	229.64 secs.	—	—
High jump	2.09 m	2.14 m	2.10 m	1.82 m
Pole vault	5.06 m	5.34 m	4.80 m	4.11 m
Long jump	7.52 m	7.47 m	7.46 m	6.55 m
Triple jump	15.50 m	15.52 m	14.94 m	13.51 m

Women world record holders in track would be very competitive in California boys' high school track, and indeed they would have won some events in

2015. They would have been crowned 2015 high school boys' champions in
Louisiana, the median state in 2015. Women's world record holders would be
competitive in Division III (i.e., non-scholarship) men's athletics, though they
would not have won many events in 2015. These findings support studies that
find that fewer than 10% of women are as strong as the average man.[33]

In a decisive sense, the body limits everyone—there is probably a speed to
which no human being can aspire or a height over which no one can leap. People used to say that the four-minute mile was impossible, but then a flood of
people broke that barrier. I say that the unaided three-minute mile is impossible for human beings, and I will bet against the strength of the human spirit.
Human beings will never be faster than a speeding bullet or more powerful
than a locomotive. The body limits men and women differently in athletics.
Internal structures, traceable to well-documented sex differences in body,
limit the imaginings of feminists. This difference is traceable to measurable
and consistent differences in muscle mass, fat concentrations, certain hormones (and especially testosterone), and other biological features.[34]

In 1979 Donald Symons, an evolutionary biologist, wrote that human
beings "grow up in an environment in which everyone believes that men typically are larger and stronger than women and yet few of us would ascribe
this sex difference entirely to tradition."[35] The same probably holds true today,
though feminists shame those who say it. These differences are also traceable
to a male psychological trait, one that does not necessarily cover men with
glory: a single-minded devotion to one thing at the expense of other things
related to their competitiveness.

Aggression and Agreeableness

Women are more competitive than they once were, especially American
women. The trait of competitiveness in women is much more celebrated in
America than it was in the past. Some consider that progress.

What Steven Rhoads wrote in 2004 reflects the ideas about men and
women from time out of mind: "males are more competitive and females more
cooperative."[36] Studies on how men and women talk reinforce what we see
with our eyes in sports. Women speak, as Carol Gilligan notes, "in a different
voice," one feminists ignore (a man's word) or downplay (a woman's). Women
tend to understate, while men tend to overstate. Women politely suggest
("perhaps you might consider . . ."), while men assert, order, or lecture ("You
will immediately . . .").[37] Women tend to manifest an ethic of care, feelings
of empathy and compassion, and concern for building and maintaining relationships, while a man's talk is more likely "clearer, more direct, more distinct,
and sharp-edged."[38] "Certain aspects of male play, such as dominance struggles and themes of heroic combat, may be cross-culturally universal, or nearly

so," writes Eleanor Maccoby in her *Two Sexes* (1999). Boys dare, challenge, shout, boast, refuse to yield—and "this is the element of the male agenda that most distinguishes their interactions from those of girls."[39] From an early age, male friendships arise through competition and sharing common projects, less based on intimacy, conversation, and emotional connection with other men.[40] Tracing sex differences to brain formation and hormones, Marianne Legato concludes, among other things, that "women are better at multitasking, while men are better when concentrating on a single task from beginning to completion."[41] Dominance and aggression (and sports success) accord with being single-minded or wanting to have your way, while doing several things is informed by a desire to please, be agreeable, and accommodate.

Nowhere is this aggression more pronounced than in crime and violence. "The overwhelming maleness of violence," writes evolutionary biologist David Barash, "is so pervasive in *every* human society that it is typically not even recognized as such." Over 95% of homicides worldwide are committed by men with male victims. "This difference between the sexes is immense and universal. There is no known human society in which the level of lethal violence among women even begins to approach that among men," relates Martin Daly and Margo Wilson in their treatise, *Homicide.*[42] Hanna Rosin, chronicling the "rise of women," has a hopeful chapter on how women are catching up to men as violent criminals—"A More Perfect Poison: The New Wave of Female Violence."[43] As feminism deepens its influence, women will keep closing the crime gap. That's progress! What Rosin shows is that women have become more violent than in the past (a small increase in a very small number), but that men's numbers have remained constant.

Let us not get carried away with sexual difference in aggression, however. Women want their way too, but they go about getting it in more accommodating, indirect, less violent (and sometimes more manipulative) ways.[44] The single-minded or aggressive woman is more social and cooperative than the single-minded man and hence less prone to violence and addictions, though she is more prone to disappointment, anxiety, and depression (and antidepressant use among girls and women continues to climb in the Western world). Boys commit suicide more than girls, while girls attempt suicide more than boys (as a plea for help, perhaps, or as a way of gaining attention).[45] Another application of this, characteristic of life in the 2010s: since girls are more social, they worry more about being left out; social media, which attracts females at higher rates than males, increases anxiety and depression and the fear of missing out and of being left out in females.[46] Applications of this thought can be multiplied, including in sex differences in how achievement relates to happiness (for men it is more crucial to happiness than for women).

Hormones and brain structures explain the tendencies in males to aggression and females to sociality. Testosterone is associated with the building of muscle mass and with aggressiveness in males of all species. Oxytocin and prolactin, hormones released into women's bloodstream especially during breastfeeding and pregnancy, facilitate bonding and make women more prone to obey and please. Estrogen, another hormone typically in females in much higher doses, facilitates soothing social relations, and especially counteracts testosterone. When men breathe in oxytocin mists, studies show they become quite nurturing and cooperative and less aggressive. When women have less estrogen (after menopause, for instance), studies show that they are more apt to take on traditionally male characteristics, since estrogen counteracts testosterone in their bloodstream. Women can move the needle on aggressiveness (and men can move the needle on nurturing), but short of castration and comprehensive hormone therapy, expect no sameness in aggression or nurturing.

Gender—in this case, how society institutionalizes or imagines aggression—arises from tendencies in sex; that gender construction also rebounds in the other direction to affect how men think of themselves as men and how women think of themselves as women. If we pretend that there is no difference between the sexes on aggression and agreeableness, society is less intentional in civilizing both sexes. Societies can harness aggression toward warfare and conquest, other acts of courage, gang membership, commercial competition, sports, family success, service, or other things. With these gendered options laid before men, they come to know themselves as "men"; their aggression is thereby shaped and may be made more peaceable and social. Men are more likely to dream of their future as football or basketball players, priests, hedge fund managers, video game designers, fathers, generals, or U.S. marines. Gender, the product of a time and place, grows in the grooves of sexual difference. Maleness could go in any number of directions—and gender tutors. Man without a city, Aristotle writes, is either a beast or a god: untamed beasts live without the gender-based tutoring provided through political life or civilization. But there are certain ways that gender will not go.

Sex and the body pose problems that gender restates, but some restatements go with the grain of nature and the body. Turning men into kindergarten teachers is difficult; though men may love children, they love them differently than women do. Women truck drivers, electricians, and plumbers are rarer than female CEOs; feminists, for some reason, rarely seem concerned about that. If feminists love equality, they should be concerned about the gap in dangerous, manual labor. If feminists want to gain power for themselves indirectly and without asking (appealing to guilt), they would express themselves as they do. The way they criticize disparities *selectively* is profound evidence of womanly indirection in the effort to get their way.

Sex and Sexual Desire

Women are more social or plastic than men. As women are more sociable and malleable than men, so they have less of a "nature" than men, by nature, or their nature is more social than men's and hence society determines it. Would a feminist welcome this finding as proof of the prominence of gender and hence celebrate women's flexibility, or would the prominence of gender among women *by nature* incline feminists to reject the characterization as the more malleable sex?

Few things reveal our bodily difference and animal nature as intensely as sexual desire and sex. Even in sexual relations gender mediates how we experience what the sexual act means and even what it is. Society's prevailing ideas of how much sex one "needs" and how active each partner will be in initiating sex, for instance, affects the experience. Evidence from the sexual revolution shows that women can be more sexually adventurous (e.g., engage in sex outside of marriage) than they once were, and women have more partners than they used to during the course of their lives; both of these things are true of men too. In a nod to gender, societies can move the needle on sexual desire in terms of both quantity and qualities, and make it relatively more central to a good life.

How much can the needle be moved? Feminists of several sorts compare the male's penetration of the female to a violation, suffered, on her back, in a "posture of defeat." Womanly passivity in sex makes her an erotic object for men, and, on this view, she aspires to become an erotic object. Sex makes her "the second sex." To put an end to this, women should become more active, controlling sex partners or take initiative or shun fidelity.[47] Women should use sex to achieve independence and seek pleasure and power where they can. Perhaps a woman can reimagine an erect penis penetrating her as an expression of transcendence. Perhaps, as some of today's feminists hold, the hookup culture allows women their short-term trysts while encouraging them to use sex to further their independent-minded goals. Beauvoir's most complete discussion of how women escape objectification in sex is found in part 7 of *The Second Sex* (entitled "Toward Liberation"), in chapter 25, entitled "The Independent Woman."[48]

Just such a "feminization of sex" is imagined in *Re-Making Love* (1986), a book written by three feminists celebrating the sexual revolution. Sound science seems to support aspirations for the "feminization of sex." No less an authority than Alfred Kinsey and his colleagues writes, "In spite of the widespread and oft-repeated emphasis on the supposed differences between female and male sexuality, we fail to see any anatomic or physiological basis for such differences."[49] Feminists also appeal to sexology for the idea that "orgasm is a phenomenon which appears to be essentially the same in the

human female and male."[50] Women, our three feminists promise, would come
to have as much sex as men, have as many partners as men, become as adventurous in sex as men, and enjoy it as "enthusiastically as men are said to."[51] The
old "drama of female passivity and surrender" would give way to "an interac-
tion between potentially equal partners."[52]

The "battle for orgasm equity" shakes patriarchal social forces.[53] This
battle has secured many victories, as our three authors believe. Women are
going to strip clubs, purchasing and using sex paraphernalia, masturbating
as much as men, and loving sexual role-play and sadomasochism as much as
men. Marriage is more sexualized than in the past. Women are becoming ever
less modest, relatively less interested in having children or in raising them if
they do, and less suited for or interested in marriage than in the past. Younger
girls watch or consume more pornography than their recent female relatives.[54]
They perform and receive more oral sex. They engage in more sex without
commitment.[55] That's progress! The daughters and granddaughters of those
sexual revolutionaries and feminists confirm many of these revolutionary
expectations: "the ideal sexual script for women has changed toward a greater
valuing of sexual agency, especially with respect to sexual initiation."[56] More
broadly the sexual dance is now a work of art, a joy, as women enter into its
pleasures in equal numbers as men.[57]

Hannah Rosin's *The End of Men and the Rise of Women* frames the issue
of sex differences as "Plastic Woman and Cardboard Man." Women adapt,
change, take on new characters and new patterns of existence, while men
seem stuck with the same ambitions, desires, and lifestyles.[58] Women "tend to
be more malleable sexually," which leads to more sexual experimentation (i.e.,
lesbianism) among especially younger women and also more sexual absti-
nence than among men.[59] Women are more cue-taking animals than men.
While "men incline to polygyny," women "are more malleable" in this respect
and "depending on the circumstances, may be equally satisfied in polygynous,
monogamous, or polyandrous marriages"; men tend to be more jealous, while
women, "more malleable," can be as jealous as men but are usually less so.[60]
Legato agrees in her summary of the sex difference literature: "as women's
opportunities for education and career expand, so can the characteristics she
seeks in a mate," and she must not seek merely a "good provider," but Legato
sees no simultaneous change in what young men are looking for.[61]

For the most part and for better or worse, men have a stronger desire
for sexual pleasure—or "stronger libidos"—than women, are more stimulated
through seeing women's bodies as opposed to being touched, value physical attractiveness more than women, have a greater taste for sexual variety
than women, and are more inclined to take initiative in sexual relations and
romantic relations (or at least to think they are).[62] "Men—historically, and
on average—tend to want sex more and pursue it with greater abandon and

single-mindedness" than women.[63] Men separate emotional from physical intimacy, and use women's penchant for the former to pursue the latter. Most seducers are males in our literature, from the suitors surrounding Helen in the *Odyssey* to the series of men that conquer Emma Bovary in *Madame Bovary*. This is sex more than gender.

Plastic Woman, it seems, has moved more than a little in the direction of horny Cardboard Man since the sexual revolution. Many women sense great empowerment in this revolution, or, as Rosin writes, "young women are more in control of their sexual destinies now than . . . ever before."[64] Though they have made progress in sexual adventurism, they still trail men in having sex, in desiring fewer partners, and in initiating it. Women are sexual gatekeepers (in a testament to sex),[65] but after the sexual revolution they mind the gate somewhat differently than in the past (in a testament to gender). As casual sex becomes more accepted and expected, women offer it more and men rise to supply it. Are women thereby also more in control of their sexual destinies and relationships? That is less certain. Supposedly plastic women are also more inclined to see sex within the context of a relationship or as contributing to building somewhat enduring bonds.[66] As Rousseau divines, "the two sexes have so strong and so natural a relation to one another that the morals of one always determine those of the other."[67] Women are more empowered and encouraged to have sex outside of marriage, but the sex difference in sexual desire means that women cannot make as many demands on men for enduring relations and intimacy when sex, for men, is easily gettable, and hence women are less able to achieve their goals through sex.

Differences in sexual desire may reflect sex differences in the presence of particular hormones grounded in sexual biology. Men's sexual desire and willingness to take the initiative in sex seems related to their greater penchant for aggression. This is the long-standing, traditional view about the troubling character of *eros*—connected as it is to tyrannical ambition, sexual desire, and the love of wisdom.[68] Testosterone, the hormone prompting the testes into action, lies at the root of both sexuality and aggression. Castrated men are docile, more social, asexual, and hairier,[69] while elevated testosterone makes men more into loners. The opposite also seems to be the case. Physical attributes that make women more nurturing and relational assist them in subordinating sex and sexual desire within sustainable relationships; and it is a for-the-most-part universal that women are more interested in finding a subordinate place for sex than in unconnected sex, while men are more interested in sex without much commitment. The structure of sexual relations broadly conceived belies the assumptions of the post-structuralist world: sexual differences are managed and channeled to make them consistent with the natures of each.

Consider other applications of this. Emphasis on sexual pleasure for both men and women coincides with the increasing importance of physical beauty, but unevenly in men and women because each values different things in the other. Women value looks in men more than they used to (and not as much security or status, which they can get better on their own than they used to), but not more than men do.[70] More pressure is thereby put on women under liberationist conditions to appear beautiful if they would attract men, since women must still be pleasing to men to gain attention and more women are willing to bestow attention on men. One may, following Naomi Wolf, see women tyrannized by the "beauty myth,"[71] but one cannot expect a concern for beauty to disappear in the age of sexual revolution when people are more likely to make judgments based on beauty. Believe me: it's a tough time to be alive if you are ugly! Plastic Woman is more sociable. This sociability affects her vision of where sex fits in with life—it's more important than it used to be. Women are more likely to find sex satisfying if they think the hookup will lead to a relationship or if a relationship appears to be a prelude to marriage; they take break-ups or being spurned harder than men too.[72] It's different for girls.

Efforts to deny this difference make it more difficult to manage it toward the happiness of each. Women are encouraged to lose the tools (such as modesty, sobriety, and making demands) that assist them in managing the difference. It becomes more difficult to translate men's sexual attraction into the enduring love that is more consistent with their concerns. More on that later.

Motherhood and Fatherhood

Motherhood and fatherhood are sexual and gender terms. Only women can have children, while men provide half the new child's genetic material. The availability of contraception makes biological motherhood more a matter of choice than it used to be, at least when it comes to timing and number, but motherhood is not pure choice—it involves biological necessity. Many men and women may want to have sex with one another, but do they want to have children, do they want to raise them, and what does each have to offer in the raising of children?

Motherhood and fatherhood are for-the-most-part universals. By *motherhood* I mean having, nurturing, and raising children. Many feminists think motherhood has been vastly overrated in the past, and that women chose motherhood only because they had few other options and were conditioned to so choose. Motherhood seemed more necessary in the past. We have seen how women in sex were, on the feminist view, humiliated and violated. Same with motherhood. A life centered on motherhood is, for women, "continued *infantilizing*," "a living death," and "a terror," wherein the mother and wife is "committing a kind of suicide" and the role is "burying millions of American women alive."[73] Let these phrases, all taken from Friedan's *Feminine Mystique*, stand in for the hundreds that could be brought forward to show that the feminist re-ranking of goods brings motherhood down more than a few notches.[74]

Women have options in the feminist world: education, contraception, and careers are available. How will they choose? The feminist quasi-answer—that every woman should decide for herself—is a cop-out: ranking derives from our way of imagining and prioritizing goods. Feminists expect that women will choose no differently than men; if they do not, then patriarchy persists. Feminists want women to "make a new life plan"—at most integrating serious, lifelong commitment to society with a less serious or less lifelong marriage and motherhood.[75] This is the image of the Independent Woman that directs our feminist education in later modernity. Some consistent feminists, we have seen, envision a world where women are freed from the dictates of motherhood through the accomplishments of human cloning and state-directed care for children.[76]

Is there a groove to prevent motherhood from slipping out of the rankings altogether? The astonishing, well-nigh universal decline in birth rates speaks to the power of gender on this matter. Modern women are less likely to have children and more likely to have fewer children if they do. This does not tell the whole story. Do childless women, nearing the end of the time when they can safely have children, educated to emphasize career to the exclusion of motherhood, regret the ticking of the biological clock? Examples of barren women with such regrets abound, even among thoroughly modern women. Book titles such as *Flirting with Danger, Motherhood Deferred,* and *An Unquiet Mind* provide glimpses into how some barren women think they bought feminism's fraudulent bill of goods.[77] Surveys show that regrets haunt "successful," childless women in the corporate world.[78] Are these lagging examples of women raised at a time when there was still more respect for motherhood? Will today's girls and young women, educated more or less without reference to motherhood, have the same regrets?

Perhaps there is a "maternal instinct," leading women to want to have children and then to spend time and energy raising them. Granting the existence of "maternal instincts," however, the question for all communities is how "maternal instincts" rank in relation to other instincts and options for women and how much to honor them. That motherhood is desired is a matter of sex; how women rank motherhood is a matter of gender. Holy Orders or motherhood or a "meaningful" career? Pretty strong desires for emotional connection and for having children exist in many women, perhaps even to such an extent that many women would rather integrate their careers into their experience of motherhood than the other way around. Not for all. Motherhood and being a wife need some cultural apparatus, since raising children and building a beautiful home requires more than a few folkways and traditions.

Fathers are less connected biologically to their children. The greater desire for sex in men is a groove. Mothering as a priority in a woman's life is a groove, though a less certain one than people thought fifty years ago. No one would suggest that there is a marriage or monogamy groove—marriage is more a matter of gender or at least quite far removed from nature. The father-hood groove is similarly weak and mores must support fatherhood. Men can have relatively free access to sex outside of marriage, thanks to sexual libera-tion. Economic reasons for marriage may have also diminished for men and women. There is today little official social pressure for men to stick around to love a committed wife or to rear children, and less pressure on women to stick it out in marriage than there once was (and perhaps some reward for women to break up their marriages). Despite the waning of support for mar-riage, most men enter into marriage and stay married, and most men in those marriages try to be responsible parents to their children, and the same holds for women. Perhaps the desires for female companionship and community (as opposed to sex) and for children are somewhat natural grooves within which a fatherhood culture exists.

How are these grooves ranked? Sparta, prodigy of the ancient world, ranked them such that homosexual relations among bands of brothers were honorable sexual outlets and expressions of martial, sexual solidarity, while procreative sex with one's wife bore more than a hint of shame; children were raised, more or less, in common at an early age, rendering the family impo-tent in light of the city.[79] A rule, perhaps: direct fathers away from the family and the political community grows in their estimation. Men tend to see their children as extensions of their relations with the mother of their children. Paternal engagement depends, in the modern context as in the Spartan, on husbandly engagement. Detach honorable sex from marriage and marriage suffers. The key groove in modern marriage, for men, seems to be the desire for feminine companionship, grounded in part in sexual desire, the need for complementary character from women, and the qualities of character that the desire for companionship calls forth from men.

The manner of husbandly engagement matters. Often feminists, notic-ing the "second shift" of housework that working mothers perform once their paid labor is done, suggest that men and women are interchangeable when it comes to housework (and all work) and parenting. The "sexual division of labor" must be abolished, they hold.[80] Though men now spend more time on household tasks generally than they did generations ago (testifying to the power of gender), the gap between men and women is still substantial and men do different kinds of tasks than women (testifying to the power of sex). Fathers spend more time with children than they did a generation ago (testi-fying to the power of gender), but the gap between men and women remains and men and women tend to act quite differently with children (testifying to the power of sex).

Differences persist between fathering and mothering and in the jobs men and women choose to make for a complementary, common life. These differences relate to the characteristics of caring and aggression in the two sexes. These characteristics are more variable than the specific contributions women and men make to sexual reproduction. The grooves in this area relate to two pertinent facts. First, as David Barash, reviewing the literature, describes, "there is no society in which men do more fathering than women do mothering; in fact none in which men and women are even comparable."[81] Second, men and women do not make exactly the same contributions to "parenting": women tend to mother, while men tend to father.

Mothering and fathering integrate sex differences in aggression and nurturing.[82] Mothering seems to comport with the bent women have toward caring and noticing important elements in their context. These elements are sometimes, erroneously, called "emotionalism" in women. Actually, women are contextual and subtle, taking in unspoken messages such as facial expressions and tones, and anticipating needs.[83] They smile more than men and seek to make people and especially children comfortable; they show more affection to their children than men, providing assurance that the potentially hostile world is welcoming.[84] Mothers adapt their ways of treating children to how their children act, integrating their ways with the child's ways.[85] In this way women seem more willing to accept the present and notice its beauties and provide what is necessary for the context. Building intimacy, even the housework that women tend to specialize in builds the home and makes a common life possible.

Fathering lines up with man's tendency to aggression and violence. Fathers seek to get children's attention to the outside world (making faces, distracting with toys), instead of reconciling the child to the world as it is. Men play rough with children of both sexes.[86] Fathers communicate much more with imperatives and rules, mothers with suggestions and through manipulating the situation to make rules less necessary. Fathers tend to govern the actions of their children to bring about progress toward productive adulthood, while mothers engage and celebrate each achievement on its own terms, more in the moment.[87] Somewhat more independent themselves, men seek independence in their children—sometimes too much. The household tasks of men tend to be outward-facing and mechanical, more concerned with things rather than with nurturing and caring.

The family thus appears as a mixed regime itself. Mothers observe present needs, reconcile, welcome, and nurture, while fathers mind the long term and disrupt the comfortable present to bring it about. Mothers seem more democratic, while fathers assume a more hierarchical or aristocratic stance toward

their children. Mothers are concerned to notice what it takes to preserve harmony and to carry it out, while fathers do not mind disrupting this harmony
sometimes. Mothers work with their children; fathers are demanding. Perhaps this is why children thrive best with engaged mothers and fathers—each
brings something distinctive and complementary to the job of "parenting."
Children need comfort and risk, acceptance and ambition, stable identities
and disruption, support and prodding, affirmation and challenge: each one
of these pairs makes the other side more possible. We all need that in our
relations. Such a mixed regime works differently in the workplace, with results
that need exploration.

Conclusion: The Dialogue between Nature and Feminism

Sexual grooves in men and women limit the feminist project. We will not get
a fifty-fifty world even especially in an atmosphere of freedom, prosperity, and
equal opportunity. In fact an atmosphere of freedom and equal opportunity
does much to reveal the different natures or preferences of men and women.[88]
The human body is not simply standing reserve to be manipulated at the
behest of bureaucratic authorities or self-determining individuals. Bodily differences between males and females suggest that characteristics of each may
be bent, but only up to a point.

Disparities or differences between the sexes do not necessarily mean that
we have a patriarchy or a matriarchy. The characters and ambitions of all individuals are shaped by many different traits, including (but not limited to) their
upbringing, the laws, their bodies, their subculture, and their broader culture.
There is flexibility in the nature of each; our bodies constitute grooves that
lead us to expect something different from men and women. Some grooves,
however, are more determinative than others. As the rolling revolution shapes
our world, we will not see independent human beings, but men and women
reacting, in accord with their natures, to changes in gender construction. The
sexual grooves manifest themselves in a new way in our new sexual regime.

Or perhaps we just have not tried hard enough to dull these grooves.
In taking an adversarial stance toward nature, feminists see all grooves as
socially constructed and remediable. All aspects of our identity must be
willed—and willed autonomously—for human beings to experience freedom
and independence. Erasing difference and inequality requires more than just
consciousness-raising classes and changes in education and child-rearing. It
requires an abolition of the family. The final frontier of feminism is reached,
as Firestone sees, with the conquest of the body—a fundamental restructuring of human being through hormone therapies, brain manipulation, genetic
engineering, and perhaps other things. Anything less would mean that feminism would have to define an acceptable end point where its goals had been

achieved. A restructuring of human nature is fraught with risk: what lies on the other side of this latest and greatest Tower of Babel?

No respectable inquirer opposes equality of the sexes, properly understood. It is not just, on the modern account, that human beings are born women or men; we do not make our own being. Modern justice and justice strictly speaking, then, while powerful explainers, are not the sole explainers. Is it a matter of justice that men and women are different—and that each has a body? Justice has nothing to do with it. Does our love of justice demand that we consider such differences as insignificant as the difference between baldness and having hair? No. With sex difference, modern justice reaches a caution sign about human power and must raise questions about the goodness of its experimental mode. Modern justice cannot on its own terms provide an account of phenomena such as birth and sexual difference, yet these are probably some of the most important and rewarding experiences in human life. Being born seems pretty crucial—and among the first things we notice about newborns is their sex.

Those who oppose efforts to try harder to remake human nature face accusations of old-fogeyism as they defend the necessity and the goodness of the sexual grooves. These grooves are given in that they are part of our physical and moral nature as embodied creatures, and in that they contribute to the sweetness of human life and to the love and life women and men would often share. Evolutionary biologists may speak to the origin of these differences in our genetic heritage. Social science can speak to the pervasiveness and durability of the grooves across cultures even especially in advanced democracies. Neither of these groups speaks to the goodness and desirability of such differences.

Let us focus on the goods that these different attributes serve, not in their excesses and isolation but in their relation to the others. Differences contribute to the good life. These contributions may be better captured through literature and art than through argument, yet this book is an exercise of argument, so that is its limit. Each element is valuable, though differently. Strength and speed and grace and elegance are valuable, and men's sports can be appreciated for some while women's sports for others. Women cannot compete on men's terms, and men do not want to compete on women's terms. Direct speech is part of getting things done and seeking to understand things clearly, while conversation and relationships grasp ambiguity and counsel caution. Some are interested in things; others are interested in people. Concern with both is necessary to make one's way through life well: concern with things fosters improvements in the world and defense of the innocent, while concern with persons suits those improvements to a human context. Caution and initiative are needed in all endeavors, so let us enjoy both. Progress can come through conflict and competition, but sole focus on conflict makes for a heartless world. Single-mindedness is important to human accomplishment in and beyond competition, as is keeping everyone relatively happy and on board. Men are demanding; women are welcoming—both seem necessary to life. No one celebrates male violence as an end in itself, but perhaps society cannot do without some degree of physical heroism much more likely to bring forth the qualities of men and attract the fairer sex. Single-minded men can destroy and build, but women make building beautiful.

No one can say for sure what woman is or what man is, since gender always intervenes to make sense of sex. That is the beginning of wisdom. The dialogue between nature and culture continues—and it yields wisdom and appreciation. The problem with feminism is that there is no dialogue: there are forces of Darkness and oppression and forces of Light and equal liberation. We need an approach to women that acknowledges limits and is willing to say to radical feminism that enough is enough (at some point).

POSTSCRIPT TO CHAPTER 5

On the Nature of Moderate Feminism

There could be a moderate feminism, which would not embrace the principles of radical feminism. It must accept that sex provides grooves for gender and that independence is not good for men or women. It would recognize that the fifty-fifty world of the radical feminist imagination is neither possible nor desirable. Nor would it look for "independent" love and sex, knowing that love and sex imply dependence. Conventions that lead men and women in different, *gendered* directions (e.g., images of fatherhood for men and of motherhood for women; conventions emphasizing competition in boys and sociality for girls) help men and women fulfill for-the-most-part different traits. What feminists dismiss as patriarchy or social construction helps foster happiness in each, since those institutions register and educate differences between the sexes.

There are pseudo-moderate feminists on the retail level. Some pseudo-moderates worry about what people will think if radicals demand feminism's whole loaf. These pseudo-moderate feminists would take a half a loaf (for now!), and then ask for the next half of the half loaf, and then the next. Also appearing moderate are those who emphasize that there *may* be biological limits on the feminist project, but who think that human beings can flexibly overcome those limits with proper education or more technology; these pseudo-moderates say, "Yes" to limits on feminism, but also say, "But" because they embrace Beauvoir's basic claim about becoming a woman. Let us survey these two pseudo-moderate feminisms before turning to the character of a genuinely moderate one. The first of these pseudo-moderate feminisms says,

"Not yet" to radical notions, while the other says, "No," but always wants to move closer to a world consistent with radical principles.

How odd to have a postscript in the middle of a book. Feminism, raising the central issues of modern political thought and modern life, is endlessly challenging. Stepping outside of feminism requires that we step outside the dominant stream of modern thinking and consider the world anew. To what extent does nature limit the ambitions of human power or autonomy? How should human beings conceive of these limits? Are limits remediable? Must we submit to limits grudgingly or with a smile on our face? Do those limits point to higher things? Can and do limits limit us morally instead of just "realistically"? None of these questions can be answered with geometric certainty. In fact answers to these questions are, for most, treated best in art and in religion, since philosophic reflection leads most to philosophical doubts and melancholy. Yet it is mortifying to think that reason cannot continue the dialogue about feminism and its limits, and explore what those limits might mean for human life and for our politics.

Friedan's Feminist Principles and Activism

Each of these pseudo-moderate feminisms emerges from the career of Betty Friedan, America's most influential second-wave feminist. We explore pseudo-moderate feminisms in her achievements. Her *Feminine Mystique* accepts Beauvoir's intellectual framework and conclusions regarding human identity. Friedan affects to have been just a simple suburban girl when she ran across Beauvoir. "It was *The Second Sex* that introduced me," Friedan later reflected,

> to an existentialist approach to reality and political responsibility—that in effect freed me from the rubrics of authoritative ideology and led me to whatever original analysis of women's existence that I have been able to contribute to the Women's Movement and its unique politics. . . . When I first read *The Second Sex* in the early Fifties, I was writing "housewife" on the census blanks, still in the unanalyzed embrace of the feminine mystique.[1]

Friedan uses the term "the feminine mystique" to describe the complex of laws, opinions, and pressures that turn women into sexually passive, intellectually stunted housewives. The "feminine mystique" generally makes women the "second sex." Friedan brings Beauvoir's abstract endorsement of transcendence, suggestive of making human beings into gods, down from the heavens, and packages it in terms more consistent with America's dedication to individual rights. The prevailing Progressive ideology, captured in America's universities, would put the new science in the service of cultural reconstruction that would support healthy, chosen human identities.

Science has, for Friedan, long reinforced the "feminine mystique." It counsels women to find fulfillment in distinctive wifely and motherly tasks. In Friedan's day that science would have predicted that women would be satisfied, as they were fulfilling their destinies as wives and mothers during the baby boom. Friedan diagnoses a discontent traceable to a disjunction between society's expectations and women's real dreams. Women of the 1950s and early 1960s yearn to escape their wifely and motherly fates, she claims, and they suffer from boredom, feeling trapped, and sensing that they have nothing important to do. They suffer from what Friedan calls the "problem that has no name."[2] Doctors, counselors, scientists, psychiatrists, and the popular press have all failed to identify this problem. A woman who allows society to define her life for her has what Friedan calls a "forfeited self," with "no goal, no purpose, no ambition patterning her days into the future, making her stretch and grow beyond the small score of years in which her body can fill its biological function." Such a woman commits "a kind of suicide."[3]

Stirring next to the old science that thinks women of the 1950s and 1960s will be content in their matronly roles is a liberating science that shows how old ideas actually disable women and new ideas could lead women to healthy identities. "The core of the problem for women today," Friedan contends, "is a problem of identity—a stunting or evasion of growth that is perpetuated by the feminine mystique."[4] Instead of living according to the feminine mystique, each woman must solve her own "identity crisis" by finding "the work, or the cause, or the purpose that evokes . . . creativity."[5] Creative work fosters genuine struggle, and such struggle fosters personal growth. Through such creativity women can become true selves and achieve "self-actualization," a phrase Friedan borrows from mid-century psychologist Abraham Maslow, whom she interviewed for her opus.

Maslow, a leading light of the new liberating science, argues that achieving the highest levels of happiness requires "giving up a simpler and easier and less effortful life" as a mother and wife "in exchange for a more demanding, more difficult life" pursuing a mission "concerned with the good of mankind."[6] Self-actualized people, Maslow writes, possess "the full use and exploitation of talents, capacities, potentialities. Such people seem to be fulfilling themselves and doing the best that they are capable of doing," and to know it.[7] They have "good self-confidence, self-assurance, high evaluation of the self, feelings of general capability or superiority, and lack of shyness, timidity, self-consciousness or embarrassment."[8] A fully developed woman strives "beyond femaleness to the full humanness she shares with males," Maslow writes.[9] At the pinnacle of human motivation is the desire for self-actualization, which Maslow defines as "growth . . . the striving toward health, the quest for identity and autonomy, the yearning for excellence."[10]

Following Maslow, Friedan sees the good woman of the future moving "beyond privatism" toward having "some mission in life . . . outside themselves"; enjoying sexual pleasures more than others because they have a stronger sense of their own individuality; and loving out of gift love and "spontaneous admiration" instead of a needy love informed by personal dependence.[11] Friedan applies Maslow's theory and concludes that old gender roles immiserate women, but that self-actualized women would be happy.[12] A self-actualized person is, as Friedan relates, "psychologically free—more autonomous."[13] Healthy human identity, for women, lies beyond the "feminine mystique" or society's prevailing notions of gender. Those with healthy identities engage in projects that make the world a better place through social reform, and lose themselves in careers that they find meaningful and rewarding and that call forth all of their capacities.[14] "The only kind of work which permits" a woman "to realize her abilities fully, to achieve identity in society," Friedan writes, is "the lifelong commitment to an art or science, to politics or profession."[15] Educators, psychologists, and others in the learned professions must adopt this vision of human happiness and encourage women conform to it, in the name of freedom.

Friedan links liberation or autonomy to what promotes mental health, personal fulfillment, and self-actualization. All is framed in a mostly value-neutral way: one can be fulfilled so long as one constructs one's own destiny, regardless of what destiny one chooses. This contains an implicit critique of women living in traditional roles, unless they independently and self-consciously embrace all that such roles entail after surveying other possibilities. The task for psychiatrists, parents, government, and educators will be to ensure that no individual simply conforms to society's notions of proper living, and that all individuals are free to make their own identities. Perhaps society will have to dismantle the whole idea of preconceived notions of proper living. The task of feminist statesmanship is one of continuous diagnosis and remedy. Exposing the influence of patriarchy and promising a new future for individual growth become linchpins for the scientific enterprise. Science uncovers the hidden power of gender in every sphere of life, and hence points to the gap between what women have been and what growing women could become. Friedan's principles are the principles of the not-moderate rolling revolution.

She put those principles into action, moderately. Friedan sought to make this vision a reality when she served as president of the National Organization for Women (NOW) during the late 1960s, as an abortion rights activist and as a prominent activist-intellectual. Preparing the way would involve reforming marriage, making sexual relations between men and women less encumbered by marriage and procreation, and changing education and the workplace, among other reforms.

On the reformation of marriage, NOW hoped to win legislative support for new divorce laws. Old divorce laws required that either the man or woman prove fault, and that women who had dedicated themselves to the family during marriage receive alimony payments to support them after the divorce. Friedan and her fellow advocates wanted at-will divorce, where either party would be able to leave a marriage at any time. They advocated for equal division of property because "as feminists . . . we didn't believe women should ask for alimony," since alimony implied that women would put themselves in a dependent position while married.[16] Divorce reform was a lever to change womanly ways. Without the crutch of alimony, more women would need to prepare for careers in case their marriages failed.[17] Moreover the threat to leave would give women especially greater bargaining power to reshape marriage to suit their interests and ambitions.

On the sexual revolution, Friedan argued for legalizing contraception and abortion as essential to the feminist project. Contraception, for Friedan, allowed women "to take control of their bodies" and "define themselves by their contribution to society, not just in terms of their reproductive role."[18] Friedan joined a coalition of abortion activists called the National Association for the Repeal of Abortion Laws (NARAL); later, when they had accomplished repeal after *Roe v. Wade* (1973), the group kept the acronym and became known as the National Abortion Rights Action League. For Friedan the right to abortion was "a final essential right of full personhood."[19] "Motherhood is a bane almost by definition," as Friedan argued at a 1969 abortion convention. Only when women could prevent motherhood through abortion and were unashamed to put their career ambitions before their biology would they achieve "self-determination and full dignity."[20]

As important to Friedan was the ending of sex discrimination in employment and in higher education. The 1964 Civil Rights Act prohibited racial and sexual discrimination in employment and in public accommodations such as restaurants or hotels. That law established the Equal Employment Opportunity Commission (EEOC) to investigate illegal discrimination. From NOW's perspective, however, the EEOC was at first more interested in racial than sexual discrimination. NOW, under Friedan, set out to change that. They complained that stewardesses were fired when they were no longer attractive, or that newspaper advertisements asked for applications from only one sex, or that companies prohibited women from performing dangerous or high-level work, or about the existence of exclusive men's clubs. In each of these cases and in others, NOW gained the attention of the EEOC, and companies and businesses changed their practices under threat of legal penalty. All of this was accomplished so that women could, as the NOW manifesto of 1966 read, have "full participation in the mainstream of American society" and "develop their fullest human potential."[21] Precisely how far this revolution against discrimination would go—and whether it would countenance arguments about "disparate impact"—was not yet an issue under Friedan's leadership.

More still needed to be done. NOW set up a Task Force on Education that called for the elimination of sex-specific school curricula, the integration of student facilities such as dormitories on college campuses, and public instruction in family planning.[22] These outmoded institutions were based on the assumptions that boys and girls had different needs or different personalities, and they formed the basis for male privilege and exclusivity. Education should instead aim to treat all as human beings with the same needs, aspirations, and abilities.

Friedan and her reforming sisters thought none of their goals would be achieved without government-provided childcare. "Without child care," Friedan learned from Swedish feminists, "it's all just talk." In 1967 NOW demanded "paid maternity leave, federally mandated child care facilities and a tax deduction for home and child care expenses for working parents."[23] These proposals would allow women to pursue creative work of their own. These proposals would form the structure of a new, gender-neutral society, where women and men would have the same level and kind of devotion to the family and each could equally devote themselves to their careers. They also called for opening up the priesthood to women and the removal of sex segregation in religious organizations and church-sponsored schools, in the hope that private organizations could be pressured to abandon their commitment to the feminine mystique.

All in all, Friedan's reform agenda could have been more radical in these years, especially when compared with the ideas of Firestone and Beauvoir. She often appealed, in good old American common sense, to complaints about a boorish boss who thought women could only make the coffee, or who thought they had to look nice in order to do a good job. Nowhere did she call for the abolition of the family, for sexualized childhood on the model of ghetto children, or for cybernetic communism, for instance. She even criticized the radicals for exceeding her ambitions. Thus Friedan flirted, even in her activist years, with a moderate feminism that stood in some tension with her own radical principles and with her radical sisters. Friedan's moderate feminism, never developed in a book, emerges from interviews and occasional pieces Friedan wrote after 1970, when Millett, Firestone, and their radical sisters were emerging as the leading edge of feminist thought.

"Not Yet" and "No, but . . ." Radicalism.

Friedan was critical of "sexual politics"—the idea that culture constructs opposite-sex sex and a woman's desire to be pretty and generally communal love to keep women in a subordinate position. Friedan worried that sexual theorists such as Firestone and Millet (and even Beauvoir) risked defining the women's movement in "anti-love, anti-child terms." If the radicals were to take over the movement, Friedan worried, "we are not going to have the power of the women and the help of increasing numbers of men who can identify their liberation with women's liberation."[24] In her memoir Friedan lamented that "the women's movement was not about sex, but about equal opportunity. . . . I suppose you have to say that freedom of sexual choice was part of that, but it should not be the main issue, the tail that wags the dog." Sexual politics was "bad business."[25] Lesbians—whom she called the "Lavender Menace"—were, Friedan worried, taking over the women's movement and turning off middle-class women, who found contentment mixing family life with careers.

Friedan emphasized prudential considerations in an interview with Beauvoir. Beauvoir, recall, convinced by Firestone's argument, contended that "no woman should be authorized to stay at home to raise her children," because "if there is a choice, too many women will make that one." Beauvoir argued that "as long as the family and the myth of the family and the myth of maternity are not destroyed . . . women will still be oppressed," and that the abolition of the family in law and opinion would be necessary for women to be genuinely free.[26]

Friedan stopped short of endorsing Beauvoir's proposal to outlaw involved motherhood. She first worried that "politically at the moment" it would be impossible to force women away from motherhood, because "we have hardly any child-care centers in the United States." Perhaps such centers should be built, though. Beauvoir's proposal to force women away from motherhood also ran afoul of the "tradition of individual freedom in America" because of which Friedan "would never say that every woman must put her child in a child-care center."[27] Perhaps that tradition could be changed—it certainly deserves no respect as tradition for Friedan. These are arguments that bespeak a "not yet" pseudo-moderate feminism.

Concerning artificial reproduction, Friedan called it an "abstract discussion" that does "no good," because the development of new life through human cloning is not possible now. "Don't talk to me about test tubes," Friedan wrote in her treatment of ideological traps for the new feminists. "We must confront the fact of life—as a temporary fact of most women's lives today—that women do give birth to children . . . and challenge the idea that it is *woman's primary* role to rear children."[28] Not yet to cloning. Tomorrow, if such technologies were developed, Friedan would presumably have a different opinion, and would welcome such technologies into her feminist teaching if it would be of help to the goal of building a self-actualized identity. Perhaps, that is, artificial reproductive technologies would be the next stage in freeing women to take on truly meaningful careers in bureaucracies or in other creative endeavors.

These are variations of "not yet" moderate feminism. Radical proposals, far in front of public opinion, risk undermining the unity necessary for a successful women's movement. Yet if the country became ready for such changes,

Friedan would welcome them and adjust. This "not yet" feminism endorses radical feminism's assumptions about the separation of gender from sex and its aspirations about the independent woman, yet proceeds prudently, harnessing public opinion and consolidating gains. Even radical feminists are coy "not yet" moderates (as we see in Firestone's predictions).

Friedan's criticisms of feminism sometimes went beyond strategy. She came to suspect that some experiences that radical feminists criticize are valuable, and that feminists should therefore be careful not to upset or uproot them from human life. She seems sometimes to say, "No," instead of, "Not yet," but her "no" is really a "no, but . . . maybe."

Against those who see sexual relations as inherently oppressive, Friedan said the experiences of "love and sex are real," woven into the human psyche, and are an expression of genuine human needs for connection and love and belonging (which the feminine mystique has exaggerated).[29] Friedan may have envisioned a feminism that would walk a line where women would or could still love a man and bear children, but neither experience would overly determine her life, and each experience would be truly chosen and free.

Friedan also went further than "not yet" feminism in her criticism of Beauvoir. In an interview with *Social Policy* magazine from 1970, Friedan held, "I think love and sex are real and that women and men both have real needs for love and intimacy that seem most easily structured around heterosexual relationships." Otto Weininger might agree! Women, like men, are not going to renounce love, and they "shouldn't be asked to do so." Friedan embraces the "possibility of sex and love combined, of joyful sex as part of a larger, meaningful relationship."[30] Much the same is true of motherhood. Against Beauvoir, who would abolish motherhood and the family, Friedan draws what appears to be principled opposition. Friedan thought that "maternity is more than a myth," and that it is "neither good nor necessarily desirable to denounce all of the values of motherhood as long as one has a choice."[31] Maternity could be a subordinate part of a life well lived, as long as it was consistent with a healthy individual identity for women, as Friedan puts it in a 1994 interview.[32]

Friedan also separates herself somewhat from the fifty-fifty aspiration put forward later in the work of Okin and underlying much of contemporary feminism taken with our reigning civil rights ideology. "There are differences between men and women," Friedan wrote in 1969, "but we will not know what these differences are until women have begun to spell their own natures and define themselves in the human dimension more than they've been able to do in the past."[33] Perhaps there could be a sexual imbalance sufficiently chosen or free to satisfy Friedan and her moderate sisters. In a similar vein, Friedan came, later in life, to regret some of what she wrote in *The Feminine Mystique*. The comparison of the suburban housewife to the concentration camp victim she regretted as contradicting her own experience as a mother and the genuine goods that came with motherhood.[34] She also thought women who made themselves beautiful in order to attract men were not desperate, pitiful sex-seekers, but rather people expressing their very human needs for intimacy and love.[35] She was blinded by radical ideology when she made those claims. Oops.

These positions point to an unstable "no, but... maybe" pseudo-moderate feminism, always tending toward radicalism. Friedan would hem in the principles and aspirations of radical feminism with other valuable human experiences. This hemming in, traceable to moral as well as physical difference, must be an essential part of any genuinely moderate feminism. How should Friedan's hemming be understood? Is it inconsistent with the radical principles or not? Friedan never relinquishes those radical principles and aspirations, including such ideas as that the body gives rise to obligations, needs, and dependence and that love involves dependence, and that the only identity worth having is one freely chosen or autonomous (i.e., one that recognizes no limits). Her principles therefore cannot yield a genuine appreciation or respect for those other experiences; her defense of those experiences reflects an unwillingness to draw out all the implications of her initial principles and aspirations, but does not revisit those principles.

Consider a point on which Friedan and Beauvoir agree, namely the claim that motherhood must be chosen instead of the result of conditioning. What is a fully chosen motherhood? All agree that women must have other options besides motherhood for motherhood to be chosen. Friedan and Beauvoir mean something more—women cannot be educated or "conditioned" to be mothers if their choice of motherhood is to be free. When is a choice a choice, and when is conditioning conditioning? If it is a genuine human need (as Friedan suggests in seemingly moderate moments), then is it "conditioning" to prepare human beings for it? Parents shape the views of their children through providing social connections; by cultivating interests, beliefs, and skills in their children; through genetic inheritance; and in forming aspirations or a love of the good and beautiful. Mothers may teach their daughters (some of) their ways, that a beautiful home is something for which one strives and sacrifices and for which one prepares through acquiring skills and ranking those skills necessary for family life (e.g., decorating, cooking, mothering) higher in one's life. All such folkways must be eliminated for Friedan and Beauvoir to hold that women have genuinely chosen motherhood. Those old folkways would have to be replaced with a new folkway, emphasizing careers and public service as central to a satisfying human identity. Friedan's feminist sloganeering—emphasizing the "feminine mystique" and freely chosen projects—prevents her from defending the ground of a genuinely moderate feminism.

The greatest concern theoretically is how she juxtaposes conditioning with choice, a typically late modern move. Social conventions register sex differences to an extent, instead of simply imposing or creating difference where none exists. The stuff of human nature is not just standing reserve to be created or shaped according to power or the human will.

Second, the revolution in human identity that Friedan endorses cannot coexist with the love, intimacy, and sex differences she also professes to respect. For Friedan and Beauvoir, to be truly human is to experience "human liberation."[36] While this may resemble a human good, it is not consistent with human love or intimacy or neediness—all of which are, from the perspective of radical feminism, traceable to immanence or dependence or a forfeited self. People who love, for instance, are incomplete without the addition of another person or another thing. Those who long for intimacy need the emotional and physical closeness of another human being. Sex is for the most part a dependent, immanent act also requiring another human being. Children are dependent, and those who experience the joys of motherhood take a pleasure in raising dependent creatures to adulthood, which is an immanent process. All such experiences ground one's identity, at least in part, in the unchosen needs and deeds of the body or human aspiration. All such experiences call into question whether reality or transcendence or independence or liberation define a good life. The radical principles have a built-in condemnation against the mixing, hemming, but subhuman experiences Friedan sometimes defends as more than myths.

While Friedan professes to think there are differences between men and women, she also thinks that "we won't know for quite a while how much of the difference between men and women is culturally determined and how much of it is real. But let's at least start with the assumption that men and women are human. Women are female, but they are not cows—they are people."[37] Woman is not a cow, but is she a god? By "human" and "people" she means "transcendent" and "historical." If you have seen one cow, you have seen them all: the cow of one era is very much like all cows. Women and people, however, are historical, on Friedan's account as on Beauvoir's; they take on new characteristics and even a new character from one time to another. A look at women yesterday tells us *nothing* about women today, just as a look at men yesterday tells us *nothing* about men today—or so Friedan suggests. It is one thing to say, for men and for women, that anatomy is not destiny—that difference is a testament to gender. It is quite another—and quite beyond the scope of available evidence, or the idea that we are human beings and limited—to say that anatomy is nothing—the lingering effects of the body are a testament to the influence of sex. This is the incipient radicalism in the feminist slogan, present on Subaru bumper stickers across America, that "feminism is the radical notion that women are human beings." No sex differences have a basis in nature, if what it means to be human is to overcome nature. Despite Friedan's protestations, the feminist hope for a fifty-fifty world (or for a new world where women rule) proceeds from her embrace of radical historicism and independence or transcendence, because her theory accepts no "stuff" and no limit derived from nature. Friedan's "no" to radical feminists, therefore—if that is what it is—is in each case, it seems, overwhelmed by her embrace of their principles. Revision at the level of first principles is necessary to a moderate feminism.

Confronting Radical Feminism with a Moderate Feminism

Let me give more inches to feminism. Women have more options for employment and education than they have had in world history, and easy access to technological family planning fosters these options. Cads have less room to operate in the workplace than before. Teachers are made to feel guilty if they steer girls away from math classes or philosophy, which might prove too stressful for their dainty charges. Many today celebrate how marriages are entered into on more equal terms. The feminist movement takes credit for these adjustments. In some ways feminist reform coincides with democratic moral progress. Yet none of these supposed advances is traceable to the principles of the rolling revolution. None requires the celebration of individual transcendence or a fifty-fifty world where the human body is thought to be meaningless stuff subject to technological manipulation. None demands the abolition of gender. We can secure moral advance without the inhuman transcendence of radical feminism.

Many disparities between the sexes are traceable to the different bodies and psychologies men and women have and the different choices they make. Not a few contemporary disparities—wage gaps between men and women, differences in the kinds of jobs men and women take, differences in the amount of time men and women sink into jobs, differences in personality and strength, and so on—result, partly, from their different decisions and character traits. Feminists do not let people get away with a lazy acceptance of disparities, and for their service to human understanding they should be thanked: all disparities between men and women are opportunities to learn about the sexes and about our society. However, no one should let them get away with the hidebound analysis that feminists lazily, persistently, and despite mounds of evidence and common sense put forth: all disparities have multiple causes, and some causes reflect different tendencies of the sexes. It is neither all socialization nor all natural, and the "natural" and the "social" are not so easily discerned.

As we have seen, a moderate feminism arises from the feminist view of how sex and gender relate to one another. Language traps us inside the feminist view of the world, so we need a new world for such moderation. No one hates neologisms more than I, but when words capture a false view of the word new words are needed. I will call this new view *womanism*, despite the baggage of such a word, because such a word grounds the question of womanly identity in the bodily and psychological grooves specific to women. We womanists proceed from the assumption that men and women are human beings, not cows. I learned that from Betty Friedan, among other places. We womanists understand the human in vastly different terms than Friedan, Beauvoir, and the advocates of human transcendence and liberation. No womanist aspires to "independence" or "transcendence," or thinks all previous practices are simply patriarchal, distorting nature and hence oppressive. Conventions express nature, to some extent (at least). Acknowledging respect for conventions is the other side of the coin that rejects the aspiration for transcendence and independence. Human beings are always guided through conventions; arguments can be made on behalf of one set of conventions against other sets of conventions, but there is no "beyond convention" for any society.

There is no simple starting point for womanism: there are starting points. Human beings are pulled in many directions and seek to achieve many goods during their lives, including, but not limited to, love, family life, companionship, a lovely home, friendship, career accomplishments, artistic successes, intellectual challenges, moral virtue, wisdom, piety or love for God, successes in invention or novelty, distraction, and fitness. Women before feminism had before them many, if not all, of these possibilities. Developments in modernity may have had the effect of increasing the number of such options, or at least of attaching honor to more of them. Such results can be celebrated, or not, as they conduce to a wider experience of human thriving. We womanists do not condemn the opening of possibilities when they promote human flourishing.

Feminists have contributed to the opening-up of more professions to women—this could have been accomplished without its ideological baggage. Women have had to be convinced to abandon their old feminine ways and take up new career-oriented ways. Careerists elevate the good of career (for men and women) at the expense of other things that are good. Encouraging careerism has meant investing careers with a species of romance. Friedan and her feminist sisters have contributed to the invention of the career mystique—a set of ideas that tries to convince men and women that changing the world through their careers is the paramount path to fulfillment, growth, and happiness. Before Friedan's feminism people worked jobs, suggesting a task to be done or a necessity to work to serve something else; jobs were means of provision for other goods. Since Friedan's feminism many people have had careers, around which their lives revolve and through which they find their meaning and, step-by-step, fulfill their personal and professional ambitions. Perhaps Friedan has opened a new moral possibility—or perhaps an artificial chain and enslavement.

We womanists accept the opening-up of jobs, but question the career mystique as the primary vehicle of human accomplishment and happiness. Most jobs give some fulfillment; jobs can be as workaday and disappointing as children, husbands, and dirty laundry. Literature like Tolstoy's *Anna Karenina* and *The Death of Ivan Ilyich*, calling into question the satisfactions of bourgeois labor, weighs in here for us womanists, and against the idea that careers are the source of human fulfillment. Radical feminism is an obstacle to human happiness, in part because the fulfillment that men and women gain from careers has been vastly overestimated under its auspices and the importance of career fulfillment has been blown out of proportion. The modern university, in America at least, has become a major vehicle for the career mystique and hence, through its alliance with radical feminism, a source of human misery. Womanism recognizes the panoply of human goods toward which human beings aspire, but it is leery of blowing any of them out of proportion. For us womanists, human happiness for most in both sexes depends on pursuing many goods, and crucial among these goods are human community and love. We expect that the sexes will order their ways differently from one another. Individuals within each sex will order their ways differently. There will be sexed patterns to this pursuit, but there will be exceptions.

We womanists would remove obstacles that might inhibit people from pursuing goods of life. None of the particular goods should be shunted aside as immanent and infantilizing or as baby steps to a suburban Auschwitz. The promise of transcendence or independence betrays the human condition. A womanism wherein women want to have it all (to experience many such goods) instead of a feminism bewitched by the career mystique or the aspiration of transcendence or independence is moderate. Cows want just a couple of things, and always the same things. Human beings want many things. A moderate way of looking at things is open to the moderating influence of the observation that one cannot have it all; all people must range among human goods and dedicate themselves to a mixture of such goods in order to achieve happiness (and few are better off ignoring the human community involved with marriage and family life). Know limits!

Perhaps womanism recognizes the importance of female independence in some ways or spheres, just as it recognizes the importance of male independence in some ways or spheres. Womanism can embrace independence up to a point, not as the defining trait of human being. Much the same is true of "choice"—it is something valued in both men and women, but only up to a point. Independence and choice are, taken to their extreme, incompatible with corporeal life, education, habit, and political community: our independence is traceable to prior dependencies where our character is formed, just as our choices are shaped through our education and habits; each little platoon that shapes our individual character exists, in turn, within a broader community or regime. Men and women do not choose to be men or women. Nature shapes men and women, and their political community notices and respects that difference. Everyone is for equality, independence, and choice, but no one professes to give a sufficiently detailed account of what these concepts mean for women or men. Ultimately what feminists argue for, though they do not admit it, is *a certain way of prioritizing the goods that human beings pursue*, or a new regime. If so then they can drop the abstract language and aspirations for a more moderate feminism of prioritizing genuinely human goods. Much progress can still be made within this universe of meaning—women can use their rational faculties in careers just as men do—but without the false, ambiguous promise of human liberation and a new humanity.

We womanists reject disparities between men and women traceable to the idea that women cannot do one thing or another (i.e., laws prohibiting women from practicing law, for instance), but we can live with disparities that arise in an open legal atmosphere; we reject the need for quotas or affirmative action to bring men and women into rough alignment in professions or schools because there is every reason to think that rough alignment is not what men and women choose; we think men and women should be prepared for living lives together in marriage and as parents; we expect that men and women will provide different, valuable goods for their children and in their relationships; we reject efforts to label some crimes as crimes of one half of humanity against the other half of humanity; we never seek to reconstruct an environment where an inflated conception of human choice is demanded; and we celebrate the deflating, civilizing irony of a woman just as we celebrate the risky manliness in a man. Our rule of thumb is this: treat all people like they are spouses, parents, and citizens or future spouses, parents, and citizens.

With sufficient coercive power, we could engineer a fifty-fifty world where equal numbers of men and women are criminals and plumbers, kindergarten teachers and lactation consultants. Would we want to create such a world? Some early evidence suggests, as we have seen, that pushing science and high-pressure jobs on women leads to more women taking these jobs and then leaving those professions in much higher rates than men. In Scandinavia and in the upper reaches of American income groups, women who have a choice generally choose more traditionally than feminists had hoped (even after investing lots in education).[38] Submitting to necessity, women chose differently in the bad old days. Preconceived notions, derived from feminism, about how jobs should be distributed compromise happiness and fulfillment for women. It may be wrong, for us womanists, to see such preconceived notions as cultivating a false character among many women, placing

ambitions and goals where none would naturally be. The moment encouragement fosters disenchantment is a bridge too far.

Yet this account of womanism is still insufficient, for it considers only
one side of the sex difference equation. What effects do feminism generally
and its careerist ambitions for women have on men? A deeper womanism
must consider not just the point at which encouragement fosters disenchantment among many women, but the point when the arrangement of goods for
women, propounded through feminism, compromises the ability of men and
women to form enduring, fruitful relations with one another, and thus to contribute to human happiness on a broad scale. Since these are genuine human
goods, no political community, concerned with the pursuit of happiness and
securing the blessings of liberty, can ignore all that it takes for women and
men to respect and honor one another on a personal level. This issue demands
more and deeper rethinking.

Above all womanism recognizes the truth that women are not simply victims and men simply oppressors: as Alexander Solzhenitsyn writes, the line
dividing good and evil does not run between ideological classes, but through
the heart of each man and each woman. Just as the line between good and
evil runs through each of our hearts, it runs through each way society tries
to arrange gender and sexual relations. Knowing the goods and the bads of
each way is part of wisdom. A feminism based on the assumption that such
differences are made makes the pursuit of such wisdom impossible. All the
world was not previously mad. It would be better to see all ages as partly mad
and partly sane, and to learn about the differences between men and women
with them.

6

THE PROBLEMS OF CONTEMPORARY LIBERALISM

Contemporary liberalism aims to secure autonomy under a state that is neutral on moral controversies, and to secure personal independence under a state that provides security through generous provision. Liberal feminists would reconstruct the moral and economic environment so women and children can enjoy as much moral and economic independence from the family as possible. Each strand of liberalism points toward the abolition of marriage and toward replacing it with state-created, state-regulated units responsible for caregiving.

Critics of contemporary liberalism have dogged it since its inception. Many have worried that contemporary liberalism saps the political community of its capacity for self-government.[1] Others find the idea of dignity at the heart of contemporary liberalism to be facile and incoherent. Contemporary liberals proceed from the demand that others affirm or dignify our actions or lifestyles. When another demeans one's actions or one's lifestyle, it does one a "dignitary harm." Such an idea of dignity, at the heart of identity politics, is neither dignified nor liberal. It presumes the existence of a weak creature, without sufficient pride or self-government absent an affirmation from others. In demanding such affirmation, such persons overreach in making demands on others that none should be bound to meet in a political community dedicated to liberty and resisting tyrannical ambitions.[2] These cogent criticisms strike at the heart of contemporary liberal theory as political and philosophical doctrine, but are not my main concern.[3]

I focus on how contemporary liberal theory fails to treat marriage and family life. Its aspiration for neutrality is an impossibility, since no truly neutral stance exists within politics. Contemporary liberals seem to think that only the parts of our identity traceable to choices are worthy of concern and respect. Contemporary liberalism thus ignores and misconceives important unchosen and unchoosable parts of our person, including our bodies, our religious conscience (which binds individuals), our sexuality, the habits that shape our choices, and our formative communities. Contemporary liberalism gets the person not wholly correct, gets the community not wholly correct, and misunderstands its central theoretical aspiration. No theory can give an adequate account of human life or public philosophy with such prominent, intractable errors.

The Pretension to Neutrality

Contemporary liberals promise a modus vivendi whereby people who disagree about the meaning of marriage can get along. As the state withdraws from moral conflicts, the state remains neutral and all remain free to follow their chosen life plans. Neutrality accommodates diversity. It promises that individuals will be autonomous and that their autonomy will be respected.

Such a public philosophy may foster public peace and a species of social cohesion, but it peddles a morality. Contemporary liberals assume that human beings are less social than they are, and they fail to recognize, officially at least, that laws embodying autonomy educate on matters of marriage and family life and on a whole host of matters. Some autonomy advocates recognize this. Lawrence Friedman, a libertarian, embraces "'the republic of choice' . . . a world in which the right 'to be oneself,' to choose oneself is placed in a special and privileged position; in which *expression* is favored over *self-control*."[4] As it relates directly to the family, Joseph Raz, who welcomes the ethic of autonomy, recognizes that monogamy "cannot be practiced by an individual. It requires a culture which recognizes it, and which supports it through the public's attitude and through its formal institutions."[5]

Marriage and family life are shaped by what the laws do and by what they leave undone. Examples from other areas of human life illustrate how seemingly neutral laws promote a particular moral worldview. Tocqueville marvels that previous political thinkers have "not attributed to estate laws greater influence on human affairs."[6] By "estate laws" Tocqueville means laws concerning primogeniture (which devolves property to the firstborn, legitimate son) and entail (which requires that estates be bequeathed whole). Feudal societies depended on such laws to build familial attachment to the landed estates, which were home to the extended, intergenerational family. Patriarchal feudal families seemed permanent, thinking of themselves in light of obligations to great-grandfathers and great-grandsons. Such laws were abolished in modern societies.[7] Equal partition among heirs, Tocqueville writes, "succeeds in profoundly attacking landed property and in making families as well as fortunes disappear with rapidity."[8]

Laws abolishing primogeniture and entail "privatize" the question of inheritance, allowing parents to divide estates as they see fit: those attached to feudal ways can keep estates intact; more egalitarian parents can divide estates. Under feudalism laws aided inclination and shaped it so estates passed intact to the eldest. In democratic societies that abolish primogeniture and entail, parents either spend their money before they die or divide estates evenly among their children; this encourages wealth to circulate and abets the formation of temporary, nuclear families, while it erodes enduring, patriarchal, cross-generational families. Formally neutral, these laws all but bring the democratic society into being and doubly reinforce its tendencies toward individualism.[9]

Divorce is another complicated example. Before America's no-fault divorce revolution in the late 1960s, divorce was rarer, relatively difficult to secure, and a matter of no small cultural stigma. Perhaps people in unhappy marriages stuck it out because the law limited their options; perhaps fewer could imagine deserting or divorcing because the law so shaped their opinions; perhaps the idea of marriage was more connected with marital obligations and duties to one another. Adopting no-fault, at-will divorce laws changed actions and thoughts, unsettling marriage further by undermining expectations of permanence and removing protections for now risky devotion. The result in America was a marked increase in the number of divorces within a short period and the rise of an even weaker marital culture.[10] Concern about the effects of divorce long prevented the move to no-fault divorce, but after its acceptance it was increasingly difficult to express concerns about divorce since so many people had divorced.[11] Legal acceptance presaged much more cultural acceptance. At roughly the same time, statutes proscribing adultery, enticement, and fornication were either repealed or fell into desuetude.[12] Those things also became more thinkable and acceptable as those laws were de facto and de jure repealed. (I consider the case of divorce and the law in chapter 10.)

Countless examples illustrate this classical view that law serves as a form of educator. The anti-discrimination provisions of the Civil Rights Act of 1964 stigmatized racial discrimination and encouraged the public to embrace integration. The Americans with Disabilities Act brought issues surrounding the handicapped into such fields as architecture and education so that the needs of the handicapped come much more immediately to the mind than before: it helped to build a more disability-friendly culture. The Supreme Court's *Lawrence v. Texas* decision coincided with and encouraged America's greater acceptance of homosexuality. The legalization of same-sex marriage has encouraged many who opposed it only several years ago to accept it.

Laws always reverberate throughout the culture.[13] Laws affect behavior and attitudes by attaching honor or shame to actions or detaching shame from actions. The choice of whether to allow choice in any area is itself a choice, shaped by particular moral considerations and with predictable long-term moral ramifications. To decide that the state should leave people free to choose in a particular realm is to decide either that the realm in question is truly private—like the choice of hairstyle—or that one elevates individual choice over the common good—as has happened, largely, on how to define marriage—or that the common good is differently understood. As Harry Clor argues, "The law teaches by promulgating, in a decisive manner, the message that certain ethical standards have public status—that they are norms *of the civic community* and are not merely private opinions."[14] Public pronouncements aim at behavior, but ultimately aim at shaping the opinions and habits of a people, since political animals identify with their community and their country.

Not legislating on the purpose or character of marriage teaches that the form of marriage or the goal of marriage is a matter of public indifference. This shapes morals and social conduct toward greater openness about marital form. A country accepting of divorce and cohabitation and embracing the goals of liberal feminism would countenance same-sex marriage, and a country accepting same-sex marriage would consider plural marriage. If the *law* no longer supports a monogamous marriage, the *culture* will be less supportive of monogamous marriage and there will consequently be fewer monogamous marriages. This is true of other aspects related to marriage as well. When civil government withdraws laws concerning adultery or fornication, it provides a kind of blessing to those actions, partially removing the stigma attached to them and diminishing expectations that sex will take place within marriage. Laws that permit the sale of contraception affect—and are intended to affect—how women approach careers and how men and women approach sexual relations.

Imagine a contemporary liberal placed amidst a patriarchal people (in ancient Rome, for instance) taken with an attachment to the land and with an undisputed commitment to property rights, and with family headship inhering in the firstborn. Under these circumstances abolition of entail and primogeniture would not upset the previous property or family arrangements. Patriarchs in such a situation would be ostracized if they did not endow their oldest son with the family estate, nor would they genuinely want to break up the estate. Transported to such a circumstance, my guess is that contemporary liberals would seek laws *requiring* the equal partition of land or a steep inheritance tax to break up the estates and foster a more dynamic economy, greater equality in society, and a thinner experience of family life.[15]

The purported commitment in contemporary liberalism to withdrawing the law from marriage is not evidence of a genuine commitment to neutrality. Contemporary liberals know that such a withdrawal in today's context fosters particular marital outcomes. Liberals would not embrace "neutrality" if it led to illiberal results such as patriarchal arrangements or a Puritanical censorship. Laws cannot be considered "in the abstract" as reflecting principles such as neutrality. Those who advocate for the contemporary liberal approach to law know that "neutrality" is, in this context, most congenial to sexual liberation, personal independence, and deinstitutionalization of the old family. The apparently neutral halfway house of contemporary liberalism is but a Trojan horse to advance a commitment to greater personal independence, if I may mix metaphors. Liberals can change culture and affect marital and familial practice without having to argue on behalf of the vision of the family they favor.

Laws shape political or familial situations. Today's debates about state "neutrality" to marriage and family law take place in a context shaped by previous laws, which took place within a context shaped by other laws. Tocqueville's discussion is again germane. Democratic people will abolish primogeniture and entail at a certain time. America was "eminently democratic" from its birth and it is "even more" democratic in Tocqueville's day.[16] Only after Americans had thrown off religious authority and hereditary monarchy did they apply democratic principles to civil matters such as inheritance. This made more democratic changes possible.

Laws may, as Rousseau observed, still uphold "morality by preventing opinions from becoming corrupt; by preserving their rectitude through wise application; [and] sometimes even by determining them when they are still uncertain."[17] Laws must account for human weaknesses. Though adultery, fornication, and homosexual sodomy may have deleterious effects on a sustainable republican public morality, enforcing laws against them requires that government transcend its legitimate limits. Laws regulating some forms of obscenity, some gambling, drug use, polygamy, incest, the age of consent, public nudity, or indecency continue to discourage and stigmatize, at the margins at least, actions and thoughts that might further disrupt devoted monogamous marriage and erotic sensibilities. Social consensus on these matters still exists, and such laws probably discourage ways inimical to personalized, monogamous love.

Laws *depend* on preexisting opinions that laws, among other things, shape, and laws *shape* future opinions, actions, behaviors, and possibilities. Laws can probably only do so much to damage family life, though the extent of that damage is difficult to gauge. Something in the human spirit escapes the law. The existence of this element of the human spirit points to a partial truth in the aspiration for neutrality. If, after all the liberal reforms to marriage and family life, some men and women still choose to live dependently within permanent, faithful, monogamous marriage, contemporary liberalism tolerates them. Perhaps, no matter what, some people will find fulfillment in being married, having children, and raising them, though perhaps fewer when the laws do not support such actions and when the mores are not supportive or mildly hostile. Some people find that marrying, having children, and raising them are not for them no matter what, but perhaps more when the mores and laws encourage the neglect of such things. When laws and mores are hostile, expect more alternatives to marriage, fewer marriages, fewer children, and less parental involvement in education of children. When they are favorable, expect more. The law is not strictly determinative, especially in the short or medium term. Other aspects of law and a complicated system of mores—both hallmarks of a mixed family regime—provide support for individual action and can make marriage and family life healthier in practice than it is in law.

The Aim of Contemporary Liberalism: The Pure Relationship

If law is an educator, what do the laws of contemporary liberalism *educate* toward? The contemporary liberal vision of marriage fosters what sociologist Anthony Giddens calls the "pure relationship." A pure relationship is "a social relation . . . entered into for its own sake, for what can be derived by each person from a sustained association with another; and which is continued only in so far as it is thought by both parties to deliver enough satisfactions for each individual to stay within it." Pure relationships manifest an intimacy where "development of self is a first priority," where partners share "wants, feelings and appreciation of what your partner means to you," where each embraces the individuality of the other, where the "relationship deals with all aspects of reality," where each provides care for the self, where "sex grows out of friendship and caring," and where all practice a "loving detachment" in which partners support each other's growth and are willing to let go (so there should be no jealousy). If pure relationships are exclusive, it is because the partners believe that faithfulness grows out of contentment and trust.[18]

To establish pure relationships, people must be free to form relationships that they want and to exit relationships when they no longer serve their life plans: no-fault, at-will divorce and the public acceptance of cohabitation nourish the pure relationship. Nor can any demands be made about what form marriage takes. "Marriage" or close, intimate relations (as they are styled) are open on the form and number of partners and the extent of their commitment. All partners must be able to revise the terms of an ongoing relationship.[19] Trust among partners is generated from the actions and beliefs of the individuals in the relationship, not through external supports in the culture or religion or from social expectations that one might do one's duty. Roles and the division of labor between (or among) partners are subject to renegotiation as the partners' needs, talents, and interests change.

Pure relationships reimagine procreation, sex, and parenthood. Marrying to have children and raise them appears to be a classic example of an archaic marriage structured through "external" laws or considerations. Giddens in fact, writing in 1992, sees that "orthodox marriage" has already become "just one life-style among others," but the "institutional lag" that keeps it existing by a kind of inertia makes this development difficult to see.[20] Procreation is outside the purposes of the pure relationship: those of the same sex, in fact, form pure relationships that do not involve external factors such as making or educating children and are much more likely to involve mutual support of each partner toward independence and the development of each.[21] Day care eases the formation of pure relationships, but children always complicate it. Parents in pure relationships are intimate with their children instead of exercising authority over them. Children are mutual projects of spouses, perhaps, but do not impose duties. Sensitivity, mutual respect, mutual understanding, keeping one's distance, and a parent's hope for their children to achieve self-discovery and spontaneous growth come to define parenting, not rulemaking. It has a framework of children's rights. Children will have not only rights to be "fed, clothed and protected," but also "rights to be cared for emotionally, to have their feelings respected, and their views and feelings taken into account." Parents encourage children to "break with the past" (when they were dependent creatures) as they enter into adulthood, less a coming of age and more like a divorce or break-up.[22] The highly subsidized and celebrated modern university, where kids shift for themselves away from mom and dad, is a vehicle for realizing this break. At university, newly liberated individuals can begin a special narrative of self-discovery without any of the routines of dependent childhood. Such students will always have a hard time coming home.

Sex, while pointing to human dependence, lurks closer to the heart of pure relationships as an avenue for self-exploration, pushing the boundaries of one's identity, and reconstructing the self. Achieving "reciprocal sexual pleasure" determines whether the relationship is fulfilling—all must have their expanding sexual needs met.[23] The ability to supply sexual pleasure to one another must become the topic of open, honest conversation, perhaps with advice from experts. Whereas in the past men were thought to be more interested in sex, the equally strong, if not same, sexual desires of women are now imagined or acknowledged. Sexual escapades are part of one's narrative of self, either carrying with them the promise of intimacy or generating that intimacy. Plastic sexual desire, divorced from reproduction through contraception, accommodates diverse visions of the pure relationship.[24]

Economic support must be available within the relationship so both can leave without compromising their independence. This economic support can come in the form of prioritizing career ambition over sacrificial love, so that people do not enter a pure relationship without first achieving success and independence. Government assistance also supports the purity of relationships. With outside support available, each stays within the relationship out of inclination (not necessity or duty). No one stays to take advantage of another's health insurance or because the other is a good provider. Men will no longer want to be providers, since provision is outside the demands of the pure relationship. Nor, more importantly, will women want men or need men to be providers, since an expectation of provision compromises the pure feeling on which pure relationships rely.

Giddens imagines what the road to pure relationships will look like, as "orthodox marriage" fades away. "Some marriages may still be contracted, or sustained mainly for the sake of producing" and educating children. Children, however, will strain the relationship as much as "shore it up." Heterosexual marriages that do not approximate the pure relationship will, he believes, "devolve in two directions." One will be "companionate marriage," where spouses are not involved sexually but sympathize with each other on the model of friendship. Spouses will be "best friends." The other will be partners who use their relationship as a "home base," with less emotional investment in each other (much as the man, as Giddens sees it, used the home as a base for his career success under the old dispensation of the feminist imagination). Both these movements toward the pure relationship are only just underway.

Pure relationships arise from the free, unbounded will of each person. People in a pure relationship may still forge bonds with others, but these bonds must continually be re-willed and renewed if they are to last; consent must be an ongoing act of creativity among or between partners. If bonds were "natural," "corporeal," "habitual," or "divine," liberty would not proceed from our will alone, and individuals would be less than autonomous.[25] Autonomous, pure bonds are untainted by imperatives of the body, economic necessities, the requirements of the species, the demands of universal morality, custom, or public opinion.[26] Let me conclude provocatively: every action of contemporary liberalism abets formation of the pure relationship and the displacement of the impure.

Contemporary Liberalism and the Problem of Social Cohesion

Lay this aside, and take contemporary liberalism on its own terms. Perhaps contemporary liberal moralism fosters social cohesion in an age of increasing marital and familial diversity. If people would respect the life choices of others, society could get on with a common commitment to the autonomy of each to form a relationship. Sexual preferences and marital arrangements are like soda pop preferences, and society has hardly collapsed because some prefer root beer and others prefer white soda. In practice, those who would live lives of obligation and dependence are burdened somewhat or dishonored, and have a more difficult time raising their children to that kind of life, but, perhaps, this is a small price to pay for getting along with one's fellow citizens. A sufficiently common spirit could survive a profound diversity on family matters because of a more general commitment to tolerance and neutrality leading to different relationships.

How much unity is necessary to sustain a political community? All political communities have commonly accepted, authoritative norms. "There is a society," writes Tocqueville, "only when men consider a great number of objects under the same aspect; when on a great number of subjects they have the same opinions; when, finally, the same facts give rise in them to the same impressions and the same thoughts."[27] The modern celebration of family diversity gets part of its plausibility from the not illegitimate concern about a totalizing politics. There is a danger in the other direction too, however, since common political life depends on holding things in common and that commonality is a product of laws and education broadly conceived. Aristotle's moderate conclusion guides thinking about social cohesion: "a city should be one in a sense, but not in every sense."[28] There is no way to know when a political community has reached a level of diversity on fundamental matters where it cannot survive as a community. Could a society exist as half heroin addicts, half responsible adults? Could a society continue to exist with a third of its populace supporting exclusive, enduring man–woman marriage, a third for open marriage, and a third for traditional patriarchal polygamy? Would such a society ever arise under the seemingly tolerant auspices of contemporary liberalism? Precisely when does diversity on marital, familial, and sexual matters equal—to use Lincoln's phrase, borrowed from a somewhat higher authority—a house divided against itself that cannot stand?

Perhaps today we still have sufficient unity in practice even in family matters. Most Americans embrace the idea of lifelong love with a person of the opposite sex. Most think marital fidelity important. Most of those who have a child together feel responsible for his or her well-being. Most believe that children should not be treated as sexual beings too early and most endorse some idea of the age of consent. Public nudity is frowned upon almost everywhere in the country. Most tolerate homosexuality. I could go on. With the contemporary liberal approach to law afoot, however, it does not suffice to project today's marital and family practice into the future. Nothing in liberal public law stops relationship and family practice from becoming more dynamic and diverse.

Good examples are more important than good arguments when it comes to establishing that toleration is the modus vivendi around which political community can unite. Decades of liberalizing, privatizing tendencies on issues surrounding marriage and family life suggest that our political community encounters dangers, now, from underestimating the value of unifying beliefs. Modern communities that embrace the "neutral" idea often find it increasingly difficult to confront and resolve problems arising in the course of normal politics. Perhaps citizens in such an environment have a stunted ability to think through and govern on common problems. A minimalist community has never yet existed. Perhaps important elements of human nature go unfulfilled in the absence of such communal expressions of value. There may come a time when, as a practical matter and for the purposes of mere survival, moral diversity on this or other issues makes anything but the most minimal, functionalist shared morality viable. Yet history shows that such political communities have a compromised ability to face their problems, and such strains threaten their existence in the long term.

A Contemporary Liberal Blindness: Parenthood and Procreation

The aspiration for neutrality promotes the ideal of the pure relationship, though it tolerates other kinds of relationships. Liberalism imagines itself to present a modus vivendi for living in a diverse republic, but contemporary liberal political practice shows signs of devolving into degeneracy or social corruption and disintegration or social disunity. Yet, as we have seen in chapter 3, contemporary liberalism professes not to care about these possibilities.

While it pretends to give a rational, neutral account of the human phenomenon, contemporary liberalism ends up hiding or distorting all that is not based on choice in human life, to the detriment of our understanding and of our policy on the family.

This blindness is most problematical when contemporary liberals seek to conceptually separate procreation (the having of children) from parenthood (the raising of them). For liberals the connection between procreation and parenthood compromises the independence of women, who give birth to the children and often take the lead in caring for them. With the separation the person having the kid need not take care of the kid—making women independent. The aspiration for separation generally, born of modernity, expresses the rolling revolution in family life. People can add up human experiences according to their will. Modern reproductive technologies such as artificial insemination, modern legal concepts such as adoption and surrogacy, and modern social developments such as the rise of single-parent families seem to sever biological reproduction or procreation from the education and nurturance of the child. Legal decisions on the nature of marriage erode the "procreative prejudice" in parenting, so that the two are not secretly united within marriage, a third connection.

Despite efforts to sever procreation and parenting, the connection nevertheless persists in what we do and in what we leave undone. The law assumes that those who give birth to children will care for them—and exceptions to this norm (such as adoption and surrogacy) are at the margins of our experience and undergo heightened state scrutiny. A woman who gives birth to a child in a hospital and then leaves the hospital without that child is guilty of child abandonment. "Deadbeats" who shirk their duty are subject to moral disapprobation. Even after much family decline, in most cases, biological parents raise children. Such numbers are consistent across the world. The frequency of children living with a birth parent or two birth parents is so high that I am bold to think it is not due to chance or choice.

Why should those who "have" children raise them? What does recognition of this relationship imply about marriage, family life, and the public's interest in those institutions? These questions cannot simply be ignored: children do not come out of nowhere and, when they arrive, they need some intense care to thrive. Let us explore some of the alternatives that might be employed at the nexus of having children and raising them to expose the limits of contemporary liberalism.

Parental Licensing

Parental licensing[29] calls into question whether those who bear children are qualified to raise them. Like drivers, teachers, or medical doctors, who are licensed professionals, two individuals (or whoever) would need to demonstrate basic competence to gain a "license" to parent a child. Advocates of parental licensing differ on what basic competence is. Some say licenses are negative, disqualifying "incompetent" parents who would abuse their children.[30] Others say there should be positive requirements, involving a conception of "moral" parenting such as allowing children to choose their religious or sexual identity, or teaching racial justice or environmental awareness, or more generally providing "equal access to opportunities to develop their potentials in life."[31] Advocates also differ on who would grant licenses—the state or a board of acceptable parents, perhaps—and how those on the license-granting board would be appointed. Should parents be licensed?

Under the old understanding of marriage and parenthood, marriage is not a license to have children or raise them per se, but it is a formal, publicly recognized way to provide entrée into parenting.[32] Husbands and wives marry and both are transformed some into people able and willing to be responsible for making and rearing a child. Some advocate for licensing more in sadness than with the zeal of reformers. With marriage, the old preparation ground for

parenthood, eroding, licensing can promote competent parenting.[33] Others
see the old approach of "licensing" parents through marriage as eroding a ves-
tige of slavery and inequality. Hugh LaFollette, a pioneer of parental licensing,
describes the belief that leads benighted folks to oppose licensing schemes:

> The belief is that parents own, or at least have natural sovereignty over,
> their children. It does not matter precisely how this belief is described,
> since on both views parents legitimately exercise extensive and virtu-
> ally unlimited control over their children. Others can properly inter-
> fere with or criticize parental decisions only in unusual and tightly
> prescribed circumstances–for example, when parents severely and
> repeatedly abuse their children. In all other cases, the parents reign
> supreme.

Parental licensing advocates eschew marriage as the form that responds to
parenting and favor a state focused on the caregiver–dependent relation.[34]
The negative, prevent-abuse justification for licensing gives way to a positive
conception that teaches, supports, and subsidizes caregiving by whomever.[35]
Licensing would continue to serve the child's best interest, just as compulsory
school attendance laws, delinquency laws, some health laws, and housing laws
do. Licensing might leverage better parenting through the threat to withhold
government benefits.[36] Society would, licensing advocates promise, benefit
from the boon to productivity, from curtailing child abuse, and from the fact
that more individuals would be better taken care of and reach their potential.
The whole scheme would pay for itself, many times over!

Advocates point out its similarities to adoption or foster care, where parents apply and where children are placed after state or state-approved agencies
analyze the home situation.[37] In this sense, licensing advocates revise the "normal" case (parents being responsible for their biological children) in light of
the extreme case (adoption). This comparison fails to acknowledge that adoptive or foster children are almost always in a desperate way (either orphaned,
or "unwanted," or otherwise beyond parents' ability to raise), suggesting that
the link between biology and parenting is already broken. Such revision sees
"parenthood as a privilege for which one is qualified rather than as a right that
accompanies the event of childbirth. It would define parenthood realistically
as a relationship rather than as a biologically determined state."[38] Licensing
breaks the link between giving children life and raising them, and then compares itself to a process where the link is already broken. It calls eggs an omelet
and then breaks them to prove it.

Nothing in these licensing proposals explains why or whether birth parents should have the first chance to rear that child. Licensing advocates seem
to assume that biological parents, for some reason, get the first stab at being
the licensed parents. The link between biology and education persists, even

among licensing advocates who would separate the two. They acknowledge that link—and that acknowledgment is the ground for thinking the family is a pre-political institution. Those who would conceptually separate procreation and parenting cannot explain why the connection is almost always respected and at other times severed. If the link should be erased, then the scheme to separate them must go further. Licensing advocates are not radical enough.

Parental Licensing Plus

Plus what? Plus procreative licensing. Since radical-seeming proposals to license parents *still* take for granted the existence of the babies and hence the supply of babies that would need licensed caregivers, perhaps the licensing should move back another stage to require state licensing for procreative sex. Some advocates for parental licensing indeed take the more daring step of requiring a license also for those who make babies. "The next logical extension of this process," Edgar Chasteen writes, "is to make it a privilege to *have* children."[39] Calling procreation a privilege (a matter of public right) means that it is not a right (a matter of personal discretion). Procreative sex, surrogacy, cloning, genetic reproduction, or whatever reproductive means would require prior permission and may be subject to prior restraint (i.e., sterilization or temporary sterilizing methods that could be relieved after demonstrating mastery of procreative and parental subject matter).

Let us limit ourselves to proposals based on sexual reproduction. Such proposals combine the problems of a simpler licensing scheme—that it mistakes parenthood for a predictable skilled-based endeavor and conceives of family life as a means to social ends—with the mysteries associated with sex, marriage, and love. Translating lovers into friends, parents, caregivers, and providers is not a predictable or spontaneous endeavor. Much in relationships is surprising, and personalities are not as static as licensers presume. Both the arguments for parental licensing—the one that allows for procreation or at least conception before the licensing and the one that requires licensing for procreation and then parenting—continue to be stodgy and stupid in assuming that those who make a child should take care of the child.

More fundamentally, even if the public somehow could determine which couples or groups should reproduce, no public authority can bless bringing an individual into the world with legitimacy. Political communities lack the legitimacy to identify competent lovers and parents, even if they could. Children do not authorize the public to do so, any more than children authorize their parents to do so. Mythical children cannot be said to authorize the public to decide from behind the veil of ignorance. Contemporary liberalism cannot on its own grounds of choice produce the legitimacy for a parenting-plus licensing scheme.

All other schemes to separate procreation from parenthood partake of these same difficulties, laying aside the not insubstantial problem that they are unlikely to work. Communal allocation of children (private birth, with children then assigned to different parents) presumes that private parents or someone can bring children into being without a child's choice, and it assumes that parents will still produce children even though those children may be seized when they are more rationally allocated. Communal provision, built on private procreation with the community directing education, has the same problems. A child market, where birth parents could sell children as they saw fit, does not adequately establish the legitimacy of the original parental ownership and it presumes birth establishes some property right.

Those who separate procreation and education *presume* the legitimacy of bringing children into the world through procreative sex and *presume* that birth parents are de facto parents. The link between sex, pregnancy, and parenthood, obscured in law and ideology and through birth control, persists—and cannot but be protected in any order. Liberalism cannot explain these links on its own terms. Contemporary liberals provide a picture of sex unrelated to pregnancy, of a child brought into the world without strings attached, without any prior personal identity; and a picture of the mother (and father) as detached and asking, earnestly, perhaps, in the best interest of their children, how children should be allocated according to the principles of justice and public reason. Then liberals sneak in the connection between procreation and parenthood that they had "conceptually" separated.

No theory accounts for the legitimacy of procreation and for the link between procreation and education. Human societies do not and could not allocate child-rearing responsibilities or justify them on the basis of contractual reasoning or other brands of radical reform. Political communities arise to protect and foster the enduring, *pre*-political relationships between biological parents and children. Political communities acknowledge and protect these actions and connections.[40] Any political community that subverted the idea that parents should take care of their children would rightly be considered tyrannical, and would require a comprehensive remaking of human nature.[41]

We *acknowledge* this reality antecedent to moral reasoning and public philosophy. Parental duties and rights flow from the natural, biological relationship. This obligation, so widely felt, is inexplicable on the grounds of autonomy since parents cannot choose their children and children cannot choose their parents. Edmund Burke uses parental duties to illustrate duty as such and how parental duties provide a glimpse into the human situation:

Dark and inscrutable are the ways by which we come into the world. The instincts which give rise to this mysterious process of nature are not of our making. But out of physical causes, unknown to us, perhaps unknowable, arise moral duties, which, as we are able perfectly to comprehend, we are bound indispensably to perform. Parents may not be consenting to their moral relation; but consenting or not, they are bound to a long train of burthensome duties towards those with whom they have never made a convention of any sort. Children are not consenting to their relation, but their relation, without their actual consent, binds them to its duties; or rather it implies their consent because the presumed consent of every rational creature is in unison with the predisposed order of things. Men come in that manner into a community with the social state of their parents, endowed with all the benefits, loaded with all the duties of their situation.[42]

It seems likely ideas of parental duty, obligation, and connection are rudiments for human life (akin to a definition of a line, point, or plane in geometry).[43] This connection reveals human nature—a complex mixture of choice and natural obligation—to us. Some connections arise without our having chosen them or without full knowledge of what choosing them will entail. They are no less obligatory for being unchosen.

Few have proposed that political communities distribute children randomly to caretakers, or that society distribute children on the basis of parental merit, or that children should be sold to the highest bidder. Nor is the idea that children should be birthed privately yet raised in common, as in Engels' postrevolutionary world, on the public agenda. Cloning followed with public supervision à la Huxley's *Brave New World* or Firestone's ambition has hardly been proposed. We are "stuck with stupid," a mortifying reliance on nature to generate parental duties, a conclusion most at odds with contemporary liberalism.

Marriage and Family Life after Contemporary Liberalism

There are few signs of contemporary liberalism disappearing from the human scene. Even after decades of the most prominent contemporary liberals conceding to their critics that their supposedly neutral theories are not neutral, judges, lawyers, and theorists alike continue as if nothing has happened. The "wise" are "wise" who the "wise" say are wise. If today's "wise" say that liberalism is neutral and that neutrality is good, *that* is wisdom. The apotheoses of contemporary liberalism in public life have coincided with the greatest contemporary liberal thinkers conceding that their theories legislate a particular form of morality and have no claim to universal validity. Even the author of *The Myth of Autonomy* embraces a vision of the family based on autonomy. That's their story and they are sticking to it.

While it might be tempting to bemoan dishonesty, it is better to see those advocates of contemporary liberalism as advocates for the pure relationship, based on the seemingly autonomous will of each person. This vision may undermine social cohesion. The fundamental point against the liberal vision is that it is neither neutral nor reflective of human being. Those who would defend the family in the modern world must build from the ground up; that is, they must begin with the recognition that parents have a legal and moral obligation to mind the children they bring into the world. Public law acknowledges this reality. Public opinion expects such a thing. Attempts to conceptually separate parenthood from education run up against and end up *assuming* this fundamental fact of human life. This fact illustrates how the family is a pre-political institution, acknowledged by the state rather than created by it. Even in our late modern republic, where the state does so much to support and define human life, the state does nothing but acknowledge this fact, no matter the mental gymnastics whereby the clever seek to explain it away.

This acknowledgment suggests a limit to contemporary liberal reform and a floor from which to expose the deleterious assumptions within contemporary liberal theories. It reveals the family as a community to be protected through government action, instead of permeated in the name of the public's ideas of what a child should be. It puts limits on the pure relationship by showing that an "impure" relationship always arises in society (even if increasingly rarely as fewer people have children). There are probably more such pre-political bonds—including the sexual bond between the man and woman that bring the child into the world. Much interrupts that bond in the modern world, but nothing can altogether erase it. The aspiration for independence runs up against at least this tough nut, which it cannot crack.

Instead of ignoring this bond or wishing it away, a responsible, truer public philosophy would acknowledge that the bond exists and seek to find ways to make that bond serve personal and public happiness. As we shall see in chapter 8, a public morality must grow up around these pre-political institutions to make them suitable for politics and to make them suitable for individual thriving. No political community can promote the pure relationship and survive or thrive.

7

THE PROBLEM WITH ENDING SEXUAL REPRESSION

The sexual revolution aims to take human beings beyond repression. Feminists agree, thinking that female sexuality has been directed toward reproduction, marriage, and love, and that much sexual repression is central to the oppression of women. Liberation from such repression serves the goals of equality, thus feminists seek to make sex about pleasure and not reproduction or "commitment." The sexual revolution requires, to revert to Millett's phrase, "an end to traditional sexual inhibitions and taboos, particularly those that most threaten patriarchal monogamous marriage: homosexuality, 'illegitimacy,' adolescent, and pre- and extra-marital sexuality." Equality requires an end to female modesty and shame; an end to taboos against childhood sexuality and incest; the rise of an adventurous sexuality in women; the erosion of the sexual double standard; cultivation of the idea that sex is for pleasure; and other innovations. The feminist hope is that eliminating repression would liberate female sexuality and empower women. Thus Rosin sees that "feminist progress is largely dependent on the hook-up culture" (i.e., on the separation of sex from emotional attachment, enduring relations, and responsibility broadly conceived),[1] so women prioritize careers, genuine achievement, and independence during their nubile years. Men will probably remain the same horny devils they have been since the initiation of patriarchy, but women can manipulate this for their liberation.

Contemporary liberals, occupying comfortable chairs in judges' chambers and academe, affect not to care about the sexual revolution. To them, or so they say, all should be able to make their own sexual life plans without laws, society's opinions, and nature's dictates getting in the way. They affect to be no libertines; they are just interested in neutrality. Freedom from the *law's* repression is the rule for contemporary liberals, unless a sexual practice violates a law that serves a compelling state interest. Anti-sodomy laws must go, for instance, not in the interest of sodomy but in the name of neutrality. Laws against adultery or fornication must go, not because liberals advocate adultery or fornication, but for the sake of neutrality. Laws discriminating against illegitimate children must go because of the stigma they represent, not as encouragement to illegitimacy. Perhaps incest laws and statutory rape laws can remain, liberals might say, if they serve compelling state interests; but if they do not, they too must go.

At the same time, however, neutrality is a fiction: loosening the law's repression abets the establishment of the "pure relationship," contemporary liberalism's preferred mode of association. The dismantling of laws and opinions favorable to sexual repression contributes to the move from the bourgeois marriage, to the "companionate marriage" (where couples are friends based on romantic attachment),[2] to the pure relationship. To be pure, nothing outside the will of each individual can determine the nature of the relationship. Pure relationships can be same-sex, can involve more than a narrow couple (if trust survives this expansion), can probably involve younger people than we expect and accept today, and involve a destigmatizing of illegitimacy and premarital sexual performance. Partners require openness about sex. Sexual performance must be mind-blowing: this need may lead to a "sexual-industrial complex" of how-to books and pornography. No laws should restrain the availability of such sexual aids. Pure relationships are based on a love that flows together, or what Giddens calls "confluent love": relationships are founded on always revocable human will, based on equality, grounded in emotion and contingent tastes, and aimed at artistic performance, mutual satisfaction, and discovery.[3]

What is sex liberated from? The greatest source of sexual repression comes from the monogamous family and from society's support for it. More broadly revolutionized sex must be freed from traditional morality, which buttresses the traditional family. The aim of sexual revolution is the revelation and expression of the real self beneath what political communities have repressed with traditional morality, in all its forms. Sexual liberation would allow for the expression of desires that traditional morality has pent up within the individual.

At stake in the teaching of sexual liberation is the nature of human being. The modern tendency is to deconstruct what we accept from the past so that we can own it and make it our own: this is the thrust of modern autonomy as we have seen it in the teaching on feminism (chapter 2) and sexual liberation (chapter 4). Is sexual desire so malleable (like teachings about gender from gender theorists) that any teaching on sex can be brought into being through history or human will? If so it is raw material in the hands of human makers or creators, and human beings can be as sexual or as asexual as our teachings propose. Or, on the other hand and against the stream of modern thinking (like my argument that the grooves of sex limit gender creativity), does sexual desire have a nature and does it run in grooves? How can we know its nature? It is one thing to rearrange the deck chairs on the ship of human destiny; it is quite another thing to make and remake the ship and chairs out of our own wills. Is the sexual revolution a rearranging or a recreating? If it is a rearranging, what guides the rearranging? If a recreating, what guides the recreating?

The Nature of Natural Sexual Desires

Criticisms of sexual liberation spring from a defense of traditional morality (against the modernizers like Kinsey) or a defense of civilization (against the liberationists like Marcuse and Reich). Criticisms correspond to doubts. Perhaps sexual liberation is impossible to achieve. Perhaps sexual desires are not so nice as sexual liberationists assume. Perhaps getting beyond repression would require such a revolution in the nature of human beings and society that it is difficult to imagine its accomplishment. Perhaps sexual liberation undermines other important human goods so that sexual revolution would on the whole be bad for human beings. We must ask, Have the liberationists understood what "repression" is? Could we take human beings "beyond repression," as liberationists suggest? Would we want to?

Liberating sexuality from traditional morality is more radical than liberationists conceive. Advocates for sexual revolution seek to liberate sexual desire from the repression of traditional morality, but with the proviso that people act on sexual desires only with the consent of the willing. Thus the liberated sexuality of the sexual liberationists is never as liberated, threatening, or chaotic as it could be. It is a civilized sexual liberation bending to the slippery concepts of consent and safety. Men, for liberationists, want orgasms, untainted by aggressive violence or possessive ownership; it is the difficulty of securing the women who foster male orgasms that makes men aggressive and possessive.[4] Make access easier and men will become less competitive; rape and sexual harassment will wane in an environment of liberation (liberationists affect to believe). Here is a paradox: Strictures against rape and ungentlemanly behavior are part of traditional morality, yet liberationists aim to flush traditional morality as such away. Whence the authority to pick and choose among tenets of traditional morality, retaining some proscriptions but releasing much else? Whence their inconsistent embrace of civilization, since normally it is repressive but sometimes it is protective? In any event those emphasizing sexual plasticity have not taken full account of the problems inherent in making men's sexual desire respectful of consent—and they escape the problem by assuming the best about sexual desires in their teachings, without worries that they will get a much worse type of human being because of their teachings.

We should understand what liberated sexual desire is before we liberate it. Sexual desire, private in some ways, is shaped and conjured through living in a political community that tells particular stories about the who, what, where, and when of sexuality.[5] Similarly the rank of sexual desire in human life is mediated through the particular time and place—some regimes emphasize sexual performance, satisfaction, or progeny more than others. On the other hand, sexual desire is not simply conjured up by any political community. Sexual desire is a given with which every political community must work. Human beings are desiring or longing or erotic, and sexual longing is a well-nigh universal expression of human desire (this is a testament to its nature). Political communities do not create sexual desire, but they do shape it, invest it with pride, give it direction, and rank it in a good life (this is a testament to its plasticity). Must human beings be taught to make sex about pleasure, conquest, consent, or loving bonds? What is natural and what is "cultural" about sexual desire?

Accessing "raw" sexual desire, on the modern notion, requires stripping away the accretions of the political community—just as "state of nature" theorists stripped away "social man" to reveal "natural man."[6] This is what Freud and his followers tried to do—interpreting children as inherently sexual beings from infancy.[7] Those theories have not exactly stood the test of time.[8] Perhaps what they did badly we can do well. It does not hurt to try! Would it be best to turn to the ethnographies of pre-Western people? Would that yield a defense of a liberationist ethic? I leave this to others.

Universal practice or history yields a teaching on "natural" sexual desire, if we keep things sufficiently general. Let us test the proposition that natural sex concerns pleasure, while all other interpretations of sexuality are impositions of "traditional morality" or culture. Must sexual desire be caught up with issues of right and wrong? Does sexual desire aim merely to scratch an itch or satisfy a hunger? Such is the query that underlies Michel Foucault's *History of Sexuality*, a three-volume set. Foucault, no prude,[9] reveals the genesis of changing sexual norms: sexuality seems to be plastic, shaped by those doing the defining and repressing. The conclusion that history shapes sexuality mirrors the basic pattern in Foucault's other genealogies, including the genealogy of criminology. There, he argues, scientific public opinion took the place of torture, characteristic of feudal regimes, when it came to instilling social discipline. Bourgeois society invented "crimes," "madness," and mental disorders to defend itself from those who would rock the boat. Bourgeois "truth" and "reality" henceforth determined what people saw as crime and mental illness.

Perhaps what happened with crime happened with sexual mores.[10] Did bourgeois morality and previous moralities similarly shape how people viewed sex and sexual desire? Foucault goes back to ancient Greece, aiming to show, it seems, that Greeks equated sex with pleasure and engaged in sex for its own sake (thus Foucault's title for volume 2, *The Uses of Pleasure*): the Dionysian Greeks could serve as a model for modern sexual liberation. Foucault's Greeks always "problematized" sex and mingled sex with ethical judgments, however, even in Foucault's telling. Norms governed sex with boys and women in Greece: there were always honorable and dishonorable people with whom to have sex and ways to have sex. For Foucault this reflects the deep-seated idea that "sexual activity is sufficiently hazardous and costly in itself," that "sexual pleasure might be an evil," and that it is "sufficiently linked to the loss of vital substance to require a meticulous economy that would discourage unnecessary indulgence," or at least that it required a "strategy of moderation and timing." Foucault seems disappointed to find that "the principle of a rigorous and diligently practiced sexual moderation is a precept that" antedates Christianity and the Stoics and even late antiquity: it is already around in fourth-century Greece.[11] Foucault had read his Nietzsche: the pre-Christian Greeks were supposed to be the fun guys!

In volume 3, *The Care of the Self*, Foucault explores the "problematization" of sex in the early Roman Empire, where sexual ethics became a private matter. For Foucault privatization bespeaks a deeper austerity: the discipline provided through public teachings about "truth" and "reality" is more subtle and powerful, since informal mechanisms of language form an iron cage for thought. No longer governed through notions of public honor and shame, private individuals consulted their publicly shaped consciences and constructed or cared for themselves. Purity and fidelity reflected, they thought, their best selves. The sexual act appeared to be "dangerous, difficult to master, and costly," and its involvement with the valorized other required self-control, moderation, and an idea of worthiness. Sex was not condemned under the Romans or in the writings of Plutarch; it directed toward the development of relational or familial mores (even in the decadent Empire).[12]

Foucault's *History of Sexuality* shows that the concerns about getting sex right in the modern era, expressed medically and psychologically, have analogues in the ancient world. If Foucault intended to show that the Kinsey–Marcuse reading of plastic sexual desire antedated Christianity, the books fail. For Greeks and Romans, sexuality was a problem—they thought sexual passions were strong, unruly, ungovernable, dominating, and potentially disruptive to political harmony, enduring relations, self-respect, and individual happiness. All sought limits and directed sexuality toward education and enduring relations. Foucault, to his credit as a scholar of sorts, refrains from talking a pleasure-centered society into existence when he describes these civilizations, yet he does not deny the pleasure-centered possibility. Foucault may still think that there could be an "unproblematized" sexuality (and hence one focused on the self and pleasure or a more plastic sexuality). He imagines transgressive sexual heroes fostering a genuine sexual liberation and he celebrates, when he can, the transgressives of the Greek and Roman worlds as precursors of such heroism.[13]

Sexuality among the ancients shows that sexual desire is inherently "problematic"; the problems and the ethics center around mostly the same issues. Sexuality does not appear to be perfectly plastic nor simply focused on pleasure. Sexuality is problematic (without the scare quotes) from the standpoint of personal relations, love, and affection. Those involved in sex are tempted to objectify each other, to see each other as useful for their own purposes, or even to dominate one another. These purposes are not simply scratching the itch of pleasure. Sexual passions can be dangerous, mysterious, and problematic, through being possessive, unstable, domineering, and aggressive, and making the other vulnerable in different ways. Sex may involve the fleeting promise of conquest as an element of the excitement.

Robert Stoller, the psychoanalyst, even suggests that sexual passion involves hostility. "One can raise the possibly controversial question," he writes, "whether in humans (especially males) sexual excitement can ever exist without brutality also present (minimal, repressed, distorted by reaction formations, attenuated, or overt in the most pathological cases). . . . If hostility could be totally lifted out of sexual excitement there would be no perversions, but would normal sexuality be possible?"[14] Even advocates for pure relationships see that sexuality opens a dangerous vista of ecstatic experience not often available in the rationalized, modern world.[15]

The existence of sexual desire is a groove in human life. Sexual desires can be destructive or constructive, satisfying or exploitative, unstable and difficult to govern. The liberationist's natural sexuality is usually pretty tame, in the sense that it is respectful of a partner's equality and consent. However, contra the liberationist's view, certain questions arise in sexual practice (Am I worthy? Did I do right? Was that done right? Should I have waited? Is this all there is?). The existence of these concerns and questions is another for-the-most-part universal groove. Those questions are answered differently from time to time and from place to place. "Sex as pleasure" is not the only groove in the human sexual constitution, if it is among the most important of them. "Sex as problematic" for relations and for self-government, and the idea that "it is problematic to reduce sex to pleasure," are also for the most part universal. Fruitful debates about the character of such a complex, mysterious phenomenon exist. The sexual liberationists are among the only ones who think that sexual passion could be "unproblematized" as a pure pleasure or as a desire for release.

If the modernization of sex is the isolation of sexual desire and the reduction of sex to pleasure, Foucault's "problematizing" shows that such isolations and reductions are not found in civilization. Such "problematizing" would have to be brainwashed out of human beings. Why? Sexual pleasure is *directed* toward another.[16] Sexual desire, while private, is also public, in a sense: our *teaching* about how sexuality is directed toward others (and which others) shapes the experience of sexuality, the ranking of sex in a good life, and our self-evaluation from sexual experiences. Sexuality cannot escape the odor of relations between people: ideas of self-respect, respect, self-image, personal honor, shame, regret, worry, and guilt accompany it. It is not just sex. Foucault's forays into the San Francisco bathhouses for the pleasures of anonymous, sadomasochistic sodomy do not constitute a genuinely human and humane model for sexual activity, but rather seem to be a morality play for a future sexual regime.

These two conclusions—that sexual desire can be possessive and otherwise not benign, and that sexual desire is in its nature social or directional—may seem at odds with one another in our egalitarian age. The implication of the first is that one partner, usually the man, could exercise a tyranny over the other partner, usually the woman, and that the sexual act itself subordinates women (as feminists worry). In a larger sense, however, even possessive, non-benign sexual encounters are directed at other human beings, informed through social mores and directed at intimacy, which would tend to soften such non-benign sexual expressions. The entire justification for traditional morality was to translate or direct possessive, non-benign sexual passions into enduring, intimate relations that subordinated sex within a larger realm of common goods. The teaching of sexual liberation compromises such translation.

In any event the fact that everyone must be carefully taught, even especially those who would live by the dictates of sexual liberation, is a principal exhibit against the ethic of sexual liberation. Sexual liberation represents a teaching about sexuality that emphasizes some grooves (sex as pleasure) at the expense of other grooves (e.g., sex as relational), while dismissing those other grooves as inventions and repressions. A better teaching would account for all the grooves.

The Intractability and Desirability of Relational Ways

If human beings are thought to be social or political animals, it is more likely that we will think of sexuality as transcending individual pleasure and as shaped through a political community for personal, marital, and communal ends. Modern individualists may think sexuality aims at the goods of the self; sex for them is more likely to be a matter of physical pleasure to be enjoyed as the individual sees fit; efforts to limit the pursuit of pleasure they see as tyran-nical. Traditional morality recognizes the danger of isolated, ungoverned sexual desire and the desirability of pointing sexual desire toward stable and civilizing—or at least less debilitating—ways. Sexual desire is partly, at least, relational, aimed at other people. With traditional morality sexual attraction, sexual desire, and sex itself point to a relationship that subordinates sex within a relation pursuing a common good. Sex provides grist for that relation. Is this a superior way of thinking through sexual desire?

Imagine sexual liberation theory as an experiment taught to citizens. Tell people that sex is just an animal function; that no shame attaches to any sex-ual activity and no judgment follows from a following of one's strong pas-sions; that satisfying sexual desire is a human need; that long-term exclusivity in relationships is debilitating and boring; that morality or self-government is repressive; that the sexual double standard is an unjust social invention; that sex need not mean anything; that pornography, masturbation, and other means of sexual gratification will not affect interpersonal relations—teach cit-izens, I say, all of these deliverances of sexual liberation theory, and they will move toward such a teaching with predictable results, but, if I am correct, *few will fully adopt these teachings*. Elements too central and valuable to human nature would have to be eradicated in order to achieve the new humanity envisioned by sexual liberationists.

First, sex differences. Modernizers must above all change the minds and ways of women—the more traditional sex on such matters is also the more plastic, so maybe modernizers can succeed. We have seen in chapter 5 that these two angles on sexuality—the relational and the pleasurable—are tenden-cies in each sex. Women are keener on subordinating sex within a relationship generally, while men tend to see sex as an expression of possession and plea-sure. Thousands of observations prove the point; novelists and political think-ers before 1970 rarely doubted it. Consider a couple of such observations from today's social sciences. Sexual promiscuity in all its forms is more accepted in the twenty-first century than it was in 1950. Laws and mores have changed in the direction the sexual liberationists had hoped; this has especially affected mores around sexual activity among women. Sex is more casual: a hookup culture exists to some extent. Yet still "feelings about casual sex seem to be among the most stubborn of sex differences," as women have unattached sex to little or less sexual or personal satisfaction.[17] No matter how plastic sexual pleasure is and how plastic women are, this womanly sexual groove appears to be a for-the-most-part universal—and an obstacle to the realization of sexual liberation (so far!).

This is confirmed also in "homosexuals . . . the acid test for sex differences in sexuality," as Donald Symons writes.[18] Homosexuals present an experiment about this sexual groove. Remove the "correcting" tendency of the opposite sex and the maleness and femaleness of sexuality is more pronounced. Sex differences persist on these matters among people who transgress bourgeois society's marital approach. Lesbian relationships tend to have much less sex than relations between men and women, while men who have sex with men tend to have a lot more sex than either lesbians or those in opposite-sex relations. Put two sexual "gatekeepers" into a sexual relationship and one tends to get what Pepper Schwartz and Phillip Blumstein dub "lesbian bed death" in their study of *American Couples* (1983); much evidence from randomized studies and ethnographies suggests this persists today.[19] Male homosexuals have more sex than the other groups, including more anonymous sex, more sex early in relations (mostly right away), more sexual partners, more open relationships, and less conversation.[20] Put two "initiators" and "pleasure-seekers" together and you get more initiation and more pleasure-seeking. The liberationist, modernizing approach to sexuality requires an eclipse of the womanly approach to sexuality or its reconstitution. Testifying to the plasticity of sexuality, men and women (and especially women) have changed their sexual expectations and accept more casual sex. Testifying to the limits of such plasticity, sexuality still manifests itself differently in men and women.

Let me raise another indecent question that reveals something fundamental about human sexual desire. Why is sexual assault different from any ordinary assault? If sex is just like any other act (as the scientific sexual liberationists hold), then sexual assault is a subspecies of physical assault and there is nothing particularly important about that violation. Perhaps rape causes more trauma. Is that trauma reasonable or is it a remnant of the old view, embraced unwittingly by the victim, that sexual violation is something other than physical assault? If rape causes more trauma than other assaults, on the sexual liberationist's view, one could ask, Is the perpetrator to be blamed for the victim's "benighted" opinion? To hold that rape is different from simple assault, which is the traditional view and my view (but cannot be the rolling revolutionaries' view), is to hold that sex is different from other physical encounters and that it is not just an animal act. It is deeply personal, and implicates love and honor and shame. Rape is forced sex against a woman's will; it is an assault that violates personal honor and integrity; it is a violation of love and its relation to sex. All so much worse than getting punched in the nose. Ambiguities in interpreting sexual actions are bound to creep in once sex is taken out of its cultural context or if the cultural context is confusing. Sexual revolutionaries have wanted to have it both ways—sex is just an animal desire and sex is special as an instrument of oppression. Traditionalists are more consistent: sex is connected to love and through love to marriage; and sex crimes dishonor those connections and thereby offend the personal integrity of the victim in a way that punching someone in the nose does not.

Sex differences highlight a third valuable aspect of human ways protected under traditional morality, as evidenced by the persistence of modesty and shame. Sexual modernizers see modesty as a remediable cultural invention. Shame or guilt appear as the price people and especially women pay (or have imposed on themselves) for violating that invention. Animals do not feel shame or modesty; nor would humans who understand how animal their sexuality is. Openness about sexuality is both possible and desirable; reticence is repression and distortion. Or so goes the theory of sexual modernizers. Modesty and shame serve relational sex, as opposed to casual sex. Women tend to be less satisfied and inclined to see sex as casual, hence modesty and shame are more parts of women's sexual system. Modesty, relational attitudes, and shame would have to disappear from the human character to achieve sexual liberation, but the persistence of each plank—and their interrelation—suggest that these matters are inherent in human nature. These traits support womanly efforts to cultivate mutuality or relations, and have the effect of harnessing men's initiative toward building a common life. Women may no longer demand such things as much as they had (i.e., sex has become more casual), but this is still limited by modesty and shame. Men and women in relation to one another still mostly demand fidelity to their bonds once they enter them.

Two for-the-most-part universal grooves in human sexuality tell against the debunking of modesty and shame. Modesty and shame persist in both sexes. They persist unequally in the sexes because sexual desire manifests itself differently in the sexes. Shame, modesty, and embarrassment about "dirty" bodily functions, including defecating and urinating, are for-the-most-part universals. Much the same is true, if modernizing pioneer Havelock Ellis is to be believed,[21] about the human tendency to hide private parts under clothes and to withdraw behind closed doors for sex. People dress. Dogs will pee or poop or lick themselves anywhere, without embarrassment, though sometimes to their owner's embarrassment. People close the door when they do their duty. Conventions like closing doors and taboos serve these for-the-most-part universals, but these conventions and taboos point toward persistent grooves of shame and modesty. It is difficult to teach even immodest and shameless people out of these modest habits. The difference between trained dogs and people, both of whom live comfortably in civilization, points to the naturalness of *some* shame and modesty beneath our culture and breeding. People are generally uncomfortable with public fornication or such things.

Modesty persists unequally in the sexes—another groove. Rousseau, the greatest modern psychologist of modesty, tells why modesty adheres more to women than men, but he tells a different story than the one I tell. Female modesty, for Rousseau, governs a woman's naturally insatiable sexual appetite. Governing herself, she uses modesty to govern men, indirectly, by making men work to gain her allegiance and favors. A promising lover governs more effectively than an easy lover.[22] Modesty suggests distance between men and women, which paradoxically draws them more closely together in love and the hard work of building a common life. Wanton intermingling of the sexes—thinking men and women to be the same—fosters loose or shameless women, who give themselves up too easily, do not earn men's respect, and do not call forth men's strength. This leaves nothing but "weak men and disreputable women," in Tocqueville's phrase.[23]

The virtue in Rousseau's explanation lies in its recognition of human difference with respect to sexual appetite and desire. Rousseau's account sees women with limitless sexual desire requiring first their self-government before they use modesty to govern men. On most accounts men have sexual appetites more difficult to satiate, but Rousseau shows the greater plasticity of female sexuality. Women today bristle at Rousseau's central contention that women exercise a soft, indirect empire over men and morals, since modesty appears a stratagem for the weak that contains condescending compliments of woman's natural superiority and that offends human equality.

Bristling is not an argument, however. Less a stratagem than an immediate response, modesty and shame are natural or normal reactions—supported more or less through mores and conventions—when something private becomes public. Shame and modesty attach to particular situations, where one's vulnerability, and especially sexual vulnerability, faces exposure and violation. Nakedness per se is not the problem. Children can walk around naked, shamelessly. Patients strip naked before surgery.[24] Nakedness combined with a sense that there is something that can be disrespected or used conjures up feelings of modesty. Voyeurism would be a victimless crime, were it not for the violation of making the private public or of offending modesty. Men are more likely to violate, disrespect, and use women in sexual relations, so modesty appears more necessary to protect women. Modesty protects deeper, personal relations by keeping attention away from mere sexual organs and objects and drawing attention to our individuality. It reflects a hope to be respected and loved in a relation, not simply as a sex object: "my eyes are up here." Men react in sexual relations, becoming erect from a vision or promise, with the hope of physical satisfaction. Few actions are as physical or animal as such standing at attention. Usually not feeling the same reactive sensuality or the same physical release, women are more likely to experience and enjoy sexual relations with a promise of emotional closeness or of seeing sexual relations within enduring personal relations. Modesty transforms male sensuality into a species of respect for the sexual individuality of the woman.

How sensuality, emotional closeness, and modesty express themselves varies somewhat across time and place, with effects for relations between the sexes. For sexual modernizers the separation of sexual desire from love makes modesty superfluous and less to be practiced. Women today, following these dictates, acting sensually more like men than in the past, may use sex to pursue their careers. Testifying to the power of gender, women can be and are more sensual than they once were, though, testifying to the power of sex, the average woman is still not as sensual as the average man. Testifying to the power of gender, women make more of their bodies public than they have in the past, but testifying to the power of sex, neither women nor men show everything. Removing social support from modesty puts women at a disadvantage in translating sex into relations. Decrease the modesty, and male responsibility declines and sensuality increases. The logic of modesty is a persistent groove in human affairs. Advice from sexual modernizers and feminists affects degrees more than kinds, which means that there will be no end to their frustration and demands for reform as the grooves of sexual desire persist.

Consider the persistence of the sexual double standard. Male promiscuity and infidelity are never celebrated (except, perhaps, by sexual liberationists), but they are more tolerated than womanly promiscuity. This double standard proceeds from the fact that men and women desire sex in different quantities and they experience sex differently. Men pursue women more than women pursue men. The question of sexual mores is, What are we going to do about this fact? Will we demand more self-control from men or more self-indulgence from women? The liberationist ethic imagines more sexual indulgence from all. What is the effect of this? Women who allow themselves to be easily caught are more likely to be plagued by self-doubt or regret than a man who can be easily caught. Few women brag about their sexual conquests, though bragging is a typically male vice. Women tend to underreport the number of sexual partners they have had, while men overreport. Change and continuity exist in the sexual double standard, which exists in the consciences of each sex. It's different for girls. "Try as they might to feel like men, women's greater ambivalence about sex and their more poignant experience of its emotional consequences are a stable heritage and an enduring component of the stubborn sexual double standard."[25] Plenty of women try to realize the goal of relationless sex, but many fewer sustain such ways over the long haul. Movies such as *No Strings Attached* (2011) and *Friends with Benefits* (2011) depict this reality better than a thousand essays.[26]

The sexual double standard works in a different, more alienating way under conditions of sexual liberation. The idea that sexual satisfaction is a crucial human need, popular since the world of Freud and ascendant still today, gives sexual satisfaction more importance as an aspect of happiness than it has often, perhaps ever, had in the past. Sexual pleasure ranks high (is it the highest value?) as a determinant of human happiness. Therefore sexual attractiveness becomes a more important element of status in libertine societies, and growing old becomes increasingly intolerable (unless one's erectile dysfunction is addressed). Statistics and theories tell part of the story.

No one can fully capture this consequence of the sexual liberation without the aid of literature, yet our art and literature have some catching up to do. The film *The Ice Storm* from Ang Lee is a good place to start in the depiction of the emptiness of suburban lives convulsed with sexual desire and intrigue.[27] On the topic of sexual winners and losers, the controversial work of French novelist Michel Houellebecq is essential reading. Sexual liberation affects people differently, to be sure (this diversity is what must be explored), but the milieu reveals a syndrome of problems. The main character of Houellebecq's 1994 novel *Whatever* (*Extension du Domaine de la Lutte*) reveals something about the losers in the sexual revolution. The book depicts a hero, Harel, an engineer in information technology. Harel is a bit overweight, ugly, and without emotional attachments or family ties. He is sent with Raphael Tisserand, an ugly 28-year old virgin, to give seminars in a new city—and the two men are increasingly frustrated in their vain attempts to find some girly action on the road. The careerist women hardly turn Harel on. Harel muses to himself about liberated societies:

> In societies like ours sex truly represents a second system of differentiation, completely independent of money; and as a system of differentiation it functions just as mercilessly. . . . Just like unrestrained economic liberalism, and for similar reasons, sexual liberalism produces phenomena of absolute pauperization. Some men make love every day; others five or six times in their life, or never. Some make love with dozens of women; others with none. It's what's known as "the law of the market." . . . In a totally liberal economic system certain people accumulate considerable fortunes; others stagnate in unemployment and misery. In a totally liberal sexual system certain people have a varied and exciting erotic life; others are reduced to masturbation and solitude. Economic liberalism is an extension of the domain of the struggle, its extension to all ages and all classes of society. Sexual liberalism is likewise an extension of the domain of the struggle, its extension to all ages and all classes of society. . . . Businesses fight over certain young professionals; women fight over certain young men; men fight over certain young women; the trouble and strife are considerable.[28]

Raphael, when encouraged to murder a woman who has rejected him, demurs, knowing that spilling blood does not solve the problem. Houellebecq provides a testable hypothesis about sex differences under conditions of liberation or casual sex. Women, as sexual gatekeepers, can now decide for themselves with whom to have sex. Women will choose powerful, handsome men (trading up to find men who suit their vanity) and attractive, sexually compulsive men can, hither or yon, get satisfaction. Other men, less handsome and powerful, fail to attract and are consigned to lonely lives of monism. Yet most women (those who do not lasso a man at the top) will tend to be unsatisfied with this arrangement, as will many men. Sexual liberation has winners and losers. Redistribution may remedy this, as Aristophanes showed in his *Assembly of Women*.

Houellebecq's *Atomised* (1999) also treats the effects of sexual liberation. Two of the three main women characters—the mother of the two male protagonists and their respective lovers—die by their own hand, each (for different reasons) failing to find enduring love and intimacy in the world of sexual liberation. The narcissistic mother, Janine, a full participant in bringing about the liberated regime in sexual matters, having abandoned her two sons, dies alone after a life of serial lovers. Bruno, the older brother, is the product of Janine and Serge, a vain plastic surgeon. They abandon Bruno to be raised by elderly grandparents, and upon their death he is brutalized in boarding schools and marries. Lecherous and sexually compulsive, Bruno loses his teaching job for masturbating in front of a young student. After losing his job and marriage, he has a relationship with a liberated woman, Christiane (who had a liberated mother similar to Janine), begun at a New Age commune. Christiane is a fully liberated woman, though also an absentee mother after an accidental marriage. She takes Bruno to swingers' clubs and pleasures him and others morning, noon, and night. They seem to be falling in love, with sex as the centerpiece of their pure relationship. She is, however, paralyzed trying to complete a difficult move at an orgy. When she turns to Bruno for love and acceptance as a nonsexual being after the paralysis, he balks; she takes her wheelchair down a set of stairs because she no longer can enjoy what was at the center of her life.[29]

Michel, the brother raised by conservative maternal grandparents, would be happy with the sweet, seemingly chaste Annabelle, his childhood friend, but his rejection of his mother's sex dalliances leads him to forgo sex altogether, and he takes up inventing a new kind of asexual human reproduction that, he thinks, might provoke a new humanity. Annabelle, beautiful and capable of love but unable to find love as a beauty in a sexualized world, has two abortions and remains a lonely woman of 40. Michel comes for a visit, and she begs him to make her pregnant. But the pregnancy is cut short by uterine cancer, and she too kills herself in the face of long odds without the prospect of motherhood.[30]

These suicides in Houellebecq's novel point to women rendered unhappy in times of sexual liberation. Christiane, for instance, stands for the worry that love will not endure once one's looks and sexuality decline, for people need to build on something above and beyond sexual gratification if they are to live together happily. Christiane, with Bruno, confuses sex with love, but they have no language or experience taking sex toward love (both their parents being liberationist precursors). Annabelle, in contrast, is a good girl from an intact family (with three children, no less), and she joins the sexual revolution with the advantages of overwhelming physical beauty; she attracts the most confident and successful men, none of whom loves her. She stays with a young Michel after he is beaten up on the streets. Only Michel takes the time to love and know her, but he cannot find words or thoughts with which to articulate the love he might feel for her. Virtuous, loving women like Annabelle, forced, in a sense, into the sexual revolution by their beauty and agreeableness, find that it compromises their happiness. Only Janine dies naturally, though piti- fully, scorned by her children and at the tail end of a vain search for meaning- ful convergence with someone, her lifelong search for eternal youth ending in the grave.[31]

As society elevates sexual desire, orgasm, and genital pleasure as pinna- cles of human relations, other ways of experiencing relations wane. This is a social project, one that promises all a chance to satisfy themselves sexually, but which leaves some behind and others miserable:

> Pleasure and desire, which as cultural, anthropological secondary phe- nomena explain little about sexuality itself; far from being a determin- ing factor, they are in fact themselves sociologically determined. . . . In the liberal system which Bruno and Christiane had joined, the sex- ual model proposed by the dominant culture (advertising, magazines, health education groups) was governed by the principle of adventure: in such a system, pleasure and desire become part of the process of seduction, and favour originality, passion and individual creativity.[32]

Everyone must be carefully taught! Sexual liberation promotes an "atomized" society, one where moral bonds between individuals are difficult to build. This "atomized society," Houellebecq writes, is akin to Huxley's Brave New World: families destroyed, sexual liberation, celebration of youth, and unbelievable material abundance.[33]

Huxley's unforgettable Brave New World (1932) is a more complete vision of a world without the traditional family and its connections than even Houellebecq depicts. Babies are cloned. Sex is more completely with- out consequences, attachment, or reproduction. Enduring love is discour- aged through public opinion. The state provides the blueprint for a child's education—including sleep-time indoctrination and state-provided child- care. Parents are not responsible for children. A home is seen "as squalid psychically as physically," where a mother broods "over her children (her chil- dren!) . . . brooded over them like a cat over kittens"; the old world with the family, displaced by the brave new world, was "full of fathers . . . therefore full of misery; full of mothers—therefore of every kind of perversion from sadism to chastity; full of brothers, sisters, uncles, aunts—full of madness and sui-cide."[34] Sex, worries about children, parental care, and erotic longing destabi-lize the individual. Since families connect individuals to their past, this brave new world seeks to erase history and memories of the past—the destruction of the family serving the destruction of the past and the promotion of plea-sures in the here and now.[35] It wipes out the joys and sorrows connected to human attachment and achievement and replaces them with ecstatic drugs, meaningless orgies, rootless relations, and distracting amusement.

Yet Huxley's teaching is ambiguous. Despite the cloning, the abolition of the family and the home, the demystifying of sex, the erasing of the past, and the conditioning toward sexual liberation, many are anxious. This brave new achievement is not satisfying, and people are restless in this world of pleasure. Sex and orgies relieve anxiety among some of the conditioned. Others take the drug soma whenever they feel uneasy or unhappy or like something is missing. Leaders in the brave new world understand that pursuing stability costs the intense, somewhat disorienting attachments typical of family life and romantic love. Such leaders pay homage to the structure of human goods as they rearrange those goods and upset the previous balance in human nature. There are wilderness areas in the brave new world for the rebellious lot of old humanity that practices monogamy, lives married lives in families, has procre-ative sex, experiences vaginal childbirth, embraces tragedy, and suffers natural death. Human nature cannot so easily be vanquished, it appears.

These human experiences reveal our social nature, our anxiousness as incomplete creatures, our longings for completion, our ability to control the future and its limits, our hopefulness about the future. These traits are, Huxley indicates, linked to the fact that human beings have bodies and sense their mortality. Birth, death, sex, the drama of human love, children—these are ineradicable parts of the human psychological landscape. In the old world, marriage and family life allow for the growth of larger communities, for the development of character through a recognition of human limits and from suffering, for experiencing euphoric highs and tragic lows, and for intense love, devotion, and commitment not seen in market transactions or politics. Leaders in the brave new world, like sexual liberation theorists, would distract people from this psychological landscape and its troubles.

Marriage and family life are, for Huxley, associated with suffering and limits. The family and traditional morality are standing reproaches to human autonomy and the technological view of the world. Intense focused love, sac-rificial love, the sufferings and untold joys associated with the stuff of living, the highs and lows, and the love of one's own are central to the human expe-rience; learning to deal with them magnanimously or charitably is central to a life of character and wisdom. Marriage and family life bring with them "the pain of living,"[36] and hence also its joys. In *Brave New World* the elimination of the traditional family and its connections produces (mostly) a breed of happy animals, easily controlled by state power, unable to love another, unable to appreciate the past, undisturbed by suffering due to heavy doses of medication. The elimination of marriage and family life points to the elimination of human depth.

The most remarkable exchange in Huxley's book takes place between John the Savage (who was born and raised on a reservation for humans living according to traditional morality) and the World Controller Mustapha Mond, who understands the costs of the brave new world. When confronted with this issue of costs by those who have seen and appreciated Shakespeare's *Othello*, Mond gives a remarkable speech:

> Our world is not the same as Othello's world. You can't make flivvers without steel—and you can't make tragedies without social instability. The world's stable now. People are happy; they get what they want; they never want what they can't get. They're well off; they're safe; they're never ill; they're not afraid of death; they're blissfully ignorant of passion and old age; they're plagued with no mothers or fathers; they've got no wives, or children, or lovers to feel strongly about; they're so conditioned that they practically can't help behaving as they ought to behave. And if anything should go wrong, there's soma.

When confronted with how *Othello* surpasses pornographic feelies in artistic excellence, Mond concedes the point, but holds that sacrificing high art and the tense form of human life for stability and superficiality is worth the cost.[37]

Some movements toward the brave new world of Huxley's imagination are in evidence. Certain drugs resemble soma, and the prominence of those drugs may signal a willingness to embrace distraction and eschew certain kinds of misery. Sex without consequences is more easily practiced today thanks to advances in birth control and sexual liberation. Consumption of pornography is on the rise and real-life sex dolls are in production. Cloning may be in our future. There has been a prominent critique of thick, concerned motherhood and private parenthood that leads, in principle, to greater public control over socialization. Knowledge of tradition and history have declined in the past generation. Our new world informed by the teaching of sexual liberation feeds sexual desire: sexual desire and preoccupation with sex correspondingly grow. Sex, as Giddens predicts,[38] becomes compulsive, and people, especially men, may turn to new, less relational ways of satisfying their surplus sexual needs.

Sexual liberation changes the moral environment in which men and women pursue and imagine sex. As a result the plastic element of sexuality in each is bent. The grooves continue but in different ways. Sex is desired, but in a liberationist context and in a liberationist way. Some, indeed many, are immiserated through this elevation of ecstatic experience. None of this *proves* beyond all doubt that the principles of sexual liberation cannot win the day and eradicate persistent grooves from human nature. Nor can I prove that any individual human being is mortal, though there has been a strong tendency toward mortality in the human species. One cannot prove that the future will resemble the past, though one can appreciate what would be lost if the future does not resemble the past.

Sexual Liberation, *Eros*, and Higher Things

The isolation of sexual desire that sexual modernizers promote reduces sex to pleasure and orgasm; liberationists see this as joyous release. Anything that stops joyous release is repression. Sex for self-conscious human beings is usually, if not always, intermingled with their imagination, reason, and actions. This connection between the body and the mind means that sex is difficult to divorce from the communities that most people imagine are grounded, somehow, in sexual relations. Sexual longing and attraction show that human beings imagine themselves to be incomplete and that they long for completion, but the longing does not stop at sexual satisfaction. Human beings wonder about what sexual longings mean for a life well lived, no matter how much modernizing and liberationist dogmas prevail in our public teachings. Sexual modernizers and liberationists err in seeing sex as pleasure or release, not as a solid expression of human *eros* that points to higher and other longings. Sex alone cannot and should not satisfy human beings.

Ancient wisdom on the issue of *eros*, sex, and the higher things clarifies what is at stake in the teachings of sexual liberation. Only a fool would claim to present the Platonic teaching on *eros* definitively in such summary form, but a few observations drawn from Plato can order thinking about *eros*. *Eros* appears as a yearning or a desire—a recognition that something is lacking in one's character or life and a hope giving rise to action that that lack might be filled.[39] Sexual desire, as the Athenian Stranger observes in Plato's *Laws*, is *eros* at its sharpest and most maddening. One can also have, as he tells us, *eros* for food and drink, for perfecting one's profession, for fishing and hunting, for endless acquisition, for moderate and just political rule, and for wealth and riches.[40] Elsewhere in Plato, the man taken with *eros* has a thirst for political rule, for becoming a tyrant, for wisdom, for virtue, for immortality, for glory, for artistic accomplishment, and for friendship. Not for nothing does Socrates' putative teacher, Diotima of Plato's *Symposium*, say that *eros* is the "desire of all good things and of being happy."[41] *Eros* is also linked to desiring bad things and being made miserable. *Eros* grounds human striving. Its domain seems infinite. In the dialogues Plato presents a Socrates interested in pointing his friends and fellow citizens toward desiring virtue and wisdom and away from tyrannical ambitions and merely physical existence.

Sexual liberationists reduce *eros* to a desire for sex. Kinsey takes joy, purely scientific, in identifying ways human sexual desire mirrors animal behavior. Gratifying sexual desire or the new *eros* (think erotica) is a national project for sexual liberationists. Any effort to tutor sexual *eros* in the old sense, to show that it points beyond sexual desire to higher things, violates the isolation or separation of sexual desire from every other human experience. Sexual liberation impoverishes and misunderstands *eros* in delinking it from the high and dangerous in human life. Pornography and other hallmarks of the liberated sexuality are the new opiate for the masses.[42]

The effort to separate or cordon off *eros* appears reasonable against Plato's almost maddeningly vast teaching on *eros*. That effort not only robs human beings of imagination, greater striving, stable relationships, and the best things, but it underestimates connections at the heart of human experience. Here we must turn to first principles of the human soul. The highest things, the aspiration of all our passions and actions, is to be happy (not to be sexually free or sexually equal); while happiness is probably not opposed to human pleasure, it is also not reducible to it.

Eros must be made consistent with respect, self-respect, love, responsibility, and fidelity. None of these happens without social tutoring; none of these is against the manifest tenor of human sexuality, which is relational as well as concerned with pleasure. *Eros* is made consistent with respect and self-respect through conventions that go with this groove in human nature. As sexual liberation theories undermine these conventions, they lead to a species of unhappiness and are inconsistent with some of the grooves in human nature. They reshape human nature in predictable ways—illustrating both the plasticity and the durability of human nature.

It is a mistake to see sexual passion divorced from other human experiences, just as it is a mistake to think that social problems around abuse and rape will be solved through the liberation of sexual desire. The idea is not to repress *eros*, but to educate it and improve it toward higher human goods, including those goods around nuptials. Efforts to channel and improve sexual *eros* (though not to squash it) are central to traditional morality, though the traditional family is not the only destination for human *eros*. Erotic desire, so understood, is enslaved when it is contained only within sexual life. This is what sexual liberation does, and for this reason, even if we could liberate sexuality, we would still want to govern it.

Part III
The Post-Rolling Revolution World

The rolling revolution is in principle and in practice unfinishable, so it will always run up against limits. It is best to know those limits that contribute to the human good and to self-government, as we have seen in the previous three chapters. It has become increasingly difficult to see and appreciate those limits, as the ideology of the rolling revolution spreads. Intellectuals who defend the family rightly spend much time exposing blind spots in the contemporary ideology. All this time in the defensive crouch, however, distracts them from thinking through where these limits point in our particular time and place. Seeing the goodness in those limits, it is necessary also to reconstruct a public opinion and a public policy that appreciates those limits.

Much Old Wisdom needs to be recovered. Recovery alone is not enough. We must understand what we are seeking to accomplish with a family policy for a liberal society—and also appreciate the limits within which that family policy necessarily operates. Too much focus on the limits imposed by the rolling revolution makes the job of reconstructing public opinion and public policy seem quixotic. Too little focus on what could be done and where we are going has made family advocates appear opportunistic and guilty in public debates. That there are sex differences is one thing to show—but precisely what those sex differences mean for public opinion and public policy is quite another. Without an acceptable answer to the second, the answer to the first appears to be a defense of patriarchy. That the public legislates morality is one thing—but showing what type of morality is suited for a liberal society is much more difficult. Without a defensible answer to the second, the answer to the first appears like the complaints from yesterday-ville. That there is more to sex than scratching an itch or liberating the spirit of orgasm is one thing—but precisely how society goes about translating sex into love and respect is much more difficult. Without accomplishing that last task, opponents of sexual liberation will appear as uptight fuddy-duddies, unwilling to allow others to have a good time.

The subsequent chapters contain an attempt to map out what marriage and family advocates should aim at in our situation. It begins with a treatment of what family policy in a liberal society aims at—why the state is concerned with marriage and family life and how the state can help to shape an environment where natural passions are ordered toward marital and parental duties. From there, I seek to identify several areas of policy where traditional ways have been upset and to demonstrate that a return to a modified traditionalism is necessary if human beings are to live happily and freely in light of their limits.

8

A SKETCH OF A BETTER FAMILY POLICY

None of the theories of the rolling revolution does justice to the phenomenon. A better orientation must be based on an accurate account of who men and women are and how human beings aspire and must account for the interrelation between the individuals, the family, and the political community. Without new citizens capable of taking on the responsibilities of freedom and citizenship, no country can survive and thrive. John Adams *understated* the importance of families when he suggested that the "foundation of national morality must be laid in private families."[1] The very existence of a political community rests on the sexual behavior and procreative purposes of especially married couples.

Civil governments depend on marriage, procreation, and responsible parenthood, yet government cannot direct these matters overmuch; its power is limited. Civil government neither can nor should require people to marry, to have children, or to stop having children. It cannot and should not choose marriage partners for anyone or prescribe the careers toward which parents should raise children or do a lot of other directing of parenting. This tension between the great interests of civil government and its circumscribed power makes family policy a most difficult field to understand. The public depends on the private to produce the next public, but the public has limited power over the private to achieve the public's goals. Paradoxically, perhaps, private decisions are not entirely private either in origin or in effect—the actions of people arise in large part from the predominant mores, manners, and opinions in a particular time and place and these mores, manners, and opinions are in part informed through the law. The public shapes the private without controlling it.

Liberal democracies resolve this incongruity *indirectly*—not by forcing decisions on people but by encouraging people toward the goods of marital unity and protecting the environment within which decisions are understood and made so that goods are more likely to be chosen. A political community protects marital and parental rights to promote its interest in the procreation and education of children. Civil government thereby provides space for people to do what they are often inclined to do. Marital and parental rights, while the beginning of a sound policy, are not enough. The protection of a particular marital and familial form also promotes an environment where couples achieve the public goods. Modern democracies protect such rights and have promoted a monogamous, enduring, man–woman marital form on the assumption that securing these rights and protecting that form fosters the responsible exercise of marital and parental duties. The construction of a congenial marital and familial environment helps translate natural passions into civilized practices that promote personal happiness.

The rolling revolution's progress has undermined gentle indirect policy to no small degree. Thinkers of the rolling revolution recognize the influence of marital form and seek to undermine the traditional form and replace it with different ideals. Feminism not only seeks the abolition of family as a means of securing human liberation, but it denies that men and women make unique contributions to the family and that they benefit from different habits and mores to lead flourishing lives. Contemporary liberals rule out the accomplishment of state interests even indirectly because the policy of indirection entails legislating morality (that is not the pure relationship) and because they seek to promote individual independence from marriage and the family in the service of accomplishing pure relationships. Sexual liberationists seek to detach sex from procreation and to teach people that sexual expression is the key to human happiness.

Recovering the policy of indirection requires first that we overcome the aspirations of this rolling revolution and ground our theory on a marriage and family culture that accounts for the aspects of human nature that I described in part 2. Contrary to the views of feminists, sex provides grooves for gender, and a more livable public morality would direct, instead of bury, these somewhat different grooves toward peaceful, fruitful harmony between men and women. Contemporary liberalism aspires to a chimerical neutrality and an extreme, inhumane vision of personal independence; a more livable public morality would honestly seek to impart a healthy, human public morality based on a broader range of human aspirations. Sexual liberationists propound a vision of human sexuality at odds with the relationship between sex and love and overestimating the importance of sexual expression for human happiness; a more livable public morality would see that which liberationists view as repression as the self-control at the basis of morality that fosters enduring relations.

Understanding the radical political teachings of the rolling revolution, the object of part 1, is not enough. Exposing the half-truths in the political teachings of rolling revolution and recovering the experiences that they seek to blot out, the object of part 2, is not enough. Such critical work prepares the way for a teaching, centered on a policy of indirection, the protection of marital form, and a public morality aimed at channeling human beings toward lives of self-control, virtue, and happiness.

Marital and Family Form and the Idea of Duty

Responsible family policy begins with a political community protecting marital and parental rights. Civil government protects rights so that important duties can be better executed and it protects the joint marital form to realize of important public duties. How do governments provide a framework that protects a workable marital form, connects rights to duties, and thereby indirectly accomplishes its interests in marriage and family life?

American courts, in the name of securing freedom for people to marry and procreate, have, for instance, swept away laws that restrict the right of inter-racial couples to marry,[2] that interfere with the ability of those behind in child support payments to marry,[3] and that called for selective sterilization.[4] Protecting marital and parental rights cannot be detached from the reasons for it. Government protects marital and parental rights so that the concerns that make up marriage and family life can be realized, expecting that enough spouses and parents will do them well enough. Government thereby protects space for couples to marry and to take responsibility for children in the hopes that enough couples will marry, have children, and take responsibility for them. Governments forswear the power to accomplish these goals directly, never forcing people to marry or have children. Indirection is a crucial policy of all governments. Civil government protects and shields many of the great institutions of civil society—private property, educational corporations, economic enterprises, and religious organizations—with the hopes that they will produce indispensable public goods such as prosperity, civic knowledge, and self-governing citizens.

James Madison's discussion of property in *Federalist #10* is illustrative. Instead of directly shaping people's faculties and talents, Madison counsels protecting the products of their faculties and talents. "The first object of government," Madison writes, is the protection of the diverse and unequal "faculties" of citizens. Faculties come from a person's innate abilities, acquired talents, background, and education. Some people are flute players or writers, others have a talent for banking, farming, or making manufacturing products. According to Madison the "different degrees and kinds of property . . . immediately results from . . . the different and unequal faculties of acquiring property."[5] Governments police the boundaries of property and thereby provide a framework of stability and protection within which people can cultivate their own faculties. By protecting private property, governments create a safe environment within which people can pursue natural inclinations such as the desire to cultivate one's faculties and thereby often create useful inventions or economic prosperity.

Much the same is true of the protection of the rights of conscience, which governments protect in order to provide space for vibrant religious life. More can be accomplished indirectly on these scores than could be accomplished directly. Protecting property allows for a diverse range of faculties to arise, but seeking to cultivate faculties directly leads to a thicket of problems concerning governmental competence and legitimacy.[6] Governments are incompetent to direct people to certain kinds of careers or to organize the production of most economic enterprises through rational planning. Protecting rights of conscience allows for religious practice to rely on people's natural sentiments, inherited traditions, and religious practices, but efforts to foster religious practice through state churches leave religion moribund and the state conflicted.[7]

According to this indirect policy, the protection of marital rights promotes the formation of marriage and secures its integrity, so the individuals in the marriage can pursue a common life with confidence. For mothers and fathers, the protection of parental rights provides space for procreating and educating children so parents can fulfill their duties. The protection of such rights requires different actions at different times and in different situations. For example, it can mean shielding parents from laws intruding into the proper sphere of parental independence, like mandatory sterilization laws from the Progressive Era, proposed laws to prohibit children from playing in public parks or from roaming around without adult supervision,[8] or laws that all but prohibit homeschooling.

Parental rights and civil interests can clash in the sphere of education. Parents have responsibility for directing their child's education and shaping their child's character. At the same time, modern political communities play a significant role in providing and administering education.[9] The family clashes with the state when parents want something different for their children than does the state. Two Supreme Court cases from the 1920s, *Meyer v. Nebraska* (1923) and *Pierce v. Society of Sisters of the Holy Names of Jesus and Mary* (1925), limn the divide between parents and the state and illustrate the policy of indirection through which the conflict is partially regulated. In *Meyer,*

Nebraska had outlawed teaching foreign languages to children before the 8th grade, while the Oregon statute at issue in *Pierce* required Oregon parents to send their children from age 8–16 to public schools. The *Meyer* court declared the Nebraska law to be an unconstitutional infringement on individual liberty and parental power. Protected liberty, the court held, was more than

> merely liberty of bodily restraint, but also the right of the individual to contract, or engage in any of the common occupations of life, to acquire useful knowledge, to marry, establish a home and bring up children, to worship God according to the dictates of his own conscience, and generally to enjoy these privileges long recognized in common law as essential to the orderly pursuit of happiness by free men.

The state could "go very far indeed" as it seeks to "improve the quality of its citizens" but this state power must also respect parents' "fundamental rights."[10] Preventing parents from sending their children to a school teaching German, in this case, went beyond government's legitimate interests in improving the "quality of its citizens."

Pierce follows *Meyer* in protecting parental rights. During an era where John Dewey and others promoted state-directed, Progressive education, and where there was movement toward compromising religious, especially Catholic private education (as the Oregon law itself attests to),[11] the Court again defended parental rights.

> The fundamental theory of liberty upon which all governments in this Union repose excludes any general power of the State to standardize its children by forcing them to accept instruction from public teachers only. The child is not a mere creature of the State; those who nurture him and direct his destiny *have the right, coupled with the high duty*, to recognize and prepare him for additional obligations.

The court in *Pierce* links a right "of parents and guardians to direct the upbringing and education of children under their control" with a duty to use that freedom well. The fact that the Society of Sisters, a holy order of Catholic nuns who ran a private school, provided education that was "not inherently harmful" and even "useful and meritorious" made it easier for the unanimous Court to defer to parental rights in this case.[12] The inclusion of such an analysis suggests that there are limits on parental rights. The state can require that children be educated, regulate teacher qualifications, and require the integration of certain competencies into education, yet the state could not remove parents' ability to direct the education of their children.[13] Every instance of state action risks eroding parental duty to some extent—and a more activist state poses a greater threat to parental duty. Indirection is effective so long as citizens have a sense of duty to fill the space civil government protects with responsible actions and the exercise of marital and parental duties. Private citizens use their freedom to fulfill these important duties, because those duties and functions are sufficiently grounded in natural sentiments.

Duty is an obligation that at times constrains or tutors passion or can demand the performance of a task even when that performance goes against a person's immediate desire or interest. One's understanding of duty shapes and prioritizes one's interests and passions. Duties often attach to, and derive from, institutions or forms such as marriage, which themselves are not solely products of human choice and are partly products of civil society. Duties are essential to marriage and the family, and involve getting married and staying married, having children, and raising children.

Some duties are enforced through laws (i.e., a duty to pay a tax). Duties surrounding marriage and family life—especially duties related to raising children—would be imperfectly executed if the community depended on legal incentives to get parents to take care of their children or to require spouses to love and cherish one another. Duties do not arise spontaneously or naturally; they must be carefully taught. A political community's reigning idea of marriage supplies a notion of duty that tutors interests and passions. People come to act upon duties that are in line with some human passions and interests and to ignore other passions and interests. The reigning idea of marriage—the predominant marital form, that is—shapes or "forms" our understanding of which passions should be followed and what is in our interests, of what is right and what is wrong. Duties thus appear to be, and indeed often are, in one's interest and consistent with one's desires. Duties associated with marriage and family life can arise from conscience and religious obligation (i.e., a duty to be "fruitful and multiply"). Duties may in addition arise from nature, habits, mores, and opinions, or from a worry about shaming oneself or one's family. In any event those duties arise from a form of marriage that channels nature, shapes habits, molds opinions, and grounds obligations.

The form of marriage and family life is important because human passions and interests point in any number of directions. Rolling revolutionaries do not have much time for duties that derive from a traditional marital form—such duties are seen as tyrannical tools of patriarchy designed to keep women down, as compromises to the pure relationship, or as instruments of sexual repression. We do well to understand the complexity of passions and interests on the key issues of having children, raising children, and attaching adults and especially males to family life because so much of today's simplistic thinking takes for granted responsible human actions and assumes they will continue into the future.

The Ambiguous Givenness in Nature

Nature provides the stuff out of which marriage and family life grow, but it does not provide them unambiguously. Nature provides the building blocks, and political society participates in the building. From the perspective of the political community hoping to perpetuate itself through a somewhat traditional form, it is a matter of translating natural passions into civilizing ones leading sufficient numbers to enter marriage and family life. From the perspective of the individual, such manners and mores, formed indirectly, foster a species of human happiness, love, and responsibility not inconsistent with their nature.

Consider first the issue of whether women have children or sense a duty to do so. Securing space for consensual sex is relatively easy as human beings have some desire for sex or intimacy,[14] but the advent of modern contraception has made it easy to avoid having children in that space. First, women must have sex, while nubile, within the space they are provided. Second, they must have sex without contraception or abortion. Even if there is a natural desire for sex, there seems to be no natural duty for women to reproduce, though women may have some natural inclination to have children[15] and though there are divine injunctions to be fruitful connected with the Jewish and Christian traditions. Having a child is a real commitment—involving sacrifices of time, energy, and care and great bodily sacrifices—during a time in life when young women are filled with great individual vibrancy and a multitude of attractive lifestyle options. A political community that protects sexual and marital freedom expects enough women to give birth to enough children so society can perpetuate, though perpetuating society or being a slave to the species can hardly be a woman's motivation to have children. How can the political community's interest in having future citizens be vindicated now that motherhood is much more optional for women?

Consider second the parental duty to invest the time, treasure, and care into shaping a child's mind and character. Parents love their children as their own, which makes providing for a child's care seem an almost natural or innate human characteristic. Many parents bear the costs of parenting without counting them. Things are more complicated, however. No society relies exclusively on natural feelings to accomplish such goals because duty and passion do not perfectly coincide. There may be an interest in parenting: parents are connected to their own and every society respects the connection between procreation and parenthood on some level. Yet, these late modern times have proved to us that limited creatures with limited time on earth must give priority to some natural passions or duties over others. Individuals have many rights and conflicting passions (selfish, communal, etc.) as well, so exercising certain rights and following certain passions are matters informed through public morality. The question for the political community is how to get enough adults to prioritize parenthood so that enough children are reared to responsible adulthood and citizenship to secure the perpetuation and health of the political community.

Third, there is the thorny question of men becoming interested in marriage and fatherhood. There is often talk of "maternal instincts" (that supposedly kick in after women have children) but rarely do people depend on "paternal instincts." Since mothers know their children biologically and nurture them physically, motherhood has a more natural basis than fatherhood; this physical basis provides a sturdier grounding for the exercise of maternal duties. While motherhood is not for all women, mothers find it to be a rewarding source of fulfillment and happiness.[16] Still the partial detachment of sex from getting pregnant abetted through contraception has had the effect of freeing female sexuality more than a little from civilized restraints.

There is a bigger problem with men. Most mothers feel attached to their children once they have children.[17] Men seem less interested by nature in being husbands or fathers, or in having other long-term commitments. Fatherhood arises more from culture and opinions about what is honorable and noble than it arises directly from nature.[18] Some men seem more interested in sexual satisfaction, personal ambition, and vainglorious violence than in becoming fathers. Nor is it necessarily best if men who follow their fleeting desires stick around. John Locke, for instance, catalogs the "sports of men"—including incidents of cannibalism, child sacrifice, exposure, feeding children to wild beasts, and burying children alive—when men are freed from law and censure.[19] The difficulty of encouraging male responsibility manifests itself in several subcultures in contemporary America.[20] Neither the meandering nor the primitive man constitutes a civilized and civilizing family. The acts of establishing and protecting legal rights to be a member of the family are the beginnings of a marital form in this respect. How do men especially move from disorderly sexual desire and male nonfamilial, nonmarital ambition to a sense of marital and parental duty?

A man and woman walk up the aisle on an airplane. The woman cradles a young baby in her arms, ensuring its safety and caring for its needs. Behind this woman comes a man, clad in the uniform of a suburban father, carrying baby bags with extra formula and diapers and a car seat for their little idol. They work together to raise a child. This picture, a source of mirth, is an accomplishment of civilization, a consequence of makin' whoopie. Each element—the motherhood, the fatherhood, and the marriage—has a foundation in natural desire, but no natural desire points directly and unambiguously to this motherhood, fatherhood, or marriage. That man could be playing video games or be a member of a gang or watching pornography or doing high finance. That woman could be running a human resource department or be a pathbreaker of reform or be a nun. Natural desires are problems and solutions, at the same time—and they point in many different directions.

The answer to the problems of having children, prioritizing parenthood, and cultivating male responsibility, for modern governments and for all time, involves interesting women in such things and attaching men to such women and children through the promotion of an enduring, monogamous marital form between a man and a woman. Such marriages are most likely to be fecund, where a child cements and expresses a loving relationship between a husband and wife. A monogamous marriage between a man and a woman is most likely to coincide with a trusting relation where two people live a common life that includes having children.

Consider the case of the man, something respectable people can talk about. Consensual, monogamous marriage attaches the wandering male to a wife and family while taming him and elevating him some sense of responsibility. It can tame domineering tendencies with the demand that women genuinely consent to marriage. Continued relations between the husband and wife reflect respect for that consent, with the expectation that partners will be willing. Men, rather uninvolved in the actual birthing of children, find their importance in providing support to their families and in sharing much with a wife. A man's identity comes to be melded with responsibility to support and his ambition is likely aimed toward the goods of family. Within the context of marriage, a man is more likely to take responsibility for his children as a means of keeping and deepening marital harmony and out of genuine concern for the future of each child and for the happiness of his wife. Thus a man's duty comes to match his understanding of interest and his passions.

Such marriages also make space for women to have children and raise them, if they want. (It will be necessary, in chapter 10, to consider the obstacles to women wanting marriage and children—a less respectable topic.) In fact the very existence of that marriage suggests that men and women share something, and that suggestion is the basis for having children and raising them in common. Women tend to be more interested in such people, and hence are more likely to use the space provided to have children and then to make friendships with other women who are also raising children. This is the basis of community, often.

Since marital forms shape how people understand their interests and prioritize their passions, civil government has an interest in promoting some forms at the expense of other forms. Marital forms such as polygamy and (some think) coverture tend to undermine the affection, consent, marital friendship, and trust central to a well-functioning marriage. The state's interest in procreation, education, and tutoring male sexual ambition may not be promoted well under these forms. Men and women are both prone to adultery and discontent under polygamous arrangements, and children are less well raised to self-government. Today's weak marital form emphasizing the pure relationship, at best, sees provision and children outside the purpose of marriage. Today's image of the independent woman abets marriages modeled on the pure relationship, seeing children outside its purpose if not a burden to travel, dining out, and recreation. The pure relationship model produces fewer children than did the marital regimes of the past and those children tend to have less capacity for self-government. The pure relationship "form," that is, teaches parents to look out for themselves (their careers, their looks, their recreation) and to be independent more than it centers on care for children.

The state trusts that many couples will marry, have children, and raise children when marital and parental rights are secured *and* when the joint marital form most conducive to these goals is protected in law and held honorable by public opinion. Seeing marriage and parenting as high duties means that they are supported and reinforced, indirectly, for the most part, through interest, conscience, law, and public morality.

Despite the rolling revolution, many people still marry, have children, and raise them to honorable adulthood. The policy of indirection depends on the attractiveness of these experiences or how they rank in human life.[21] These experiences arise from more or less spontaneous, universal passions, but these passions do not unambiguously point to marriage, parenting, and family life centered on marriage. Many human beings desire sex with people of the opposite sex and intimate, enduring relations with others,[22] so marriage has a natural basis. Human beings desire to have sex, to live beyond themselves, and to express their love for another concretely, so procreation has a natural basis. Human beings desire to care for children and to take on responsibilities, so education of children has a natural basis. The line from some of these natural desires to duty is straighter in some instances than in others. Passions are most likely to be instructed toward the exercise of marital and parental duties when laws and opinions support the enduring, exclusive man-woman marital form.

Religious beliefs point natural passions to the discharge of duties. Those who faithfully attend church services, for instance, are more likely to marry and stay married, have children, and direct the education of their children.[23] On this score duty and responsibility seem to come from outside of liberal principles in a manner that reinforces the hopes of the political community. In contrast, the mildest forms of feminism call into question the joys and duties of family life that involve dependence of one person on another. The successes of the rolling feminist revolution consist in changing mores and expectations and elevating other human goods such as careers while dethroning motherhood and family life generally. Try defending the family and suggesting that couples have more children and you are sure to hear the following: "I am not going back to the kitchen." The answer: "You don't need to cook, but someone must if the family is to share a beautiful meal as part of its common life."

Whether the feminist reeducation constitutes a suppression of nature, an exchange of one culture for another, or the subversion of a partly natural, partly cultural political order, under its influence the pure relationship and its ways more often win out over the mutual dependence and community of marriage that ground parental duties. In such cases parental rights may be secure but underemployed and perhaps are less important to individuals than in the past. Just as property rights and rights of conscience are most vulnerable when fewer own property or practice their faith, parental rights are most vulnerable when fewer avail themselves of those rights or when fewer are interested in the attendant duties.

The Challenges of Indirection

Rolling revolutionaries undermine nearly every plank of a sound marriage and family policy, and they stigmatize indirect efforts to translate natural passions into civilized, marital, and familial duties. Their successes are notable, especially in the destruction of the marital form and in the transformation of the moral environment that does not support the translation of natural passions into marital and familial duties. Men and women are free to have procreative sex; they are free to marry; they are able to raise their children—yet they all do so at increasingly lower rates and these actions are not as honored as they once were. Passions, interests, and goods are less pointed toward marriage and family life—and they are often pointed away from it. More and more twenty-somethings, imagining that they are independent minded and following their passions and dreams, mostly "choose" against marriage and children and for careers, delayed childbirth or none, and the pure relationship. What a coincidence! This re-creation of the moral environment is the astonishing feat of the rolling revolutionaries. Thus the challenge for those who would mix this family regime and sustain our political regime.

Part 2 put forward the limits in the rolling revolution. Efforts to make those limits effective involve sustaining and rebuilding a public morality that supports the enduring, monogamous marital form between a man and a woman. A better public morality translates and prioritizes the natural passions that lead to enduring, monogamous marriage between a man and a woman and to responsible, involved parenthood, while deemphasizing and perhaps stigmatizing the rolling revolution's way of translating natural passions. Sometimes efforts to do so involve clearing the underbrush of bad arguments and false assertions that rolling revolutionaries put forward. Sometimes such efforts involve protecting against further rolls of the revolution. Sometimes they involve finding ways to limit the effects of the rolling revolution in particular areas. The subsequent chapters lay out various ways to limit the rolling revolution.

Natural passions, interests, and goods run in a number of channels. The passions, interests, and goods that lead men and women away from marriage and family life are often expressions of natural passions as well. The rolling revolution has a way of translating these natural passions on the road to a seemingly autonomous human future, toward a world of the pure relationship and beyond. The goal of a better policy is the cultivation of a public morality that defends monogamous, enduring marriage between a man and a woman because this situation increases the likelihood of translating natural passions into civilizing ones. We have spent some time identifying the relevant natural passions, interests, and goods, and hence the limits of the rolling revolution, in part 2. Now we must bring these perhaps still too abstract ideas down to the level where they touch our lives and our regime.

9

TOWARD A NEW, NEW SEXUAL REGIME

America, like most countries in the modern world, once upon a time, had, as we have seen, a regime of laws and mores supporting the procreative, monogamous marital form and encouraging responsible sexual self-control. Laws and mores proscribed contraception and abortion; sodomy, adultery, and fornication; and the trafficking of pornography, or strictly limited access to indecent and pornographic works. Laws and mores made divorce difficult and required an assignment of fault to one or another party. People generally had many children. Most planks of this old sexual regime have been removed, through judicial actions, legislative adoption of a new set of laws, changes in regulations, and the dismantling of previous mores and opinions in accord with the rolling revolution.

Those who would support the family must hope to revive some ways of the old system through the policy of indirection. Much reconstruction of public opinion, mores, and perhaps even laws is necessary to accomplish such a revival to any substantial degree. The opinions and mores supporting the old way are, in many quarters, stigmatized and labeled irrational prejudices. Those who question the rolling revolution can, in some circumstances, face charges of puritanism, misogyny, homophobia, or transphobia.

Chapters 5 and 7 call the basis for this new sexual regime into question. Feminism and sexual liberation do not contain the whole truth about human nature: they ignore, misinterpret, and obscure aspects crucial for understanding human nature, love, marriage, and family life. Advocates of feminism and sexual revolution have every interest in putting a stop to such debates, and they are, in the 2010s, increasingly successful in preventing honest assessments of their theoretical claims and practical reforms. No progress toward a reconstruction of public opinion is possible without first piercing through the syndrome of opinions and partial truths undergirding the rolling revolution. A necessary step in dealing with the assumptions of the rolling revolution today is dealing with the idea that all disparities between particular "victim" groups and the majority culture (differently defined) are traceable to discrimination—what I call our reigning civil rights ideology. The fact that fewer women are CEOs or plumbers or truck drivers or mechanical engineers or murderers, according to our civil rights ideology, for example, is taken as proof that there is systematic sexism and misogyny preventing opportunities for women. Similar arguments are used to show that modern societies are homophobic and transphobic and other things.

Subsequent steps in the reconstruction of public opinion proceed after the underbrush of our reigning civil rights ideology is cleared. I chart some of these subsequent steps in this chapter and the next. It is crucial to keep in mind the goals of such policies in a liberal society—to secure forms and space for people to translate natural desires into civilized discharge of marital and parental duties. I try to articulate pro-family policy goals for a late liberal democracy and suggest ways of getting there amidst the rolling revolution. The short- and medium-term prospects of reconstructing public opinion are pretty dismal, given the successes of the rolling revolution and the iron grip it has on respectable debate (in some cases). The pretty dismal prospects in our rolling revolution combined with a blindness about what the goal should be would doom policy doubly. It is essential to think through how laws and opinions would best be arranged on a host of issues such as same-sex relations, population decline, and consensual relations if family advocates are going to suffer losses worth having or perhaps gain victories worth having.

Are there ways of simulating mores from the old sexual regime without reviving its legal regime? Should those who would rebalance our family regime, playing a long game, aim to restore the old legal regime or are we better off without it? Let us pry into same-sex relations, population control and contraception, and issues related to consensual sex to think through the manifold goals of a responsible policy that would take things in the direction of balance and the old mores.

Disparities and Discrimination: Problems in the Reigning Civil Rights Ideology

The reigning civil rights ideology considers disparities or inequalities detrimental to aggrieved minorities traceable to a culture of discrimination and oppression. "Racial disparities," in unemployment or income, for instance, according to a 1977 statement from the U.S. Commission on Civil Rights, "provide strong evidence of the persistence of discriminatory practices."[1] A recent anti-racist scholar-activist, Ibram X. Kendi, articulates this principle with admirable clarity: "Racial discrimination is the sole cause of racial disparities in this country and in the world at large."[2] Blacks earn less income; therefore, the country is racist up to the point of disparity. Blacks are disciplined more in school; therefore, the school system suffers from institutional racism up to the point of the disparity. Common in race relations, this ideology is applied to all aggrieved minorities: selective disparities between the aggrieved minority and the "dominant culture" are taken as evidence for discrimination. It pertains, as chapter 2 shows, to discrimination against women, where anything less than a fifty-fifty split on issues deemed important is evidence of patriarchal discrimination.

This reigning civil rights ideology prevails among homosexual rights scholars and activists as it does among anti-racists.[3] Disparities between those who have sex with people of the same sex and the rest of the population have existed and continue to exist, as many studies show.[4] Youth attracted to those of the same sex, for instance, are said to have suicide rates two to eight times higher than the rest of the population.[5] Men who have sex with men are between four and eight times more likely to suffer depression than men who do not have sex with men. Men who have sex with men are significantly more likely to abuse and use drugs, abuse alcohol, contract sexually transmitted diseases, suffer from anal cancer, contract AIDS/HIV and smoke, among other things, than men who do not have sex with men.[6] Life expectancy for men who have sex with men seems to be somewhere between eight and twenty years shorter than men who do not have sex with men.[7] In a larger sense, the reigning civil rights ideology could see the fact that same-sexers (as I will call them) are a significant numerical minority as itself discrimination. Perhaps half of men would be having sex with men but for subtle pro-man–woman-sex discrimination!

Why such disparities? The answer for homosexual activists is homophobia, a term therapist George Weinberg coined in the 1960s. Homophobia, Weinberg writes, is a "conventional attitude of revulsion and anger toward things homosexual," which, when directed inward toward homosexuals themselves, yields a "condemnation of self" that proves its status as an aggrieved minority.[8] Weinberg endorses the disparity-equals-discrimination ideology:

> If the disadvantages, disabilities, and penalties which the homosexual faces are a result of society's prejudices—*and of course they are, in their entirety*—then suggesting that the homosexual improve his lot by submission to those prejudices, at the cost of his personal integrity, is fundamentally immoral.[9]

This idea endures. M. Ryan Barker, author of a 2008 literature review on these disparities, traces disparities to heterosexist oppression, "an ideological system that denies, denigrates, and stigmatizes any non-heterosexual form of behavior, identity, relationship, or community."[10] Nearly every study, advocacy group, or government website endorses this formulation. A 2017 report from the Center for American Progress, for instance, purports to show that "LGBT people across the country continue to experience pervasive discrimination that negatively affects all aspects of their lives," despite the "unprecedented progress toward LGBT equality."[11] The Centers for Disease Control echoes this: "Homophobia, stigma (negative and usually unfair beliefs), and discrimination (unfairly treating a person or group of people) against gay, bisexual, and other men who have sex with men still exist in the United States and can negatively affect the health and well-being of this community."[12] Most publications lack a conclusive statement claiming that homophobia causes *all* such disparities; yet most entertain no other factor as a possible cause of disparity aside from the general homophobic or heterosexist culture.[13] They leave the impression that it is homophobia alone that causes disfavored disparities.

Perry Halkitis, writing on behalf of the American Psychological Society, makes such an argument in "Discrimination and Homophobia Fuel the HIV Epidemic in Gay and Bisexual Men."[14] Men who have sex with men contract AIDS/HIV at a much higher rate than men who have sex with only women. How does a homophobic or heterosexist culture cause this physical disease? The broader homophobic culture makes it so families, schools, friends, and others do not accept a child's same-sex orientation; children then turn to risky behaviors as a way of coping with their "nonacceptance"; these behaviors persist into adulthood. Nonacceptance results from thousands of acts ranging from ignoring someone, unkindness to violence; after repetitive nonacceptance, men who have sex with men internalize the hatred of society into a species of self-hatred or depression. Risky behavior is the reaction of those who are not accepted, and certain kinds of risky behavior (unprotected sodomy) increases the risks of contracting AIDS/HIV. Much the same argument applies to anal cancer. Men who have sex with men are eighteen times more likely to contract anal cancer than the rest of the population. The larger culture of oppression, enforced through a legal and regulatory regime, undermines

access to health care services. Men who have sex with men are ashamed to go
to doctors, who look down on their lifestyles. Low self-esteem, depression,
and self-loathing induce men who have sex with men to retreat into self; they
forgo regular checkups. Such lesser access then causes bad sexual health, violence, drug abuse, and other disorders and maladies, including anal cancer.[15]
Or so the argument goes.

There are good reasons to reject the reigning civil rights ideology as it
is applied to these dramatic same-sex disparities. The reigning civil rights
ideology has an incoherent theory of oppression and a risibly simplistic
understanding of causation, ignoring the prevalence of nature or the body
and subculture; it selectively focuses on issues where supposedly aggrieved
minorities do poorly when compared to the majority population and it
ignores or selectively applies areas where supposedly aggrieved minorities
have "favorable" disparities.[16] A broadly hostile culture, if such a one exists,
may play some role in creating physical and mental diseases, but same-sex
actions themselves, supported through a homosexual subculture, also contribute to most physical and mental diseases.

Suicide illustrates the incoherence and risible simplicity of the reigning
civil rights ideology. Elevated suicide rates among same-sexers is a quintessential sign of the homophobic culture and oppression, for homosexual advocates. According to this nonacceptance argument, same-sexers experience
rejection from parents, bullying from school, alienation from previous relationships. Even if they are not rejected, they worry about rejection. Instances
of rejection and worries about rejection contribute to mood disorders, anxiety, substance abuse, low self-esteem, and depression. These mental disorders
make same-sexers, especially same-sex youth, more likely to attempt suicide
or commit suicide.[17] Evidence for this reasoning includes higher suicide rates
in states that had banned same-sex marriage by referenda than in states that
accepted it and lower suicide rates in states that protect same-sexers through
anti-discrimination laws, among other things. This line of thinking leads to a
demand to recognize same-sex marriage, adopt anti-discrimination laws for
same-sexers, beef up anti-bullying laws, adopt hate speech laws, adopt different safe school's policies and so on.[18] Dismantling the culture of homophobia
will eliminate disparities on suicide. These victims have only society's negative
attitudes toward their orientation rattling around in their heads—no natural
conscience, no positive feelings from society, no reinforcement from a subculture. Or so the argument goes.

This narrative does not capture the whole truth. Same-sex men have higher
suicide rates than same-sex women, for instance, suggesting that something
other than the supposedly homophobic culture—something related to sex, gender, or both—contributes to elevated suicide rates.[19] Same-sex youth are more
likely to commit or attempt suicide than older same-sexers, which suggests that

the time one spends in the supposedly homophobic culture (and previously even more homophobic culture) does not lead to greater suicide. Suicide rates seem to be just as high in Sweden, Denmark, and the Netherlands, all countries whose laws have aimed at dismantling the supposed culture of homophobia for much longer and with more apparent success than in the United States, as they are in the United States.[20] If dismantling the culture of homophobia does not lead to a decrease in suicides and suicide attempts among same-sexers, the larger culture of homophobia seems not to cause elevated suicide rates. Nowhere have I found longitudinal data to show that as society becomes more accepting of homosexuality suicide and suicide attempt rates go down.

However this may be, other factors in addition to supposed homophobia play a role in disparate suicide rates: social attitudes affect suicide rates and such but a little.[21] Perhaps sexual rejection, an unhappiness or depression traceable to past experiences of sexual abuse or sexual trauma (associated itself with producing a same-sex identity), one's natural conscience, sexual compulsiveness, the volatility of same-sex relationships, a cry for help about the direction that youth or person is thinking about going, and the *anticipation* of rejection and homophobia (as opposed to genuine homophobia itself) play no small role in heightened suicide rates and suicide attempts among youth.

On a broader note, suicide ends up being an unreliable canary in the coal mine for aggrieved minorities, especially racial, gender-based, and homosexual groups. Assume that victimized groups becoming depressed as a result of their victimization and depression is a mechanism on the road to suicide. If so, victim groups would commit suicide at higher rates than the dominant population against which they are compared. This is not the case. Many of those who think America is homophobic also claim that America is racist and misogynist.[22] Blacks would have a much higher suicide rate than whites and women would have higher suicide rates than men, if it were true. Just the opposite is the case as both blacks and women have lower, even significantly lower suicide rates than white men.[23]

A constellation of factors, as students of suicide from Emile Durkheim onward know, explains suicide on the social science model. Phenomena like suicide, crime, and mental and physical health are *always* the result of *many* causes. The risibly simplistic understanding of our reigning civil rights ideology obscures more than it reveals when it traces disparities to a single factor and holds out hope that removing the root and sole cause will alleviate human misery for the supposedly oppressed groups.

Consider some health examples such as AIDS/HIV. Lesbians and men who have sex with men live in the same culture and hence are subject equally to its debilitating discrimination, we are told. If American homophobia causes AIDS as the theories of our reigning civil rights advocates presume, then lesbians and men who have sex with men would have the same rate of AIDS/

HIV infection (and of anal cancer). They do not, however. Something in addition to homophobia explains disease rates. Perhaps it is the specific character of sodomy among same-sex men. Perhaps it is the penchant of men who have sex with men to engage in risky or unprotected sexual behavior, in which case the diseases, to some extent, result from the act. Nor is there any reason to trace this riskiness to depression; it could be part of the risqué life of same-sex men. Unprotected sodomy is *ipso facto* more unhealthful and riskier than unprotected vaginal intercourse. Baker vaguely suggests that "there are biological factors associated with male-to-male sexual activity [i.e., anal intercourse?] that increases the risk of contracting HIV."[24] Presumably he means unprotected sodomy. The dangers associated with sodomy may indeed be a cosmic injustice (to use a phrase from Thomas Sowell), but very little can change things ingrained into the embodied life.

The nonacceptance mechanism provides another revealing complication. Substance use, alcohol use, and unprotected sex are, on that argument, "coping mechanisms for social stressors and depression,"[25] and, perhaps, there is a long, crooked road, with many exits, from such abuses to suicide in some cases, especially among youth. Such an interpretation belies the seemingly genuine Dionysian joy many same-sexers experience or claim to experience living the way they live. Drug and alcohol use, smoking, and unprotected sex are often celebrated aspects in the subculture of those men who have sex with men, not signs of retreat and depression. They are fun (for some), despite what social science scolds say. "The fantasy of the gay liberals," Edmund White writes in his *States of Desire: Travels in Gay America* (1980), "is that all homosexuals are basically the same as everyone else."[26] Not so, says that gay American. Social scientists affect to see the use of hallucinogens, tobacco, alcohol and cocaine as "coping mechanisms," but men who have sex with men often see these such uses as partying, reveling, and having a good time: the gay bar, with its drinking, drugs, and revelry, is part of the gay subculture in America. The boys of Fire Island are not shirking in shame, nor seeking approval from the bourgeois culture. Peruse works of gay literature as a window to this world,[27] in order to test the hypothesis that Dionysian joys are really coping mechanisms. Such characters are liberated precisely from what they take to be the staid, boring culture enslaved to workaday concerns. Those who affect to think that "the alcohol and tobacco industry" target "the gay community" with advertising campaigns[28]—and this special targeting is the cause of increased alcohol and drug use among men who have sex with men—should rethink the relation between cause and effect. Those who prioritize transgressive pleasure over long-range, humdrum bourgeois survival turn to booze, drugs, and smoking, but not out of depression from homophobia.[29] Health disparities also result from mores of the prevailing homosexual subculture and the intrinsic nature of some sex acts.

As activists see it, those in the dominant culture, responsible for these disparities and pathologies, must be made to feel guilty and change their ways, since the moral responsibility for the disparities and pathologies cannot lie in the victim group. Homophobic actions thus cause AIDS/HIV, anal cancer, suicide, and depression.[30] Efforts to complicate this picture are said to diminish feelings of guilt and moral responsibility and to let the dominant culture off the hook. State interventions to minimize the alleged discrimination that fosters disparities must become a central object of politics. Political thinking becomes "subordinate to the ideological precepts of political action" to act in unison with one's fellows toward the eradication of difference and inequality. Thus, as Polish professor and statesman Ryszard Legutko affirms, a totalitarian temptation lurks within the simple democratic ideology.[31]

The broader heterosexual culture, if such a thing exists, is not solely responsible for the disparities involving men who have sex with men. Such disparities are partly, at least, traceable to the homosexual subculture, to physical and psychological risks intrinsic to the ways of those who have sex with those of the same sex, and to experiences that contribute to people becoming homosexuals. No group of people is exactly like another group of people. Claims of homophobia are used to immunize these supposedly aggrieved minorities from self-criticism or honest analysis. They prevent societies taken with the reigning civil rights ideology from accurately identifying risks, problems, and ills and their causes and from considering other public goods aside from alleviating the supposed grievances of certain identity groups. If we should not approach homosexuality through our reigning civil rights ideology, how should a liberal society approach same-sex relations? What should be the aim of policy and opinion toward same-sex relations in a liberal society?

Nature's Customary Policy

For Montesquieu crimes against heresy and performing magic are inconsistent with free, gentle political rule in modern republics. Crimes against heresy and magic lack a sound baseline for non-heresy and non-magic; countries that countenance such crimes are always inviting tyranny and injustice from those making trumped up accusations. Given the prevalence of human weaknesses—in this case a desire for revenge and a tyrannical desire to rule over others—Montesquieu would have polities rescind laws against heresy and magic.[32]

Montesquieu favored decriminalizing sodomy, which is, like magic, among the hidden crimes. What it takes to discover sodomy is beneath the dignity of a legitimate government to collect, for the most part. Convictions of such crimes involve the murky evidence (what we call "he said, she said" evidence). Convictions may depend on the evidence of an easily manipulated or vindictive witness. The standard for sodomy could be murky: would a wink suffice, or a solicitation, or would it need to be "open and notorious"? Sodomy charges could be a pretty easy way of getting rid of people who are otherwise "undesirable," as it has no doubt sometimes been in the past. Since prosecutions for sodomy (and heresy) invite such abuses, limited governments refrain for the most part from prosecuting such crimes.[33] This approach guards against moral purists who would do too much to stamp out heresy or sodomy (both within the law and perhaps even beyond the law) and aspiring tyrants tempted to abuse murky laws for their own benefit to get rid of "undesirables." Rule number one: no legal proscriptions on sodomy.[34]

Habits are a different matter. Montesquieu calls sodomy, among other things, a "crime against nature" that "religion, morality, and policy" condemn.[35] He writes:

> I assert that the crime against nature will not make much progress in a society unless the people are also inclined to it by some custom, as among the Greeks, where the young people performed all their exercises naked, as among ourselves where education at home is no longer the usage, as among the Asians where some individuals have a large number of wives whom they score while others have none. Do not clear the way for this crime, let it be proscribed by an exact policy, as are all the violations of mores, and one will immediately see nature either defend her rights or take them back. . . . [Nature] prepares us with our children, through whom we are born again, as it were, for satisfactions greater even than those delights.[36]

Montesquieu criticizes customs among Greeks, English, and Persians for indirectly promoting sex between men. This makes same-sex sex more prevalent than it would otherwise be and corrupts other well-functioning, necessary institutions. Greeks not only exercised together naked, but spent much time in military bunks and even seemed to think of sodomy as a means of building camaraderie and softening or humanizing mores in a warlike time.[37] English boarding schools isolated young men from marriageable young women; they discouraged men from developing a taste for women and for enduring relations with women, and kept sexually curious, bold young men in tight quarters with one another. Persian polygamy dried up the supply of women, so that men had few sexual outlets except with other men or becoming eunuchs.[38]

According to Montesquieu same-sex customs blind men to greater joys. English boarding schools, among other practices, discouraged Englishmen from prioritizing the joys of married life (other practices include prostitution, dirty literature, and excessive suspicion between the sexes). Hence awkward Englishmen were less likely to become interested husbands, lovers, and fathers. Curtailing these joys, English customs promote dour, dismal Spartans instead of the joyful lovers of France and Athens.[39] Their non-procreative same-sex ways form a standing insult to the necessitous, workaday ways of the father and form part of the ways of the English that deprives fatherhood of honor.

Greek practice is especially illuminating. Same-sex relations among the Greeks are associated with the corruption and depopulation among the Greeks and with the dishonoring of marriage. Montesquieu's arguments turn on how sexual desires and habits support political health. Some Greeks, the Cretans, as Montesquieu relates, referring to Aristotle, encouraged sodomy—a "vile means . . . to prevent too many children" from being born. The Cretans, whose institutions imitated Sparta's, lacked manpower, like Sparta. This lack of man-power, combined with the practice of infanticide, depopulated and disrupted Sparta's regime, though the Cretans were spared the military consequences of disruption by their isolated position.[40] In Sparta, it is reported,[41] so common were pederasty and same-sex relations that newlyweds consummated their marriages under the cover of darkness and with no little amount of shame; nubile women dressed and appeared as boys to ease the transition to opposite-sex sex. After discussing how the Romans encouraged the propagation of the species, Montesquieu announces a general rule drawn from nature:

> The more one decreases the number of marriages that can be made, the more one corrupts those that are made; the fewer married people there are, the less fidelity there is in marriages, just as when there are more robbers, there are more robberies.[42]

This reasoning, supported through sex ratio analysis today,[43] suggests a simple mechanism based on assumptions that men are less likely to marry unless they must. The greater the acceptance and practice of same-sex relations, the fewer the number of married people; the fewer the marriages, the more likely depopulation.

Do America and the Western world generally have customs akin to the British, Romans, Persians, and Greeks? Maybe. Perhaps the sexual revolu-tion combined with the reigning civil rights ideology and our celebration of diversity constitute a pro-same-sex custom. Ethical education baptizes same-sex relations with approval more than in the past, as liberationists intended. The reigning civil rights ideology may undermine the confidence and abil-ity of those who would cultivate a fecund marital culture. The popularity of gay liberation theory (one that actively denigrates conventional opposite-sex relations and envisions no limits on sexuality) would constitute a pro-same-sex custom, though it is difficult to know precisely how far gay liberation has advanced in American opinion.[44] Comprehensive studies find that the num-ber of men who have sex exclusively with men is about 2.5% of the population and women who have sex exclusively with women is 1.5% (for studies pub-lished in 1992 and 2000).[45] Those numbers held roughly level in 2012, though the numbers of experimenters with same-sex relations in early age seems to have risen among women.[46] Will that number increase as same-sex love is seen as a love like other loves or at least not wrong and as such diversity is more and more celebrated? More people, especially the more plastic women, may experiment with same-sex sex, but will most return to opposite-sex sex after graduation?

Why should we care about such habits? Political concerns such as depopulation and developing a culture that prepares the way for happy private life head the list of reasons. Montesquieu refers to moral arguments against same-sex relations and habits as well. Sodomy's "delights," Montesquieu suggests, among other things, give "to one sex the weaknesses of the other" and prepare "for an infamous old age by a shameful youth."[47] Nature's customary policy suggests, if Montesquieu is right, that unhappiness tends to follow such lives (for a variety of reasons) and other ways seem more consistent with deeper human "satisfactions" for love, children, and responsible community with others. Montesquieu may have Old Wisdom about the effects of sodomy on character and happiness in mind. What could be more painful than to recount such Old Wisdom? Sensitive readers may want to skip this treatment and rejoin the discussion in a few paragraphs.

Old descriptions of homosexuality from before the rise of our reigning civil rights ideology prove valuable artifacts in reconstructing the Old Wisdom from which Montesquieu may, regrettably, perhaps, draw. Excavating this Old Wisdom is neither to endorse nor to condemn it. A crime against nature, it seems, compromises self-preservation, the most natural of desire. Symons' *Evolution of Human Sexuality* (1979), as we saw in chapter 5, aims to show how men and women complement one another in sex. "The sex lives of homosexual men and women—who need not compromise sexually with members of the opposite sex—should provide dramatic insight into male sexuality and female sexuality in their undiluted states."[48] Men who have sex with men and women who have sex with women manifest exaggerated and uncompromised male and female sexuality respectively.

Symons turns to studies on the sexual styles of same-sexers to test his theory. What follows may be a partial litany of Old Wisdom, buttressed by science. Men seek greater sexual variety, are more likely to initiate sexual encounters, spend more time fantasizing about sexual adventure, desire more sex, and emphasize physical attractiveness and youthful vitality more than qualities of character when compared to women. A sexual marketplace arises to satisfy male same-sexers (e.g., gay bars, baths, public restrooms, parks). This marketplace emphasizes risk-taking sexual relationships—the pang of discovery, the public nature of the sexual display, even its danger. One-night stands tend to prevail. Sexual partners are less likely to converse—a system of signals arises for men who have sex with men to find one another and convey their desire for a few minutes alone. Relationships are more likely to begin with sex and to focus on orgasm. Such men try to look beautiful and flamboyant for one another—knowing that their potential partners love plumage, and they worry about their waning looks. One man, illustrative of these tendencies, was sodomized forty-eight times in a public bath, Symons relates, in sex that "presumably was fairly indiscriminate."[49] Sex among men who have sex with men has a tendency to become compulsive, addictive, all-consuming, primal, and most un-bourgeois.[50] Such men may desire stable relationships—but most do not sacrifice sexual variety for stability. It is difficult to know exactly what Montesquieu means by "one sex" taking on "the weaknesses of the other." Perhaps it is this: the moral weakness of vanity; Symons shows that such men are particularly concerned with outward appearances and having shapely bodies. Once looks fade, more misery tends to follow. Perhaps the act itself is more susceptible to disease and reflects a general disposition toward unhappiness.

For lesbians, in contrast, emotional intimacy generally precedes sex; lesbians generally aim to subordinate sex within a relationship. Few lesbians embrace sexual variety along the lines of homosexual men. The few lesbian-friendly establishments that there are emphasize socializing rather than anonymous sex, since lesbians, like women in general, tend to find impersonal sex unsatisfying. There also seems to be less sex among lesbians than among male homosexuals, since women are less likely to initiate sex—something that came to be called "lesbian death bed" in years after Symons' book. What sex there is tends not to focus exclusively on genitals but emphasizing bonding and loving the whole person. Knowledge of a lesbian partner's character is relatively important for lesbians, especially when compared to physical attractiveness.[51] Women may also be a bit more fickle than men, so one would expect those lesbians who form relationships that aspire to last would have double the trouble of making them last. Perhaps there are more divorces or breakups among lesbians in a same-sex marriage world than among men. This is all by the by.

Montesquieu's modesty on same-sex relations reflects his modesty generally. He does not draw any pictures, reflecting a desire to keep the private from the public—a species of public morality: he trusts a not-so-plastic nature, uncorrupted by customs, to guard herself and customs and mores, uncorrupted by ideology, to allow people to respect nature. Montesquieu points the way toward a public opinion that neither celebrates nor takes pride in same-sex things, neither punishes nor proscribes same-sex things. Discretion is the watch-word for a modest, limited regime—one that subordinates sexual matters and sexual identity.

This view contrasts with the views predominant among those taken with the reigning contemporary liberal ideology. Today, we are told, as we saw in chapter 3, it has become necessary to respect the choices that people make in asserting their rights, regardless of what that choice may be. Lifestyles demand equal concern and respect, and they get their meaning from the concern, respect, and recognition they receive; pride and dignity comes from public recognition and approval of one's choice; choices are without meaning unless they are recognized by the public, both in laws and in opinion. When choices are sexual, the demand for public approval reflects a publicizing of sexuality that is inconsistent with its private nature.

This ideology of recognition, supplemented with the reigning civil rights ideology, undermines public harmony and limited government. What is to be done? The approach toward religious beliefs points the way to a modus vivendi on same-sex ways.[52] The separation of church and state means that one's citizenship is not determined by one's religious beliefs. Atheists can be citizens as much as orthodox Christians, for instance. Atheists may disapprove of Christians, thinking them weak-minded or afraid of autonomy or easily duped by priests and pastors. Christians may disapprove of atheists, thinking them lawless anarchists, rebels from God's law, or willfully blind to the call of the Spirit. Antagonism between the two is built into the nature of each. Each will think that the other is overly recognized in public affairs and public opinion as long as the other endures: atheists will object to Christian aspects or remnants in our laws or culture, while Christians may think their beliefs are being dishonored when religion is not given more of a place in the public square. Atheists will demand secularism; Christians something more akin to a Church-State cooperating. Both groups are correct, in part, as I argued in chapter 6: there is no neutral ground from which to adjudicate their dispute about public law and public opinion.

The same fundamental repulsion need not define the relations between same-sexers and opposite-sexers. Religion is Yankees–Red Sox (a big-time rivalry); sex is Yankees–Dodgers, though sex becomes Yankees–Red Sox when it reproduces the orthodox-atheist conflict. Perhaps a father, who sacrifices much to create a family, will be quite disappointed if his children do not follow his footsteps, taking some same-sex ways to be inimical to the workaday life of fathers. Perhaps mothers will feel that children who shun family life are secretly condemning their ways and therefore react against it. Perhaps parents, believing in God, think same-sex actions a road to a loss of faith. Perhaps each had hoped to be a grandparent, with its joys and lessened responsibility. Perhaps both parents, looking at the statistics, worry that same-sex lives are less likely to be happy. Gay liberationists think "exclusive heterosexuality is f@#*ed up,"[53] and they dishonor it. These are antagonisms, to be sure. However, a modus vivendi can be worked out on sex. There will still be no truly neutral solution to the tension between the two: opposite-sexers might tend to think their ways are dishonored and that same-sex ways are intrusively praised and promoted; same-sexers may think the predominant culture is less than fully accepting if it is not celebrating.

Neither same-sexers nor opposite-sexers think their way is meaningless or an insignificant part of who they are, yet all can continue to favor their ways despite what others do and despite what the others think. How can and should the public occupy the contested ground? The public has an interest in promoting responsible self-control in sexual matters so that sexual passion can be a subordinate part of a life well lived. It also has an interest in ensuring its continued existence with the reproduction of responsible citizens. Could there be a social consensus in a liberal society around responsible self-control and modesty in sexual matters, along with the gentle rule Montesquieu recommends? Those promoting same-sex love and those promoting heterosexual love would agree to responsible self-control and modesty. Sodomy would be decriminalized in the interest of limited government. Neither law nor opinion would tolerate violent intervention or legal intervention to stop same-sexers from meeting one another and commencing relations. Domiciles could legally be bought or rented. Property could be bequeathed to one another. Visitations could be guaranteed. Partner benefits could be earned from employers. Rule two: sexual self-control and modesty would be favored as public morality.[54]

The idea that Americans and other modern peoples generally are loathsome bigots on matters relating to same-sex love cannot be the basis of education, public policy, or public opinion. The object of dismantling stereotypes or combating institutional discrimination (at the least) cannot be the object of public policy, much less the insistence that all lifestyles and assertions be affirmed. We cannot know exactly where disparities traceable to subculture or nature end and disparities traceable to "phobias" begin. When is a country done dismantling a stereotype? The Danish are still beating themselves up about their supposedly homophobic culture because disparities exist. It is tyrannical to demand that one's fellow citizens approve of one's lifestyle or choices, partly for the same reason that sodomy laws are beyond the pale and partly because it risks turning the dispute into the religious dispute. *Lawrence v. Texas* and *Obergefell v. Hodges*, as based on the reigning civil rights ideology, must be overturned if a reasonable society accommodation is to be found. The outcome of *Lawrence*, which declared all anti-sodomy laws unconstitutional, is consistent with the proper outcome for our time and place, but its reasoning tempts toward this tyrannical demand to affirm the lifestyles of each and civil government is prohibited from favoring opposite-sex sex over sodomy through a reading of the equal protection clause; thus the principles of the sexual revolution become a constitutional mandate. That is a bridge way too far in a liberal society. Rule three: dismantling stereotypes cannot be the object of public policy or education.

Laws aimed at rooting out supposed discrimination and supposed stereotypical homophobia—Sexual Orientation and Gender Identity (SOGI) laws—invite abuses that, properly diagnosed, argue for limited government. SOGI laws posit that private and public actions taken by schools, businesses, charities, or other entities that discriminates against people based on their sexual orientation or gender identity would be subject to civil penalties and perhaps, eventually, criminal penalties. The precise character of sexual orientation, however, is somewhat amorphous (just as heresy is somewhat amorphous) and the evidence used to accuse and convict is open to abuse. It can even be trumped up as a species of intimidations—better to remove that temptation from all citizens. Sometimes, perhaps especially in our current environment, accusations are akin to convictions. Disparity-equals-discrimination claims, since they are grounded in incorrect and even tyrannical assumptions, could not, at the least, form the basis for an anti-discrimination policy, even if such a policy could be liberal or open or tolerant.

Can same-sexers and opposite-sexers come to tolerate criticism in the same way atheists and Christians tolerate criticism of one another? The hate speech movement, insofar as it represents same-sexers generally, suggests that the answer is no. If the answer is no, it is traceable to wide acceptance of our reigning civil rights ideology. Public opinion based on our reigning civil rights ideology is a recipe for continual civil disharmony. One must go further. The future of every society depends on fruitful opposite-sex relations. On responsible self-control rests stable marriage and family life and hence not a little of human happiness. Society maintains that preference for a variety of reasons, none of more public importance than the prospect of population decline.[55]

Population Decline and the Policy of Nature

Nearly all countries have total fertility rates below the replacement.[56] The fact that it is a global phenomenon means that the overall trajectory is not traceable to a country's particular situation or complex of laws. China's "One-Child" Policy and Singapore's feminist indoctrination programs may have yielded lowered birthrates more dramatically and quickly than those birthrates have fallen in America or Europe or Iran, but most are falling. The nearly universal nature of this decline provides food for reflection about the nature of human being.[57]

All human choices presuppose a horizon or context, though human beings are not reducible to that context because nature is varied and regimes themselves are complex wholes. As Montesquieu writes, propagation among human beings depends on "the way of thinking, character, passions, fantasies, caprices, the idea of preserving one's beauty, the encumbrance of pregnancy" and many other factors. Women, moreover, as we have seen, tend to be more plastic than men; hence, the idea of what it means to be a woman is more likely to change as women are encouraged to live one way or another. How women rank their options is more a product of honor and shame or "socialization" (as we say today) than it is for men. The more the image of the career-focused independent women is accepted or glorified, the fewer women find their identity and meaning in marriage and motherhood. Nowhere is this more evident than in the Near East, where modernity, careerism, and declining birth rates seem linked in an indissoluble chain.[58]

Feminists generally explain the decline in birth rates as a product of women having choices: the availability of contraception and of higher education for girls came along with steeper declines in birthrates and marriage rates. Let a recent newspaper article stand in for scads of explanations for why feminists celebrate and take credit for the birth dearth. Why the decline in birthrates across the world? "Here's the answer: choices. For the first time in human history, women truly have them. A lot of women don't feel pressured to have kids they don't want. [Here the author cites a quotation from an expert:] 'There's so much out there to help child-free women feel good about themselves, to not feel shamed.'"[59] Women are free enough from the feminine mystique, many have been reared to value careers more than motherhood, and they are now affirmed in finding meaning in creative work of their own in the workplace.

What is a choice? Generally, for modern peoples, a genuine choice proceeds from one's autonomous, undetermined will. Choice implies a prior independence. A choice is affected by no legal pressure, no social pressure, no religious stricture, no incentive structures, no biological imperative, and no habituation or education to shape "proper" choices. Immanuel Kant, the discoverer of it, was skeptical that such a choice could exist in human life,[60] but, he thought, only this choice fully vindicates the principle of human freedom or liberation. Kant is skeptical that human liberation exists because he accepts the standpoint of modern natural science, namely that human beings are shaped in a world of social pressure and biological causes. All human choices seem to be shaped through a social environment or "laws of nature"; it is precisely the dependability of such causes that allows the study of human relations and permits the construction of an environment conducive to human profit.[61] This scientific view is what Montesquieu has in mind when, writing of depopulation, as we have seen, he suggests that having babies depends on ranking "the way of thinking, character, passions, fantasies, caprices, the idea of preserving one's beauty, the encumbrance of pregnancy" and thousands of factors.[62] Kant the philosopher put forward, in effect, two worlds: one, a world of mind or noumenal world where human beings were free; another, a world of social science and things or the phenomenal world where human beings are caused through nature and nurture.

This Kantian formulation of choice as independence and liberation lacks precision. America, and indeed the entire modern world, is where the works of Kant are perhaps least understood, but where the effectual truth of his dichotomous teaching explains or shapes how we think and live. We see this in many guises. In the feminist hope to escape sex and make our own identities unbounded by body we see the desire for independence or autonomy. In the contemporary liberal hope to make government and indeed the culture gender-neutral we see the hope to make the individual independent of all pressures so they can make their own lives. In the contemporary liberal emphasis on consent as the grounding of legitimate relations we see neither the body nor civilization can create an obligation; only one's consent can. Sexual liberationists hope to endorse a plastic sexuality subject only to human will and creativity and to see even a very bodily function in terms of individual spiritual power.

Taken to their logical conclusion the ideas of autonomy and independence point to the idea that human beings are not and cannot be part of an order outside of human will: there is nothing outside human will that human beings serve. Before people discovered this capacity to will, "all the world was mad," as Nietzsche has Zarathustra inform Last Men or all the world was living through a self-imposed immaturity, as Kant puts it. This madness, for Nietzsche's Last Men, was a belief that there was a God or gods, or heroes or a natural order or a political order outside each individual's creative will. With Kant's conception of independence and autonomy comes the idea of historical progress—the idea that we are moving beyond the time when the world was mad or when human beings imposed immaturity upon themselves or even thought there was anything beyond themselves. The past is a place to visit and perhaps even admire, not a fount of wisdom or of motives that produced its most profound works or lives (works which have been exposed as based on illusions). A forceful human will finds itself precisely in overcoming the limits as nature and culture present themselves.

A syndrome of trends connect with the belief in autonomy and its commitment to historical progress.[63] Included among these are the rolling revolution generally; the decline in religious belief and divine law, especially among the most refined; a decline in attachment to the country as a political unit and the rise of a global corporate elite, especially among the refined; the decline of constitutionalism as adherence to a permanent solution to a set of political questions and the corresponding rise in the "Living Constitution"; our fascination with technological progress; the decline of the university and the humanities in particular as repositories of Western civilization's wisdom; and the decline of birthrates to below replacement across the Western world. Talk about a general idea!

Real choice does not come from the proliferation of options or from the elimination of external influences; it comes from aligning one's choices to the goods and the Good available in human life. Among those are responsible work, family life, marriage, service to God, perfection in art, philosophy, and a few other things. For each of these goods there is a season. Children exist outside of one's own will; the obligations and duties people have to their children are grounded above all in the body—in the very bodily acts of procreative sex and the even more athletic event of giving birth. No matter how much human beings seek to control the physical aspect of human procreation, it is biological. No matter how much we sever the relation between sex, procreation, and parenting, it persists and must persist in our ways and is acknowledged in our laws. Our way of handling this tension between our civilization's self-understanding and the reality of children is to bury our heads in the sand: our regime defines our reality and it cannot notice how the body creates obligations. Nature in the old sense fails us because we conceive our nature as overcoming nature in the old sense. Also remarkable is how few pay attention to unprecedented global population decline. Compare the exploding number of monographs written on the lingering problem of patriarchy or even on transphobia with the small number written on the demographic decline. Few even celebrate or acknowledge the reality of this issue. (Perhaps more will take notice when American universities collapse for the failure to have enough students.[64]) Why? Reckoning with the demographic collapse would force people to rethink the foundations of our reigning civil rights regime or our regime as such. That is too painful to imagine.

This is by the by. The First Demographic Transition was when birthrates went down, infant mortality lowered, and mortality itself declined.[65] Children were, according to many, previously sources of labor, but once the demands of labor could be served with fewer children, parents had fewer children. Children thus appear as means of production and retirement plans. The move to cities and the creation of large corporations to harness human power are part of this move away from the raw, primitive world where people had many babies. Contraception is as much an effect of an effort to secure human autonomy as it is a cause of declining birth rates. The Second Demographic Transition is the movement, following the 1960s, to birth rates below replacement rates, abetted through abortion and contraception and marked by the rolling revolution.[66] Later marriage, abortion, contraception, postponing childbearing, at-will divorce, acceptance of living together outside of marriage go together everywhere with population decline—all mark "shifts in values, away from group-oriented values (family, nation) and towards individual, often post-materialist ones in which self-fulfillment is a key goal for most people."[67] Lives of pleasure, not duty.

What is to be done? Proposals to "reverse" the trend of declining birth-rates through economic incentives assume the sufficiency of the human world. Perhaps, as some think,[68] there are environmental problems that have led to a plunge in sperm counts and a crisis in male fertility. Fewer plastics would mean more sperm and hence more children. Perhaps children are expensive, so the state can relieve the cost (how depends on what incentives the proposer thinks will move people).[69] Few of these modest programs do more than nudge the timing of births. "*People cannot be bribed into having babies*."[70] Incentives mediate through values, so trying to leverage birthrates with economic incentives fails to reach people at the level that decisions are really made.

Or perhaps we have not really tried yet. Does not every woman have her price? If demographic collapse calls for greater production of children, per-haps we could pay women sufficiently to encourage breeding and then turn those children into wards of the state, for purposes of education. Perhaps sufficient wages will, eventually, attract sufficient laborers. Pay $100,000 or $1,000,000 or whatever it takes and someone might sign up for such employ-ment. Such a proposal severs the link between procreation and marriage. In removing the norm that parents should have an active role in educating their children, it severs the link between parenthood and education. In mak-ing labor a matter of wages, it removes any expectation of love or sacrifice or enduring, exclusive relations between husband and wife. Peoples do not even conceive of such a policy because they remain, unbeknownst to the regime as a whole, committed to the marital form and its attendant understanding of duties. As an inverse proof of this, birth rates tend to be most robust in places where marital norms are strongest.[71]

Our modern regime is not purely modern (yet!): religious citizens have more children than the nonreligious. According to Jonathan Last, the Republic of Georgia reversed its declining birth rates when Georgia's patriarch prom-ised to baptize children born to parents who already had two children. Amer-ican states with higher weekly church attendance rates have higher birthrates than states with more "secular, enlightened, self-actualized" citizens.[72] Phillip Longman worries that fundamentalist believers are out-procreating secular liberals so that we may be facing a "fundamentalist moment" led by "relent-lessly pro-natal" monotheist religions.[73]

This points the way forward. Successful efforts to reverse declining birth rates require the mixing of the modern regime more generally. Governments cannot and should not order people to have children. Nor should govern-ments create children. Unsuccessful modern programs aimed at increasing fecundity have aimed their benefits at women alone (detached from mar-riage) and at reducing the burdens of parenthood (through government sup-plied day care); let us learn from this lack of success. These approaches fail to move the needle because they are detached from the family form that shapes desire and duty. Mothers and fathers must bear the burdens of motherhood and fatherhood if they are going to take these aspects of life more seriously. Incentives must *reinforce duties* (not relieve them) and the view of the world that accounts for duties. Giving the family more to do (i.e., choose how to educate their children) may be the route to increasing a family's sense of its own responsibility.

Indirection is the policy with the aim of prioritizing some not unnatural desires (such as the desire to have children and the desire to love another human being) in the lives of women and men. To wit, perhaps some combination of the incentive programs predominant in many countries and supporting the marital form could yield results. Governments could forgive student loans or some student loans for graduates who (1) marry and (2) have children before age twenty-six. This would affect the timing of childbirth perhaps, and moving that timing up can increase the amount of time women have to stay married and have children. Governments could also put money in a retirement annuity for those who marry, stay married, and have a certain number of children, two or three. This involves discriminating in favor of the married and fecund. Married couples with a certain number of children could receive housing allowances or other benefits, to offset the high costs of living in a world with so many childless. Laws and regulations that encourage women to have children apart from fathers must be repealed if we are to rebuild a culture indirectly supporting the marital form.[74] When labor shortages arise, governments should refrain from encouraging those who might mind the home and have children (i.e., women) from entering the workforce for the good of the economy. Perhaps such available options would encourage parents to point their children toward more responsible and earlier marital ways during their lifetimes and encourage students and schools to learn how marriage and happiness can go together. Incentives detached from marriage have failed; perhaps incentives attached to marriage will fail less.

Public honoring of marital fecundity also makes sense, though this case is complex and depends on a myriad of factors. Consider the case of Russia. The Soviet Union instituted an honorary medal in 1944 called the "Order of Maternal Glory," including state benefits for women who bore over five children.[75] This policy coincided with a major collapse in the Soviet and then Russian population, one that exceeded normal declines throughout the modern world, suggesting that a paucity of national or political pride has some role in making people sufficiently hopeful to have children. Russia never had a total fertility rate over 1.4 between 1993 and 2006. Russian rates exceeded 1.7 each year from 2012 until 2017, however. Perhaps the general religious revival and national pride (including some revanchism) engaged in by Vladimir Putin combined with his policy of celebrating large families are responsible for the unforeseen, and perhaps temporary, reversal of Russian demography.[76] Putin declared September 12, 2008 "Family Contact Day," where parents could have the day off of work to get it on and nine months later he declared "Russia Day" when those who gave birth received fabulous merchandise, including a washing machine or a brand new car.[77] Parents with more than seven children receive the "Order of Parental Glory" and are invited to the Kremlin to receive the medal from Russia's somewhat popular and feared president.

Penalties for childlessness? They are of ancient provenance, but they do not seem very availing. Caesar Augustus taxed unmarried, aristocratic bachelors. Much the same happened in England. Nor does shaming those who fail to have children seem to move the needle in the modern environment, or at least not in Japan where they tried to stigmatize "parasite singles," jet-setting women who prefer fashion, cats, their own sultry looks and athletic bodies, and careers to marriage and children.[78] (A cat penalty might be passed by a coalition of dog-people and fecund couples.) What is honored matters, but notions of honor and shame cannot be created out of whole cloth: they must comport with human nature and coexist with the horizon. Gentle persuasion toward maternal concerns, backed, perhaps, by art, literature, and evidence, may be a better ticket.

We do well to consider the amazing, unprecedented steep declines in birth rates among East Asian countries. What explains this precipitous drop especially in a segment of the world where family loyalty is thought to be so important? An obvious misfit exists among norms in these countries. On one hand, the culture embraces family and a modified patriarchy. On the other hand, these Asian cultures socialize women toward careerism, fashion, and economic productivity. The contradiction between these cultural norms leads to a marital form that the advanced women shun and the cultivation of women that the relatively traditional, lonely men will neither love nor accommodate. The independent women are not lovable, and the men are not interested. "Asia's looming problem right now is . . . the threat of industrial-scale sexual indifference," as the feminist Rosin writes.[79] Sexual indifference cannot be unrelated to the birth dearth.

Contraception presupposes sexual interest, something we can no longer take for granted. If the Second Demographic Revolution is a problem and that problem is abetted most fundamentally through hormonal contraceptives, then would not limiting access to contraception be a viable option? Contraception is like nuclear weapons in that it cannot be dis-invented or un-discovered. It exists, and making it illegal would simply create an underground market for this much desired good. No legal proscription is then possible or (hence) desirable. Many studies throughout the years have called into question the health and psychological risks of oral contraceptives.[80] This fact is crucial: Only through calling into question the ways of life that have grown up around contraception (rearranging honoring and dishonoring) could the existence of contraception become consistent with a more sustainable total fertility rate and perhaps other human goods. Beauvoir knew that contraception had to be invented and *then honored* for it to be of use; its use depends on the honor attached to the independent woman it promotes.[81] We must revisit Beauvoir's vision of womanly fulfillment through independence , as it has become one of our most sacred, unquestioned opinions.

The religious believer/atheist and same-sex/opposite-sex conflicts inform our thinking about this problem of honoring and dishonoring types of women. Can women dedicated first and foremost to mothering and women dedicated first and foremost to careers coexist peacefully in a society? Yes! What one woman does need not affect what other women do; private choices should be made privately and according to an individual's choice; we can celebrate both. "Every mother works hard, and every woman deserves to be respected," as a politico's wife once said. Second-wave feminists themselves rejected such a "live and let live attitude," thinking that there was no neutral ground on this matter. Beauvoir writes: "What is extremely demoralizing for the woman who aims at self-sufficiency is the existence of other women of like social status, having at the start the same situation and the same opportunities, who live as parasites."[82] Why else were traditional women labeled "the second sex"? Contented, married women present temptations to those aspiring toward self-sufficiency; it is not easy to resist the temptations of a maternal culture or, perhaps, one's nature. On the same score, women who put mothering first may, on some level, see career-oriented women as forfeiting valuable human experiences that define contentment. When career-oriented women are most visible and honored in public opinion, mothers to some extent will feel left behind or less than beautiful; career-oriented women are left seeing their sisters as "only mothers," not achieving true humanity and choice. As women's pride and identity—indeed, as her vanity—is invested in a career, looks, and personal independence, and as men are no longer viewed as important for providing or for love, as women wait longer to have children and to marry (but still want to have children and marry, perhaps) but still seek to make themselves attractive in the eyes of others, pregnancy will not fit so easily into their life plans. When mothering predominates, career-oriented women are subject to suspicions and sniping from their maternity-minded sisters; the maternal may even gently call the womanhood, apparent happiness, and the priorities of their careerist sisters into question.

These and other hostilities are bound to exist between these two sets of women. The tension also exists in the souls of many women as they navigate these poles of womanly existence in the late modern republic. One sees this deeper conflict superficially in the different voting patterns of married women with children and unmarried, childless women throughout the Western world: those primarily concerned with creating and sustaining another generation act and think differently from those interested in improving the world through public action or themselves through meaningful careers or whatever.

Tolstoy depicts this confrontation between two visions of womanhood vividly in *Anna Karenina*. Anna begins the book as a happily married mother, who befriends and even leads her sister-in-law Dolly, a mother of seven who has, as the French saying goes, let herself go, back to her marriage; Dolly's husband has cheated on her and Anna saves their marriage (such as it is). After Anna commits adultery, gains a new set of womanly friends, leaves her husband, jet-sets to Italy with Vronsky (her lover), shuns her duties as a mother and lives a life of womanly independence (such as it was before human resource departments), Dolly comes to visit her on her estate to show her loyalty and love for Anna.[83] Dolly worries, as she travels, about her children, and seems to regret all that she has sunk into her troubled life as a mother, even comically envisioning herself once again being the object of amorous attentions, inspired, no doubt, by Anna's dazzling, full life. Dolly plans to stay for a spell. Yet her visit lasts only a matter of days, because her ways and Anna's are incompatible: Dolly cannot respect Anna for her vanity, her farming out of maternal duties to a series of nurses, her emphasis on worldly projects such as a hospital, and Anna's use of contraception. Her discovery of Anna's use of contraception "leads to consequences and deductions so enormous that at the first moment one only feels that it is impossible to take it all in."[84] Anna is miserable (sleeping only with *morphia*). Dolly is insulted at Anna's betrayal, and she is convinced that Anna's misery reflects well on her own complicated domestic life. Anna and the doting mother cannot sustain friendship if they take their visions seriously. Do these different kinds of women form and keep friendships today? There is bound to be not a little animosity between such women, and few intimate friendships: this opposition seems to be more fundamental even than the opposition between same-sex and opposite-sex ways.

The ideology of liberalism professes the untruth that society can cultivate both kinds of women at the same time. Feminism professes the superiority of the career-oriented, independent woman, and our education is mostly feminist. Public necessity and possibly human happiness require a different public opinion. No solution to this conflict of public honor can exist without first reestablishing the truths about sex and gender discussed in chapter 5: differences between men and women persist and add genuine joys to human life for most human beings. Public opinion must take its bearings from these manifest tendencies and help each sex to realize its for-the-most-part universal traits.

Certain things would henceforth be expected and celebrated instead of lamented and condemned. For instance, cross-cultural studies show that most women prefer part-time employment, while most men prefer full-time employment; this gap widens as people and political communities become wealthier.[85] Practice follows this preference as well. Full-time work for women is less likely to be a positive good than part-time work, and when women work full-time it is more likely to be tolerated as a necessity. It seems unlikely that we are matching our career preparation for girls and women to the reality that many more women would rather enjoy part-time work and working with people and fewer actually desire the rat race of highly competitive jobs, whether they have children or not. A more prudent and satisfying policy to accommodate this sex difference might involve encouragement to create part-time jobs, on the assumption that women will probably fill most of these as time goes on. A new social bargain would be necessary: feminists would not complain about the pay gap (which would remain, as today, in its raw form when not controlled for work experience and longevity) or about pigeonholing women into caring, allegedly meaningless or menial work, and men would not complain that women are freed from clocks and the burdens of a job that never gets put down. This is the way of life that the upper classes generally lead in America and in much of the West, but that they are loath to celebrate amidst their dreams that "leaning in" makes a better life. Part-time work could replace universal day care as the object of public policy debates. Let us praise part-time work, instead of seeing it as a sell-out or failure.

One must go further. With the advances in feminism come paradoxical declines in female happiness and with advances in the workplace and in female pay comes less life satisfaction.[86] Many factors contribute to these relative and sometimes absolute declines in happiness and the ballooning use of antidepressants, but let me suggest one: women are more plastic than men, and this means that they imbibe social cues more than men; when social cues contradict important natural aspirations, people are dissatisfied. The idea that every disparity equals discrimination informs our ways of counseling many young women today—toward more engineering, toward making law partner, toward the ambition to have a corner office (but never plumbing, for some reason). What this means, however, is that more than a few women will pursue fulfilling career ambitions, but leave those professions or leave their ambitions behind once they achieve their goal. Women leave engineering careers at two to three times the rates of men. Women are more than 50% of law school graduates in America, but fewer than 20% make law partner. The sexual paradox is that men and women choose differently in an atmosphere of freedom. No solution to this conflict of public honor can exist without putting happiness and fulfillment, as opposed to power and discrimination, at the center of reflections about human life, and acknowledging that men and women for the most part pursue happiness and fulfillment differently.

A significant majority of women will act differently than most men if they are free to do so, whether or not the women are married or have children. One of the ways they will, in general, act differently is that they will prioritize close relationships (including family) over monetary ways—and they are happier if they do. Any solution to the birth dearth means celebrating the grooves that limit the ambitions of feminism.

Toward a New Modern Family

Nature is durable, as conservatives never tire of reminding us (usually quoting Horace). Nature is corruptible too and nature is not enough, since nature depends on healthy mores and can go in several directions. Equally problematical is the belief that it is all mores all the way down, and that nature provides no grooves for human life—this is the problem manifest among the rolling revolutionaries. What we want out of nature is always a matter of public reflection and priority—a truth that confounds the revolution and qualifies tradition.

No state is neutral on the goods promoted through its family policy. No state can resign itself to whatever sexual practices its population might happen to have. The public aspect of private desire demands attention directed toward the long-term health of the political community and the happiness of its citizens. A long-term healthy policy of indirection, informed by our womanism and skeptical that the sexual revolution has given an adequate account of sexual desire, serves the goods associated with the enduring, fecund marital form. The "pure relationship" would not be honored. Civil society and government must encourage procreation through its laws and through its public honoring. Our new sexual regime must resemble the old in its mores, if not in its laws. Support from the laws, where possible, would not be superfluous.

10

CHOOSING ONE'S CHOICE

Consent's Incomplete Guidance for Public Policy

All rolling revolutionaries appeal to consent as providing a standard to guide private relations in a liberal society. Feminists want women to have an expanding array of lifestyle options ranging from an openness to careers to marital and sexual choices, and ultimately to an undetermined will freed from socialization and anatomy. Contemporary liberals hold that all relations based on consent are equally legitimate and that no public pressure to choose one thing over another is legitimate; consent emerges as *the* neutral principle to guide relations under contemporary liberalism. Sexual liberationists baptize sexual relationships between consenting adults, with the thinking that less pressure to choose exclusive opposite-sex sex (i.e., bourgeois sex) rather than other forms of sex would remain as time goes on.

Widespread public agreement about consent masks deep, important disagreement over what consent means. Consent is not a neutral principle after all, since the question about consent is over when and whether a "yes" or a "no" *really* reflects a person's consent. Consent contributes to the rolling revolution in three intertwining ways.[1] First, rolling revolutionaries see culture and nature compromising consent. A "yes" or a "no" can be shaped by one's education, religious beliefs, societal norms, socialization, or even one's body. A "shaped" choice is, from the standpoint of rolling revolutionaries, not genuine freedom, since a subtle power external to one's will informs the choice. The only freedom worthy of its name reflects a choice proceeding from one's undetermined will.

One is genuinely free to marry, for instance, only when marriage has no public status higher than non-marriage or drinking a soda pop.

Second, for rolling revolutionaries who insist on our reigning civil rights ideology, all disparities reflect compromised consent. This idea assumes that a society of consenting adults, free of external forces, would be a fifty-fifty society, a society with no disproportionate inequalities between supposed victim groups and the supposed dominant culture. The reigning civil rights regime and the rolling revolution prefer genuine consent (which should result in a fifty-fifty world) to apparent consent (where differences only appear chosen). There is always a temptation toward social engineering in the name of consent because we can know authentic consent only when no disparities exist between the sexes (for instance). It's all social engineering anyway; we might as well socially engineer an egalitarian, genuinely free society where individuals can consent. Or so the radical argument for "consent" goes.

Third, for rolling revolutionaries, previous choices cannot constrain subsequent choices. Human beings have choice; they must continually re-will their choices in order for such choices to be genuinely theirs. Continuous consent is especially needed as people come to understand how their "choices" are shaped through culture and nature. Education involves the eclipse of the old, seemingly determined self and the rise of a new, seemingly liberated self, and the freedom to announce and act upon one's independence. The allegiances and duties contracted under a previous self (say, a choice to marry or to pursue a profession) cannot bind a new self without alienating one's will and forfeiting this liberation.

The seemingly modest and neutral principle, consent, as understood by rolling revolutionaries, unsettles preexisting relations; unsettles love, virtue, and family life; and presents a partial, inhuman vision of human being. Taken to its logical conclusion, continuous consent presents the view, adverted to in the previous chapter, that there is nothing outside human will that human beings serve and that there is nothing outside the human will that can, legitimately, make us what we are; only what human beings have themselves made is worthy of human respect.

Human experiences like birth, death, and sleeping refute the sufficiency of liberation so understood. Human beings literally do not make themselves; life is bestowed upon each of us. Human beings die, though they can put it off and affect its timing. Other experiences limit and define a human life. Against feminism, human being is embodied and our cultural and personal ideas of "gender" never can be divorced from bodily sex, a biological reality. Against contemporary liberalism, all laws embody some controversial moral position; hence arguments about what goods our laws serve are inseparable from political life just as political life is part of human life. Human beings do not invent happiness or morality: there are a limited number of human goods toward which human beings strive. Against sexual revolutionaries, sexual desire and sex without a body is absurd; and almost all people think about whether they are doing the right thing in matters sexual, even under conditions of liberation. Human beings are free to choose in some sense, but not in the sense that our rolling revolutionaries think. "No limits!" the revolutionaries assert. No. Know limits!

Rejection of consent as rolling revolutionaries understand it does not send me careening into the position where all people are simply determined by culture or nature or where there are no illegitimate disparities traceable to cultural oppression or where no human choices can be revisited. Consent presupposes some realistic number of options for human beings and the ability to pull oneself out of the stream of nature and culture and make reasonable decisions for one's life. Consenting adults survey and serve many human goods and ways of life as they approach their lives, and their eyes are, to varying degrees, open to what goods they are pursuing. Consenting adults live in a particular time and place, so their options and ways are limited. Consent does not oppose education—institutions and mores always arise to deal with birth and death just as they arise to deal with sex. Genuine consent, recognizing limits, opposes force, fraud, and artificial burdens, but its lineaments cannot be drawn precisely. How many realistic options must one have to consent? How much must one govern one's will through reason to have consent? What goods can one pursue or how much must one know about those goods before one can finally say that consent is achieved?

Questions over the meaning and demands of consent persist while our public deals with a host of issues implicating consent. We have laws about the age of consent (i.e., at what age people can assent to sex and marriage), rape (i.e., how to know when people consent to sex), and divorce (i.e., how people remove consent from marriage). Rolling revolutionaries have, in some cases, reformed laws consistent with notions of consent implicit in the ideas of a radical notion of liberation. Laws, as they currently exist, reflect, at best, a mixture of the rolling revolution and the durable consent and "shaped" consent recognizing human limits. It could hardly be otherwise. Statutory rape laws have changed, but are not overly revolutionized (yet!). Rape laws are being revolutionized. Divorce laws have changed more completely than the others. What do each of these areas of law seek to accomplish? What should shape law and mores on these topics?

Consent and Rape

Stephen J. Schulhofer, an architect in the latest rape reform laws (affirmative consent laws), testifies to the reciprocal relationship between law and culture. "Law itself influences society's view of what sexual abuse is," Schulhofer writes in *Unwanted Sex: The Culture of Intimidation and the Failure of Law* (1998), "and the relationships between law and culture are complex. Social attitudes sometimes control legal outcomes, but those attitudes are shaped in turn by legal rules."[2] Exactly so. We begin to make ourselves what we want to be through laws, though laws must take into account who we are. Rape law is a question of social value, Schulhofer rightly begins. It is a question of great human interest to determine what social values anti-rape laws should serve.

Rolling revolutionaries disagree among themselves about what to accomplish through rape laws. Feminist revolutionaries think all or most sex is rape if patriarchy persists. Not absent in Beauvoir's or Firestone's work, Catherine MacKinnon articulates this position with the greatest clarity. "Rape," she writes, "is defined as distinct from intercourse, while for women it is difficult to distinguish the two under conditions of male dominance."[3] Conditions of patriarchy exude subtle social coercion just as brute force does. Men possess status, economic power, and the expectation that they will take the initiative, and women are taught to be sex objects, to acquiesce, and to like it.[4] Women cannot resist sexual advances and survive or thrive. Opinions hold women down and get them to lie down. Andrea Dworkin runs with this line of argument:

> Men have social, economic, political, and physical power over women. Some men do not have all those kinds of power over all women; but all men have some kinds of power over all women; and most men have controlling power over what they call *their* women. . . . The power is predetermined by gender, by being male. . . . Intercourse remains a means or the means of physiologically making women inferior.[5]

Sex under conditions of male privilege expresses male tyranny. Marriage enshrines patriarchy, so marital sex is coerced. Economic and social disparities reflect patriarchy, so sex is subtly or not-so-subtly coerced outside of marriage too. Free love is not free, under patriarchy. A radical restructuring of the world may eliminate disparities between men and women inside and outside of marriage and that could make sex genuinely consensual, but, barring that, evidence of sex seems sufficient to prove rape. Only a world beyond gender could be genuinely beyond rape.

Other rolling revolutionaries admire such forceful, blunt reasoning. Schulhofer thinks it may "represent the dominant strand in feminist thought about rape" and is full of "insight" and is "well intentioned." Schulhofer continues:

> Feminists *rightly* stress the distortions of women's preference and deplore the interference with autonomy that result from cultural pressure, economic dependency, and women's justified fears of violence

from male strangers. Feminists *rightly* note that under these conditions, women's consent to sex, even when given to a trusted, nonthreatening male friend, may not be the result of a true and authentic choice."[6]

Schulhofer nevertheless objects to these feminist notions. All sex before the Beatles' first LP or so may have been rape. With the advances in feminism "we can no longer be certain that women's desires and choices are inauthentic." Progress has, apparently, been made in creating women's independence and hence space for women's freedom and choice. These successes complicate the feminist definition of rape. Workable laws must draw distinctions between different kinds and degrees of pressure.[7] Yet Schulhofer goes further than these piddling criticisms. The rolling revolution, he seems to think, is ill conceived. "We cannot expect (even in theory) that a person's preferences can be entirely self-generated, because complex preferences, beyond the basic appetites for food, shelter, and sexual release, can hardly form at all in the absence of social influence."[8] Those who demand undetermined individual will are, it appears, unreasonable and inhuman. Perhaps consent can be shaped and rape laws must recognize this. Know limits?

For Schulhofer, autonomy does not, strictly speaking, exist. Socialization matters and makes human things possible. Pressure and expectations shape actions within relationships and marriages. Power disparities do not mean relationships are coercive and perhaps differences are not just about power relations—and women can manipulate men as men can manipulate women. Men and women universally, for the most part, approach sexual relations differently, men taking the initiative and women using suggestive, indirect ways of indicating their interest; men more interested in sating desires, women more interested in forming bonds.[9] "No," per Schulhofer, may mean "yes" or "go slower" or "try harder" or "not yet, but keep going."[10] Deception and self-deception are hardly unknown in affairs of the heart and flesh. The line between good and evil runs through the heart of all men and women. (This is an impressive list of obstacles to achieving an enduring love with another. Parts of the despised sexual regime, including its respect for modesty and its buckling of sex to marriage, arose to ameliorate these tendencies.) Schulhofer, reasonably enough, uses the list to show the limits of autonomy as feminists understand it.

What then should guide rape policy, for Schulhofer? His lodestar is *sexual autonomy*, surprisingly, given his deconstruction of it. "Sexual autonomy" is a "legal entitlement" with "three distinct dimensions." Sexual autonomy involves (1) "an internal capacity to make reasonably mature and rational choices"; (2) "an external freedom from impermissible pressures and constraints"; and (3) "the separateness of the corporeal person" (i.e., respect for the bodily integrity of the other person).[11] Schulhofer's sexual autonomy can provide guidance once we find acceptable definitions of "reasonably," "impermissible," and "respect." We will have to reason backwards from his proposal.

Current rape laws, which I call the "totality of circumstances" approach, fail to recognize sexual autonomy sufficiently on these scores. As Schulhofer presents it, current law asks whether, given all the relevant circumstances, sex is forced upon the victim or is the result of willing consent. The devil is in the details. Before 1950, proving rape meant proving that a woman put up the utmost resistance. Those alleging rape also were subject to character witnesses who could impeach the woman's veracity or tendency to have sex with little commitment on the assumption that it was easier to excuse men with a woman of easy virtues. Victims had to corroborate their accusation with evidence such as promptly reporting the crime or physical bruises. These three planks were toned down after the advances of feminism, but the general framework emphasizing all relevant circumstances remains. "Active resistance," indicating to a reasonable person a woman's lack of consent, suffices today. Rape shield laws (passed during the 1970s) limit inquiries into women's sexual past, but a women's and a man's actions prior to the encounter are used to determine whether a reasonable person could infer consent, so juries can have access to some prior actions in forming judgments about what happened. Corroboration is easier so long as accusations are made in a timely way.[12] Such an approach, revising previous law but sticking within its confines, purports to vindicate each party: a woman may falsely accuse and manipulate while men may misread a woman's indirect signals or to take what he wants against right.

Schulhofer and other seemingly moderate feminists think that this approach yields too few accusations and convictions and that it does not properly shape the culture toward feminist ends. "No" does not always mean "no" under the "totality of circumstances" system—that is its failure though it is a truth; and this old system therefore encourages men to persist and override and perhaps force and it allows women to be coy. That system accommodates gender stereotypes. Furthermore, as the principles of sexual liberation inform the attitudes of girls and women, the volume and ambiguities of sexual encounters multiply. Compare the hookup culture of casual sex to the old courtship regime. Under the old regime, women were less frequently in compromising positions: being in the compromising position was seen as rebuttable evidence of a willingness to engage; going up to a man's hotel room invites more than playing pinochle in the lobby. A woman's caution and modesty, under this old system, reflected worries about male sexual desire and invited attempts to harness it toward warmer, perhaps marital relations.

According to our rolling revolution, girls and women no longer grant sexual access as part of exclusive avenue to marriage, love, and commitment, while men must govern their lust through the private, individualized assent of their partner. What guides assent of women and girls under these conditions? Answer: Whatever they choose. Imagine the situation of a young woman. She is taught that she has a right to sex as she wants it, with no duties to her family, God, her church, her community, or the man. There is no official public teaching about what she should want out of sex or life or about how sex should fit into her life, which means that there is no support for her "no." No social rules or expectations like readiness for marriage or love are guiding their wills. Passion, attraction, personal need, vanity, whim, convenience, future relations, a desire for pleasure, a desire for acceptance and a weighing of social goods guide her sexual actions, in shifting proportions. Sometimes she may not even know her own will or her will is confused. In any event, in many cases, women must today explain their "no," without reference to widely accepted answers. A girl cannot as easily say, with the assistance of social support, "I am saving myself for marriage," or even, "I am saving myself for love," under conditions of sexual liberation. Imagine the situation of a young man too. He thinks about sex a lot, and he is also taught that the differences between girls and boys are negligible or socially constructed. This must mean that girls too think about sex as much as he does. He too is taught that people are entitled to sexual freedom, with the exception of rape, of course. Throw in a little alcohol, co-educational dormitories, and withdrawn parental supervision, and the hookup culture, with its ambiguities, emerges.

What provides guidance under these circumstances? For Schulhofer it is sexual autonomy, which, as he thinks, demands affirmative consent laws. Affirmative consent laws demand, according to Schulhofer's model legislation, that there will be "actual words or conduct indicating affirmative, freely given permission" to sexual intercourse. "Silence, ambiguous behavior, and the absence of a clearly expressed *un*willingness are evidence that affirmative consent was absent." Ambiguities mean rape. Verbal or written communication is especially an indication of affirmative consent. This is a bit stifling, perhaps, so Schulhofer loosens up. "Unambiguous body language" would "signal affirmative consent." *Not* included among unambiguous body language is "heavy sexual petting" (which is no more suggestive of sexual interest, Schulhofer thinks, than "inviting a man in for a cup of coffee"). Nor does intense sexual foreplay count. Does oral sex count? Does disrobing with an intent to arouse count? He proffers no example of "unambiguous body language."[13] Partners (read: women) can remove consent at any time during sex or the run up to sex. Affirmative consent laws thus reflect the idea of continuous consent, a continually revisited and revisitable "yes."

Sex with a woman who says, "No," is rape. Sex with a woman who remains silent is rape, unless it is accompanied by unambiguous affirmative body language. Sex with an explicit "yes" or accompanied by unambiguous (yet unspecified) affirmative body language is lawful.[14] No decent human being living in a decent society would analyze rape laws in detail, but, as we live when we live we must seek to understand and know. (I will have more opportunities to offend the protocols of decency.) Affirmative consent laws are based on continuous consent—consent can be withdrawn at any time and whatever happens on the other side of the withdrawal is rape. This is the import of Schulhofer's claim that heavy petting and foreplay say as much and as little about one's intentions as having a cup of coffee together. Let us take an example from real life. A drunk man and woman go into a private room. They undress each other. Each is aroused. The woman performs fellatio. The man thinks she would like to go all the way. He puts her on her back and begins to thrust and to penetrate her, the wind-up and the pitch. She moans with plea-sure. After winding up and pitching a few times, the woman comes to have regrets and says "no." She has withdrawn consent, as is her right under the logic of affirmative consent. Does any wind-up and pitch after her withdrawal of consent become rape? Even, let us say, one pitch after the unexpected no? That pitch was unwanted, after all.

Continuous consent sees no logic to sexual encounters that cannot be suspended through an autonomous, creative act of the will. Even the staunch-est advocates of affirmative consent laws would probably not call the situation that I have described rape. Why? They accept *some* notion of durable consent, where past actions bind or limit future ones. They must accept that sex has a logic, otherwise one would need affirmative consent to each wind-up and pitch. Some stable invitation is presumed in sex. The word foreplay suggests that some acts are part of a sexual dance that comes before. Rape laws cannot defy the logic of sex. "Heavy sexual petting" indicates more of a willingness to engage than "inviting a man in for a cup of coffee." Identifying precisely where it is reasonable to draw this line cannot be divorced from the "totality of the circumstances"; juries should be involved in making such judgments.

Affirmative consent laws legislate morality: "*Any* legal rule will favor some of these women over others," Schulhofer writes, "Inevitably, the law must choose sides."[15] Affirmative consent laws purport to bridge sex differences in communication: men must clarify any previously ambiguous intentions, while women must drop the coy, indirect ways of relaying their intentions and come to know and articulate their own wills. Men must worry about being bold and taking the initiative, while women must be bolder. As journalist Ezra Klein writes, "To work, 'Yes Means Yes' needs to create a world where men are afraid."[16] Perhaps when becoming the active, controlling partner women can provide unambiguous body language (e.g., hopping on top), since lying in the "posture of defeat" provides only ambiguous body language.

Affirmative consent laws are instruments to combat "the culture of intim-idation" (Schulhofer's subtitle). Schulhofer thus joins feminists MacKinnon and Dworkin in seeing rape as an example of sexual harassment, a broader concept. Reforming rape laws is part of combating the broader and deeper, more controlling imposition of male power over women. "Sexual harassment," MacKinnon writes, "eroticizes women's subordination. . . . It acts out and deepens the powerlessness of women as a gender, *as women*."[17] Elsewhere: "The entire structure of domination," MacKinnon writes, "the tacit relations of deference and command, can be present in a passing glance" or in a compliment that she looks beautiful in a dress. As a practical matter, putting an end to the "culture of intimidation" requires ending the "hostile environment," with women and victims as judges of the hostility. Precautions must be made to restructure sexual relations, as Daphne Patai catalogs in her survey of sexual harassment training manuals. Stereotyped perceptions, for instance, are sexual harassment because they intimate that a woman may not want to do something or might not be good at something. A one-time overture can create a hostile environment for the woman who rejects the overture or the one who accepts; a compliment is beyond the pale—it may make a woman feel as if she is a woman and hence different from a man. A joke with sexual implications could be grounds for dismissal. Training and policing against sexual harassment must start early, with the hope of creating a welcoming culture.[18]

We have an unprecedented situation, with males and females freely mingling at school, at university, and in the workplace. What rules should govern their mutual relations? Feminism has provided "sexual harassment" as the answer. Everyone is equal and the same; those who act as if difference is present are subject to remedial action. When men act like cads (who can deny that they sometimes do?), they violate equality and become sexual harassers. Men acting in accord with the ways of gentlemen and who would treat women as ladies will also frown upon caddish behavior and would not defend it. The gentleman, however, can be caught in the same web as the cad—he "harasses" when he compliments a coworker or opens a door. The sexual harassment revolution provides a big question mark for the idea of male as initiator and female as evaluator and chooser. Women now are also encouraged to accuse and sue, and sensitivity training helps them to identify when they are singled out as members of a sex. When people (read: men) recognize sexual difference or when a man has sexual desire for a woman, he is asserting power[19]—and hence he is contributing to a hostile environment indistinguishable, in principle, from rape or sexual violence.[20]

Rape and sexual harassment are not crimes of one half of humanity against the other—this is among the ploys used to show that a problem is an "epidemic" or a "crisis" that demands a restructuring of human relations. All exercises of power or experiences of inequality are on the same level, on this theory. This reduces male-female and sexual relations to *power relations*. It denigrates the private life and realities such as love, building a community, pleasure, attraction, and family. There is no route through the sexual harassment ideology or affirmative consent policies toward a better, more mutually respectful society: it leads instead to a breakdown of trust and initiative; it sows suspicion between the sexes, it encourages false accusations as a means to achieve a modicum of self-respect, and it praises and cultivates ever-thinner, more sensitive skin. Such laws encourage female vanity and indulge female narcissism, while punishing male initiative and cultivating fear. What is more, those taken with the sexual harassment ideology, a growing minority of the population, are as unlikely to achieve community and self-respect as they are to achieve happiness.

I say little about the problem, prominent today, that the movement from "beyond a reasonable doubt" standard for guilt in cases of rape to a "totality of circumstances" standard constitutes something akin to a witch trial on campuses, or the other problems associated with due process.[21] At stake in the question of affirmative consent (as in the case of sexual harassment) is what the problem is and whether women should implicitly be trusted with accusations and whether characteristics of each sex demand such a fundamental restructuring of our world. The totality of the circumstances approach defines rape better than the new affirmative consent law. Blackstone sees rape as a crime against persons and defines rape as "carnal knowledge of a woman forcibly and against her will."[22] Before Christian and English law on this, as Blackstone tells it, the Romans counted on the honor of men and presumed women were seducers—so incidents of rape (hardly unknown to the Romans) rarely led to charges. The English code, informed through Christianity, presumed that either the women could seduce or make "malicious accusations," or the man may ravish against a woman's will: it therefore marked a "liberalization" of Roman law, though they assumed that both men and women could go wrong and a jury must sift through the whole circumstances to identify guilt.[23]

Affirmative consent laws presume the deterioration of mores consistent with a reasonable, human idea of consent, and they overpromise protections that are best advanced through mores harnessing sexual difference and through marital forms. Healthy mores recognize male initiative and its associated virtues and vices and provide moral support for women to say, "No," by encouraging respectful behavior from men and modesty among women. Such mores condemn rakes, cads, or libertines, and recognize the difference in sexual interest between men and women. They accept the logic of sex, so that all know what a compromising position is (for instance). Many bromides are inconsistent with this Old Wisdom.

Affirmative consent laws are not ignoble attempts to provide support for women to say, "No": her "yes" being sought explicitly will make her consent, pure and simple, the trigger for sex; being asked directly, she will be more likely to say, "No." Or so goes the reasoning. More than a few studies on sexual relations, common sense, and great literature show that community support for the saying of, "No," for the sake of a woman's honor or chastity or virtue or personal integrity or building a loving relation is a great help. Women for the most part tend to like such mores or at least to dislike their opposite. Such a community is inimical to rolling revolution, but there are resources sufficient in the differences of the sexes (see chapter 5), in what we value as a civilization (chapter 6), and in the nature of sexual desire (chapter 7) that make such a different public teaching desirable. Rape is a crime against bodily integrity different from being punched in the nose, as I argued in chapter 7, because it involves something that strikes closer to the heart of deep personal meaning. Fighting it most effectively requires the Old Wisdom that sex is special because it is related to love and through love to personal integrity and marital community.

Love and the Age of Consent

Two feminist tendencies complicate rape law: the MacKinnonite tendency to see individuals as products of patriarchy that compromises individual consent points to the impossibility of consent; and the more moderate tendency of affirmative consent advocates to social engineer through an explicit, ultimately untenable idea of continuous consent. Questions about statutory rape and the age of consent are more fundamental; they force our attention toward what we expect to get out of consent. Age of consent laws, prevalent in every American state and in all countries of the world, set an age or an age disparity for when sexual conduct is *ipso facto* considered rape.

Radical feminists such as Firestone see childhood sexual independence as crucial to the rolling revolution. Recall that Firestone thinks women will not be free until the family is abolished. Modern mothers task themselves with rearing children. This requires supervision to cultivate self-control, including sexual self-control. Only when mothers learn to let go and liberate their children are they free from motherhood. Liberation includes a willingness to tolerate and encourage childhood sex.[24] This feminist world would, presumably, be shorn of statutory rape laws or fornication laws. Sexual liberation leads to the same place. Since repression causes rape and other distortions, the elimination of repressive laws concerning childhood sex is consistent with genuine sexual liberation.

The leading edges of the rolling revolution point to the eclipse of statutory rape laws and an open embrace of childhood sexuality. Is there not a manifest tendency in this direction? A time traveler, dropped from almost anywhere in history, would be surprised at the sexualization of children in late modernity—and at the fact that sexual education is now the responsibility of the state whose emphasis is safe sex and consent. Movements encouraging ever younger teenagers to become comfortable with their bodies and to

experiment with them proceed. Expecting sexual experimentation and exploration from kids, the emphasis on positive body image in education, the easy
access and widespread use of pornography at earlier and earlier ages—these
aspects, I say, of progress in sexual liberation are evident from scientific studies and our own eyes.[25] Will our advanced society identify a stopping point
and keep enforcing an age of consent?[26]

Such laws could fade away. Enforcement of age of consent laws could
become laxer than the letter of the law, until such laws fall into desuetude much
like fornication and adultery laws. Then laws would be revised downward. But
we still treat statutory rape differently from run-of-the-mill physical assault.
There is something special about sex, as we noted above. There is something
special about children too. People are still outraged when high school teachers, for instance, have sexual relationships with their students, even when it
is female teachers preying on boys. The law prosecutes such actions. Scandals
within the Catholic Church also show that people remain opposed to pedophilia chic and older men of the cloth preying on young boys.[27]

Part of today's support for statutory rape laws comes from within the
idea of consent itself. Statutory rape laws and laws surrounding the age of
consent for marriage are part of a slew of laws that made young age a disabil-
ity for entering into *any* contractual obligation, marriage, or sexual relations.
Youths lack the discretion, judgment, and moral independence to decide
upon entering into marriage. This logic covers sexual relations.[28] Children did
not know enough and were too vulnerable to being dependent and manipulated to assume that a child's consent is genuine. Statutory rape laws may
allow informed consent, based on independence, to govern without judging
how sexual desire is directed. Sexual desire must be directed independently
without any influence from outside of a person's own will, and children are
not mature enough to be independent and to have their own will.

Changes in the approach to statutory rape and age of consent do not
upset this view. In the beginning, there were age of consent laws, proscribing
sex and marriage with those under a particular age. At first, in early parts of
the last millennium, that age was set around 12, but in the early part of the
1900s the age was raised to 16–18 in most of the Western world. The assumptions in these laws are manifold. Liberal critics of such laws often suggest,[29]
mistakenly, in my view, that these laws were designed to protect youthful vir-
ginity, valued more then than now, for marriage. More likely is this. In the
beginning, ages of consent for sex relate to ages of consent for marriage, since
marriage was buckled to sex. Age of consent thus shifted up with the age of
marriage, always with the proviso that the married were not covered by the
law.[30] The law enforced and reflected the norm buckling sex and marriage.
Fornication laws covered sex among the unmarried, while statutory rape and
seduction laws covered instances where adults seduced children. Seductive

women on the boundary of adulthood were "jailbait," as the old slang goes, luring men to jail with their siren looks and invitations. When second-wave feminists sought to unbuckle sex from marriage through, among other things, making contraception widely available, American jurisdictions reformed laws relating to statutory rape. Beginning in the 1970s, states jettisoned "gendered" language in their statutes and jettisoned an age of consent approach for age disparity approaches to statutory rape (sex by someone 18 with someone under 16 or 15, depending on the jurisdiction, is a misdemeanor; with someone under 12 a felony, for instance) partly because they thought age difference implied power difference.[31]

While our respect for genuine consent or independence partly explains our adherence to statutory rape, it cannot explain the whole. Consider some variations on the theme (again let me remind the reader that no decent human being, living in a decent society, would raise these questions). Everywhere in the modern world sexbots are available for purchase, yet more than a few jurisdictions prohibit the selling of child-like sexbots. On what grounds are such laws permissible? Such practices do not compromise the independence, consent, or moral independence of human children. Society could continue to prosecute men who purchased child sexbots when and if they turned their passions to actual children: anti-child sexbot laws could not survive the liberal wringer. People also treat access to pornography for children differently than access to pornography for adults, and see child pornography (even digital child pornography) as especially problematical and proscribe it accordingly. Each of these cases show that there is something about childhood itself that justifies the special protection of the laws.

The sanitized language of statutory rape should not blind us from the broader, deeper issue of pedophilia, the sexual attraction that some adults (especially adult men) have for children (especially boys). The prohibition on the selling of child sexbots shows that we think pedophilia is bad for the adult in question, just as we think children watching or participating in pornography is bad for adults. None of the cases can be explained by the principle of consent alone. Pedophilia is a taboo, like many others, and we might still be able to say that pedophiles are perverts. It is not their exercise of power that offends: it is their enthusiasm for violating the innocent, for treating sex entirely apart from love or its potential growth, that marks them out for censure and jail.

No one portrayed this issue better than Thomas Mann in *Death in Venice*, a novella where an aristocratic Gustav von Aschenbach becomes progressively more obsessed with Tadzio, a young Polish boy. Gustav follows the beautiful boy around Venice, dreams about his erotic attraction to Tadzio, and idealizes the innocent boy as a Greek god dedicated to innocence and beauty. At the moment that Gustav believes Tadzio is inviting him to swim in the sea, Gustav cannot arise from his beach chair—he dies suddenly from a bout of cholera sweeping through Venice. Though Gustav and Tadzio never speak or touch in the book, Gustav's passion for the young boy is degrading to him and reveals why he is lonely, incapable of love, commitment, or transcending his passion. Mann's portrait of modern decadence puts pedophilia, though never consummated, at its center. Gustav's voyeurism is as deadly and as disturbing as his hoped-for relation with the boy.

Pedophiles, like those indulging in sexbots themselves, would connect themselves with a beloved that they can control and define. This desire to initiate an innocent child sexually reflects a disordered sexual desire in the pedophile—he longs not for the love of another person, but for forbidden, innocent fruit. Pedophiles love not another person or even the child, but rather they confuse the lovely, seemingly pure innocence of a child for a species of beauty and think all beauty is sexualized. They do not want to attract or possess that beauty, but to despoil it. Nor is it to be expected that a child will grow to love a patron in any enduring way—with memories of the taboo violation and manipulation so central to the child's premature initiation into adulthood. Children are likely to feel resentment toward their supposed patrons and to have disordered souls themselves, making it most difficult for them to love later in life. Underage sex, especially with older people, may be related to depression and disorder among young girls who have sex with men and among sodomized boys.[32]

Opposition to child pornography—both viewing it and the participation of children in it—falls under much the same rubric: an interest in preserving childhood innocence and purity; and an interest in producing the kind of character that can love, trust, and sacrifice for another. Its portrait of sex divorced from enduring love amounts to a reduction of love to sex. Our worries about children watching pornography involve not just preparing children to consent intelligently later in life, but also protecting their innocence and their future. Exposure to pornography makes it more difficult to trust, love, marry, and exercise a healthy sexual self-control. It affects the character of children and teens—it affects their brains' structure. Pornography use is also associated with child enticement and molestation.[33] These are violations. Allowing such violations is bound to increase their number and scope, and to normalize otherwise unloving, unenduring, particularly impersonal forms of relation.

Age of consent laws are thus tied to the issue of whether those engaging in sex are ready for a genuine, enduring love. The downward pull of the age of consent follows from the earlier sexualization among children: revealingly dressed urchins invite a lowering of the age. Society may have unbuckled sex and enduring love, but the two experiences nevertheless cling to one another in our demand that children be exempt from such pressures. Much of the enterprise of making young boys and girls ready to love another human being has been left behind, forgotten, or devalued; our willingness to teach the beauty of personal integrity and honor is dissipated. The age of consent is an element of the old vast education project that remains. Liberalism obscures the genuine nature of the law by seeing age of consent laws as navigating the twin shores of consent and power. Age of consent laws are designed to protect marital character.

Understanding Divorce and Consent

Legal divorce is central to the story that contemporary liberals tell about marriage. In the beginning legal marriage was indissoluble and many other features of marriage were borrowed from the Christian vision (e.g., coverture). Modern ideas percolated. Sovereigns could grant divorces on somewhat biblical grounds (e.g., adultery) that Protestants observed by the time of the American Revolution. Then later sovereigns established administrative processes to effectuate divorce on somewhat broader grounds (e.g., abandonment, insanity, abuse, and others), usually finding fault in one spouse or the other: sometimes at this stage sovereigns would seek to encourage conciliation or imposed waiting periods; sometimes not. People soon found this fault-based system too constraining. Parties either invented violations or lied as their marriages broke down; courts modestly, in the spirit of limited government, preferred not to get involved in confirming domestic details in any event. A situation where perjury abetted consensual divorce was intolerable. Divorce by mutual consent was contemplated and then accepted throughout the Western world. Divorce for "irreconcilable differences" with very short waiting periods (or none) and no mandatory conciliation became the norm around the Western world (starting with California in 1970). Generally, waiting periods for divorce and remarriage are shortened and conciliation processes are hollowed over time. "At-will" divorce, where one party can leave marriage whenever he or she wills, arose. Sometimes parties must give a reason; sometimes not. Remnants of fault-based divorce appear at the settlement stage as couples negotiate child custody and support, but equal division of community property is the rule.[34]

Nothing new exists under the divorce sun. Those who opposed the liberalizing changes thought indissoluble marriage (or its rough equivalent) deterred divorce and acted as a bridle on unruly sexual passions;[35] allowed human beings to remain in love and deepen that love even with the minor irritations that inevitably come with married life;[36] served the interests of children;[37] and (sometimes) protected the principle of a man ruling the household.[38] Divorce liberalizers, in contrast, argue that divorce follows directly from the principle of individual consent: the right to enter a marriage carries with it the right to exit the marriage; continuous consent is more consistent with individual

freedom and spontaneous love than durable consent; marriages with a preponderance of hatred, cruelty, abuse, and other ills undermine the happiness
of individuals; the public sanctions cruelty, unhappiness, and perhaps death
itself when it forces people to stay married; permanent, exclusive marriages
are stultifying and repressive; strict laws force those with unsatisfied sexual
passions or unsatisfying relations into illicit relations instead of allowing
for their satisfaction within new licit relations; children will do better with
one parent without the conflict of a tumultuous marriage than they would
with unhappy quarreling parents; what is good for the adult in a marriage,
as judged by that adult, is good for the children, since generally happy and
fulfilled adults make better parents than unhappy, unfulfilled adults; marriage
presupposes love and love is not a mandate of law but the result of individual
feeling and when it is gone the marriage is expired anyhow.

The divorce revolution, now mostly complete in law and opinion, is part
of an effort to "free sexual union from the bonds of governmental regulation and to treat them purely as affairs of free individual love" or "individual
sex love" just as Frederick Engels had described for the postcapitalist world.[39]
Feminism is both a cause and an effect of the divorce revolution, loosening
the marital bond and making the new independent woman a matter of self-
interest. The pure relationship demands it. States now tolerate and may even
be on the way to recognizing only relations based on subjective feelings (as
opposed to necessity) arising from free consent.

Divorce and Love

Easy divorce reflects a pure, Romantic vision of love—spiritual, shunning
necessities, and alienating duties and obligations, where persons can live
together as long as their love shall last. "Consent" in this circumstance is *continuous*, where an "I do" must be reaffirmed every moment and hence can
be withdrawn arbitrarily. Nothing such as habits, religious or legal duties, or
previous promises alienates the individual will or compromises one's passion.
A common dedication to common love unites people. David Hume warns of
the dangers of uniting

> two persons so closely in all their interests and concerns, as man and
> wife, without rendering the union entire and total. The least possibil-
> ity of a separate interest must be the source of endless quarrels and
> suspicions. The wife, not secure in her establishment, will still be driv-
> ing some separate end or project; and the husband's selfishness, being
> accompanied by more power, may be still more dangerous.[40]

As a practical matter, a thinner common life means that spouses are less dedicated to being fathers and mothers and to building a home together. Couples

invest less time and energy and identity in marriage when it can be ended easily, studies, following logic, show.[41] As a divorce culture is more strongly entrenched, people are less likely to stick it out in a marginally unhappy marriage for the children.[42] Married couples become less efficacious and more willing to transfer their duties to the state or to hire them out to private agencies. The availability of at-will divorce makes cohabitation or "experimental" marriage more viable as an option for organizing life with another. Experimental marriage is an appearance of marriage—it involves living together without necessarily assuming obligations, especially without an enduring commitment to having and raising children. The very character of this experimentation means that the parties never, strictly speaking, attempt a genuine marital experiment.

The kind of character associated with a divorce ethic emphasizes the value of experimentation; individual independence, autonomy, and self-sufficiency; a greater emphasis on adult interests as opposed to a common life or a child's interest; and, perhaps, a greater emphasis on romantic, passionate, and hence unstable love. The freedom to divorce coincides with the emergence of the modern, independent woman—and women initiate more divorces than men in the United States and worldwide.[43] Women especially find the courage to follow their own dreams instead of subordinating their own lives to the lives of their children or their husbands or their marriage. Divorce provides women with opportunities for growth, individual expression, and for building a new sense of identity,[44] while providing them with leverage to change the arrangements of domestic duties within the marriage: the credible threat of divorce, wielded by women, can get men, who depend on their wives for happiness, community, and access to children, to do more housework and defer to women in the arrangement of domestic affairs;[45] it changes the "balance of power" within the home. Divorcing may spring from an inner dissatisfaction: marriage for the new independent women cannot be subject to external constraints like children or alienating societal expectations like an expectation of permanence or the idea that divorce is a personal failure.

Enduring marriage is less spiritual, less free, and less pure, more grounded in habits and necessities, where two people grow together into one community so that it is difficult to imagine oneself apart from it. Consent in this circumstance begins with an enduring vow or promise to stay together "for better or worse, as long as both shall live." The kind of character associated with enduring marriage forms a sober sense of expectations; exercises self-control; recognizes the goodness and meaning in obligations, duties, and dependencies; steadies itself on habits, familiarity, and working things out; and keeps long-term, time-resource intensive goals firmly in mind as the couple navigates the difficult shoals of life. Feelings, arbitrary and capricious, take on a subordinate place in a common life, as couples come to feel more alike as they grow together. Marital character seems based on an ability to love a good and to share that love with another person. That good may be grounded in satisfying the necessities of daily life, yet those necessities are satisfied in ways that involve an understanding of the good life and a manifestation of certain virtues.

Natural human passions can point in different, incompatible ways, both toward and away from enduring marriage. Public morality shapes how individuals think about the noble and shameful, the good and the bad, and hence which reasonable passion seems to be more in a person's interest. Before the divorce revolution in the 1970s America, divorce was considered a personal tragedy, a matter to hide, and a source of shame. No more. As more people divorce, it becomes more difficult to discuss the perils of divorce for children and for adults. An ethic accepting of divorce—or one where divorce can often in fact be celebrated—affects how human beings approach their relations with others. The more temporary relations are, the less loyalty and investment they call forth. The less obligatory those relations are, the less stable they are. People perceive these problems and possibilities as they form relations; this affects how each understands marriage. At-will, no-fault divorce goes hand in glove with a conception of marriage as pure relationship, its celebration of individuality, and ultimately the rolling revolution itself. If the rolling revolution is an incomplete vision of the human good, so must be the Divorce Revolution. Its basis in continuous consent fails to take account of stability, duty, and necessity. What can be done to acknowledge these goods in our divorce law and culture?

Rollback?

There have been successful, and in some cases sustained, rollbacks of liberal divorce laws.[46] Previous to the French Revolution, French law reflected for the most part Catholic canon law. The marriage bond was indissoluble. Revolutionary France in 1792 sought to effect its vision of marriage as a "civil contract," allowing divorce by mutual consent or for incompatibility of temper and other situations such as cruelty, desertion of two years or more, incurable insanity, and notoriously dissolute conduct of life. Divorces would be registered with administrative officers after a somewhat elaborate process whereby a family council, consisting of three close relatives of each spouse, would be convened three times to seek conciliation. A waiting period (first of one year, then shortened to six months) followed the granting of divorce. "While extensive use was made of divorce in Paris, the Law remained a dead letter for wide districts of rural France" where 80% of the population lived.[47]

Rollback of the civil divorce law began under Napoleon (1803), whose code embodied a vision of divorce involving punishment for a proven fault.

Gone were incompatibility of temper as grounds for divorce and the concilia-
tory process involving family councils. Instead the Code adopted a woman's
adultery, a husband's open and notorious living with a mistress in the marital
home, conviction of a crime, and maltreatment or grave injury committed by
one spouse against the other as grounds for divorce and allowed divorce by
mutual consent. The rollback Napoleon started deepened after his abdication,
when a restored Bourbon monarchy reintroduced much from the old regime
with respect to divorce, including most prominently ending divorce on these
grounds and eliminating divorce by mutual consent. Marquis Louis de Bonald shepherded the law and defended it with a treatise that comes down to
us as *On Divorce*. No one made significant changes to French divorce law for
about seventy years after Bonald's changes from the mid-1810s.

Assuming Bonald deserves credit for this restoration, what arguments
worked? At the crucial points in his case, Bonald makes empirical arguments,
echoing and deepening Old Wisdom about divorce canvassed above. Indissoluble marriage, Bonald contends, acts as a "public bridle" to steady the incon-
stant tastes and violent penchants typical of human sexual desire. Allowing
divorce, even for grounds, causes the eye to wander, the mind to lose its focus,
children to be neglected, and encourages depraved actions.[48] Proponents of
Revolutionary divorce opposed Bonald with New Wisdom also canvassed
above. Divorce law does not create marital breakdown, but acknowledges it;
makes a concession to the weakness of human nature and especially to that
in rich, modern societies where artificial passions and opportunities for wandering eyes abound; and provides a way to let people out of unhappy, perhaps
even dangerous marriages while allowing them another chance at marital
happiness through remarriage.[49]

Boland's emphatic response to these arguments mixes Stoical resolve,
Christian hope, and assisting virtue through law. Boland grants that liberal
divorce laws would be safer in poor, more faithfully religious times (during
the sixteenth century) because people then would not divorce even if the law
allowed it.[50] Perhaps some would separate from a spouse, with the hope that,
after prayer and time, reconciliation would await. Perhaps some would take
religious orders, spending the rest of their time in prayer and service to others.[51] There are alternatives to divorce for a good life, after all. In the nineteenth century, however, when there are larger cities allowing for anonymity
and opportunity; where commerce, novels, democratic politics, and theaters
provide a profusion of titillating public or forbidden pleasures; when men
appear in public with few clothes on, showing off their bodies like barbarians;
when women insult modesty without shocking the ever lower standards of
propriety overmuch; when the "sexes disappear beneath the dignity of expressions we are all . . . males and females" (i.e., animals); when religion loses its
terrors; and when philosophy defends libertinism—when these attributes of

the nineteenth century become evermore the norm, Boland writes, tolerating divorce makes bad mores worse. Allowing for divorce is "to command prostitution and legalize adultery" and "to conspire with man's passions against his reason, and with man himself against society" and leads to the "community of women and the promiscuity of beasts." It brings a "distaste for marriage,"[52] which builds and presupposes control of desires and voluptuousness and which appears mundane and necessitous compared to the free love available elsewhere. Children will be neglected.[53] Once equality is introduced in the divorce law with the idea of mutual consent, the subordination of the wife to the husband will end making it more difficult for the man to run the household.[54] Legal divorce becomes thinkable when a syndrome of passions, practices, and pathologies are prevalent, and then the adoption of legal divorce makes the syndrome even worse.

Prohibiting divorce is a hard doctrine for his dissolute age. "Laws must be more severe in proportion as society is more advanced and man looser," Bonald writes,[55] just as an adult's duties are greater than a child's.[56] Is it "for the legislator to attend to the pleasures of the individual at the expense of society?"[57] Boland would reintroduce order into the marital and sexual relations; deterring dissolute actions will, with time, reorder the mind and the imagination of the French. A short-term pain against freedom for a long-term gain for virtue and society.

What kind of a people would acquiesce in this apparently hard doctrine? Loose divorce laws could be passed in the "ruder" state of society, when the population was deferential to the Church or its doctrines and when necessity made life hard enough to preclude wandering eyes. Perhaps most of France was still, despite Boland's belief that things had gone to hell in a handbasket, in such a "rude" state in 1816 so that the liberalizing laws had not been particularly relevant to how most people lived married life.[58] Perhaps strict laws were made for a people whose mores were at least as strict.

An experiment of sorts can prove this, since Catholic Belgium kept a relatively loose code that permitted divorce by mutual consent as it obtained independence from France in the early 1800s. In Belgium, there were over 1,700 marriages per one divorce in 1840 and 739 marriages per one divorce in 1865; the numbers increased somewhat rapidly thereafter all the way to 83 marriages per divorce in 1900.[59] Numbers in France under the reformed law were little different. (Comparable numbers for the United States in the twenty-first century are 2.9 marriages per divorce.[60]) This hardly represents a Belgian epidemic of divorce. Each generation availed itself of divorce more readily, however. France seems to have, in effect, consented to Boland's hard law as a reflection of its strict mores just as Belgium ignored its soft laws because of its strict mores. This interpretation suggests that laws play a lesser role than mores in restraining the passions when it comes to divorce in the short run.[61]

Such findings seem to justify Max Rheinstein, a legal scholar and the most morally serious of the divorce reformers during the early 1970s, who sees little to no connection between loose divorce laws and the frequency of divorce. More evidence could be adduced for the conclusion that mores trump laws. American laws on divorce were by and large unchanged from 1870 through 1950, but America's divorce rate increased by a factor of seven during that period.[62] France was not ready for the widespread practice of divorce when Boland legislated.[63] Boland's rollback succeeded, but the prevalence of strict mores and strong, Catholic faith made the reform manageable and somewhat beside the point.

Lest we be tempted to see these cases as speaking to impotence of laws, keep in mind that laws themselves had no small role in making those strict mores over generations. Catholicism was established, for instance, and that establishment had more than a little influence over how the French believed or how the Belgians acted. There is no neat way to isolate "law" from "mores." For every Belgian case where mores are stricter than laws there are many American cases where the adoption of liberal divorce laws (at-will, no-fault divorce in the 1970s) precipitated an increase in divorce. The fact that no-fault divorce laws were passed with little opposition in most American states demonstrates that people either were reconciled to the proposed changes in law in the United States or did not understand what was happening. Divorce rates were, after all, rising in the century before the profound change and the profound change in law hastened divorce revolution in practice. The no-fault revolution pushed the envelope through a greater emphasis on adult fulfillment in law throughout the Western world and by undermining the idea of marital unity that could provide a justification for counseling or waiting periods.

What Is to Be Done?

Boland's jeremiads could not win in today's late republic where laws restricting divorce would have to win acceptance from democratic majorities. If Boland thought the mores were loose in 1815 Paris, visiting the Las Vegas strip or a random college dormitory on a weekend might give the poor man a coronary. Do we again want to see divorce as a tragedy and source of personal loss and shame? Would we insist on a fault-based system? Would courts be required to dig deep into the faults to confirm that they are genuine? Would courts be required to discover whether the couple is indeed estranged one from another? Would we countenance the perjury of couples who would assert faux faults in order to split? Could a genuine conciliation mechanism become a state mandate and responsibility? Could we make divorce more difficult without causing fewer people to enter into marriage for fear of their inability to get out of it? Is there a mechanism or a "collective reflex" that might help put matters right or turn back the clock?[64]

One way to end divorce, for instance, would be to rid the world of divorce through the abolition of marriage. Simulacra of this solution are, perhaps, seen in Sweden and some other European countries, where the number of marriages is so low that divorce has become increasingly rare, though divorce rates are rather high.[65] Yet it could never be more truly said that this remedy is worse than the disease. It would be as foolish to abolish marriage because it can lead to divorce as it would be to wish the annihilation of air because it imparts to fire its destructive agency.[66]

There is no question of reintroducing indissoluble marriage: such measures would require tyrannical authority against an unwilling populace (for now!). Boland's extremism is out. There are good reasons to oppose the abolition of marriage. We are left in a large gray area, between no marriage and indissoluble marriage. The rolling revolution broadly conceived is part of the fatal circle of late modernity. That fatal circle cannot shut human beings out from the small recesses of the heart and the vague sentiments that the principles of the rolling revolution discourage us from seeing. The stable and stabilizing attractions of enduring marital love, the presence of children to whom parents are responsible and to whom parents make unique contributions, the differences between men and women, and the proper ordering of affections involving the subordination of sexual and other fleeting desires in a properly ordered soul—these elements, I say, can and do limit the attractiveness of divorce and a divorce culture. None of these elements is directly a product of law, though law did much to reinforce them and has done much damage to these experiences and could indeed do more through upsetting, for instance, the presumption of parental responsibility over children. Perhaps the law can only avoid doing further damage under contemporary conditions.

Could a healthier set of opinions regarding divorce be reconstructed? Could we seek a healthier practice? Imagine the range of divorces, from high conflict divorces involving high-frequency and high-intensity fighting, addiction, serial adultery, or violence on one end of the scale to low conflict divorces, where parties divorce over the most frivolous inconveniences on the other. Divorces in cases of high conflict, even when children are present, are not about to be prohibited, nor, perhaps, should they be. Yet the public could encourage sticking it out when levels of conflict are low and when children are present (over half of divorces involve children). The importance of marriage for children must once again become a more important element in public morality. This could involve honoring and rewarding parents who stick it out and, perhaps, dishonoring or stigmatizing those who leave their responsibilities. In emphasizing children, spouses would be emphasizing the obligations that they undertook when they embarked on marriage together.

Some of the best literature on divorce suggests that professional marriage counselors who renew efforts to save marriages, discuss benefits of marriage for both spouses, emphasize the importance of two parents for children, and, in total, seek to salvage especially low conflict divorces make a difference.[67] More than a few institutions in civil society involve themselves in saving troubled marriages. Evidence suggests that only a few of those who find themselves unhappy in their marriage but stick it out are still unhappy in their marriages some time later: Hume's somewhat stoical thoughts about people finding happiness when they reconcile themselves to staying together seem vindicated in this.[68] Stoicism, so far from the spirit of the age, heals many wounds. Divorce itself provides no guarantee for happiness and fulfillment—the grass is usually not greener—and the problems that gave rise to the divorce compound, in some ways, with the divorce. The only legal reform that might be of assistance in these cases is a cooling off period, especially for low conflict divorces, but this only works if there is a will to heal or stick it out. Cultivating such wills is crucial.

Another reform might indirectly favor sobering second thoughts. Women initiate most of the divorces (60–70% or more) in the Western world.[69] Why is this? It is not because of domestic violence, which, surveys suggest, ranks well down the list in factors that contribute to divorce. Jennifer Roback Morse suggests that divorce for modern women allows them the continued fulfillments of motherhood (since they win custody much of the time) with child support, and less interference from a bumbling father.[70] Perhaps, Morse continues, "switching the award of custody from the mother to the father would decrease the probability that the mother files for divorce" by disrupting the benefits that women can keep through divorce[71] and by minimizing the amount of leverage women have in the relationship.

The predominant vision deemphasizing the sexes plays no small role in our inability to resolve marital conflicts. Let us remember a foundational principle: the line between good and evil runs through the heart of men and women. Responsibility for marital problems does not lie only with irresponsible, cheating, addicted, emotionally distant men—men have their vices. Women are not without their typical vices too. Generally, women have a greater need for harmony; a lack of harmony and agreeableness strikes more deeply at the center of womanly personality than it strikes at a man's. Women, more than men, hold on to stress and sour feelings in the aftermath of a disagreement. As one book on a different topic holds, *Men Never Remember, Women Never Forget*. Men seem less affected by conflicts within relationships, welcoming conflict if they cannot get their way and forgetting about conflicts rather quickly afterward. Qualities of character such as magnanimity from men (aided by a recognition that women see conflict differently and more existentially) and patience and forgiveness from women (aided by an equal recognition of how men differ) help to keep conflicts from escalating or arising. Women may be more likely to initiate divorce because conflict itself shakes their confidence in the relationship more than it shakes the confidence of men: no-fault divorce allows women to act for light and transient reasons that they are more likely to feel.

Sex differences at the level of psychology, when coupled with the feminist emphasis on empowerment and self-assertion, have made women the more volatile partners in marriage. Another speculation is in order. Generally, men are tempted by pleasures, and women are tempted through vanity. Vanity fosters a fear in women that they have not chosen well enough or that they could do better. The more our public philosophy teaches that fulfillment is found outside of marriage and family life and the more marriage is liberated from day-to-day concerns, the more such vanity unsettles the attachment to marriage and family life. The vain would like to mate with the best and then keep the best man for themselves. They would like their souls to be filled with fulfilling activities, but such fulfillment always seems just out of reach. They may find a better man or find genuine fulfillment in human resource departments or wander from San Diego to the Canadian border, barefoot, taking in the beauty of nature. Not a few popular books today celebrate the fulfillment women sense from leaving a good-enough man.[72] Vanity fosters volatility, as the greatest literature on marriage and family life (i.e., Tolstoy's *Anna Karenina*) shows. The freedom to divorce allows women to act upon their vanity more, to the detriment of men who earned, worked, and became overly dependent on them. Divorce is difficult on men too. Even emotionally available men may lose their home, access to their children, their connection to community through their wife, and the time that they have put into making their marriage work. Enduring marriage teaches responsibility to men *and* women—and it educates against a tendency in each.

Divorce is a concession to human error and weakness. Concessions to weakness weaken commitment—that is a moral hazard. The concession to error can make tough, but manageable problems seem unmanageable. Seeing the bond as necessary can help to stabilize men and women, and bring with them a species of happiness that is found in enduring relations. Laws cannot square this circle. The circle can be squared best if we recognize elements of truth that contemporary liberalism willfully blinds itself to—the centrality of children to marriage, the benefit to children of having a mother and a father, the obligations of marital life in a community, and the differences between men and women. In serving these goods and reflecting them opposition to at-will divorce finds its raison d'être.

Consent Is Not Enough

Each element shows problems in seeing relations merely in terms of consent. First, the very idea of consent is controversial: Is consent durable or continuous? Does consent reflect the autonomous act of the will or can it implicate one's "socialization"? If it integrates education and socialization, how and to what extent can these elements shape one's will before it ceases to be one's will? Rolling revolutionaries make the most radical and inhumane assumptions about consent, yet their radical thought need not lead us to deny the importance of consent. Consent must be situated and pointed in the direction where human actions promote to personal happiness, fulfilling lives, stability, and social goods.

Second, consent alone is not enough to account for human happiness. Rape and statutory rape are violations of consent, but the violation of consent does not alone show why we single these violations out for special censure and prosecution. Sex properly involves ideas of personal integrity and honor. Statutory rape violates childhood innocence and incapacitates all concerned from building an enduring love. At-will, one party divorce contains a controversial conception of consent, but also cannot account for the habits and community that form around an enduring marriage.

Each of these issues with consent ultimately ignores the fundamental question for understanding marriage and family life. What kind of character can undertake a successful marriage? That the person would consent to the marriage is not at issue: that the person would be fit for marriage and be able to stick it out is the issue. Laws, while they point to that kind of character and support it, do not of themselves create it. We must come to grips with the kind of marital character that can consent to an enduring marital community.

11

THE NEW PROBLEM WITH NO NAME

Second marriages represent, as Dr. Samuel Johnson quipped, "the triumph of hope over experience." This understates the role of hope. All who marry must hope to fulfill the demands of living, in close quarters and in common, with another human being. Marriage as such requires hope and faith, for people never really know that they have found a person with whom they can be bonded. People who marry have some thought of projecting marriage and common life with another into the indefinite future, for better and for worse—this projection is what I mean by *responsibility*. Such *marital* responsibility seems on the wane. Each generation since the emergence of the rolling revolution marries later, in the main, marries less frequently, has fewer children, puts marriage further from the core of their lives and so on. New men and women, less suited to marriage, are emerging under our new sexual regime under the influence of the rolling revolution. The eclipse of characters fit to marry and stay married is the new problem with no name.

Take the most basic institution of the rolling revolution—the pure relationship. Love and responsibility drain faster out of pure relationships. Partners deemphasize lifelong love and sacrificial giving. Partners are less interested in pleasing or serving one another in the long term; they settle for manipulating or using one another. They may fail to enter marriage as a school for parenthood. They may, on the lower end, have few good job prospects, a poor work ethic, or no sexual interests or options. People may lack personal integrity, industriousness, and honesty; they may be addicted to alcohol or narcotics; they may have lower levels of education and religiosity.[1] Those with nonmarital character may not aspire to the good of another, either because people are mired in necessity or because they believe themselves to be mired in necessity. It reflects "life at the bottom."[2] Horizons shrink. Many lack the capacity, mores, habits, vision, dreams, character, and most other stabilizing norms for marriage.

There are two different kinds of nonmarital character, one uncivilized and the other "pure," hypercivilized. New men and women emerge, and sometimes old problems emerge under new conditions. Gender itself is being reconstructed under this new sexual and marital regime, but always within the sexual grooves. Our new regime produces a New Woman, but she is still distinctively a woman, and a New Man, also distinctively a man. This aspect of the rolling revolution is among the least well understood, but most important.

The New Problem with No Name in "Two Americas"

The problem of "uncivilized" nonmarital character is as old as politics. Great lawmakers concerned themselves with marriage laws to prepare people for a common life. Social scientists and careful observers recognize the problem of "uncivilized" character in late modernity. Books such as Charles Murray's *Coming Apart: The State of White America, 1960–2010* (2012), Andrew J. Cherlin's *Love's Labor's Lost: The Rise and Fall of the Working-Class Family in America* (2014), Robert D. Putnam's *Our Kids: The American Dream in Crisis* (2015), and Kay Hymowitz' *Marriage and Caste in America: Separate and Unequal Families in a Post-Marital Age* (2006), among others, catalog the rise of nonmarital character in the American context, especially among men. The same problem frames James Q. Wilson's *The Marriage Problem: How Our Culture Has Weakened Families* (2002). Wilson sees "two nations" divided along marital lines, one with relatively strong neo-traditional marital norms and one where fewer marriages form and last. Sociologists and activists noticed the same problem since the 1950s. Michael Harrington's *The Other America* (1962) and Ken Auletta's *The Underclass* (1982), while they do not only trace the two Americas to marital differences, allow for such a reading.

Few describe the differences between marital and nonmarital cultures with greater clarity than Wilson:

> In one nation, a child, raised by two parents, acquires an education, a job, and a home separate from crime and disorder by distance, fences, or guards. In the other nation, a child is raised by an unwed girl, lives in a neighborhood filled with many sexual men but few committed fathers, and finds gang life to be necessary for self-protection and valuable for self-advancement. In the first nation, children look to the future and believe that they control what place they will occupy in it;

in the second, they live for the moment and think that fate, not plans, will shape their lives. In both nations harms occur, but in the second they proliferate—child abuse and drug abuse, gang violence and personal criminality, economic dependency and continued illegitimacy.[3]

Harrington's pre-Great Society call for national action against poverty sees two Americas too. He characterizes the poor in the following terms: "their horizon has become more and more restricted"; "the other America is becoming increasingly populated by those who do not belong to anybody or anything"; the "new poverty" destroys "aspiration" and is "impervious to hope"; the new poor are "rigid, suspicious, and have a fatalistic outlook on life. They do not plan ahead, a characteristic associated with their fatalism. They are prone to depression, have feelings of futility, lack of belongingness, friendliness, and a lack of trust in others." Such "fatalism" and "pessimism" permeate "every aspect of an individual's life; it is a way of seeing reality." In the more innocent world of 1962 (before the poisoned reaction to the Moynihan Report compromised our ability to discuss such matters), Harrington traced these problems in part to "the family structure of the poor," where there are "more homes without a father, there is less marriage, more early pregnancy, and . . . markedly different attitudes toward sex." The ability of many men to be fathers, enter marriage, be responsible parents, and have loving attitudes toward their fellows is compromised.[4] This problem of "two nations" is a grave and growing problem in the United States.

Other Western nations experience the same problem.[5] Theodore Dalrymple, nom de plume for the British essayist Anthony Daniels, describes a blend of passivity, immersion in the present, and aggression in his *Life at the Bottom*, a treatment of Britain's new problem with no name. A "dishonest fatalism" and a "passivity and refusal of responsibility" defines the "lower" British.[6] Those living at the bottom see themselves as victims of circumstance. Many are unable to conform their lives to another. Families among the working poor rarely eat common meals. Common meals require advanced preparation in the service of common life. Cooking itself indicates that the family shares its time and experiences. People are obliged to subordinate their own separate plans to eat with others. Common meals are hassles, perhaps, from the perspective of individual convenience. Common meals require self-discipline and placing value on solidarity. People incapable of eating in common experience a "loss of dignity," a "self-centeredness," and a "spiritual and emotional vacuity" akin to a "poverty of soul."[7]

I run up against the limits of science in describing this uncivilized non-marital character. Art in film, novels, and television shows captures what it is about people that makes them unsuitable for marriage. Television dramas including *The Wire* and *Justified* depict a culture of hypermasculinity; violence;

a selective passivity or victimhood; honor; misogyny; materialism; contempt for merely physical, bourgeois work; contempt for honest, law-abiding labor; hedonism; presentism; and fatalism (especially among men) so that few characters can build enduring bonds of love or friendship. Male characters lose themselves in video games, drug use, drug dealing, alcohol, sports, gang violence, violent sexual relations, pornography, passing sexual relations, relations on the edge of violence, and more—anything to distract themselves from the hopelessness, anomie, habitual boredom of their solitary lives. Female characters are rightly suspicious and jealous. Without families many sink.

Work does not suit the men because work means working on someone else's time: employment presupposes punctuality, and punctuality demands governing oneself by a rule outside one's will. Following rules at work or exerting the self-discipline and concentration necessary to accomplish tasks is unmanly and scorned. If such work is to be done, it is not done with joy, creativity, engagement, or even much interest. Work brings forth little or no pride and its earnings serve one's passions, not one's duty to provide for a family. These habits are consistent with poor capacity to manage money—to foresee emergencies, to recognize the problems of credit card debt in the long term, to store up capital in a residence. The toxic mix arises: declining marriage, declining industriousness, lost religiosity, and greater dishonesty among those with the new problem with no name.

Orlando Patterson's lead essay in *The Cultural Matrix* (2015), which compiles contemporary sociology literature on African American youth, describes how America's African American community manifests this character. Let me limit myself to his description of the decline in marital character among what he calls ghetto culture.[8] Most children in ghettos are born out of wedlock; most first marriages end in divorce; a significant portion of men cannot be fathers because they are, for a variety of reasons, unable to provide; and, what is most important, they manifest a "hypermasculinity" that lies at the "core of self-identified 'bad boys.'"[9] Male pride comes from the "disruption of mainstream normalcy, and fighting":

> In the culture of the street, being able to "pull the girls" and then "cutting" or "hitting" them are essential attributes of masculinity. Women are commodified; objects to be played, "hoes" to be fucked, pimped, and (if they have the goods) trafficked; "bitches" to be impregnated, violently put in their place and discarded, along with the culture they produce who simply become notches on their phallocentric poles to brag about with other predators on the corner and to enhance feelings of control.[10]

Many boys reject the mainstream educational values, use of language, style of clothing and deportment, gentle parenting techniques, and sexual egalitarianism.[11] Obtrusive tattoos proliferate. Sports prowess is overvalued as expressing manliness. Men emphasize an extreme, sometimes violent demand for respect in "one's space and manhood."[12] Gang leaders in this subpopulation replace absent parents; gang members support the gang, not families.[13] Mothers, in turn, recognizing the threat coming from such boys and men, "armor" their daughters to be suspicious of men. A girl's education emphasizes "protection and deportment over affection, resulting in intense and sometimes antagonistic relationships."[14] African American women still hold to the ideal of having children as a sort of "emotional imperative invested with great personal value," but they often do so alone, sensing that having the child's father around might make matters worse.[15]

"Street culture," as Patterson describes it, exacerbates the long-standing conflict between African American men and women traceable to slavery and lingering belief in racial subordination. This street culture seems to be a new cause, extraneous, strictly speaking, to the history of discrimination.[16] Regardless of how this culture came about, Patterson's work stands for the idea that the new problem with no name pervades a not insignificant part of street culture and sets the tone for the broader African American community: the pre-civilized men he describes are not marriage material, nor are the manipulative, suspicious women.

Variations on the same problem are seen in white America—as Murray's *Coming Apart*, J. D. Vance's *Hillbilly Elegy: A Memoir of a Family and Culture in Crisis*, and Sam Quinones' *Dreamland: The True Tale of America's Opiate Epidemic* (2016) show and as depicted in the television series *Justified*. Vance's memoir concerns hillbillies of Appalachia; these folks have a difficult time holding down a job, shun punctuality, do not value hard work as much as their forebears (though they are in denial about this and tend to blame others), take drugs, devalue success in school, are unlikely to have much of a work ethic, do not take care of themselves (suffering from "Mountain Dew mouth," for instance), parent in abusive ways, abuse spouses and partners more, are skeptical that God has a providential plan for humanity, and live more and more in short-term, mutually suspicious relationships. Today's hillbillies, as Vance tells it, "rarely cook" or eat meals together.[17] This lack of togetherness relates to fundamental debilities, Vance concludes: "American working-class families experience a level of instability unseen elsewhere in the world."[18] The wide-open hollers of Harlan County in *Justified* resemble the mean streets of Baltimore in *The Wire*: different subcultures, but the same uncivilized problem with no name.

The failure of men to rise to marital character is traceable to the rolling revolution. Stephanie Coontz, a celebrant of the new sexual regime, thinks marriage has become "a discretionary item" and "more optional and more fragile" since the victories of the rolling revolution; she celebrates how "men and women can customize their life course," but she soberly recognizes that the decline of marriage has costs. The "barriers to single living and personal autonomy gradually eroded," as did "society's ability to pressure people into marrying" and, I add, ability to teach people, through law and culture, about how manhood and womanhood can contribute to a common life.[19] "Some people" are liberated or think themselves liberated "from restrictive, inherited roles." The beautiful, "privileged" people in the first nation rise above their stodgy ancestors toward greater heights of love, bliss, advancement, and happiness: "Marriage has become more joyful, more loving, and more satisfying for many couples than ever before in history" because it is finally freely chosen and constructed. They have invented happiness! "Others" in our second nation have been "stripped . . . of traditional support systems and rules of behavior without establishing new ones." This is a bummer for them, Coontz continues. "We cannot turn the clock back in our personal lives any more than we can go back to small-scale farming and artisan production in our economic life."[20] Never have so many suffered so much so that so few could be so happy!

Coontz connects the decline of marital character among "others" to the decline in "traditional support systems and rules of behavior" or the decline in marital form. Forms elevate and extend people's interests and passions toward long-term projects and toward thinking about long-term happiness and interests. Perhaps, Coontz and her allies think, many adults can live together in love with or without marriage, children will be cared for despite the way their parents relate to one another, or people will choose a better marriage without social pressure. Perhaps, that is, they think forms get in the way of happiness.

Tocqueville thinks forms "serve as a barrier between strong and weak."[21] Forms are salutary restraints that elevate those who need their assistance. People who might be taken with irresponsible exercises of passion or who would forgo long-lasting relations with their children are tutored to their long-term interests under the old marital form. It brings with it the expectation that men and women might live together happily and share deep common interests. Under the new sexual regime, men, who might have been providers, may wander, unattached, irresponsible, lacking industriousness, loving honor in an uncivilized way, untouched by female influence. Under the new, women, who might have been wives and mothers, may seek vanity, live suspiciously, use sexual ploys for advancement, shun modesty so that translating sex into love is compromised, and value independence over community. Under the new, fewer women have children, women have fewer children, more people simply live together without marriage, fewer adults marry, fewer stay married, and more live alone—and this makes for many wandering, aimless human beings. Many men and women have difficulty, when the old marital form dissolves, rising to the level of having character capable of sustaining marriage.

Coontz, who, in theory, embraces the idea of mixed blessings, thinks that the new marriage with fewer "restrictive, inherited roles" is superior to marriages found in tradition. The new woman, not obedient or dependent like her older sisters, but career-focused, financially independent, and sexually experienced and hence, in Coontz' view, finally capable of love, is fit for the best marriage. What appears in some sense as a decline, when looked at from below, is a cause for celebration, when we appreciate its new supposed heights.

The New Problem with No Name in "Beautiful" America

Remove the old marital form and new visions of men and women arise—and if marriage remains it too will change. The for-the-most-part universal traits of men and women remain, but they are shaped differently after the old marital norm is dethroned; a new teaching about what a woman is arises. What Coontz describes as the greatest marriage in human history is what Robert Putnam calls "neo-traditional marriage." Among beautiful Americans, marriage seems relatively healthy, less often ending in divorce; spouses, soulmates and best friends, seem to put their children at the center of their lives and sacrifice, as they understand it, to raise them to successful adulthood. The traditionalism is "neo," reflecting the feminist victory, as spouses shun chaste sexual norms before marriage, respect those who adopt alternative lifestyles, consciously reject the sexual division of labor, and ignore legal or traditional norms that might guide them toward or in marriage.[22] Feminists hoped for a revolution in politics, society, economy, and education of young women so that a new kind of woman, an independent woman, would arise. She is arrived! This new woman seems more ambitious and aggressive, more independent economically, more emotionally independent, more self-confident, and sexually adventurous with fewer taboos when compared to her mother and grandmother. Is she marriage material? How does this new character arise from female sexual grooves?

Among the treatments of this New Woman is Barbara Dafoe Whitehead's *Why There are No Good Men Left: The Romantic Plight of the New Single Woman* (2003) and Rosin's *End of Men and the Rise of Women* (2010). This "new single woman" is the product of a "girl-rearing" revolution that Whitehead calls the "Girl Project." The Girl Project prepares young women "for adult lives of economic self-sufficiency, social independence and sexual liberation"[23]—all planks of the rolling revolution. This new education emphasizes the "alternative path" of achievement and a new set of assets that dethrones marriage and motherhood as aspirations for women. "What defines" this New Woman, Whitehead writes, "is not her relationship to marriage, but the remarkable path she follows virtually from cradle to career."[24] Hers is the "New Girl Order."[25] She is single for longer, bespeaking her independence, her confidence, and her desire to stand on her own. She does not need someone or profess to want someone to provide for her. Mature, professional, and responsible, she earnestly gets the job done as it is defined. As a young girl, she makes herself a "to do" list and checks items off, hoping that, at the end of the list, she has a fulfilling career. What a marvelous dream! Advanced education and professional achievement are keys to the new honorable womanhood. She identifies mentors. Check. She stays up late to study and earn high marks, always pleasing her teachers with her conscientiousness. Check. Standardized test prep. Check. Her education leads to the right schools and internships. Check. She enters her dream career, climbing the ladder of credentials and meeting expectations. Check. She practices safe sex, because unplanned children could mess up educational achievement or professional advancement. Contraception, check. Sex can be fun, exciting, and pleasurable. First some recreational dating, next perhaps living with someone, then, if the time is right (after she is set in her career), marriage. This marriage "Check" is a little harder to control.[26]

More than a quarter of all women aged 25 to 38 in the early 2000s are college-educated *single* women, whereas before the sexual revolution that category was less than 2% of women.[27] Women attend college in numbers exceeding men, a trend that dates to the early 1980s.[28] The womanly ethos of gaining credentials and meeting expectations, where those who please are rewarded and which rewards focus, organization, self-discipline, defines much of the modern university, the natural habitat for the New Girl.[29]

What makes for a successful, honorable life for a woman has changed from an emphasis on marriage and motherhood to an emphasis on educational or career achievements. New Girls are not prepared with the same kind of intensity to be mothers or wives (to enjoy the art of cooking, for instance, as part of a family meal). Such a preparation is so much bunk: "I am not staying in the kitchen eating bon-bons all day!" as a prominent retail feminist, Hillary Clinton, said. The Old Girl learned folkways of her sex, "to cook, grocery shop, and care for children," while New Girls stress "precocious performance and achievement, the acquisition of time management and goal-setting skills, early exposure to the world of paid professional work, an academically challenging school career," a college, a graduate school, community service, and so on. The Old Girl was educated to such traits as "helpfulness, charm, niceness, thrift, patience, personal sacrifice, and forbearance," while New Girls are taught to "speak up for themselves, to compete and strive for individual excellence, and to take initiative and responsibility for their economic lives."[30] Résumé building, not home economics.

This Girl Project may, as Whitehead stresses, be a rational reaction to the "divorce revolution," which unsettles communal marriages.[31] But this is backwards too. The divorce revolution is a tool used within the broader feminist revolution to bring about the New Girl Order.[32] Divorce improves the bargaining position of women in marriage because men usually depend upon their wives for their connection with their children and for their social circle and hence for their happiness; the fact that she can leave at will (and, as we have seen, she does at high rates) puts her in the driver seat to make demands. Many New Girls marry—and their marriages are often of the stable "neo-traditional" variety with female happiness at the center; happy wife, happy life! This cliché contains a threat. Men must serve womanly happiness if they want the marriage to continue. This is new marriage, "hers" not "his" (to use Jessie Bernard's formulation).[33]

Marriage and love for the New Woman follow from individual independence. In the emerging relationship system, people are more likely to pair off "for intimate relationships that range from marriage to living together to serial monogamy and casual sexual partnering"; "sex, childbearing, and parenthood are separate from marriage"; and "commitment" is left "to individuals' private understandings and mutual consent." The old "marriage system is deeply communitarian, while the "relationship system is profoundly libertarian" and feminist.[34] Rosin praises "see saw marriages," in which each partner pursues "individual self-fulfillment and each partner can have a shot at achieving it at different points in the marriage" and each "privileges self-expression over duty."[35] The new marriage see-saws serving individual fulfillment for the sake of better self-expression: the self-fulfilled are happy together because they can be happy apart in a pure relationship. New Women formally shun the idea of male provision.

The Girl Project seeks to reconcile independence with love, a tricky project. This New Love is coeval with feminism. The Old Love implied an individual insufficiency or a lacking, first a belief that one's life would not be complete or whole without another (or something) and then a finding of (or settling for) that other. Old Love involved dependence: men and women depended on each other for love and community—as love was a sign of one's mortality and insufficiency when alone. From the perspective of individual interest, this Old Love involves self-sacrifice, but it really involves the transformation of the individual into a new unity, as two become, in a decisive sense, one. Married couples informed by Old Love do not think overmuch about where mine begins and yours ends. The New Love is dispensable and arises only *after* individuals achieve self-sufficiency. They have no need for one another and hence no need to join something greater than themselves: this New Woman is already all she needs to be, in her mind. "The ideal," Beauvoir writes, "would be for entirely self-sufficient human beings to form unions one with another only in accordance with the untrammeled dictates of their mutual love."[36] Men, she seems to think, are already self-sufficient; it is high time for women to join them and stop being the second sex. Neither should sacrifice dreams or ways—and the New Woman's self-image of independence, as she understands it, cannot be compromised in the marriage. Love in the new dispensation is an act of generosity that does not compromise independence and does not demand the transformation of either individual.

Rosin is of two minds on whether self-sufficient human beings would share a life with another. A lot seems at stake here. On one hand, the "desire for a deeper connection always wins out, for both men and women," even, apparently, in the atmosphere where self-sufficiency, careerism, and independence are glorified. (If a desire for "deeper connection" is always there, perhaps a public teaching on the marital form helps nature. That is the old idea.) On the other hand, the sexual, marital, and childbearing norms of East Asian countries suggest that sex, marriage, and childbearing could fail to engage the human heart and lead to a deflation in marital life and "deeper connection" as such. The "looming problem," she writes, is the "threat of industrial-scale sexual indifference," as the high-achieving women fail to engage or interest men and even poison the relationship well and relationships with men do not interest the careerist women.[37] East Asian men, Rosin implies, may go for me-time, pornography, prostitutes, and sex robots, instead of the highly competent and seemingly independent, but also neurotic, manipulative, vain, unlovable New Girls; these self-satisfied New Girls will not be sufficiently appreciated as pearls of great price by mere men. Why settle?

The New Girl is just as sociable and plastic as the Old Girl, but she is pointed toward career rather than family life, marriage, and community. How do the for-the-most-part universal female traits manifest themselves in this new order? Womanly sociability or plasticity, of which Rosin and others are proud, has a dark side. Plasticity springs from a deep-seated anxiety or self-consciousness about how one looks, seems, and is—a trait that itself transforms work environments and marriage; social media does much to arouse and heighten this anxiety. This anxiety is, in the psychological jargon, labeled as neuroticism—so let's stick with the literature.[38] Neurotic employees want to be admired for what they do or have achieved; they have not done something unless it is observed and praised; they will do what pleases responsibly and in a timely way: conscientiousness and neuroticism feed one another in the workplace, and heighten demands in the home. Another way of thinking through this psychology is through the lens of Rousseau's vanity—where one sees oneself through the eyes of others. Vain neurotics demand more affirmation from their workplaces (workplaces must be more cooperative and less competitive; more mentoring and affirmation than in the past). And from spouses: they demand more emotional closeness, if not rule, in marriage, and men, who need women for community, cede, because much is at stake for them. Women still think they deserve handsome, high-status spouses worthy of their credentials. There is some evidence, grudgingly collected, that this new workplace, new marriage, and new education—all manifestations of the new gender—compromise womanly happiness. For instance, increasing percentages of women under our new dispensation are unhappy,[39] suffer from depression, take antidepressants,[40] are more likely to self-harm through suicide attempts or eating disorders, and other things. Their childhoods are less happy and more filled with anxiety. Women under the New Girl Order, after all, value equality and autonomy more than happiness anyways. Its purveyors seem to think that securing equality and autonomy so understood results in happiness. The promise of autonomy may not keep anyone warm at night, or happy during the day. Perhaps a bit too much promise and hope has been invested in careerism and too little in the workaday aspirations for happiness through communities grounded in nature. If so, then New Girls and single middle-aged women can be forgiven for thinking that they have been sold a false bill of goods.

New Girls, seeking an alternative to traditional love and marriage, sometimes ask themselves, "Why are there no good men left?" Whitehead's book, with this elegiac title, poses an ambiguous question. Does the New Girl bemoan the decline of chivalrous Old Men who provided for the Old Woman? No way. Men still provide for the New Girl by giving her what she demands in the workplace (e.g., clear rubrics, protections against harassment) and in the marriage (e.g., independence and buying power). New men of quality respect "woman's equality" and encourage womanly independence, from their marriage and from their family. These men embrace their own dispensability or disposability and respect women's choices. Womanly independence, competence, and confidence are what make these women interesting and attractive, men of quality come to think. New Men find traditional manliness unneeded, perhaps toxic, in today's controlled and managed world.[41] They may also be high achievers, because soul mates must share values and priorities, not because wives demand someone to look up to (or so all claim). Men and women are best friends in a pure relationship.

Above all these New Men accommodate themselves to the feminist critique of providing. Jessie Bernard, a feminist popularizer, puts that critique like this:

> The wife of a more successful provider became for all intents and purposes a parasite, with little to do except indulge or pamper herself. The psychology of such dependence could become all but crippling.

Such dependence prevents women from pursuing creative work and creates vulnerability and subordination—men earn the money, so they impose the decisions; men make the money, so they can abuse women emotionally and physically. Bernard continues: The provider role "delineated relationships within a marriage and family in a way that added to the legal, religious, and other advantages men had over women."[42] The New Girl Order *stigmatizes* the idea that it is a man's duty to provide for the family; instead, it empowers the New Girl to provide for herself.

Some men do not make New Girl Order home. Kay Hymowitz' observation, taken from the subtitle of her book *Manning Up: How the Rise of Women Has Turned Men into Boys* (2011), points to a decline of male responsibility among men in the New Girl Order. "Why aren't [more] young men evolving into postfeminist mensches?" Hymowitz asks (I insert the "more").[43] Much evidence from around the modern world suggests that education, health, suicide gaps between boys and girls under twenty are growing and life expectancy gaps between men and women are widening too, to the disadvantage of men.[44] The destruction of the provider role detaches men from private life, and fatherlessness creates its own snowball effect (boys without fathers do especially bad, and are less likely to be involved fathers themselves). No longer needed as providers for a family and entering marriage at great personal and financial risk to themselves, they have fewer reasons to enter marriage (especially when men need not buy the cow when they can get the milk for free). These observations resemble George Gilder's in *Sexual Suicide* (1973) and his related works. As women rise to careers and (in a sense) to independence, men, who need to feel needed and whose economic power (as feminists see it) is really about familial provision and service (as most husbands see it), feel less needed and let themselves go apart from women or they take a tremendous risk in marrying a fickle independent-minded woman who can, at any time, end the family. Rosin develops the same theme, with the added Machiavellian twist that unchanging "Cardboard Men" can become more like today's Plastic Women; they can change into "postfeminist mensches" in the New Girl Order—so she thinks or hopes.[45] Some men, however, find the New Woman unlovable—and they turn elsewhere for meaning, fulfillment, or a good time. They drop out of the mating game. This decline in marital character and responsibility among men is another downside of the New Girl Order.

Male strength comes, in part, from female resistance and expectations, as Rousseau argues and some studies show.[46] Some male ambition is grounded in satisfying and subordinating sexual *eros*. The expectation that men will provide for a family aids in this translation. Under conditions of sexual liberation, Gilder writes,

> males find it increasingly difficult to observe long-term erotic horizons. Their sex lives become increasingly oriented toward the next conquest of a tempting body. And because their social and work motivations are so profoundly intertwined with their sexuality, they find

their commitment to their jobs and communities also eroding. The emergence of impulsive male sexual patterns leads to adoption of a general pattern of hedonistic opportunism and impulsiveness.[47]

The New Woman leads some to an old problem. Civilized ambition, for good and ill, depends in no small part on the discipline, training and expansion of *eros* that comes, in the modern context, through enduring relations connected to marital form. That discipline comes from women demanding that men conform to heightened demands of a marital community—but today's plastic woman both wants and does not want that community and she needs and shuns provision from the outside. A better feminism—a womanism, in fact—would account for all of her aspirations.

A Return to a Womanism

Feminists have moved the needle toward the relationship system and with the careerism of the modern woman. If in 1970 one had offered Simone de Beauvoir, Betty Friedan, or Kate Millett the woman of 2005 or 2017, each might have thought the New Girl Order an extravagant dream. Friedan, who died in 2006, liked what she saw in the new women and thought, per a "not yet" pseudo-moderate feminist, that important reforms of the future would come from outside feminism and required the building a stronger state to regulate the market more. Yet each may have considered the New Girl Order just a step toward the final accomplishment.

Is the New Girl Order a destination or a halfway house? The New Girl Order accepts sex differences when it celebrates the way women remake professions as women come to rule them, but it decries the idea of sex differences in most other contexts. Feminist aspirations for independence and its denigration of the order of love, care (in the old sense of bearing burdens), manly provision, and human dependence complicate the very human hope to achieve happiness and community. Women want to be undefined and to have careers, and they want connection and love and to be pleasing to others. The New Girl Order complicates love because it ignores or stigmatizes the loving expression of male provision and attachment. Some women aspire to New Girl Order, but hardly all. For these reasons the New Girl Order is not the final word in human happiness, relations among the sexes, or our political community's aspirations. There will be some "return" or some "progress."

A return from New Girl Order begins with emphasizing the old human desire to "have it all" as opposed to desiring autonomy or independence. Reality tames this desire and forces upon all the question of priority and honor. Girls and boys should know from the start that a good life consists of having valuable, honorable work fostering individual accomplishment and also, often, a decent-enough communal life, an experience of love and self-giving aimed at a particular person, and many other goods. Feminism is not the story of our lives. People are embarrassed when they try to structure their sexed family lives according to the principles of liberal justice or autonomy. As our vision of the liberal state expands to regulate private arrangements, we are ever less able to articulate and defend familial partnerships. Men and women often have different reasons for entering this communal life in the main—men tend to want to be important to someone and hence to provide, while women tend to want to belong and, often, to be the hub of community. That difference is not defensible on the principles of liberal justice, so our modern poets would have us pretend the difference is a benighted prejudice. We emphasize career preparation, which can be conceived, I suppose, in terms of liberal autonomy. Almost nothing in our culture helps us see that "career preparation" fosters familial provision and community instead of autonomy and individual fulfillment. Almost nothing provides marriage preparation, spouse preparation, and parenting preparation. It is almost indecent to ask what character suits boys and girls to be future spouses.

For such preparation we womanists must hold up a vision consistent with marriage and motherhood and "having it all"—one that rejects feminism's starting point. Womanism is consistent with marital character. We need a summary statement of womanism as a contrast to Okin's statement about a world "beyond gender." I suggest the following:

> A happy future for human beings will have sex differences. The sexes achieve happiness in somewhat different ways. Sex will be way more important than one's eye color or the length of one's toes, especially when we consider jobs, education, and familial responsibility. Education and jobs, while mostly open to all as a matter of justice, will not be distributed evenly between the sexes. Demands for equality and independence in public have little to do with demands that people serve a common good in a family.

Marriages and families are in trouble when husbands and wives make justice their primary concern. For the most part, women will be less inclined to work full-time in competitive jobs and in jobs that involve things rather than people and men will be more inclined to work full-time in competitive jobs, somewhat dangerous jobs, and that involve things rather than people. Most men and women will find satisfaction in living a common life with a person of the opposite sex. Our culture should expect, in the main, men and women to contribute differently to that common life and to enter common life for somewhat different reasons. It might encourage people to live such lives as a part of pursuing happiness for most because such common dedication does not arise without some regime-level intention. These desires ground our mixed regime in late modernity. Mores and our sense of honor must expand the horizon of men and women toward a common life with another.

If the "independent woman" is the ideal for the feminists, the "part-time work" model guides womanists. Do not think that womanism adopts the "part-time work" model for reasons of economic efficiency or justice or contributing just a little more to family resources. Women can refuse part-time work, of course. "Part-time work" womanism is about accommodating a variety of priorities. Part-time work allows women to spend more of their time in their families, in building a community of friends apart from work, and in making a beautiful home where children and family can share a meal and grow together, while recognizing that women are perfectly able to do things outside of that. It recognizes that the necessities of the household are not so time-consuming as they were when someone had to make the clothes, spend time finding ways to wash clothes, grow food, shop daily for fresh food, or spend hours lighting and managing fires. This woman takes on many tasks with a variety of people. She can manage a variety of schedules and still weave a common life where people and friends are made to know they are important. A "part-time work" womanist does not shun the kitchen—not because it is her place, but because cooking and eating a common meal is an act of love and community at which she is the center, just as male provision expresses love. This womanist could work full-time if she must or if she is so inclined; she is capable of doing many things. "Part-time work" allows her to lean out some of the time to prioritize important things that might otherwise fall into disuse or be ignored. A "part-time work" womanism accommodates itself to the male tendency to provide, with the hopes that providing materially is related to providing spiritually for the child and the family. Work backward from everything that a family meal involves—including having children, having long time horizons, providing, and feeling the beauty of the meal—and we have the character of womanism.

The man corresponding to womanism appreciates, contributes to, and provides for this communal atmosphere. His earnings are the family's earnings—and he will probably continue to make fewer consumer decisions than his wife. That's a division of labor that the man of womanist sensibilities has to live with: he earns most of the money; she spends most of it! Perhaps this husband and wife can even needle each other about this—with the woman showing her appreciation for what he does while showing him that he is not quite as important as he thinks he is, while he questions the wisdom of each purchase and the importance of the nest. He will work a job, perhaps even not liking it overmuch, because it is his responsibility: feminists call this male power; human beings see this as duty.

Those in authority have a complicated job promoting womanism. A statesman treats all citizens as future workers and as someone's future spouse, though of course that is a pleasing fiction. Many may not marry. Many may not work. Many may fail at marriage. Many may have unsuccessful work lives. Public morality demands such a gentle, decent drapery for life. Imagine a statesman's speech at the head of a healthier public opinion:

> Greetings fellow citizens. I speak today about our country's women. A feminism emphasizing independence is not the story of your life. No one doubts your abilities, Ladies. You accomplish many things. You work tirelessly. You do great things in the workplace. Your reservoirs of strength run deep. As you manage busy lives, you also fill our lives with beauty, tenderness, and care. We value you for making unique contributions to private and public life. Lives without the love that you make possible would hardly be worth living: you bring consolation through life's disappointments and make life's achievements more joyous. You are the fount of all life and we are proud to support our loving homes. We love and treasure you.
>
> I also speak to our men. Your work brings with it its own rewards, not only for your families but also for accomplishments that are important to our country. Never forget that you work and represent more than yourselves. You have responsibilities to your family—to support them, to protect and discipline your children, to speak your mind to them and to listen to them. As poets remind us, you are lost at sea without the ones you love.
>
> Our women and men live happier lives together, sharing meals, building and maintaining beautiful homes, and dividing the tasks necessary for a common life as you see fit. Make time for this. Each contributes something crucial to that common life—appreciate what each other does. Imagine what it will be like when you reach old age, and you can look back on the home, family, and life you have lived together and on the care you have given one another, and what you have accomplished and overcome together. That, my fellow citizens, is a glimpse of paradise!

A more erudite man might suggest the promise of Alyosha and Lisa in Dostoevsky's *Brothers Karamazov* or the strange beauty of Natasha and Pierre as Tolstoy depicts in *War and Peace* as models. Nevertheless, this orientation emphasizing both economic and familial fulfillment points from "independence" and toward "having it all," moderately. Treating each person as a worker and a future spouse complicates our mode of education, but it is the only way whereby the desire to have it all can be integrated into a life. Through such action, this new problem with no name might be mitigated, putting some tasty wine into attractive wineskins.

12

DILEMMAS OF INDIRECTION

Maintaining Family Integrity in Late Modernity

Sex differences, public morality, and a comprehensive understanding of sexual passion put limits on what the rolling revolution can and should accomplish—and the *can* and the *should* reinforce one another: because human beings cannot be so remade, no one should aim at comprehensive reforms; because they should not be done, those who respect the human cannot do them. Know limits! The rolling revolution rejects our condition as embodied and relational beings, capable and interested in attachment to community of finding meaning in sacrificial love for one another and as political animals. If the rolling revolution is not a rejection of the human condition, it is an attempt to create a new human being.

These general principles traversed in chapters 5–7, helpful and necessary, are not enough because they do not point unambiguously to a policy and a vision of marriage and family life. Embodied and relational people need conventions to mediate their embodiment and relational nature, just as we need conventions to point people to the "pure" relationship. Which conventions? Men and women are different and we should expect them to follow different paths but precisely what that means for educating men and women is not totally clear. Modern America must hew to the middle path, between those who deny that natural differences exist (second-wave feminists) and biological essentialists (existing mostly in the minds of those second-wave feminists) who think sex determines social roles. Sex matters, but how much does it matter and in what ways? Those are much harder questions. Liberal neutrality is a fantasy, but that does not tell us what morality should be encouraged in our laws. Sex without responsibility, regret, or shame is hardly a human norm, but that does not point directly and only to bourgeois marriage or enduring love. It is not enough to deconstruct the claims of the rolling revolution, as I have done (though that is essential). It is not enough to expose errors in how rolling revolutionaries stigmatize elements of a responsible public opinion and practice (though that is essential too, in our time). It is also necessary to account for the complex human life that exists once we get beyond the risible simplicity of the rolling revolution. That hard work is just beginning; it involves not a little understanding of, and appreciation for, the Old Wisdom before the revolution was entrenched.

The general framework for maintaining the integrity of marriage and the family in late modernity, established in chapter 8, calls for the protection of marital and parental rights and the ability of parents to make decisions for their children. Modern governments protect marriage and family life also through protecting or sustaining a moral environment within which the passions and interests are more likely to lead people to marriage and family life and, if need be, through building such an environment. Chapters 9 and 10 concerned various threats to such an environment, and involved some ground clearing that is part of reconstructing a public opinion more conducive to marriage and family life. Chapter 9 concerned defending civil society from charges of homophobia and misogyny and reestablishing a moderate but principled policy, accommodating human diversity, concerning homosexuality, population decline, and the woman question. No society can embrace the rolling revolution on these matters and survive in the long term. There are resources in human nature (i.e., sex differences and nature's customary policies), however, and satisfactions in human life (i.e., the joys of having children, the human desire and need for love, and of fulfilling all of one's nature) that might lead to a more balanced, mixing policy conducive to human diversity and social health. Chapter 10 dealt with consent, aiming to show how consent is too ambiguous a term to build a family policy around and too destabilizing when radicalized to form the only basis for human relationships. Consent is not enough to explain civilized opposition to rape or statutory rape; and it cannot be the only value we embrace when it comes to marriage and dissolving marriage. Some notions of honor and shame, nature and endurance, and proper sexual relations limit the consent human beings give or withhold: no public can be or really is indifferent to such notions. Ultimately, a moral environment favorable to marriage and family life would be more likely to form human beings with marital character along the lines of a moderate womanism, as I discussed in the postscript to chapter 5 and in chapter 11.

This chapter concerns other challenges to marital and familial integrity afoot today. Those challenges are attempts to roll the revolution farther. Many of these threats come from more than one wing of the rolling revolution, and hence those who would secure the mixed character of our regime must be prepared to meet multiple shifting arguments at the same time. What follows is more than a sketch of some issues facing those who would maintain marital and familial integrity in the modern world. The issues that I choose will someday be dated, but the principles underlying the issues are permanent challenges in a liberal society taken with the rolling revolution. I choose these issues for the purpose of being illustrative of the various venues of conflict, with hopes of showing how principles can be applied to practical situations. I show why various threats will emerge, how those threats have worked and will work themselves out in laws and rules, what is at stake in the particular threats, and I identify the resources within human nature and political life in our time and place that help to combat these threats. The threats concern parental rights and duties and the status of public morality, among other things.

The Rolling Revolution and Parental Rights and Duties

The leading edges of radical feminist thought, as we have seen, would prohibit mothers (and the plague of fathers, I presume) from taking primary responsibility for their own children, while most retail feminists, more moderate, just hope that mothers and fathers would be incentivized to de-prioritize their children (for now!). In response to the moderate objective, modern governments abet de-prioritizing through transferring familial duties to the state, always moving further. The feminist stated goal is independence for women and adults generally, so public education, one of the great modern innovations, is the central vehicle for feminist family policy. Education must de-prioritize marriage and family life, emphasizing the "girl project" instead of the "mom project," as we saw last chapter. Contemporary liberalism gets to the same destination, with slightly different reasoning. It seeks to conceptually separate having children from raising children, and to allow autonomous individuals to add up these features however they would like.

As we saw in our treatment of feminism, it is not clear that human beings value independence as much as feminists hope—and hence there is an opening for love and responsibility. It is good for neither man nor woman to be alone. Efforts to separate procreation from parenting always presume that there should be some connection between the two. Those who advocate for the licensing of parents still think that birth parents should be the ones licensed. No political community orders people to have procreative sex. No political community calls into question that the mother of the child physically is the mother of the child for purposes of raising the child. Few, if any, political communities call into question that the father of the child physically is the father of the child for the purpose of raising the child. These facts demonstrate that the family is not a creature of the political community: political communities recognize and protect marriages and families that exist prior to the claims of law and politics. Neither feminism nor contemporary liberalism is enough to explain these parts of human existence—and hence each runs up against moral and physical limits.

Political communities, however, also limit the power of parents. Parents do not have absolute, arbitrary power over their children. To take only the most extreme example, killing children is not, as it was under the Roman family, legal. The boundary between political and parental power is always an issue in political life, because each has a legitimate claim on the other. Political communities acknowledge parental authority, while parental authority is subject to limits in political communities. In Sophocles' *Antigone*, for instance, the emergence of *civil* gods poses a challenge to *family* gods—and civic harmony demands that family members cease their allegiance to their family gods; Antigone herself makes totalistic claims on behalf of her service to the family, just as Creon makes them on behalf of the city—and the clash of such totalistic claims is the source of the play's tragedy. Antigone's totalistic claim on behalf of her family leads to her mad love for her dead brother Polynices, while Creon's totalistic claim on behalf of the city denies that the family is a source of happiness and order. In other instances, the need to wage war calls husbands and sons away from family duties to serve the needs of the entire political community. The number of touch points between the family and the political community multiplies under conditions of the modern state, when providing health, welfare, and education become central goals of the state while also remaining the responsibility of parents. What happens when the views of parents clash with the views of the state on these matters?

Moreover, people may agree in principle on what the state's role shall be, but that agreement shatters when it is reduced to specifics. All agree that child abuse is wrong, but what constitutes child abuse? More than fifty countries, as of this writing, beginning with Sweden in 1979, ban spanking children or any form of corporal punishment; many do not ban it. Is spanking abusive? All agree that parents should not neglect their children, but we disagree about how far parental inattentiveness must extend before it is actionable. Does it extend to "free-range" parenting as it is called? Most agree that parents should be able to pass on their ways to their children, but does that extend to a belief in faith healing for a sick child or a rejection of immunization shots or the adoption of homeschooling as opposed to public schooling? Some governments decide that a child's life is not worth living, and hence end treatment for that child, while parents are more willing to make uneconomical decisions in such situations. Must governments help parents to hand their ways down to their children? Can the state undertake medical care on behalf of a child against the wishes and judgment of parents? It is one thing to know what parents should do; it is quite a different thing to assume direction in these matter as state policy. How can the boundaries be negotiated?

This question cannot simply be treated on an issue-by-issue basis; all questions arise in a political moment and contribute to the making of another moment. Ignoring the direction of the political regime risks opening a host of uninvited problems in the medium term. If the wind is blowing in the direction of excessive parental or familial power (as it often has), then the statesman should be concerned to limit those powers, within reason, through actions of the public. Early anti-patriarchal liberals like John Locke limited the power of fathers by divorcing political power from parental power, among other things. If the direction of the regime is toward greater notions of public power in these matters, then the statesmanlike mixer must protect the vulnerable provenance of parental power. This is often the situation of those who would defend the family in late modernity, since even many of those with families have a thinner conception of parental duties and therefore invite much state supervision and provision.

Under liberal governments, as we have seen, parental rights are protected so that parents can understand and exercise their duties. The rights that are being protected are designed to protect the integrity of the family as a community based on loyalty, obedience, sharing, and trust. Every defense of such parental rights risks a defense of child-raising that does not meet the best interests or the needs of a child. Protecting parental rights may mean protecting the parent who serves a two-year-old Mountain Dew and the father who cusses. The good that parents do will in the main outweigh the bad, probably (and the state, no matter how rational we think it is, would make many mistakes). Acknowledging parental rights involves acknowledging the parent–child bond, apart from their good or bad use.

There was a healthy ambiguity in early liberal thinking on the family on whether the family community was respected in principle or for the good of the children. That ambiguity is resolved in later modern thinking in favor of a "parental rights-child's needs" framework, where states decide whether parents are meeting a child's needs. Consider this from a rather conservative defender of parental authority, who defends the family as a natural, pre-political community: "Organized society has the right and the duty to supervise the provision of welfare benefits for the child, to enforce the fulfillment of parental duties in this regard, to supplement the efforts of the parents when necessary, with or without their consent."[1] Under such a vision, the state limits parental rights and authority in the name of physical, mental, and sexual health. It's an ICGU, it seems. This approach is too one-sided to solve the conflict between the family and state. It creates a porous boundary between parents and the state that the state can cross at will when it thinks it has discovered what the "best interests of the child" are.

Let us take stock on parental rights and authority, since we assume so much. Let us go to the fabled example from Soviet days of children informing on their parents as a means of preparing to think thoughts contrary to today's approach. Pavlik Morozov, the boy hero celebrated in poetry, song, plays, and opera, was held up as the example of honesty and integrity for turning his father in for treason and for hoarding; the boy was said to be shot by relatives in retaliation for his alleged treachery against his father.[2] It was precisely to upset familial loyalty that the Soviets promulgated such propaganda.[3] Could that happen here? No respectable person has (yet) suggested that parents could be turned in for hate speech behind closed doors. Why? Would demanding that children inform on parents contradict principles of public policy? Glorifying children-informants would eliminate the family community as a means of protecting the public—and it would be an instrument of tyranny that seeks to sow divisions and distrust among its population as a result.[4] It compromises trust, loyalty, love, fidelity, and gratitude. Family and friends are those with whom one can share thoughts that become unutterable under totalitarian regimes and their ilk; this confidential sharing of thoughts builds trust and loyalty and reflects it. Many slights and small irritations occur in family life; no decent community would provide opportunities for members to use those episodes to disrupt the bedrock institution even when public justice is implicated. Furthermore, obedience is a virtue among (especially young) children; encouraging childhood informing would make the state complicit in fomenting rebellion within the family while sapping the vitality from the private sphere. Spousal privilege exists in our system of courts precisely to protect the trust of the home—and this same justification extends to prohibiting state authorities from requiring or encouraging children to inform on their parents.[5] Parents are not low-level civil servants delegated powers by the state to carry on the state's projects or duties as the state understands them. Families are not ICGUs.

There are cases like incest or extreme physical abuse where the integrity of the family community must be abridged. Incest (a father or stepfather with a daughter, for instance) is not simply bad for the gene pool—if that is even any part of it. If it is a stepfather, after all, no gene pool problem exists. Incest is a violation of parental love and responsibility. Families are based on preexisting bonds determined at some level through biology and birth, while loving bonds are chosen. Incest is an indication that the family is too insular and that loyalty makes excessive demands on members of the family's community. In this sense, incest is a political crime and tends toward a politics of tribalism; it implies that the insular family community has no need of the political community. In some parts of the world, kin marriage, marriage among close cousins, and the closely related child marriage, compromises the pursuit of political justice with excessive clannishness.[6] Sexual and loving bonds are incompatible with the filial respect and responsibilities of rearing children to be political animals.[7] Sex between blood relations (parents-children) and those mirroring blood relations (adoptive or stepparents-children) are abusive because the sexual intimacy between the parties threatens all the other kinds of intimacies that make up family living. Physical abuse too is a violation of trust, partaking perhaps much of a spirit of revenge rather than a concern for the cultivation of political animals who can govern and be governed in turn and whose integrity is respected in the family.

There are ditches on both sides. The proper framework for policing the border between the family and the political community concerns protecting and respecting the atmosphere of trust and responsibility central to family life while also respecting the existence of laws necessary to the political community and pointing beyond the family to a political community open to justice.

Many of today's conflicts about the boundary between the political community and the family concern practices that seem "out of the mainstream" such as faith healing, parents who oppose vaccinations, parents who would educate their own children, parents who do not support their children transitioning from one gender to another or parents who would educate their children toward sex in ways that differ from majority opinion. These questions arise in hospitals and schools. The rise of modern health care throughout the Western world reflects a decision of democratic publics to invest in physical health over other values—to make comfortable and affordable self-preservation the preeminent public value instead of virtue or salvation or the cultivation of gentlemanly affections in leisure. At the same time, infant mortality rates have plummeted which has led to a great rise in life expectancy. Childhood diseases and childbirth itself are no longer the scourges they were before 1900. Our advancing medicine makes singling out the public value of health all the more plausible. Many conflicts between the demands of modern medicine and parental rights concern the relative priority of health in a good life—and the legitimate range of disagreement over those priorities. Sometimes the state wants the parents to do something that the parents do not want to do, while other times the state does not do something that the parents would have it do.

Much has been done in progressive schooling to detach religious instruction and parental involvement from formal education through making schools free to the public in the United States. Few citizens turn to public education out of a tragic sense that education of children is best done by parents but modern parents have neither the time nor the expertise to do it well. Support for public education (publicly funded and administered) is an aspect of public justice in the American polity and in modern polities generally (responsible, affluent families provide the proper school district for their children to be educated by those properly trained to do it). Self-governing liberal societies need educated citizens capable of exercising skills in the modern workforce and using judgment in republican governments. The preeminence of public schools makes them delivery mechanisms of the rolling revolution. Consider sex education.[8] Before public involvement sex was considered a family matter and a church matter: sex implicated the holy, the virtuous, and the perpetuation of a family's ways. Public schools started providing sex education in the 1970s because, it was said, parents were not doing an adequate job, because they were too ill-informed themselves or too unrealistic about what kids do, or they imposed their ill-starred morality on their children. Far from the holy, sex education became a public health measure; safe, protected sex, the type favored in public schooling, would prevent the spread of diseases—or so it was thought; protected sex would help prevent teenage pregnancies; students need to "know the facts" if they are to act intelligently in sexual matters; and, in any event, public settings for discussions about sex helps to foster a free and open exchange of ideas and hence sex among consenting adults capable of pure relationships.

Sex education sets the pattern for how public schools generally deal with boundaries of families with children. Families cede sexual territory to public schools, which increases the boldness of state institutions generally and weakens the sense of responsibility and efficacy of parents and clergy. Education becomes not *in loco parentis*, but *in contra parentis*. Other changes are consistent with this. In the name of protecting a child's autonomy, minors can get abortions without parental consent or knowledge. In the name of protecting a child's mental health, students or young human beings allegedly interested in transitioning from one gender to another can, in some jurisdictions, do so without parental knowledge or against parental wishes if those students assert that their parents might resist a mode of transitioning.

These examples raise several issues. On the level of technique: Does sex education promote sexual health? Does immunization promote public and individual health? Does transitioning from one gender to another promote mental health? How much certainty is required in any of these areas for the public to demand crossing the boundary into parental authority? Will genuine science, as opposed to ideology and strong, connected pressure groups, answer these questions? On the level of priority and principle: Under what circumstances can parents act on different views from the public? Can parents prioritize something above or other than health even to the detriment of a child's health as the public understands it?

A fanciful example (where the shoe is on the other foot) illuminates the issue. Imagine a father, a wealthy pornographer, who forces his boy to watch two hours of pornography from an impressionable age so that, in the father's view, the boy would live without sexual repression and have a taste for the family business. Would this father be guilty of child abuse?[9] Pornographic education may compromise a boy's ability to grow up to honor and respect women instead of seeing them as sexual playthings or objects; it may render a future adult less productive, more bored and listless as an adult, and less self-controlled; this child would lead a worse life, with a stunted idea of *eros* and much lower horizons. Our laws are solicitous of the impressionability of children because of the harm exposure to obscene material may cause a child's character and prospects. A pornographic education contradicts the "best interests of the child" and compromises family integrity. Parents who watch pornography and allow their children to watch pornography are, as a result, on some accounts, disfavored in custody hearings.

However, even granting this, it may not be child abuse *in the context of our rolling revolution*, where laws and mores conform to the pure relationship, sexual plasticity, and a morality of self-expression. Something tolerated in adults cannot easily be proscribed to parents of children and hence those things will affect their children. It also may not be child abuse for the purposes of ascertaining parental rights. Parental rights assume that a political community represents a nation of families; protecting familial integrity is central to achieving the family's good, the good of most individuals, and the public good.

The fanciful circumstance of the pornographer father puts in stark relief what I mean by asking whether state action would compromise family integrity and trust instead of focusing on the question of child's needs. The political community should police and proscribe practices that disrupt the integrity of the family, perhaps proscribe practices that may lead to the disrupting of the family's integrity, and should proscribe practices that disrupt the fundamentals of a political community that transcends the family. This approach might defend the rights of the pornographic father, depending on the context. It would defend homeschoolers, so long as they took a basic competency test during their schooling and were not unduly compromising the society through organized rebellion against its laws. It would defend those who embrace faith healing as part of respecting their ability to make decisions about a child's mental and physical health generally, especially since in such situations the public is not in danger and the faith is part of the family's integrity. It would be sympathetic to those opposing modern vaccines—though it could prevent such folks from attending public schools. Parents could supervise their children's consumption of alcohol. Parents could allow or encourage their children to work outside the home, so long as some minimal education goals were met (child labor laws, that is, may violate parental rights in the name of a controversial definition of "best interests of the child").[10]

Another hard case involves whether children could give evidence in court against their parents. The parental covering of children for the purposes of the political community extends to the parent having the power to grant or deny permission to the state to uncover children for purposes of politics. Parental cover is not unlimited: the closer crimes are to incest, pedophilia, or anger-ridden or vindictive punishing, and the more crimes strike at the heart of a political community, the more the state is justified in uncovering children against the consent of parents. If dad murders mom or stepdad farms out child as a sex slave or abuses the child, testimony from children could be compelled. A minor child would not be compelled to testify against a parent hiding evidence of tax evasion within the home, unless that tax evasion is part of an excessive clannishness and continued into adulthood. When the family poses a grave and gathering danger to public order and especially to the equal application of the laws, the public steps in to protect public justice and limit the family.

Consider spanking. Even critics of corporal punishment like John Locke see it as of use in the case of a willful, *"sturdy humor"* in young children and after other kinds of discipline (i.e., explanation, shaming, isolation) fail to change a child's disposition.[11] Still many countries proscribe spanking as a parenting technique, on the basis of scientific analysis of its effectiveness and of its secondary effects.[12] Much is interesting in this example. First, public authorities in many countries are tempted to invent "needs" or proscribe "abuse" through a manipulated, ideological science, aimed at achieving results more than understanding the phenomenon. Permeating the family on the basis of questionable science, in the name of fashionable modern trends, is a permanent temptation in the typical liberal approach that emphasizes "child's needs" to determine when public authorities should intrude. Spanking, when used under the proper circumstances with a young stubborn child and after other modes have been tried, as described by Locke, may be effective in helping to shape the actions and dispositions of children—this thought is confirmed through human experience and across cultures. "He who spares the rod hates his son" (Proverbs 13:24) is a biblical injunction with metaphorical and literal significance. Children have unruly passions, including a passion for domination. If anti-spanking advocates deny this premise, they contradict the idea that good and evil run through the heart of all people. Domineering passions must be disciplined for a child to become a republican citizen. The rod is metaphorical to indicate that discipline is essential to educating a child, but it may also be literal because sometimes such discipline can best be accomplished through selective use of corporal punishment as awakening a child to the seriousness of an episode. Beatings or whippings can be proscribed as violations of the trust central to family life, but parental authority and the very trust of a family contain a legitimate sphere of discretion on how to help children achieve self-control.

The vague, easily permeable legal standards such as "parental rights" or "best interests of the child" should not be divorced from the theoretical justification for those standards. That justification relates to the things that society seeks to avoid—excessive clannishness on the one hand and interruptions of public justice on the other hand. A humble policy, avoiding such excesses, leaves parents a swath of discretion between these two ditches.

Obscenity and Maintaining Public Morality: Old Wisdom and New Frontiers

While obscenity is as old as the stage, it presents a new problem under modern conditions of sexual liberation and contemporary liberalism. Old obscenity in the vein of Aristophanes' *Assembly of Women* used obscenity to show how the natural and sexual persisted within the conventions of a political community; it opened the way toward philosophy and hence toward recognizing the limits of political reform.[13] Old obscenity persists in some modern dystopian books (e.g., Huxley's *Brave New World*).

Modern obscenity, while sometimes confused with the old obscenity, appeals to sexual passion to arouse it. Modern legislators long discouraged indulging obscenity as corrupting of public morals and inimical to individual and collective self-government. As modern communications advanced (from photographs, to mass market magazines, to videos, to the internet), publics sought either to choke off its supply or to discourage its use. Laws regulated obscenity because society has an interest in the amusements and passions about which its citizens were concerned, an interest that it achieves indirectly.

Initially, obscenity was defined through the so-called *Hicklin* standard (promulgated in 1868 first in England). Obscene material has the "tendency . . . to deprave and corrupt those whose minds are open to such immoral influences, and into whose hands a publication of this sort may fall."[14] The *Hicklin* test, first, focused on the effects of the works, not on describing what was going on in the works. This kept the public purpose of shaping the affections and passions of those who could be exposed to obscene materials front and center. Second, effects were measured on "minds . . . open to such immoral influence," not on the average person or on a person of unusual self-control or on the literary critic. These laws sought to protect children and vulnerable men from having their minds corrupted or depraved through the viewing of obscene materials. Temptations to view or read about naked bodies would be there, and the law could help protect the vulnerable from giving in to temptation and hence from being unduly influenced by obscenity. Third, there was no off-set for works with a serious literary value. Works with isolated lines or just a few infamous pictures that were intended to arouse or deprave instead of instruct, even if the rest of the work had serious literary or theoretical merit, could be and sometimes were, on this standard, prohibited through zealous prosecutions.[15]

Anti-obscenity laws were part of a system of public morality aimed at educating self-governing citizens. Sexual desire points in many directions: the fantasy of separating sexual pleasure from responsible actions is a temptation in human life, as is the possibility of connecting enduring love and sex. Individuals do not simply choose how and whether to disconnect or connect these matters. Sexuality is organized socially and privately. Human beings are imitative and imaginative animals. A public's teaching shapes how human beings think, fantasize, and act; the public is not unconcerned about whether sexual desires become civilized. The *Hicklin* standard allows the political community to protect and promote images that favor the teaching of self-restraint and self-control, that protect a sense of shame, and that consign rightly private, personal relations to the personal sphere. Fewer people are seen as sex objects if sex is kept private and mysterious. It is more likely that sexual desire can, under those circumstances, be translated into enduring love, respect for the individuality of each partner, and legitimate individual ambition and public service.[16] The *Hicklin* approach reflects a modesty, not demanding sanctity in one's soul. It contributes to an environment where the translation of sexual passion into enduring love and mutual respect is more likely.

At the onset of our rolling revolution, the United States (and much of the modern world) modified and then abandoned the *Hicklin* standard and its broader educational effort. As a matter of law, the departure came with *Roth v. United States* (1957), which put forward the following test for obscenity: "whether to the average person, applying contemporary community standards, the dominant theme of the material taken as a whole, appeals to the prurient interest."[17] Gone from the test was the special focus on the vulnerable and the focus on isolated parts a work. The new test emphasized "average person" and "contemporary standards"; the "prurient interest" to which a work appeals; and the work's "dominant theme." Obscenity could still be proscribed, but the laws were now detached from their public purpose of avoiding excessively misshapen sexual passions and they were attached to evolving standards as opposed to permanent temptations. As a permissive society arose,[18] the revolution in obscenity rolled on. As viewing of pornography spread, contemporary community standards shifted, average people become more accepting, and prurience was defined down.[19] This new environment would therefore organize or shape sexuality differently, with implications for public morality.

The deregulation of obscenity and pornography illustrates the promises of the rolling revolution in contemporary liberalism and sexual liberation—and the limits on those promises. Sexual liberationists thought the deregulation of obscenity would end sexual repression and make love between and among people flow more freely; that shame about one's body and one's sex life would erode and with it a major cause of repression and social control; that laws censoring obscenity and pornography would end debilitating hypocrisy of those who censure pornography in principle but take a peek in practice; that the end of obscenity would liberate self-expression, which is more human and precious than self-control; that consumption of obscene material would be a substitute for, not a stimulus to, antisocial, dangerous ways of acting (it would be a safety valve); that pornography would instruct in the ways of sexual fulfillment and enhance underperforming libidos, the satisfaction of which is central to human happiness; that the end of obscenity would usher in an era when people would be more adult, mature, and sophisticated about their sex lives, without alarm, titillation, or obsession; that ours would cease to be a culture of sex-obsessed voyeurs if sexual curiosity and passions were satisfied with regularity and without the need for another human being; and that that censorship has created a taste for the forbidden activity—like the snake tempting Eve with the forbidden fruit—and it may decline once it ceased being forbidden.[20]

Contemporary liberals endorsed the deregulation of obscenity in the name of freedom and neutrality: censorship is harmful to society, while an imperfect, arbitrary censorship is more harmful and corrupting still.[21] Efforts to inhibit artists, scientists or moral experimentation would rob society of benefits from free and open inquiry; artistic and scientific progress, apart from their social benefits, come from free and open inquiry. Human dignity comes from the free, conscious pure act of the will that chooses the good and true; the more alternatives before the individual the better; anything less than this is "cloistered virtue" (to borrow from Milton) and hence no virtue at all. A mature society would ignore, not suppress, obscene material: "Our goal should be to enable the public to recognize trash when they see it and to graduate from worthless literature and impersonal sexual satisfactions to high levels of personal maturity. . . . It may be questioned whether censorship is an effective means of developing good character."[22] An imperfect, arbitrary censorship of obscenity may ban classic, racy works (e.g., Aristophanes' *Assembly of Women*). Censors just seek to control kinds of vice that a majority or connected minority happens to disfavor. Censorship is based on a pretended knowledge of the supposed social harms that social scientists cannot trace indubitably to obscenity with their techniques. Censors overdo it, seeking sanctity that is beyond the demands of liberal governments. After all, in addition, one man's pornography is another man's great literature or Venus de Milo.[23]

The move from *Hicklin* to *Roth* and its progeny greatly curtailed the regulation of obscenity. Generally, sexual liberationists and contemporary liberals converge in seeing little or no harm—and much good—in such deregulation and the corresponding public acceptance of obscenity. As we are generations since a policy was initiated with the avowed object and confident promise of bringing "the end of obscenity," we should be able to ask whether that policy has delivered on its promises.

One cannot expect geometric certainty on such matters, since all social phenomena are complex. The deregulation of pornography is not the only cause of its proliferation since there is a natural interest in things sexual and pornography existed in some fashion before its deregulation. There are not a few countervailing effects (e.g., education, community norms, religious beliefs, parental oversight) that lead individuals away from obscene temptations. Nevertheless, since sexuality is partly cultural, the deregulation of obscenity affects private actions and attitudes and contributes to the erosion of a public morality conducive to the making of enduring, marital relations. The "end of obscenity" is not the sole cause for the decline of the family or of any particular social problem: many changes in laws and mores (e.g., changes in divorce law, the advent of oral contraception, radical feminism, etc.) arose at the same time and all together affect lives, relationships, and families.

Furthermore, deregulation of obscenity before the internet (roughly 1957 or 1973 until the early 1990s) had less of an impact than the post-1990s obscenity. Shame still operated when people had to purchase magazines or visit seedy nightclubs or video shops; a few furtive peeks at nakedness or sex acts are less likely to affect long-term attitudes, character, and social practice than more prevalent obsessive preoccupation and saturation more characteristic of the internet age.[24] Those born in the 1990s are the first generation of easily accessible, anonymous, affordable internet pornography. The worst fears of the most intelligent critics of deregulating pornography from the late 1960s and 1970s (i.e., Harry Clor and Walter Berns), who seemed to think American culture was a sewer then, are now more likely to be realized as deregulation meets more accessible technology.

These reasons for modesty aside, the deregulation of pornography on contemporary liberal and sexual liberationist grounds causes intrinsic problems that mirror half-truths in those theories as developed in chapters 6 and 7. Generally, against the sexual liberationists, the more radical divorce of sex from love and the reduction of sex to a bodily act involving the sexual organs initiated through pornography compromises the interpersonal, enduring-love side of sex. Consumers of pornography often have empty, compulsive, narcissistic lives. Generally, against contemporary liberalism that affects to promote neutrality, pornography shapes relationships and expectations toward the pure relationship and shapes our public morality in ways that compromise our ability to establish enduring love and community in marriage. It makes sex more compulsive and more at the heart of human relationships and marriages.

The theory that obscenity and pornography affect the minds, lives, relations, and families of those who consume them is based on the following train of reasoning. Pornography affects the senses, imagination, and minds of its viewers,[25] and its prevalence in a culture affects attitudes about sex and relations. Such changes in imagination, mind, and culture compromise the ability to form relations or bonds and the interest in forming bonds, sex, and responsibilities. The aggregate of these individual changes relates to changes in public morality—the expectations suggestive of a common ethos. Far-seeing critics saw that deregulating pornography would make it increasingly difficult to maintain the connections at the heart of marriage, enduring love, and responsible family life; that alternative forms of sexual experimentation and especially depersonalized sex would become ever more common; that women would have to cater more to the sexual fantasies of men to win their attentions; that men especially would become bored, listless, shameless, and less able to handle responsibilities in an age of obscenity; and that ending obscenity would lead to a corruption of the arts (as those who transgress boundaries would continue a race to erase the next boundary) and to the corruption of politics (as defensible lines would be more difficult to draw in many spheres of common life).[26]

Let us trace this chain of reasoning from the image of pornography to personal relations. I rely on Harry Clor's pioneering typology, based on his meticulously documented study of pornographic works, from before the internet era.[27] Certainly no decent man would conduct such a study, much less relate one at second hand, unless it was necessary to undermine the obscuring abstractions on which contemporary liberals and sexual liberationists rely to defend pornography. Let's dig in! According to the very decent Clor, pornography ranges from still shots, emphasizing sexual organs (so-called spreader shots) indicating sexual readiness and invitation; to videos with actual sexual performances going from a single act of sexual satisfaction to videos with a wide variety of sexual acts performed between and among sexual partners; to other videos with the range of sexual acts combined with humiliation, submission, and violence. Since Clor's study, pornography has moved more from pin-ups to video to online files to ever raunchier presentations.[28] Thus, a scholar in the internet era describes, "pornography typically treats gazers to a veritable fire-hose dousing of sex-act diversity, and presses its consumers away from thinking of sex as having anything to do with love, monogamy, or childbearing. . . . Add to the sharing of bodies temporarily and nonexclusively a significant dose of alternative sexual activities—different positions, roles, genders, and varying numbers of participants—and that is basically where porn leads today: away from sex as having anything approaching a classic marital sense or structure."[29]

With deregulation has come increased consumption of pornography, mostly coincident to the rise of internet as the primary means of consumption. The number of men under twenty-nine years of age using pornography doubled between 1978 and 2006 (to 54%).[30] Other studies show that in the mid-2010s 43% of men and 9% of women report watching pornography in the past week; 46% of men and 16% of women between 18 and 39 years old have watched in the past week; 24% of men in the past day; and 53% of men in the past month. Furthermore, more than 30% of 60-year-old men watch pornography.[31] Attitudes toward watching pornography have remained somewhat hostile, but it is way easier to access and therefore many who view it regret it or are ambivalent.[32] The pornography industry of the early 2000s has more revenue than any of the major professional sports.[33]

Has exposure to pornography affected people's minds, expectations, and actions? It would be a wonder in human affairs if much exposure to some kind of image did not affect the minds of the viewer. We have faith that reading fosters thinking, watching violence changes attitudes toward life, and listening to music affects mores. It would be passing strange if, in the area of sex, human beings enjoyed immunity from being affected through images. If those who affect to think that minds are not changed through much exposure to pornography, perhaps they would advocate for the end of age restrictions for children; they do not so advocate because they know the argument is insincere.

Let us start with the mind and the brain. Studies show that even short-term exposure to pornography affects the functioning and stimulation of the brain.[34] Summaries of the literature on pornography suggest the following conclusions, among others: pornography fosters "blunted affect," increases "dominating" and "sexually imposing" behavior, leads to "decreased satisfaction with a romantic partner," and fosters addiction.[35] Men come to want the cake without the calories: sex without love, responsibility, trust, or strings. Other comprehensive studies of sexual practices suggest that sex aligns with images of pornographic sex. Countries report significant increases in the number of sexual partners, increases in those reporting oral and anal sex, decreases in the number of people who say that sex should be limited to stable, loving relationships, and decreases in the age of first sexual experiences since the deregulation of pornography. Similar trends exist in America.[36] More men integrate pornographic ways into their sex lives and their expectations; women adjust their expectations accordingly.[37] Public opinion has changed, becoming more accepting of nudity and pornography. Individuals to some extent take their bearings from this public opinion: with knowledge that the standard of decency has shifted, individuals shift their standards accordingly. This amounts to a slow-motion revolution in ethical beliefs and a delicate complex of feelings, sensibilities, tastes, and expectations.[38]

The proliferation of pornography changes political attitudes about the form of marriage. Support for same-sex marriage correlates with pornography consumption, suggesting that revisions in the form of marriage track those who are open as to the form of sexual relations or who see sex detached from love and responsibility.[39] More than a few researchers trace these changes to the ubiquity of pornography,[40] though it cannot be proven with certainty.[41] Openness about free sexuality seems correlated with other efforts to change the marital form—including open marriage, polyamory, divorce, and so on. Sexual modesty, fidelity, and relations that subordinate the question of sex to the imperatives of enduring love and family life find less cultural support as pornography is more compulsively viewed. Viewpoints that seek to discipline the "energy of sexuality" or that question "more eccentric or non-conventional forms of sexuality" as practiced by the avant-garde are less likely to "be of much value" as people come to believe in sexual plasticity—and pornography helps that along.[42] Individuals seek more sexual experimentation as part of their unique cultivation of their own selves. A pornified environment supports the contemporary liberal project of promoting the pure relationship.[43]

Sexual liberationists expected the "end of obscenity" to affect marriage and character, as did the critics of ending obscenity. Both were right. Yet internet pornography and obscenity cannot be uninvented, with their deleterious effects. Censorship is less thinkable today than it was before the "end of obscenity" because of the "end of obscenity." Since solid majorities probably oppose censorship, it seems unlikely that majorities that would be willing to re-regulate obscenity will be built anytime soon, even though indirect harms associated with it are increasingly well attested to. Restoring the legal regime and the principles of *Hicklin* would aid in a healthier policy of indirection, but the circle within which we live is made by *Roth*.

What can policy accomplish? As harms become obvious, solutions could be tailored to limit them. The long-term goal of a responsible obscenity policy is helping to maintain an environment where public morality shapes the building of self-restraint as a preparatory personal virtue for collective self-government; where public morality fosters enduring love and the ability to take on the duties of family life; and where relations between the sexes could be less corrupted by images of depersonalized erotica and pornography. Obscenity is still a category in our law, though it has been drained of its significance through the evolving interpretation begun with *Roth*. Movements toward the *Hicklin* standard may be salutary, but only and first in areas where public opinion supports it. "Under-the-counter" sales of pornography—peeks and glimpses—we may have to live with; a zeal to eliminate such "under-the-counter" sales is probably inconsistent with limited, liberal government and a corresponding zeal to deny that pornography affects our moral environment is equally disrupting. Perhaps we can come to a grand bargain: no censorship, but efforts to minimize damages and harms.

Regulation may be possible as long as a bad name continues to adhere to pornography. Tolerate it as an evil, but do not promote it as a positive good. Experience refutes many fraudulent promises of sexual liberationists (i.e., the forbidden fruit theory, the idea that morality can exist without law, the idea sex without shame or honor is healthier and happier). The consumption of pornography should continue to be associated with the juvenile, the immature, and the irresponsible or shown to be part of an otherwise empty, self-indulgent life (as many of our movies have nicely done). This involves the continuation of the "old obscenity" mentioned above—an Aristophanes, Aldous Huxley or Evelyn Waugh-treatment (an art that elevates toward the good through a teaching of human limits and a ridicule of the debasing and bad) as well as the Sophoclean treatment (which shows the dead end of one's tragic errors). Seth Rogan's movies *Knocked Up* and *Zack and Mira Make a Porno* combined with P. T. Anderson's movie *Boogie Nights* (1997) show the respective comedic and tragic artistic ways to depict how pornography undermines happiness and compromises the self-control and maturity essential to living a good life. I do not expect a Society for Decent Literature or some equivalent, led by puritanical scolds, to lead to a healthy public morality anytime soon. Nor do I think traditional prudishness helps the cause of public morality in our context. Perhaps we can rally around the idea that "Porn Kills Love" though. A healthy teaching will come through the prevalence of an art that features much nudity, sex, kinkiness, and pornography and which shows that pornified individual lives and relations are empty and how the pornified life compromises the good life. Prudes who rightly recognize the problems of pornography will probably have to steel themselves to a pretty indecent art: a relatively conservative lesson can be drawn from these performances. Such works, consistent with the "old obscenity," point to a "higher prudishness" or an indirect reinforcement of a more decent public morality.

Perhaps indirect regulations of the pornography industry could accommodate the fact that majorities could no longer be constructed for the direct regulation or censorship of pornography. Jim Stoner, drawing an analogy between local zoning laws that banned strip clubs in certain neighborhoods and internet regulation, guesses "adjustments to copyright protection for obscene" materials might be a way of decreasing their profitability.[44] Gerard Bradley suggests, among other things, that laws prohibit those using government computers from consuming pornography and that those taking government contracts be subject to similar limits.[45] Regulations of working conditions in the pornography industry, to ensure safety in the workplace, could be considered.[46]

Two ideas strike me on the obscenity law front. The first involves protecting and reinforcing the lines that we still draw, the second is a narrowly tailored element of rollback of the current "end of obscenity" regime. America currently draws lines between adults and children and public and private displays of sexual acts. Liberals initially defended the boundary between adults and children in terms of "parental rights" as much as the state's interest in the welfare of the young.[47] Parental rights are not enough, however, since the public needs to be able to justify why this particular exercise of "parental rights" differs from other areas where the public does not regulate exposure to ideas and images. Instead, we should forthrightly recognize that the age requirements relate to public morality, where the public is concerned that minds and affections of children are not mis-shaped through harmful exposure to obscenity. Leave the world of adult internet pornography alone, but let us do more to protect children from exposure to it. The internet pornography industry itself could be made more responsible for policing the boundary between adults and children. Following Bradley's suggestions,[48] the internet pornography industry and internet domain holders generally could be subject to substantial civil suits if they do not develop and maintain "the most effective safeguards to prevent exposure of minors or unwilling adults to obscene material." Leaving the permissive *Roth* standard alone for adults, the definition of obscenity *as it relates to children* could move more in the direction of *Hicklin*; brain studies might help to show how obscenity and especially internet pornography tends to "deprave and corrupt" the minds of vulnerable children. Sufficiently large civil suits would place the onus on those hosting pornographic websites to continue developing technologies that keep pornographic materials out of the hands of children. Evidence of good faith on the part of such hosts would include the provision of free filtering hardware included on phones, laptops, and all other personal computer devices; and the requirement that users enter credit card information in order to gain access even to free internet pornography. Whether such laws would be effective would depend on international accords in addition to domestic enforcement.

The other line today's law allows the public to draw involves the public display of sexually explicit advertising and acts. Public nudity, public copulation, and the public advertising of pornography can be, and mostly still are, proscribed. Liberals try to justify these proscriptions on grounds of choice.[49] Such public displays force individuals to see something that they would not otherwise want to see. Seeing a couple copulating on a blanket in the park is not wrong in itself, on liberal grounds: the problem is how the sight of rutting and the sounds of the moaning may ruin the wholesome picnic of the family next to the couple. There is nothing wrong with pornography playing on the reader board in Times Square, except that several passersby would see it though they did not want to. Again, a moment's reflection shows the poverty of this merely liberal argument. Such proscriptions target some kinds of relations or displays and not others. Public handshakes or hugs are not proscribed, but oral sex on a blanket in a public park, in broad daylight, is. Why? Some acts are obscene; others are not. Public nudity, public copulation, and public purveyance of pornography make private things very public and thereby create an environment where public indecency, lewd acts, or indecent exposure would be more and more accepted, tolerated, and celebrated. Any effort to "free the nipple" (legitimize women going in public naked from the waist up), allow for nude dancing in public, allow mass mailings of obscene materials, and allow for advertising of sex toys partakes in this same public purveyance of obscenity issue. Efforts to legitimize public nudity—and then perhaps public sex and lewd acts or advertising of pornography—will probably snowball as society itself becomes more saturated with pornography.

The cases of children's access to pornography and public displays generally demand that the opponents of obscenity use public arguments to help reestablish a relatively healthy approach to public decency. These debates take place in the context of acceptance of the obscene as normal, and each line that is crossed makes it more likely that the next will be. These debates should be used to suggest that some of the things which are obscene in public may also be problematic if they are engaged in voluntarily and in private.

Those interested in securing a healthy public morality through indirection should also protect the line against child pornography. The age of consent, as we have seen, is designed not only to protect a child's capacity to consent, but also to contribute to a character where a child can eventually love and be responsible for others. Such character is compromised through sexualizing childhood and through corrupting influence of sexual predators. Thus a general principle: society should prevent children from being thought of as sex objects, both for their own good and for the good of our public ethos in general. Again, no decent citizen of a decent society would raise questions drawing us to first principles. It is necessary for us to speak to our age, however, and to uncover the implications of our modes of thinking. Pornography produced with actual children *ipso facto* violates laws against rape and child abuse so long as we have an age of consent. Should possession of computer-generated child pornography (i.e., pornography involving only virtual sexual acts by children) be proscribed? Should its generation be a crime? Should sex dolls modeled after children be proscribed? Consistent liberals, taking bearings from the principle of consent, would have to conclude that virtual child pornography and sex dolls modeled after children neither violate consent nor are related to any clear and probable harm in individual cases. Laws against such things could not survive the liberal wringer described in chapter 3.

Such instances of child pornography nevertheless violate the fundamental principle that children should not be thought of as sex objects and that childhood innocence is something to be preserved. Computer-generated child pornography may not affect any particular child directly, but its mass consumption would affect the environment in which children are reared and educated and in which they conceive of themselves: it would contribute more to the sexualizing of childhood. Child sex dolls would have the same effects. Such practices, as long as they stay marginalized and stigmatized, may be tolerated, I suppose. How do they remain stigmatized? The criminal law plays no small part in stigmatizing those practices, and such laws should be expanded in areas of virtual child pornography and child-like sexbots.

The element of rollback involves regulating *compulsive* use of pornography and thus of controlling the more obviously destructive effects of internet pornography use. It is one thing to make pornography available; it is another to encourage an addiction to pornography. Civil suits could be brought against the industry for its culpability in the creation of pornography addiction and for its attendant social costs as borne by individuals. Investigations could be undertaken to see if the industry knows about the addictive effects of its products or if certain kinds of pornography, featured on certain websites, knowingly lead consumers to consume more pornography. The industry, if it knows such addictions are not uncommon, would have to take good-faith measures to ensure that its users not become addicted to pornography or face civil penalties for the consequences of the addictions that it profits from. While no individual could or should be absolved from that addiction, nor can any supplier can get off scot-free. The culpability of those who knowingly supply addictive goods is well established in our laws, as the case of smoking demonstrates. Such an approach would have the benefit of being narrowly tailored to the social ill—compulsive pornography use—instead of aiming to purify the morals of all involved.

The liberal assumptions we purport to embrace mask the reality that the deregulation of obscenity helps establish a new image of a good relationship and a good life: the pure relationship. It also points to making public things that are best kept private and toward erasing the line between adults and children. No society can fully embrace these supposedly liberal assumptions and thrive, and our society has not (yet!) done so. Maintaining what is left of a healthy environment for children and married couples demands that we maintain the lines we have drawn and engage in some long-term efforts to roll back.

Conclusion

I am loath to close. No approach can anticipate all of the ways that all the elements of the rolling revolution will challenge marriage and family life. Generally, those who would defend the family must consistently ask the right questions and frame their opposition to the rolling revolution properly. On maintaining parental authority and marital integrity, family advocates are interested in maintaining the trust, integrity, and childhood obedience necessary to a well-functioning, happy family. On maintaining public morality, family advocates are concerned for the mores and ethos that are most likely to lead passionate, somewhat selfish people to long-term thinking, enduring, and monogamous relations that have an important place for sex but subordinate sexual relations to personal relations.

Both of these goals reflect a liberal policy of indirection. Too often we assume that the good things we currently experience will continue without legal or cultural support. Too often we resign ourselves to the vices of our time. We hope parents will use their authority well because they understand and would fulfill their duties. It is hoped that people will follow the better passions of their natures when encouraged to with public morality. The more the state takes direction in the matter, the less responsibility parents will feel. A broad range of cultural offerings are necessary for a diverse liberal people to enjoy some of the benefits of freedom, but some limits on those cultural offerings are indeed good for individuals and for the culture itself.

13

WHAT IS TO BE SAID AND DONE?

I am again loath to close. No book investigating how to reconcile family and its political community is ever complete, since the conflict between the family and the political community is inherent in the human condition. Nor can any book seeking to reconcile marriage and family life with our modern liberal order ever be complete, since marriage and family implicate deep human attachments in the private sphere and the liberal order emphasizes individual freedom and consent in the public sphere; the primary political commitments in the liberal regime upset marriage and family life to some extent. The tension is part of the human condition, and our regime exacerbates it. But the conflict is yet greater. The rolling revolution points to an autonomous world beyond gender, toward independence, and beyond repression, and thus imagines a world where marriage and family life are abolished or wither away. Marriage and family life are among the best ways to mix our increasingly democratic political regime, but due to the strength of the rolling revolution we often lack the language and ideas whereby to understand this mixture. The task of statesmanship is to assist the rolling revolution moderately where we must, to slow it down where we can, and to resist and roll it back where it threatens political health and human thriving.

Many issues need to be rethought and reimagined given the successes of the rolling revolution. Several chapters sit on the cutting room floor. I had hoped to include a limited defense of jealousy, a fear of losing what one has—so different from envy, which is a desire to have something that another has; a couple should to some extent be jealous of their community and love, and couples that envy one another for the lives they live are messing with a genuine demon, but jealousy is not necessarily such a demon. I had hoped to include an analysis of our new, more athletic vision of female beauty, one which deemphasizes maternity and even compromises the ability to conceive children: an anti-natalist, but very pro-sex vision of female athleticism, complementing radical feminism, that bends women's identity as much as our vision of law. I had hoped to include more about proposals for national day care, but I trust that my arguments in favor of a feminism based on part-time work suffice to show the pitfalls with such a narrow proposal. I had hoped to discuss transgenderism in the context of child abuse and parental rights, with the idea that the medical profession could be opened up to torts claims; it may be worse than spanking in many situations. I had hoped to include more about movements toward polyamory and plural marriage, both of which elevate sex out of its subordinate place, minimize communal love, and revolutionize the marital form. More controversies will arise: my aim is to reveal the principles that should guide thinking and acting on these matters in our late republic.

Since I have written a book intended to be useful for all who would understand it, it may not be amiss for me to provide a series of aphorisms, reflecting the arguments made in this book, in response to a sampling of slogans from feminists, contemporary liberals, and sexual liberationists, before sketching how the framework and argument I have made applies to other situations.

Advocates of the rolling revolution reduce their thoughts to slogans, which then inform all of their arguments. This is all well and good. People skeptical of the rolling revolution often run into a wall of implied arguments. They are made to feel foolish for resisting these slogans. They stand in awe of their power. They are cowed into assent, with feelings of guilt and shame in the face of publicly approved half-thoughts. These slogans give the appearance of wisdom and common sense to the rolling revolution, though they conceal as well as reveal. These slogans smuggle controversial premises into our common sense and leave people of common sense dumbfounded and tongue-tied. Feminists, contemporary liberals, and sexual liberationists cast these slogans, the shadows of our late modern cave. It is necessary therefore to combat the "common sense" of the rolling revolution, which has seeped into our everyday world, with some "common sense" of our own, also found in everyday life. Rolling revolutionaries no longer question their premises, so every chance to invite thought invites also philosophic insight. Political and philosophic responsibility combine against the cave of our rolling revolution. I offer these aphorisms and maxims—the aphorism from the rolling revolution in normal type and my response in italics—so that common people can combat rolling revolutionaries with some good humor pointing toward some depth.

Slogans and Aphorisms

Biology isn't destiny.

Biology ain't nothing.

The maleness and femaleness of our bodies create tendencies in the sexes, concerning propensity for violence and aggression, approaches to sexual desire and sex generally, dispositions to agreeableness and caring, prioritizing of personal relations, athletic prowess, tendencies to single-mindedness or many-mindedness, attraction to things as opposed to people, and many other differences. These differences are observed as for-the-most-part universals, in most every culture and epoch. It is foolish to think that "biology" and closely related psychological traits have nothing to do with these differences, and that they are the result of one universal patriarchal system. Sex provides grooves for society's particular vision of gender or as seeing social conventions as partly reflections of nature. Biology ain't destiny, but it ain't nothing either.

Feminism is the radical notion that women are human beings.

Women are human beings, limits and all.

Radical feminism, from Beauvoir on, adopts the position that to be a human being is to define oneself without limits from outside—that is, to define one's life through acts of one's undetermined will. On this notion to be human is a historical idea, and the nature of the human changes, radically, if human beings so will it, from one time to another. To be human is to create oneself from one's own will. Thus Friedan's helpful discovery that women are not cows—cows are eternally the same, but men, on this view, have long defined themselves, and women, with the help of feminism, are now learning to define themselves. This feminist notion, borrowed from radical historical thinkers, misunderstands the human condition. Human beings are limited creatures—we neither create ourselves nor are we immortal. To be human is to aspire to goods and to rank those goods according to our best reasoning and desires. We live in a moral universe that supplies the goods to which we aspire; we can reorder those goods and discover applications of those goods we had heretofore not noticed, but we rarely can invent new goods and never invent ourselves. Feminism is as subject to these limits as any intellectual movement. On this score women have never been different from men: we should not throw out what it means to be human for a dubious, fanciful notion of autonomy.

No limits!

Know limits.

The promise of human liberation from all constraints in our condition under-lies all aspects of the rolling revolution. No part of the rolling revolution can ever be completed, because elements of human nature stand in the way of liberation so conceived. Ours is a mixed condition with freedom and limits, nature and culture, and reason and passion. Sex, among other things, provides grooves for gender and limits self-creation. The aspiration for neutrality in contemporary liberalism masks an attempt to bend society to the demands of the pure relationship. Human sexual desire is directed toward people, con-nected to the conscience, and reflective of our need for community. Know limits! It is better to recognize the goodness within these limits than to seek to eradicate them from the human condition.

Believe all women.

*The line between good and evil runs through the
heart of all people, men and women.*

The attempt to understand human relations in terms of power alone—and to see women as the victims of patriarchal power alone—leaves out the reality of love, community, virtue, embodiment, and honor, among other things. It also gives rise to preposterous claims on behalf of history's supposed victims—as if they must be believed no matter what. We must clear away this underbrush and believe neither all women nor all men, nor all couples, nor all singles. In fact the mantra that a society should believe all victims is likely to increase the amount of lying and fibbing among those, since the absolute power will likely corrupt. This is a window to fixing the dominant victim narratives as well—men themselves wear white hats and black hats and the patriarchy nar-rative denies this.

The personal is political.

*Each regime is a cave, though the cave is not only a cave
and is open. And: The personal is also the personal.*

Our regime affects how we view our personal lives and live in families. The political affects the personal, but there are natural grooves within which the political subsists. The personal is also the personal! Our regime emphasizes equality and individual independence. Our regime makes it increasingly dif-ficult for human beings to recognize and acknowledge enduring individual differences, especially between the sexes, and to recognize and acknowledge the communal bonds of love that constitute marriage and family life. Our cave does not teach patriarchy or male supremacy, as feminists contend, but rather the manifest injustice of sexual inequality, sexual difference, and the construction of gender. This all shapes the family. However, there are limits to how much our regime or any regime can shape the personal constitution of each individual. Birth, death, sexual difference, a need for belonging, desires related to marriage and family life—all of these and more force the political to bend to the personal.

Feminist (noun): A person who believes in the political, social, and economic equality of the sexes.

Womanist (noun): A person who believes in the political equality of the sexes and (still) thinks they will do different things under conditions of freedom.

Word soups are not arguments. No one can expect two creatures, much the same but different in important ways, to occupy a fifty-fifty world in politics, in social practices, or in economics. If feminists expect a fifty-fifty world as a true measure of equality, they will always be disappointed, but on the bright side, they will also always have something to complain about. Feminists will never be unemployed in the world they imagine. A womanist expects differences even under conditions of equality of opportunity, and expects that conventions will arise to channel and register the differences between men and women.

Men and women are not going to be equal outside the home until men are equal in it.

Men and women will always be somewhat different inside and outside the home.

Equality within the home is less the object of human aspiration than equality outside of it. Human beings want their homes to be filled with love, joy, and support; human beings want to share their burdens, to gain consolation in times of trouble, and to build something bigger than themselves that lasts. All of these things can be done in a home, among other places. Equality in the form of a fifty-fifty world is inconsistent with human happiness and the tendencies in each sex—and this is most especially true where the most intimate and personal aspects of their lives are lived. There is, once again, a problem of definition: how does one know when people are "equal in" the home? How does one know when people are "equal outside the home"? Feminists have every interest in being obscure on this matter, since it points to tyrannical control or swimming somewhat against the sex differences that are commonly observed. Love and community are more important to human happiness than feminist justice. Feminists overemphasize equality as a source of human happiness and fulfillment.

You just want to see women barefoot, pregnant, and in the kitchen.

*Family meals are about community and solidarity, and they
require someone to shop, cook, and do the dishes.*

Feminism devalues the necessities of the home and the beauties that are associated with transcending the bare necessities. Great advances in modern technology like refrigeration and easy transportation make it easy to meet such necessities. But necessities are still necessary. Part of what attaches people to a household is a sharing of the necessities—and I suggest a deal for every family. Women used to be very practical and day-to-day in their concerns, making sure that their husbands would provide and had the space and ability to make a home livable. The more liberated all are from these practicalities, the less they share in common. This makes family life more volatile. Still, I suggest a modern new deal for household necessities: no mother should do all jobs in the home, and no father should do all jobs in the home, but there should be a genuine contribution to the common good from each and all. And working outside the home to support the home counts as work—for both sexes.

Men of quality respect women's equality.

Men can respect and love women—equality's got nothing to do with it.

Virtuous men have loved and respected and supported women since the dawn of time, and lovers of women's equality have not uniformly been "men of quality." Did Odysseus not love Penelope? Did Jesus not respect Mary? Did Harvey Weinstein, the infamous though previously famed producer of the casting couch, not "respect women's equality" and the right to choose? Respect and love are on different vectors from equality. Men can love and respect women and form enduring communities with them under conditions of equality and under conditions of inequality. Conditions of equality generally shape those communities differently than conditions of inequality, but both are consistent with mutual love and respect.

We've come a long way, but there's still lots of work to do.

How would we know when the work was done?

Every proposal for improvement carries with it a vision of the good society—and we womanists must ask about the end served by the means feminists suggest today until they can either explain when enough would be enough, or show how their demands for a rolling revolution are limitless. All should be armed with an understanding of the limitless rolling revolution implicit in the leading edges of reform and toward which most pseudo-moderate reformers tend. Since not all disparities between men and women are traceable to discrimination, it is entirely possible that the work of feminism is complete and feminists should close up shop in the Western world. As people become more equal, Tocqueville recognized, every lingering inequality becomes a cause for greater irritation and complaint. We are at that stage now when the loudness of complaints is out of proportion to the justice of the complaints. There may be no more work to do.

You cannot legislate morality.

All laws legislate morality.

The separation of church and state is often taken as a model for tolerating differences among citizens. At the same time, this separation shapes the practice of religion, emphasizing religions of tolerance and mutual forbearance over religions that insist on their way. Liberals rightly think that such an arrangement is crucial to our liberal settlement, but that model legislates morality and religious practice. All laws reverberate through the culture, and hence all laws, subtly and in the long term, shape our moral practices. The argument that Justice Anthony Kennedy made on behalf of same-sex marriage is precisely about changing the culture to make it more affirming of those taken with someone of the same sex. The question is what morality we want, not whether we should legislate morality.

Hate is not a family value. End homophobia (or misogyny or transphobia or whatever) now. Denying equal rights to other human beings based on your religious beliefs is bigotry.

Two Responses:

First, to clear the underbrush: Totalitarians speak first the language of hate, fear, and bigotry about their fellow citizens.

Second, to get to the truth: Not all disparities are traceable to discrimination.

Labels are designed to end argument by placing opposition to the rolling revolution outside the bounds of respectable opinion. Opposition is hate. It reflects a fear, obviously irrational. It is bigotry. If some advocates of the rolling revolution get their way, even true speech against the rolling revolution will be criminalized as "hate speech." These labels represent an implicit argument in favor of the rolling revolution in whatever form it then exists. No defense of traditional marriage and family life is possible when all opposition to the rolling revolution is so labeled. To admit the legitimacy of opinions contrary to the rolling revolution is to admit that the rolling revolution does not represent progress in knowledge of human beings. The willingness to shut opponents down represents the triumph of the rolling revolution over a search for the truth and public deliberation about the common good. Opponents of the rolling revolution must act and argue, first, with a sense of righteous indignation at such suggestions, though the indignation is only righteous if it establishes the grounds for a genuine discussion.

Second, the labels of the rolling revolution are traceable to the reigning civil rights ideology, which holds that all disparities between groups arise from discrimination (i.e., hate and phobias). Disparities arise, however, from discrimination, from characteristics in a subculture, from nature, from the propensity of human beings to consult their own consciences. Women produce a disproportionate number of babies, for instance, but this is traceable to nature and their own consciences rather than discrimination. Men who have sex with men suffer from certain diseases more often than lesbians or straights, and this is traceable to what those men do rather than society's opinions. The theory of oppression underlying the reigning civil rights ideology has a risibly simplistic understanding of causation, and it is applied almost randomly across supposedly oppressed groups. This orientation denies "victims" their freedom and responsibility in an effort to shift blame for failures completely to the supposed oppressor group. Since this is a lie, there is less chance that victims will better their condition. The result is anger and misery—combined with no little social disharmony.

Whatever happens between consenting adults in private should be legal as long as the consent is genuine.

Consent makes love and marriage possible, but it is not what makes it beautiful or virtuous.

Consent is either durable or continuous; it either requires the elimination of socialization and education so that an unformed autonomous will can guide choice, or makes peace with socialization and education and allows for the shaping of the character antecedent to choice. Durable consent is consistent with enduring marriage and difficult divorce, while continuous consent brings with it at-will divorce, for instance. If nothing guides the will, then a child can consent just as autonomously as an adult, though not many follow this observation to its logical conclusion (yet!). The respecting of consent also implies that there is something respectable about the choices that choice-makers make and something in addition to the "yes" or "no" that makes it respectable. We judge that children cannot consent because in their innocence they are not ready to love and we do not want to encourage adults to think that defiling a child's innocence is permissible or attractive. We judge rape to be a violation of consent when, in the totality of the circumstances, the act of sex seems forced upon a victim. Obscenity cannot be bought, sold, or viewed because of the long-term damage it does to the sentiments, minds, and actions of people capable of enduring love, but tempted toward corrupt simulacra of such love. Consent plus responsibility and love make enduring relations fruitful and beautiful.

> *If you aren't for gay marriage, then do not marry a gay*
> *person. If you don't like abortion, then do not have one.*
> *If you don't like pornography, then don't watch it.*

> *The personal is political, up to a point. Or: No man is an island.*

The libertarian and hardheaded contemporary liberal view is that "neutral" laws only make demands for privacy; contemporary liberals generally move beyond this hard-headed demand for mutual forbearance and require affirmation or recognition. Removal of the law's penalties, over the long haul, tends to mean a removal of the social stigma against previously forbidden activities, and thus a change in mores and habits. Legalizing activities changes what citizens see and what they imagine is normal and just. Removal of stigma tends to change affections, to increase exposure to images and practices, to normalize previously disfavored actions, and thereby to reshape how people act in important areas of their lives. Activities formerly shameful become accepted and acceptable. The waning of the stigma against single motherhood has led to more single mothers. Removal of stigma against contraception has led to more use of it. Society's interest in making certain actions illegal and in stigmatizing them concerns maintaining a moral environment in which marriages are more likely to form and in which more spouses will fulfill their duties. Hard-headed formulations ignore the power of example and hence ignore the habit-forming moral instruction necessary for self-government.

> *Pedophilia is based on the radical notion*
> *that children are human beings.*

> *No political community can corrupt its youth and survive.*

We again confront the question of what it means to be human. Children are human beings. On this score sexual liberationists see the key to the human being as its sexual nature, the overriding human concern for orgasmic happiness. Yet we are leery of exposing children to sex and of making them objects of sexual desire. We respect and protect childhood innocence, for the sake of both the children and the would-be perpetrators.

I was born this way. Or: "Your quarrel . . . is with my creator."

"Our laws do not allow kleptomaniacs to shoplift"
(as Susan Moller Okin writes).

That one's genes predispose one to be one way or another has little to do with the moral and political acceptability of one's way. Our laws against stealing remain in effect even though a kleptomaniac is genetically or psychologically predisposed to steal. To be born toward a sexual orientation or to have a genetic predisposition to kleptomania is not being born to blue eyes or left-handedness. A gay gene (as is celebrated) is not the same as an eye color gene. Genetic tendencies in behavioral and health matters are augmented or lessened through one's political community, upbringing, conscience, and countless other factors. Again, all social phenomena are complex. Nature can incline us in ways that our laws do not allow us to go; human law and custom must go against the grain of pernicious expressions of nature. Precisely what society's disposition is toward a way one was born forms part of the reason one either becomes or does not become that thing. This is a sly attempt to win social acceptability for a disposition (at most) by equating one's genes with what one allegedly has to be. The political community nevertheless has and should have its say.

All orgasms are created equal.

Some orgasms are better than others!

The liberationist principle of "orgasm equity" (to recall a phrase) thinks only of the animal and of pleasure; it is a principle that makes its way into many of our clichés about sex in the time of the rolling revolution. Yet virtue, happiness, respect for others, and community health point in a different direction. Return to our discussion of orgasm machines and sexbots in chapter 4. Other sorts of perversions, such as voyeurism and pedophilia, also complicate the human capacity for love and community. People who pleasure themselves in such ways are more likely to be lonely, unhappy, unattached, and unproductive. Sex and its concerns are integrated into one's life—and it forms the basis for crucial human communities. Orgasms do not equally point toward love and community—and better orgasms are more likely to foster love, affection, community, and responsibility. Political communities cannot be obtuse to those connections and should foster an environment where sex elevates and connects people, not where it leaves people alone.

Applications and Elucidations

An effective mixing of the liberal regime demands limiting the feminist, contemporary liberal, and sexual liberationist rolling revolution. Resources exist within common life to accomplish this limiting, though the successes of the rolling revolution in shaping public opinion and law makes seeing and defending those resources ever more difficult. Statesmen must begin with a wealth of knowledge in order to act effectively. Effective statesmanship involves (1) exposing the blind spots and radicalism in the rolling revolution; (2) identifying and buttressing the resources available in common life that limit the rolling revolution; and (3) translating these resources into action that slows the rolling revolution or rolls it back.

In the long term, the goal is to stigmatize the assumptions of the rolling revolution. Imagine a world beyond the rolling revolution, where our "fatal circle" of opinion reflects the fundamental truths about sex differences, love, public morality, and sexuality. A world beyond the rolling revolution would stigmatize the effort to move society beyond gender or to separate sex from gender, stigmatize the aspiration to make men and women independent, stigmatize the ideas of human autonomy and moral neutrality as undesirable and impossible, and stigmatize the inhumane idea that sexual liberation is the key to human happiness and political liberation. This stigmatizing would not involve abandoning the cause of women's equality (properly understood), or require that we abandon efforts to manage some of society's conflicts through limiting government, or mean a return to a Puritanism of the modern imagination. We need a womanism, a liberalism consistent with a public morality built for the long term, and an approach to sex that integrates it into a good life. The question of our new womanism will be, Does society's practice of gender conform to the sexual grooves, while allowing reasonable space for individual variation? The question for our renewed liberalism will be, Does public morality support industriousness, self-control, translating *eros* into responsible love, and virtue, as well as individual freedom and human equality, and does public morality see men and women as future spouses as much as future workers and citizens? The question for our sexual morality will be, Do conventions assist in the translation of sexual desire into enduring, responsible love and attached communities of devoted love? Herewith opponents of the rolling revolution take the high road that emphasizes the goods of love, responsibility, and fulfillment that human beings strive for and thrive in.

Getting to this high road is no trifling matter. Prudent statesmen must mix our dominant regime with doses of reality that we can still see and defend within our fatal circle. There are certain bottom-line areas where prudent statesmen must defy public opinion, and others where they must accommodate. Reconstituting public opinion involves arguing against the reigning civil rights ideology on questions of feminism, homosexuality, and other matters, with all the rancor that such arguing is likely to entail. It involves recognizing and showing others that there is no neutral ground in a political community, so efforts to create conditions for better marriage and family life are not castigated as "legislating morality" or dictating options to people. No progress can be made without clearing away such underbrush that confuses, debilitates, and dispirits those who would resist the revolution. Only after sweeping away our reigning civil rights ideology and our contemporary liberal pretensions can we begin to understand what is at stake in our public debates and point toward a different public opinion. This new public opinion will mix consent, and point toward a consent that allows for the shaping of consent and fosters durability. It will rediscover and appreciate the logic of sex. It will defend parental rights, except when parental rights compromise themselves or compromise the ability of the political community to execute justice. It will find ways to limit the effects of obscenity and reintroduce the protections of modesty and shame into relations. This will involve anticipating the coming turns in the rolling revolution and resisting them—and using them as a chance to point the population toward a healthier public opinion. It may in some cases be better to lose with good arguments than to win with arguments that do not point toward a healthier fatal circle. There is nobility to losing in the last-ditch effort—as long as it points to a victory worth having.

No one can predict all of the policies and mores advocates of the rolling revolution will push. What follows is a partial list of the coming turns—and the reasons why opponents should resist them.

Prostitution

Legalizing prostitution is consistent with the idea of continuous consent. No one, advocates of legalizing prostitution will say, is harmed in the narrow sense; the purchasing of sex is little different from the government's perspective than contracting with a gardener. Consenting to become a prostitute may, as feminists who see rape as endemic to sex under conditions of patriarchy, be "coerced" under conditions of patriarchy as well. All prostitution may well be "sex trafficking" under conditions of patriarchy. Has a woman consented if she is "vulnerable" yet "consents" to becoming a prostitute? The radical inhuman notion of consent may be used to convince liberals to oppose this further turn in the rolling revolution. Consent, formerly the solution to vulnerability, can be extinguished by vulnerability.

The problem with this argument, however, is that it concedes a corrosive principle—there is no such thing as consent under *our* conditions of patriarchy. There are more traditional arguments against the world's oldest profession. Legalizing prostitution will make it easier to procure prostitutes. Both the legalizing and the normalizing will, in some measure, destigmatize prostitution and the idea that sex is something that can be bought and sold. Sexual desire is shaped partly by society's images of what is good. More women might become prostitutes (and technology might help them find their customers without the inconvenient aid of a pimp), especially "on the side," when they are young and need the money. More men would avail themselves of prostitutes for a variety of reasons, none of which would point men to enduring relations. Prostitution would lead men to be less faithful and compromise the place of fidelity in marriage—one of the attributes of marriage Americans continue to see as central to it. Harms happen in the long term and through reshaping the culture. Men and women are harmed when sex becomes and is seen to become something to be bought and sold, rather than something connected to intimate, affectionate, and enduring relations.

Public Sex

Perhaps fornicating or just having sex in public is also a consensual act. If you do not like public sex, then do not watch! What happens in sex is the business of those in the sexual relationship. Shame and repression, related to the privatization of sex and the suppression of sexual fantasy, cause great turmoil in our personal lives; they make our politics authoritarian. Liberation from this privatization would create conditions for the full flourishing of human liberation. It would also release our animal nature: we allow dogs in dog parks to have sex. Since there is nothing shameful about sex, there is no reason to keep it behind closed doors. No one is free until all fornicate in the open.

Normalizing sex in public combines the problems of obscenity with the errors of the sexual liberation. Public sex makes private things public. It corrodes a sense of shame and modesty about the merely animal nature of genitals. Legalizing it may destigmatize it, which may normalize it. Normalizing public sex complicates the civilizing task of putting sex within its place in a relationship. Sex may be very important for those engaging in it, but would it not look somewhat ridiculous to those watching two amateurs go at it on a park bench? There is meaning in this ridiculousness. Sex takes place behind closed doors because it is physical, or a "low" part of a higher thing (i.e., a loving and enduring relation), and keeping the "low" part "low" allows the high part to form and thrive. Public sex encourages anonymous sex or sex without love, purely for gratification. Private sex makes space for keeping sex in its place—and allowing it to thrive in that place. It is also a special protection for women, whom few seek to pressure into public sex today, but who would be subject to such pressure in the future if this became the norm. There is a good, legal reason for saying "no" to sex in public. This protection is among the last for modesty.

Public Nudity

All of the arguments for public sex hold for public nudity. If you do not like other people's genitals or their breasts, then do not look. Public nudity helps people overcome their shame and modesty and hence be free. Dogs display their genitals; why cannot human beings too? No one is free until every nipple is free!

All arguments against public sex hold against public nudity. The political community depends on the formation of enduring relations, and sex alone cannot be the basis for such enduring relations. Generally public nudity complicates sexual attraction. People should not want to be known for their genitals; we want to encourage human beings to be loved and respected for their unique person. Prohibitions on public nudity hide the animal in us so the human can be seen and loved and relations can be formed on that basis. Such bans recognize the human temptation to elevate sex out of all proportion in relations, and fight against it by calling forth what is distinctive in all of us.

Plural Marriage

The successful accomplishment of same-sex marriage on affirming contemporary liberal grounds points to the next stage of liberal reform, plural marriage. If marriage is not confined to man and woman, why should it be confined to two instead of three?

No public harm is caused by plural marriage, after all. Recall the liberal wringer. Polygamy in Islamic countries is often patriarchal, illiberal, and abusive, but this need not be the polygamy of the American future. Transport polygamy to America, and we will get a healthier "postmodern" polygamy based on consent and equality. Our plural marriages will be virtually indistinguishable from monogamous marriages. Polygamists today in southern Utah or Northern Arizona tend to be insular, abusive, and inclined toward underage, arranged marriages, but this is just the result of plural marriage under conditions of taboo and sanction. Proscribe it and it is bound to manifest illegal practices, hierarchies characteristic of criminal enterprises, unnatural distortions, distorting jealousies, and excessively narrow education. The solution to this problem is to baptize the practice with public acceptance. Bring plural marriage out of the shadows and our liberal culture may transform it into something consensual, egalitarian, open, and liberating. Polygamists, studies show, cause problems such as underage marriage or spousal abuse. Let us improve that plural marriage experience through proper regulation of its occasional abuses such as statutory rape or spousal abuse! Liberal communities ban polygamy because they claim to be interested in gender equality, the well-being of children, and the other problems allegedly manifest in polygamous marriages. If they were interested in such things, they would also have to ban many monogamous marriages, which are not as egalitarian as liberals would like and are often abusive. This hypocrisy shows that the public is not really serious about those problems, and that we rely too much on form and structure and not enough on function. This turn in modern marriage is just what Shulie Firestone would order in our time and place.

Against this there are several things to worry about. Most disturbing about this line of argument, from a political point of view, is its narrow conception of public harm. How would public acceptance of the plural form shape the passions of citizens? Legalizing it would lead to more of it. The power of such examples erodes fidelity and responsibility in modern marriage. Fidelity, because it opens marriage up in terms of numbers, and enlarges and dilutes the circle of trust. Responsibility, because it dilutes the common tasks of husband and wife. It could thus lead men and women to think of recruiting others into their relation—an openness to experimenting could become a more important trait in a spouse than fidelity and sacrificial love. If marriage concerns pleasure or adult fulfillment, then, I suppose, nothing in plural marriage offends its purpose. If marriage is about establishing family and communal love, there are good reasons for thinking plural marriage will mostly misfire. Its form either brings patriarchy corrosive of consent or, in the postmodern polygamy of liberal imagination, disrupts community and the subordination of sex within a communal relation. One cannot give oneself wholly to another and then to still another, so plural marriage reflects a qualified attachment in great tension with communal love.

Toward a Better Political Philosophy

Family Politics, my first book, depicted the modern tendency to narrow marriage and family life. This book concerns the tail end of these "waves of modernity." Francis Bacon or René Descartes were not thinking about modern feminism, sexual liberationism, and transgenderism at the birth of the modern. Yet the idea of human power and the idea of nature as there to be controlled through human action, stripped of qualifying moderation, eventuated in these late modern ideas. Nature, on the modern view as it comes to us, does not lend direction to human will or human action; it is the stuff out of which human beings can make their future. No limits! Feminists and their epigones see gender divorced from sex, so women and men can become anything they set their minds on. No limits! Liberationists think sexual desire can take on any form and be consistent with human being. No limits! Contemporary liberals, with their pretensions to neutrality, are our current delivery system for reshaping and transcending nature, the heart of the rolling revolution. More controlling, administrative means are not ruled out.

Marriage and family life are fields of human life where the aspirations of radical modernity are playing out. Obstacles physical and moral stand in the way of its achievement of these aspirations. Nature is not so "metaphysically neutral" as our activists and hypermoderns suppose. Birth is not something that human beings can totally control. Without babies it is difficult to imagine a human future. Nor is death something that human beings can avoid. We all need sleep. The stuff of nature cannot be made alive through human will, nor stay alive simply through human will. The maleness and femaleness of human being is intransigent. The directedness of human sexuality (and the attendant feelings of shame and modesty), while not strictly speaking bodily, is intimately tied to human consciousness of our bodily nature.

Yet there is a modern rejoinder to this: We have not (yet!) brought those elements of nature under our control, but time is on the side of the human spirit! The arc of history is long, but it bends toward autonomy! Such assertions are as convincing as they are. No one can prove that a New Man, beyond what we have heretofore known as human, will not arise. Nor can the moderns *prove* that he will arise. More than a little dystopian literature concerns precisely this question, but all such novels are subject to the hope that someone could build it better.

Modern advocates have not thought through what it would mean to transcend the human as presently constituted. There are deeper, even more persistent moral obstacles to the modern in matters of love, sexuality, virtue, marriage, and family. These experiences have a logic and meaning as well. Human beings are somewhat free to choose among these and other human goods that present themselves to us, but people do not invent those goods out of whole cloth, as the theory of autonomy would suggest. There are only a certain number of ways that human beings genuinely aspire to happiness. Marriage and family life present one very common, achievable element of a happy life and a life well lived for many people. A public philosophy that acknowledges this goodness and creates an environment where human beings are more likely to enter into marriage is better suited to a great country than one that emphasizes the goodness of autonomy.

The philosophy of autonomy has no problem with the easy access to pornography today. The promise of autonomy in this area goes unfulfilled. Many people—not a majority (yet!), but an increasing percentage of modern people—become slaves to their passions, less able to develop intimate personal relations, less able to govern themselves; more men are lonely and more women encouraged either to perform like porn stars or to forgo interpersonal relations for careerism. The philosophy of autonomy has no problem with easy access to divorce, so thereby people can achieve happiness by following their own will. The promise of autonomy in this area goes unfulfilled. Many people suffer when sticking it out in marriage becomes optional and divorce becomes an honorable way of pursuing personal fulfillment and forgetting duty. Broken families compromise the lives of children. The divorce regime encourages many to wander and to invest less time, energy, and identity in a marital community. It contributes to the building of the relationships system and the decline in marital character. Divorces leave behind many broken men and women, eager to blame, less able to take on responsibility, and hurt at the depths of their being. The philosophy of autonomy has no problem demanding a fifty-fifty world in the workplace and in the home. The promise of autonomy in this area remains unfulfilling and unfulfilled. Men and women are different, and the attempt to make them be the same compromises their happiness. One could go on with example after example of the philosophy of autonomy—rolling revolutionaries defend polyamory, sex robots, lowering the age of consent, transgenderism, and other past and future cutting-edge practices, always assuming that emancipation brings fulfillment and happiness. The result is more creatures unable to take on duties, love, or responsibility, and there is no corresponding increase in human happiness.

Perhaps our revolutionaries think that autonomy is a *sufficient* condition for human happiness: as long as human beings have the freedom to make themselves or are *autonomous*, they will be happy. At least since Oedipus and Viktor Frankenstein, however, there have been warnings that within the desire for human autonomy lurks a tyrannical temptation that is itself inconsistent with happiness. Part of the unhappiness is the frustration that the world does not bend enough to human will. Part of the problem is that a will without a structure itself cannot know when it has accomplished what it seeks to accomplish. Part of the problem consists in forgetting the moral and physical limits of human beings—that the goods and happiness we aspire to are not inventions of human creativity and that the bodies we have limit our abilities. The revolution may roll on and gain in respectability, but those who oppose it serve the not ignoble causes of human happiness, virtue, and a moderate freedom.

NOTES

1 Our New Family Regime?

1 Aristotle, *The Politics*, trans. and ed. Carnes Lord (Chicago: University of Chicago Press, 1984), 1253a15. See also Aristotle's treatment of regime at 1276b1–3, 1280b30–35, and specifically at 1289a15–20, where he likens regime to "what the end of the community is in each case."

2 See, for instance, Aristotle, *The Politics*, 1292b5, 1293a30, 1294b22–25, and esp. 1310a14–36; Aristotle, *Nicomachean Ethics*, trans. Robert C. Bartlett and Susan D. Collins (Chicago: University of Chicago Press, 2011), 1158b12–19 and 1160b23–1161a2; and the account of declension of regimes in Plato, *The Republic of Plato*, trans. Allan Bloom (New York: Basic Books, 1968), 544a–569c, esp. 553a–c, 558b–c, 562e–563a, which depicts regimes as corresponding to the particular character of private men arising from corresponding families.

3 Aristotle, *The Politics*, 1280a9–11.

4 Augustine, *The City of God*, trans. Marcus Dods (New York: Modern Library, 1993), 706 (bk. 19, chap. 24).

5 Plato, *The Republic*, 514a–521b.

6 Alexis de Tocqueville, *Democracy in America*, trans. and ed. Harvey C. Mansfield and Delba Winthrop (Chicago: University of Chicago Press, 2000), 358 (1.2.10), 518 (2.2.15).

7 Leslie G. Rubin, *America, Aristotle, and the Politics of a Middle Class* (Waco, Tex.: Baylor University Press, 2018), 40–41.

8 Tocqueville, *Democracy in America*, 3.

9 Aristotle, *The Politics*, 1292b25–1293a11.

10 Aristotle, *The Politics*, 1293a12–33.

11 See esp. Aristotle, *The Politics*, 1318b9–1319b32, where he compares the "old-est" and "most decent democracy or polity" where the people's rule is mixed with a deference to the "best persons" because the people lack leisure with the "final sort" of democracy where "the base element . . . is more in the front of one's eyes" and the meanest sorts rule.

12 Aristotle, *The Politics*, 1294a35–b18.

13 Aristotle, *The Politics*, 1310a12–39.

14 Tocqueville, *Democracy in America*, 240 (1.2.7).

15 Tocqueville, *Democracy in America*, 518–19 (2.2.15).

16 Tocqueville, *Democracy in America*, 558 (2.3.8).

17 Tocqueville, *Democracy in America*, 676 (2.4.8).

18 Christopher Lasch, *Haven in a Heartless World: The Family Besieged* (New York: W. W. Norton, 1995).

19 *Obergefell v. Hodges*, 576 U.S. _____ (2015).

20 See Rémi Brague, *The Kingdom of Man: Genesis and Failure of the Modern Project*, trans. Paul Seaton (Notre Dame: University of Notre Dame Press, 2018).

21 James Q. Wilson, *The Marriage Problem: How Our Culture Has Weakened Families* (New York: HarperCollins, 2002), 192.

22 This grandiose language is borrowed from "George Washington to James Madison, 31 March 1787," in *The Founder's Constitution* (Chicago: University of Chicago Press), chap. 6, doc. 8.

23 Hopefully readers are clever enough to use the framework and examples of the book and apply them to other circumstances.

Introduction to Part 1

1 Kate Millett, *Sexual Politics* (Garden City, N.Y.: Doubleday, 1970), 62.

2 Millett, *Sexual Politics*, 62.

3 Millett, *Sexual Politics*, 62. See also Shulamith Firestone, *Dialectic of Sex : The Case for Feminist Revolution* (New York: Bantam Books, 1970), 236–37.

2 Feminism and the Abolition of Gender

1 Sheryl Sandberg, *Lean In: Women, Work, and the Will to Lead* (New York: Alfred A. Knopf, 2013), 7: "A truly equal world would be one where women ran half our countries and companies and men ran half our homes. I believe this would be a better world."

2 John Stuart Mill, "The Subjection of Women," in *Essays on Equality, Law, and Education*, ed. John M. Robson, vol. 21 of *The Collected Works of John Stuart Mill*, ed. John M. Robson (Toronto: University of Toronto Press, 1984), 271.

3 See Mill, "Subjection of Women," 297–98.

4 Much of the subsequent discussion is drawn from Scott Yenor, *Family Politics: The Idea of Marriage in Modern Political Thought* (Waco, Tex.: Baylor University Press, 2011), 175–96. For second-wave treatments of first-wave feminists, see Firestone, *Dialectic of Sex*, 15–37; Betty Friedan, *The Feminine*

Mystique (New York: W. W. Norton, 1997), 80–102; Simone de Beauvoir, *The Second Sex*, trans. H. M. Parshley (1949; New York: Vintage, 1989), 109–38.

5 Friedan, *The Feminine Mystique*, 102. See Firestone, *Dialectic of Sex*, 28–29: Women "had most legal freedoms—the literal assurance that they were con-sidered full political citizens of society—and yet they had no power. They had educational opportunities—and yet were unable, or not expected, to employ them. They had freedoms of clothing and the sexual mores that they had demanded—and yet they were still sexually exploited. . . . The cultural indoc-trination necessary to reinforce sex role traditions had become blatant, taste-less, where before they had been insidious." See also Beauvoir, *The Second Sex*, 133: "Abstract rights . . . have never sufficed to assure to woman a definite hold on the world."

6 Testifying to the kinship between herself and American radicals, Beauvoir names Betty Friedan, Kate Millet, Germaine Greer, and Shulamith Fires-tone as her worthy successors in the effort to establish a genuinely liberated society: Alice Schwarzer, *After the Second Sex: Conversations with Simone de Beauvoir*, trans. Marianne Howarth (New York: Pantheon Books, 1984), 39, 46. Firestone, for instance, the most radical and thoroughgoing of these subsequent thinkers, dedicates her *Dialectic of Sex* to "Simone de Beau-voir, Who Endured," and praises and cites Beauvoir throughout her analy-sis. Firestone, *Dialectic of Sex*, 7, sees Beauvoir as "the most comprehensive and far-reaching" feminist theorist, "relating feminism to the best ideas of our culture." Firestone herself was, in the words of one of her admirers, "the American Simone de Beauvoir": Susan Faludi, "Death of a Revolutionary," *New Yorker*, April 15, 2013, newyorker.com.

7 Beauvoir, *The Second Sex*, ixx, 267.

8 Beauvoir, *The Second Sex*, 280, 288.

9 Beauvoir, *The Second Sex*, 307–15, 321.

10 See Beauvoir, *The Second Sex*, 188ff., 548–53; Schwarzer, *After the Second Sex*, 24, 63–64.

11 Beauvoir, *The Second Sex*, 330–35. See Millett, *Sexual Politics*, 28–29; Eileen McDonagh and Laura Pappano, *Playing with the Boys: Why Separate Is Not Equal in Sports* (New York: Oxford University Press, 2008), 216–20, 222–24; Colette Dowling, *The Frailty Myth: Women Approaching Physical Equality* (New York: Random House, 2000), 42ff.

12 Beauvoir, *The Second Sex*, xxxiv–xxxv.

13 Beauvoir, *The Second Sex*, 33–34, 714, and specifically 716: "Humanity is something more than a mere species: it is a historical development; it is to be defined by the manner in which it deals with its natural, fixed characteristics."

14 Beauvoir, *The Second Sex*, xxxv, 714.

15 Beauvoir, *The Second Sex*, 387–90.

16 Beauvoir, *The Second Sex*, 322–27, 352, 359, 391.

17 Schwarzer, *After the Second Sex*, 48.

18 Beauvoir, *The Second Sex*, 695.

19 Schwarzer, *After the Second Sex*, 40.

20 Beauvoir, *The Second Sex*, 451–59, 477–78.

21 Beauvoir, *The Second Sex*, 471, 476.

22 Regarding the ambiguity of whether all or only most aspects of sexuality are socially constructed, see Yenor, *Family Politics*, 192. Some subtle indications in Beauvoir's work point to the possibility of awareness that her project is not fully possible. Sex requires the body, and how sex can be free or immanent probably involves a mystery and a compromise. She writes, for instance, that "every human existence involves transcendence and immanence at the same time": Beauvoir, *The Second Sex*, 430.

23 Beauvoir, *The Second Sex*, 697.

24 Judith Butler, *Bodies That Matter: On the Discursive Limits of "Sex"* (New York: Routledge, 1993), 4–5. Butler thinks that in "the de Beauvoirian version of feminism ... sex is absorbed by gender" and "'sex' becomes something like a fiction, perhaps a fantasy."

25 Feminist writers thus resemble the great modern philosophers who sought to transform Christianity through periodic, systematic reforms, and through planting principles within opinion that would work out in practice as time proceeded and would lead, in their case, to a secular society.

26 Millett, *Sexual Politics*, 26–88.

27 Susan Moller Okin, *Women in Western Political Thought* (Princeton: Princeton University Press, 1979).

28 Carole Pateman, *The Sexual Contract* (Stanford: Stanford University Press, 1988), 1.

29 Susan Moller Okin, *Justice, Gender, and the Family* (New York: Basic Books, 1989).

30 An entire book series, *Re-Reading the Canon*, features "feminist reinterpretations of the writings of major figures in Western philosophical tradition": "Re-Reading the Canon," Penn State University Press, psupress.org. The titles of the books give one a flavor of the work of these under-laborers: *Feminist Interpretations of Alexis de Tocqueville*; *Feminist Interpretations of Aristotle*; *Feminist Interpretations of Ayn Rand*; *Feminist Interpretations of Benedict Spinoza*; and so on, all the way to *Feminist Interpretations of W. V. Quine* and *Feminist Interpretations of William James*.

31 Friedan, *The Feminine Mystique*, 31.

32 Carol Tavris, *The Mismeasure of Woman: Why Women Are Not the Better Sex, the Inferior Sex, or the Opposite Sex* (New York: Touchstone, 1992), 212.

33 Cordelia Fine, *Delusions of Gender: How Our Minds, Society, and Neurosexism Create Difference* (New York: W. W. Norton, 2010), 27; see also 52–53, 66, 77, 87, 95–96, 116, passim.

34 Okin, *Justice*, 171.

35 See Schwarzer, *After the Second Sex*, 39, where Beauvoir accepts the way Firestone "links women's liberation with children's liberation ... because women will not be liberated until they have been liberated from their children, and by the same token, until children have also been liberated from their parents."

36 Firestone, *Dialectic of Sex*, 66.

37 Firestone, *Dialectic of Sex*, 131, 119, 136 (emphases in the original).

38 Naomi Wolf, *The Beauty Myth: How Images of Beauty Are Used against Women* (New York: Harper Perennial, 2002), 10–11, sees beauty as a tool

of patriarchal oppression with nary a nod to Firestone, though with liberal attribution to Betty Friedan.

39 Firestone, *Dialectic of Sex*, 187.

40 Firestone, *Dialectic of Sex*, 65.

41 Firestone, *Dialectic of Sex*, 67; Phillippe Aries, *Centuries of Childhood: A Social History of Family Life*, trans. Robert Baldick (New York: Vintage, 1962).

42 Firestone, *Dialectic of Sex*, 70.

43 Firestone, *Dialectic of Sex*, 93.

44 Firestone, *Dialectic of Sex*, 90–92.

45 Firestone, *Dialectic of Sex*, 185.

46 Firestone, *Dialectic of Sex*, 187, 91.

47 Firestone, *Dialectic of Sex*, 184–85 (emphasis in the original).

48 Firestone, *Dialectic of Sex*, 203.

49 See, e.g., Hanna Rosin, *The End of Men and the Rise of Women* (New York: Viking, 2012).

50 Firestone, *Dialectic of Sex*, 204–6.

51 Firestone, *Dialectic of Sex*, 213–15.

52 Faludi's significant works include *Backlash: The Undeclared War against American Women* (New York: Broadway Books, 2006). See also Faludi, "Death of a Revolutionary."

53 Thus Germaine Greer, *The Female Eunuch* (London: Book Club Associates, 1970), sometimes seems to be on the outside looking in.

54 Consider Judith Butler, *Undoing Gender* (New York: Routledge, 2004), 157; and Elizabeth Brake, *Minimizing Marriage: Marriage, Morality, and the Law* (New York: Oxford University Press, 2012), 164, as examples of feminist thinkers willing to modify or erase the incest taboo.

55 Michel Foucault, *An Introduction*, vol. 1 of *The History of Sexuality*, trans. Robert Hurley (New York: Vintage, 1978), 36–49.

56 Janice G. Raymond, *The Transsexual Empire: The Making of the She-Male* (Boston: Beacon, 1979), chaps. 2–3; Sheila Jeffreys, *Gender Hurts: A Feminist Analysis of the Politics of Transgenderism* (London: Routledge, 2014).

57 Susan Stryker sees the "wave of transgender scholarship" as "part of a broader queer intellectual movement": Susan Stryker, "(De)Subjugated Knowledges: An Introduction to Transgender Studies," in *The Transgender Studies Reader*, ed. Susan Stryker and Stephen Whittle (New York: Routledge, 2006), 1 (and, more broadly, 3–7).

58 David Halperin argues, "Queer is . . . *whatever* is at odds with the normal, the legitimate, the dominant. *There is nothing in particular to which it necessarily refers*. It is an identity without an essence." See David M. Halperin, *Saint Foucault: Towards a Gay Hagiography* (New York: Oxford University Press, 1995), 62 (emphasis in original).

59 Leslie Feinberg, *Transgender Liberation: A Movement Whose Time Has Come* (New York: World View Forum, 1992), 6.

60 Butler, *Undoing Gender*, 35. Eve Kosofsky Sedgwick, in *Epistemology of the Closet* (Berkeley: University of California Press, 1990), argues that dichotomies in the sexual world such as natural/artificial, gay/straight, closeted/

out, and masculine/feminine are recent arbitrary products of our bourgeois sexual regime.

61 Judith Butler, *Gender Trouble: Feminism and the Subversion of Identity*, 2nd ed. (New York: Routledge, 2006).

62 Butler, *Undoing Gender*, 27–28.

63 Butler, *Undoing Gender*, 26, 28–29.

64 Butler, *Undoing Gender*, 31.

65 Butler, *Undoing Gender*, 32–33. See also 8, for her contention that "a livable life does require various degrees of stability," and that a "life for which no categories of recognition exist is not a livable life."

66 For such arguments see, among others, Martha Albertson Fineman, *The Autonomy Myth: A Theory of Dependency* (London: New Press, 2005), 105–8, 134–36; Richard D. Mohr, *The Long Arc of Justice: Lesbian and Gay Marriage, Equality, and Rights* (New York: Columbia University Press, 2005), 69ff.; Ann Ferguson, "Gay Marriage: An American and Feminist Dilemma," *Hypatia* 22, no. 1 (2007): esp. 51.

67 Butler, *Undoing Gender*, 217.

68 Butler, *Undoing Gender*, 219.

69 "Gender Dysphoria," in *Diagnostic and Statistical Manual of Mental Disorders*, 5th ed. (Arlington, Va.: American Psychiatric Association, 2013), 452.

70 Butler counsels people to submit to a diagnosis for gender dysphoria "ironically or facetiously" to get the health care if it is desired, but to reject the implication that this is a pathology to be corrected; "autonomy," not pathology, is the standard by which to judge the proper choice. Butler, *Undoing Gender*, 82ff., 87.

71 Katherine Kersten, "Transgender Conformity," *First Things*, December 2016, firstthings.com.

72 Betty Friedan, "A Dialogue with Simone de Beauvoir," in Friedan, *"It Changed My Life": Writings on the Women's Movement* (Cambridge, Mass.: Harvard University Press, 1998), 397.

3 Contemporary Liberalism and the Abolition of Marriage

1 Mark E. Brandon, *States of Union: Family and Change in the American Constitutional Order* (Lawrence: University Press of Kansas, 2013); Steven Mintz and Susan Kellogg, *Domestic Revolutions: A Social History of American Family Life* (New York: Free Press, 1988); Nancy F. Cott, *Public Vows: A History of Marriage and the Nation* (Cambridge, Mass.: Harvard University Press, 2000); Hendrik Hartog, *Man and Wife in America: A History* (Cambridge, Mass.: Harvard University Press, 2000).

2 See Wilson, *The Marriage Problem*, chap. 4, esp. 83–105; David Popenoe, *Disturbing the Nest: Family Change and Decline in Modern Societies* (New Brunswick, N.J.: AldineTransaction, 2008), 3–41.

3 Mintz and Kellogg, *Domestic Revolutions*, 205, 233.

4 Cott, *Public Vows*, 197.

5 Hartog, *Man and Wife*, 312.

6 Brandon, *States of Union*, 260.

7 Steven Kautz, *Liberalism and Community* (Ithaca: Cornell University Press, 1995), 63.
8 Steven Horwitz, *Hayek's Modern Family: Classical Liberalism and the Evolution of Social Institutions* (New York: Palgrave Macmillan, 2015), 79–100, 209–40.
9 David Boaz, "Privatize Marriage," *Cato Institute*, April 25, 1997, cato.org.
10 This seems akin to James Madison's teaching on religion as described in Vincent Phillip Muñoz, *God and the Founders: Madison, Washington, and Jefferson* (New York: Cambridge University Press, 2009), 24–29.
11 Wendy McElroy, "The Grayness of Children's Rights," *Daily Anarchist* (blog), September 11, 2012, dailyanarchist.com; Murray N. Rothbard, *The Ethics of Liberty* (New York: New York University Press, 1998), 100–102.
12 See Horwitz, *Hayek's Modern Family*, 226–30.
13 This distinction between modus vivendi, or strategic liberalism, and liberalism as a matter of principle runs through all contemporary liberal thinking, with a clear endorsement of the principled approach and much scorn heaped on the modus vivendi. See John Rawls, *Political Liberalism* (New York: Columbia University Press, 1993), 147ff.; Ronald Dworkin, *Taking Rights Seriously* (Cambridge, Mass.: Harvard University Press, 1977), 14–45; Patrick Neal, *Liberalism and Its Discontents* (New York: NYU Press, 1999), 81–83.
14 Ronald Dworkin, *A Matter of Principle* (Cambridge, Mass.: Harvard University Press, 1985), 205–6.
15 Dworkin, *Taking Rights Seriously*, 269 (emphasis added).
16 I develop these elements in Scott Yenor, "Toward Plural Marriage: Understanding and Countering the Liberal Wringer," *Public Discourse*, December 7, 2015, thepublicdiscourse.com.
17 Ronald C. Den Otter, *In Defense of Plural Marriage* (New York: Cambridge University Press, 2015), 87.
18 Den Otter, *Plural Marriage*, 103–4, 107, 148–49.
19 Den Otter, *Plural Marriage*, 79, 84, 103, 106–7.
20 Den Otter, *Plural Marriage*, 77, 80, 86, 89, 105.
21 Den Otter, *Plural Marriage*, 69, 175.
22 The only restrictive practice to survive the liberal wringer is affirmative action.
23 Tamara Metz, *Untying the Knot: Marriage, the State, and the Case for Their Divorce* (Princeton: Princeton University Press, 2010), 115 (emphasis in the original).
24 See Linda C. McClain, *The Place of Families: Fostering Capacity, Equality, and Responsibility* (Cambridge, Mass.: Harvard University Press, 2006), 217, who would maintain marriage, among other similar reasons, for the "expressive benefit of public recognition of—and validation of—[a couple's] commitment"; and Brake, *Minimizing Marriage*, 174ff., who emphasizes the social support for caring relationships that extends marriage well beyond the heterosexual dyad to both homosexuals and to groups.
25 Brake, *Minimizing Marriage*, v; Den Otter, *Plural Marriage*.
26 McClain, *The Place of Families*, 193, whose answer to the question, "Should society (and family law and policy) move beyond marriage?" is, "Yes and no."

27 Metz, *Untying the Knot*. See also Steve Vanderheiden, "Why the State Should Stay out of the Wedding Chapel," *Public Affairs Quarterly* 13, no. 2 (1999): 175–99.

28 See esp. Metz, *Untying the Knot*, 134, who states that "as a legal category, marriage would be abolished"; and Fineman, *The Autonomy Myth*, 123, who states that "we do not need marriage and we should abolish it as a legal category."

29 Nearly every feminist work of contemporary liberalism pays homage to Rawls and Okin's latter-day revelation about the blind spots in Rawls' thought. Okin's glory lives on in her epigones as they recount those glory days: see McClain, *The Place of Families*, 25, 79; Fineman, *The Autonomy Myth*, 214–17; Brake, *Minimizing Marriage*, 139.

30 John Rawls, *A Theory of Justice* (Cambridge, Mass.: Belknap Press of Harvard University Press, 1971), 7.

31 Okin, *Justice*, 103: "Gender, with its ascriptive designation of positions and expectations of behavior in accordance with the inborn characteristics of sex, could no longer form a legitimate part of the social structure, whether inside or outside the family."

32 Okin, *Justice*, 104, chap. 5 generally.

33 Okin, *Justice*, 94, 97–101.

34 Earlier waves of liberalism maintained a tension on the fundamental issue of whether the individual or the family was the basic unit of society. See, e.g., Rawls, *A Theory of Justice*, 128, 146, who sees individuals behind the veil of ignorance not as "single individuals," but as "heads of families" or "representatives of families"; but see also Milton Friedman, *Capitalism and Freedom* (Chicago: University of Chicago Press, 1962), 18 , who remains agnostic on whether "the individual or the family" is the basic unit of society.

35 Okin, *Justice*, 175.

36 Rawls, *Justice as Fairness: A Restatement* (Cambridge, Mass.: Belknap Press, 2001), 167. See also 11: "To establish equality between men and women in sharing the work of society, in preserving its culture and in reproducing itself over time, special provisions are needed in family law (an no doubt elsewhere) so that the burden of bearing, raising, and educating children does not fall more heavily on women, thereby undermining their fair equality of opportunity."

37 John Rawls, "The Idea of Public Reason Revisited," *University of Chicago Law Review* 64, no. 3 (1997): 765–807. Rawls' formulation on these matters employs a certain hedging consistently throughout: "We wouldn't want the principles of justice . . . to apply directly to the family." He concedes that society may have to "allow for some traditional gendered division of labor within families . . . provided that it is fully voluntary and does not result from or lead to injustice." Only family forms providing effective child-rearing should be encouraged, or, perhaps, tolerated.

38 Similarly, *A Theory of Justice* makes no mention of abortion, for an unborn child would have a much different view of the matter than the woman seeking an abortion.

39 Fineman, *The Autonomy Myth*, 235, 273–74.

40 Thus the same-sex marriage debate was from the start to the finish part of a liberal feminist aspiration to promote a family without gender; consider Nan D. Hunter, "Marriage, Law, and Gender: A Feminist Inquiry," *Law & Sexuality: A Review of Lesbian and Gay Legal Issues* 1 (1991): 17–18; Robin West, "Integrity and Universality: A Comment on Ronald Dworkin's Freedom's Law," *Fordham Law Review* 65 (1997): 1329–34; Evan Wolfson, "Crossing the Threshold: Equal Marriage Rights for Lesbians and Gay Men and the Intra-Community Critique," *New York University Review of Law & Social Change* 21 (1994–1995): 567; McClain, *The Place of Families*, 179; Brake, *Minimizing Marriage*, 118–23. See also Mohr, *The Long Arc*, 69ff.; Ferguson, "Gay Marriage," 51.

41 *Loving v. Virginia*, 388 U.S. 1 (1967). See also Justice Thurgood Marshall in *Zablocki v. Redhail*, 434 U.S. 374 (1978), who writes "freedom of personal choice in matters of marriage and family life is one of the liberties protected by the due process clause of the Fourteenth Amendment."

42 *Turner v. Safley*, 482 U.S. 78 (1987). See Katherine Shaw Spaht, "The Current Crisis in Marriage Laws, Its Origins, and Its Impact," in *The Meaning of Marriage: Family, State, Market and Morals*, ed. Robert P. George and Jean Bethke Elshtain (Dallas: Spence, 2006), 221–35.

43 *Goodridge v. Department of Public Health*, 440 Mass. 309, 798 N.E.2d 941, 954–55, 963 (2003).

44 Stephen Macedo, "Homosexuality and the Conservative Mind," *Georgetown Law Journal* 84 (1995–1996): 279; Andrew Koppelman, *The Gay Rights Question in Contemporary American Law* (Chicago: University of Chicago Press, 2002), 87–88.

45 Ralph Wedgwood, "Fundamental Argument for Same-Sex Marriage," *Journal of Political Philosophy* 7, no. 3 (1999): 233. See the plaintiffs' brief in *Goodridge v. Department of Public Health*, No. SJC-08860, a survey of court cases in David Blankenhorn, *The Future of Marriage* (New York: Encounter Books, 2007), 13–14.

46 Adrian Alex Wellington, "Why Liberals Should Support Same Sex Marriage," *Journal of Social Philosophy* 26, no. 3 (1995): 13.

47 As part of its argument that procreation is not an end of marriage, the Massachusetts Supreme Court, for instance, has ruled that sexual consummation can no longer be a defining feature of marriage. They therefore must also deny that sexual consummation is central to same-sex marriage if they are to hold both types of marriage to the same standard. See Hadley Arkes, "The Family and the Laws," in George and Elshtain, *The Meaning of Marriage*, 130–32.

48 Brake, *Minimizing Marriage*, 144.

49 Formerly available at http://www.beyondmarriage.org/full_statement.html (and now conspicuously missing) the statement was signed by, among many others, Gloria Steinem, Barbara Ehrenreich, and over one hundred other academics. See also Kevin Noble Maillard, "Beyond Marriage, Blood or Adoption," *New York Times*, June 7, 2012, nytimes.com.

50 Brake, *Minimizing Marriage*; McClain, *The Place of Families*.

51 Fineman, *The Autonomy Myth*, 113; Cheshire Calhoun, "Who's Afraid of Polygamous Marriage? Lessons for Same-Sex Advocacy from the History of Polygamy," *San Diego Law Review* 42, no. 3 (2005): 1035.

52 See, for instance, Maura I. Strassberg, "Distinctions of Form or Substance: Monogamy, Polygamy and Same-Sex Marriage," *North Carolina Law Review* 75 (1997): 1501.

53 McClain, *The Place of Families*, 181–82 (emphasis added); Jonathan Rauch, "One Man, Many Wives, Big Problems," *Reason* (blog), April 3, 2006, reason .com, who emphasizes that polyamory will mostly be polygamy, which leads to an excess number of unmarried males who are prone to crime, gender inequality, poverty, and militarism; and Macedo, "Homosexuality and the Conservative Mind," 286, who sees dyadic marriage as serving the self-control needed for a "healthy and happy life."

54 Brake, *Minimizing Marriage*, 43, 62.

55 See Rawls, *A Theory of Justice*, 92; Rawls, *Political Liberalism*, 75–76, 178–82, 187–90. The early Rawls seems to think that the family promotes the primary goods of education for children, but the later Rawls of *Political Liberalism* seems to have accepted the feminist critique of the family and to be open to a more deconstructive analysis of marriage in terms of primary goods.

56 Fineman, *The Autonomy Myth*, 35.

57 Fineman, *The Autonomy Myth*, 123.

58 Consider Fineman, *The Autonomy Myth*, 67 ("We are at the point where we must accept that the relationship between marriage and popular conceptions about the family has changed substantially") and 107 ("new patterns of behavior").

59 Fineman, *The Autonomy Myth*, 162–64.

60 See, for instance, Thomas A. DiPrete and Claudia Buchmann, *The Rise of Women: The Growing Gender Gap in Education and What It Means for American Schools* (New York: Russell Sage Foundation, 2013).

61 Fineman, *The Autonomy Myth*, 171. See also McClain, *The Place of Families*, 107–10, who implies that a gender-neutral commitment to care for dependents will, in our gendered context, probably help women more.

62 Fineman, *The Autonomy Myth*, 169.

63 Fineman, *The Autonomy Myth*, 165.

64 See, e.g., Fineman, *The Autonomy Myth*, 200–201, 260–61, 284ff. For a very similar list securing the same goal, see McClain, *The Place of Families*, 97, 111–13.

65 Fineman, *The Autonomy Myth*, 46–53; Brake, *Minimizing Marriage*, 183–85.

66 Fineman, *The Autonomy Myth*, 171.

67 Fineman, *The Autonomy Myth*, 108, 112.

68 "Fineman's argument for bringing dependency and care to the fore is entirely persuasive. I draw from and follow much of her argument," writes Metz, *Untying the Knot*, 140. See idem, *Untying the Knot*, 120, for the abolition of marriage.

69 Metz, *Untying the Knot*, 134–37.

70 McClain, *The Place of Families*, 194.

71 Brake, *Minimizing Marriage*, 160, 158–67, 180–85.

4 Beyond Sexual Repression

1 See Yenor, *Family Politics*, 157–73, for a treatment of Freud and Russell.
2 See Wilhelm Reich, *The Sexual Revolution*, trans. Therese Pol (1945; New York: Touchstone, 1974), 40ff., on "The Influence of Conservative Sexual Morality"; and Reich's treatment of Lindsey's strange attachment to marriage: Reich, *The Sexual Revolution*, 91–106.
3 See Paul Robinson, *The Modernization of Sex: Havelock Ellis, Alfred Kinsey, William Masters and Virginia Johnson* (New York: Harper & Row, 1976).
4 Alfred C. Kinsey, Wardell B. Pomeroy, and Clyde E. Martin, *Sexual Behavior in the Human Male* (Philadelphia: W. B. Saunders, 1948), 59, 369, 373; Robinson, *The Modernization of Sex*, 56: "Kinsey refused to grant the human realm a unique place in the larger order of things. Indeed, it was precisely the pretension to such specialness, he believed, that accounted for most of our sexual miseries."
5 Alfred C. Kinsey et al., *Sexual Behavior in the Human Female* (Philadelphia: W. B. Saunders, 1953), 511.
6 Kinsey, Pomeroy, and Martin, *Human Male*, 263, see sex as a "normal biological function, acceptable in whatever form it is manifested."
7 Kinsey et al., *Human Female*, 160–64, 576–79, 625–27, 635–41.
8 Lester F. Ward, *Dynamic Sociology, or Applied Social Science*, 2 vols. (1883; New York: D. Appleton, 1897), 632–33.
9 Roger Scruton, *Sexual Desire: A Philosophical Investigation* (New York: Continuum, 2006), 16–17, 74.
10 David Levy, *Love and Sex with Robots: The Evolution of Human-Robot Relationships* (New York: Harper Perennial, 2008), 227: the modern woman has "taken an increasingly independent view of her absolute right to enjoy her sexuality to the fullest, so the vibrator has played an increasingly important role in satisfying women's sexual needs." See Barbara Ehrenreich, Elizabeth Hess, and Gloria Jacobs, *Re-Making Love: The Feminization of Sex* (Garden City, N.Y.: Anchor, 1987), for a celebration of Tupperware parties for sex paraphernalia.
11 Levy, *Love and Sex with Robots*, 220–42.
12 So thought the first great twentieth-century sexologist, Havelock Ellis, in "Sex in Relation to Society," in vol. 2 of *Studies in the Psychology of Sex* (New York: Random House, 1936), 167–70.
13 Levy, *Love and Sex with Robots*, 127.
14 Scruton, *Sexual Desire*, 155–56.
15 Scruton, *Sexual Desire*, 319.
16 Levy, *Love and Sex with Robots*, 107, 247.
17 Hilaire Belloc, *The Great Heresies* (Rockford, Ill.: Tan Books, 1938), 2–6.
18 Scruton, *Sexual Desire*, chap. 10.
19 Erwin W. Strauss, *Phenomenological Psychology: Selected Papers* (New York: Basic Books, 1966), 219.
20 Harry M. Clor, *Public Morality and Liberal Society: Essays on Decency, Law, and Pornography* (Notre Dame: University of Notre Dame Press, 1996), 191–92.
21 This pleasing euphemism for sex exists in several languages, including French (*faire l'amour*), German (*Liebe machen*), and others.

22 Such is the argument of Christopher Ryan and Cacilda Jethá, *Sex at Dawn: How We Mate, Why We Stray, and What It Means for Modern Relationships* (New York: Harper, 2010).

23 Germaine Greer, *Sex and Destiny: The Politics of Human Fertility* (New York: Harper & Row, 1984), 101.

24 Walter Berns, "Pornography versus Democracy," *Society* 36, no. 6 (1999): 7, n. 2, relates a story of a college class where four naked models performed sex acts and showed pornographic movies in order to ridicule American prudishness and help students get over hang-ups.

25 Sigmund Freud, *Civilization and Its Discontents*, trans. James Strachey (1930; New York: W. W. Norton, 2005), 53, 89.

26 Reich, *The Sexual Revolution*, xxvi.

27 Reich, *The Sexual Revolution*, 19; Norman O. Brown, *Life against Death: The Psychoanalytical Meaning of History* (Middletown, Conn.: Wesleyan University Press, 1959), 307; Herbert Marcuse, *Eros and Civilization: A Philosophical Inquiry into Freud* (Boston: Beacon, 1966), 197.

28 Reich, *Sexual Revolution*, 4, 6, 31, 34, 50, 64, 69–70, 73, 82, passim; Herbert Marcuse, *One-Dimensional Man: Studies in the Ideology of Advanced Industrial Society* (Boston: Beacon, 1964), 1–18.

29 Reich, *Sexual Revolution*, 119 (emphasis in original).

30 Wilhelm Reich, *The Mass Psychology of Fascism*, trans. Theodore P. Wolfe (1933; New York: Orgone Institute, 1946), 88.

31 Marcuse, *Eros and Civilization*, 94–97.

32 Reich, *Sexual Revolution*, 15.

33 Reich, *Sexual Revolution*, 66.

34 Reich, *Sexual Revolution*, 32, 37, 117.

35 Reich, *Sexual Revolution*, 218–21.

36 Reich, *Sexual Revolution*, 37, 133.

37 Reich, *Sexual Revolution*, 89.

38 Reich, *Sexual Revolution*, 128.

39 Reich, *Sexual Revolution*, 116.

40 Reich, *Sexual Revolution*, 15.

41 Reich, *Sexual Revolution*, 28.

42 Wilhelm Reich, *Listen, Little Man!* trans. Theodore P. Wolfe (1945; London: Souvenir, 1972), 111–12.

43 Marcuse, *Eros and Civilization*, 35.

44 Marcuse, *Eros and Civilization*, 201–2, 199.

45 See Marcuse, *Eros and Civilization*, 217ff.; Nathaniel Hawthorne, *The Blithedale Romance* (1852; New York: Penguin, 1983).

46 See Peter Hitchens, *The Abolition of Britain: From Winston Churchill to Lady Diana* (San Francisco: Encounter Books, 2000), 207–20.

47 Rochelle Gurstein, *The Repeal of Reticence: A History of America's Cultural and Legal Struggles over Free Speech, Obscenity, Sexual Liberation, and Modern Art* (New York: Hill and Wang, 1998), 258: "The non-judgmental stance is the flip side of unmasking—and both grow directly out of the emotivist moral position underlying all emancipatory projects of exposure, which holds that the judgments express nothing but private whims and subjective

preferences, and, as they belong to the individual, are always self-interested and manipulative."

48 David Hume, "Of Polygamy and Divorces," in *Essays Moral, Political and Literary*, ed. Eugene F. Miller, rev. ed. (Indianapolis: Liberty Fund, 1987), 188.

49 Anthony Giddens, *The Transformation of Intimacy: Sexuality, Love and Eroticism in Modern Societies* (Stanford: Stanford University Press, 1992), 2, passim.

50 Giddens, *The Transformation of Intimacy*, 26–27, 113–14, 179–81.

51 Giddens, *The Transformation of Intimacy*, 121ff., 124ff.

52 Mark Regnerus and Jeremy Uecker, *Premarital Sex in America: How Young Americans Meet, Mate, and Think about Marrying* (Oxford: Oxford University Press, 2011), 23–24, passim.

5 Sexual Difference and Human Life

1 Okin, *Justice*, 171.

2 Harvey C. Mansfield, *Manliness* (New Haven: Yale University Press, 2006), 26–27, shows the use of the words *sex* and *gender* has been "quite variable" in feminist and scientific literature since the 1970s, and shows that the categories both will not go away and resist clarification under the current dispensation.

3 Otto Weininger, *Sex and Character: An Investigation of Fundamental Principles*, trans. Ladislaus Loeb (1903; Bloomington: University of Indiana Press, 2005), 58.

4 G. W. F. Hegel, *Elements of the Philosophy of Right*, ed. Allen W. Wood, trans. H. B. Nisbet (Cambridge: Cambridge University Press, 1991), para. 166A.

5 E. O. Wilson, *On Human Nature* (Cambridge, Mass.: Harvard University Press, 1978), 139–40.

6 The description of spider reproduction in E. O. Wilson, *Sociobiology, the New Synthesis* (Cambridge, Mass.: Harvard University Press, 1975), 320, serves to illustrate sexual differences in humans as well:

> Pure epigamic display can be envisioned as a contest between salesmanship and sales resistance. The sex that courts, ordinarily the male, plans to invest less reproductive effort in the offspring. What it offers to the female is chiefly evidence it is fully normal and physiologically fit. But this warranty consists of only a brief performance, so that strong selective pressures exist for less fit individuals to present a false image. The courted sex, usually the female, will therefore find it strongly advantageous to distinguish the really fit from the pretended fit. Consequently, there will be a strong tendency for the courted sex to develop coyness. That is, its responses will be hesitant and cautious in a way that evokes still more displays and makes correct discrimination easier.

7 Yenor, *Family Politics*, 77–85, provides a more detailed description of this argument.

8 Consider the case for sociobiology and a "liberal sexual morality" in Wilson, *On Human Nature*, 142.

9 Beauvoir, *The Second Sex*, 404 (emphasis added).

10 Butler, *Bodies That Matter*, 10.

11 Butler, *Bodies That Matter*, 11–12.

12 Scruton, *Sexual Desire*, 274–75.

13 For a more complete discussion of contemporary feminism, see the discussion of Simone de Beauvoir in Yenor, *Family Politics*, chap. 9.

14 This idea is captured best in Aristotle, *Nicomachean Ethics*, 1094b13–1095a5, in reference to seeking the "truth roughly and in outline, as if, in speaking about and on the basis of things that are for the most part so." Aristotle speaks of the just and good things that admit of "much dispute and variability" because they appear to be products of laws alone and not nature. Since marriage and the family implicate, on Aristotle's terms, living more than living well, we may expect less variation on marriage and family life as they exist under political arrangements.

15 The best, most recent scientific work on these matters includes cross-national meta-analyses of surveys, including, among infinite others, Armin Falk and Johannes Hermle, "Relationship of Gender Differences in Preferences to Economic Development and Gender Equality" (IZA Discussion Paper Series No. 12059, Institute of Labor Economics, Bonn, Germany, December 2018); Janet Shibley Hyde, "Gender Similarities and Differences," *Annual Review of Psychology* 65 (2014): 373–98; Richard A. Lippa, "Sex Differences in Personality Traits and Gender-Related Occupational Preferences across 53 Nations: Testing Evolutionary and Social-Environmental Theories," *Archives of Sexual Behavior* 39, no. 3 (2010): 619–39; David P. Schmitt, Anu Realo, Martin Voracek, and Jüri Allik, "Why Can't a Man Be More Like a Woman? Sex Differences in Big Five Personality Traits across 55 Cultures," *Journal of Personality and Social Psychology* 94, no. 1 (2008): 168–82; John Archer, "Sex Differences in Aggression in Real-World Settings: A Meta-Analytic Review," *Review of General Psychology* 8, no. 4 (2004): 291–322; Alan Feingold, "Gender Differences in Personality: A Meta-Analysis," *Psychological Bulletin* 116, no. 3 (1994): 429–56.

16 See Scott Yenor, *David Hume's Humanity: The Philosophy of Common Life and Its Limits* (New York: Palgrave Macmillan, 2016), 199–209, for a treatment of "for-the-most-part universals."

17 Lippa, "Personality Traits," 621.

18 David P. Barash, *Out of Eden: The Surprising Consequences of Polygamy* (Oxford: Oxford University Press, 2016), 43; Mansfield, *Manliness*, 29; Steven Goldberg, *The Inevitability of Patriarchy* (New York: William Morrow, 1973); Warren Farrell, *The Myth of Male Power: Why Men Are the Disposable Sex* (New York: Simon & Schuster, 1993), chaps. 4–8.

19 Barash, *Out of Eden*, 43, and esp. Schmitt et al., "Why Can't a Man Be More Like a Woman?"; Lippa, "Personality Traits," 619, 627–28.

20 Barash, *Out of Eden*, 63–67; Mansfield, *Manliness*, 28; David P. Schmitt, "The Evolution of Culturally-Variable Sex Differences: Men and Women Are Not Always Different, but When They Are . . . It Appears *Not* to Result from Patriarchy or Sex Role Socialization," in *The Evolution of Sexuality*, ed. Todd K. Shackelford and Ranald D. Hansen (New York: Springer, 2014), 221–56; Richard A. Lippa, "Sex Differences in Sex Drive, Sociosexuality, and Height

across 53 Nations: Testing Evolutionary and Social Structural Theories," *Archives of Sexual Behavior* 38, no. 5 (2009): 631–51.
21 Steven E. Rhoads, *Taking Sex Differences Seriously* (New York: Encounter Books, 2004), 63–66.
22 See Rong Su, James Rounds, and Patrick Ian Armstrong, "Men and Things, Women and People: A Meta-Analysis of Sex Differences in Interests," *Psychological Bulletin* 135, no. 6 (2009): 859–84, for a comprehensive review of this scientific literature and new findings supporting the general conclusion that "the greatest differences between men and women are in the relative strength of the interest in working with things versus the interest in working with people" (862). See also Lippa, "Personality Traits," 630–31, 633, suggesting that the average man is about 1.5 standard deviations more interested in things than the average woman, and the average woman is 1.5 standard deviations more interested in people than the average man.
23 Eleanor E. Maccoby, *The Two Sexes: Growing Up Apart, Coming Together* (Cambridge, Mass.: Belknap Press of Harvard University Press, 1998).
24 Susan Pinker, *The Sexual Paradox* (New York: Scribner, 2008), 62–91.
25 See esp. Lippa, "Personality Traits," 621–22, who shows that many sex differences are "weaker in societies with strong gender roles and stronger in societies with weak gender roles." Other traits, like the value assigned to physical attractiveness by men and women, are simply universal, while others, like the man's willingness to take on some domestic responsibilities and a woman's willingness to earn more outside the home, follow the "enlightenment pattern" of lessening, but not erasing, sex differences. The theory that advanced democracies that protect and promote sexual equality manifest more sexual differentiation, especially on occupational choice (things vs. people; part-time vs. full-time) and agreeableness, can be found in Falk and Hermle, "Relationship of Gender Differences," 10–12, with accompanying graphs; Paul T. Costa Jr., Antonio Terracciano, and Robert R. McRae, "Gender Differences in Personality across Cultures: Robust and Surprising Findings," *Journal of Personality and Social Psychology* 81, no. 2 (2001): 322–31; Serge Guimond et al., "Culture, Gender, and the Self: Variations and Impact of Social Comparison Processes," *Journal of Personality and Social Psychology* 92, no. 6 (2007): 1118–34.
26 McDonagh and Pappano, *Playing with the Boys.*
27 McDonagh and Pappano, *Playing with the Boys*, 28–37, 114–16.
28 Dowling, *The Frailty Myth.*
29 Both these works are cited in Rhoads, *Taking Sex Differences Seriously*, 143–44. See also Beauvoir, *The Second Sex*, 333.
30 Quoted in Rhoads, *Taking Sex Differences Seriously*, 162.
31 McDonagh and Pappano, *Playing with the Boys*, 34.
32 Dowling, *The Frailty Myth*, chaps. 6 and 7, suggests that the gap will disappear as soon as women get the same training as men do.
33 Martin van Creveld, "A Woman's Place: Reflections on the Origins of Violence," *Social Research* 67, no. 3 (2000): 825–47.
34 Robinson Meyer, "We Thought Female Athletes Were Catching Up to Men, but They're Not," *The Atlantic*, August 9, 2012, theatlantic.com; Rhoads,

Taking Sex Differences Seriously, 145; McDonagh and Pappano, *Playing with the Boys*, 52–58.

35 Donald Symons, *The Evolution of Human Sexuality* (Oxford: Oxford University Press, 1979), 251–52.

36 Rhoads, *Taking Sex Differences Seriously*, 156.

37 Robin Tolmach Lakoff, *Language and Woman's Place: Text and Commentaries*, ed. Mary Bucholtz, rev. ed. (New York: Oxford University Press, 2004); Deborah Tannen, *You Just Don't Understand: Women and Men in Conversation* (New York: William Morrow, 1990).

38 Carol Gilligan, *In a Different Voice: Psychological Theory and Women's Development* (Cambridge, Mass.: Harvard University Press, 1993), 69, 160.

39 Maccoby, *The Two Sexes*, 150, 37.

40 Maccoby, *The Two Sexes*, 54–56; Aristotle, *Nicomachean Ethics*, 1157b5–14.

41 Marianne J. Legato, *Why Men Never Remember and Women Never Forget* (New York: Rodale, 2005), 10.

42 Barash, *Out of Eden*, 27, 47, 49; Martin Daly and Margo Wilson, *Homicide* (Chicago: AldineTransaction, 1988), 146.

43 Rosin, *The End of Men*, 169–82.

44 A world of womanly manipulation is seen in Tolstoy's *Anna Karenina*, the greatest novel of womanly psychology ever writ. Consider esp. part 1, chap. 19 for a study of Anna's bewitching manipulation of her sister-in-law Dolly: Leo Tolstoy, *Anna Karenina*, trans. Louise Maude and Aylmer Maude (1878; New York: Everyman's Library, 1992).

45 See Catharine Morgan et al., "Incidence, Clinical Management, and Mortality Risk Following Self Harm among Children and Adolescents: Cohort Study in Primary Care," *BMJ* 359 (2017): https://doi.org/10.1136/bmj.j4351.

46 Greg Lukianoff and Jonathan Haidt, *The Coddling of the American Mind: How Good Intentions and Bad Ideas Are Setting Up a Generation for Failure* (New York: Penguin, 2019), 148–56.

47 Beauvoir, *The Second Sex*, 371–87, 692–96.

48 Beauvoir's *Second Sex* inspired more than a few independent-minded disciples to write in favor of sexual liberation, including Millett, *Sexual Politics*, 63, who favors a "a permissive single standard of sexual freedom"; Firestone, *Dialectic of Sex*, 223, who advocates for a "more natural polymorphous sexuality"; and Ehrenreich, Hess, and Jacobs, *Re-Making Love*, 202–3: "Heterosexual sex, and especially intercourse, is a condensed drama of male domination and female submission. The man 'mounts' and penetrates; the woman spreads her legs and 'submits'; and the postures seem to ratify, again and again, the ancient authority of men over women. . . . Sex, or women's role in it, is understood as a humiliation that no man would want to endure."

49 Kinsey et al., *Human Female*, 641. See esp. the influential book denying differences between the sexes on matters of sex: Tavris, *The Mismeasure of Woman*.

50 Ferdinand Lundberg and Marynia F. Farnham, *Modern Woman: The Lost Sex* (New York: Harper, 1947), 269.

51 Ehrenreich, Hess, and Jacobs, *Re-Making Love*, 2, 164–71.

52 Ehrenreich, Hess, and Jacobs, *Re-Making Love*, 5. In fact, "women, not men, [would be] the sexually aggressive, orgasmically potent sex, capable of 'having orgasms indefinitely if physical exhaustion did not intervene.'" See also 70.

53 Ehrenreich, Hess, and Jacobs, *Re-Making Love*, 74ff.

54 Mark Regnerus, *Cheap Sex: The Transformation of Men, Marriage, and Monogamy* (New York: Oxford University Press, 2017), 116–21.

55 Ehrenreich, Hess, and Jacobs, *Re-Making Love*, 24, 170, 171ff.; Symons, *The Evolution of Human Sexuality*, 213–15.

56 Jacqueline N. Cohen and E. Sandra Byers, "Beyond Lesbian Bed Death: Enhancing Our Understanding of the Sexuality of Sexual-Minority Women in Relationships," *Journal of Sex Research* 51, no. 8 (2014): 894.

57 Consider Ehrenreich, Hess, and Jacobs, *Re-Making Love*, 94, 101, 126.

58 Rosin, *The End of Men*, 7–9, 262ff.

59 Regnerus, *Cheap Sex*, 24, 58–60.

60 Symons, *The Evolution of Human Sexuality*, 27.

61 Legato, *Why Men Never Remember*, 20. See Rhoads, *Taking Sex Differences Seriously*, 60.

62 See Symons, *The Evolution of Human Sexuality*, 27–28, 264–65; Regnerus, *Cheap Sex*, 14–15, 23, 225, n. 3; Rhoads, *Taking Sex Differences Seriously*, chap. 3.

63 Regnerus, *Cheap Sex*, 23, 225, 226, n. 3. See the review of the sociological literature on this matter in Catherine Hakim, "The Male Sexual Deficit: A Social Fact of the 21st Century," *International Sociology* 30, no. 3 (2015): 314–35; and idem., "Economies of Desire: Sexuality and the Sex Industry in the 21st Century," *Institute for Economic Affairs* 35, no. 3 (2015): 329–48. On this score Regnerus and Uecker, *Premarital Sex in America*, 27, report that "study after study of sexual partnerships, in virtually every corner of the earth, the conclusion is always the same."

64 Rosin, *The End of Men*, 19.

65 Barash, *Out of Eden*, 67; Regnerus, *Cheap Sex*, 25–26, 64; Legato, *Why Men Never Remember*, 29–33.

66 Symons, *The Evolution of Human Sexuality*, 218 (and 215–23 generally): "Studies of nonmarital sexuality in the West support the folk idea that boys typically seek sexual intercourse for its own sake while girls seek it within the context of, or as a means of developing, a relationship." Few findings are as well established as the tendency of women to elide emotional and sexual intimacy: see Rhoads, *Taking Sex Differences Seriously*, 51–55, 101–8; John Marshall Townsend, *What Women Want—What Men Want: Why the Sexes Still See Love and Commitment So Differently* (New York: Oxford University Press, 1998), 58; Regnerus, *Cheap Sex*, 100–105; Legato, *Why Men Never Remember*, 45–50; Maccoby, *The Two Sexes*, 207 (and 213, 215–19): "It is clear that in many young couples, the two partners want different things from the relationship. Males tend to be more oriented to pleasure—not just to the pleasure of sex, but to the pleasure of having fun with the partner. Girls are more often looking for a committed, long-term, loving relationship. . . . This difference has been found in a variety of ethnic groups and at all socioeconomic levels, and

seems to be characteristic of modern young people in all the Western countries where studies have been done."

67 Charles William Hendel, *Citizen of Geneva: Selections from the Letters of Jean-Jacques Rousseau* (Oxford: Oxford University Press, 1937), 81.

68 Consider Barash, *Out of Eden*, 76: "There is in any event a regrettable association between sex and aggression, which needs to be confronted." See also the great humanistic psychologist Abraham Maslow in Barash, *Out of Eden*, 76. Symons, *The Evolution of Human Sexuality*, 287.

69 John Money, *Gendermaps: Social Constructionism, Feminism, and Sexosophical History* (New York: Continuum, 1995), 54.

70 Barash, *Out of Eden*, 65–67, 72.

71 Wolf, *The Beauty Myth*.

72 Regnerus, *Cheap Sex*, 104–5. See also Legato, *Why Men Never Remember*, 41–58, esp. 47–48; Rhoads, *Taking Sex Differences Seriously*, 53.

73 Friedan, *The Feminine Mystique*, 133 (emphasis in original), 336.

74 Consider, for instance, Firestone, *Dialectic of Sex*, 74, 157; Millett, *Sexual Politics*, 161–68; Beauvoir, *The Second Sex*, 490–92, 495–99, 505–27. Even Ruth Bader Ginsburg thinks, in typically feminist false dichotomy, that "motherly love ain't everything it has been cracked up to be. . . . To some extent it's a myth that men have created to make women think that they do this job to perfection." Quoted in Rhoads, *Taking Sex Differences Seriously*, 17.

75 Frieden, *The Feminine Mystique*, 368; see also 366: women must "make a lifetime commitment . . . to a field of thought, to work of serious importance to society" (i.e., not motherhood).

76 See Firestone, *Dialectic of Sex*, 172; Beauvoir, *The Second Sex*, 525.

77 Rhoads, *Taking Sex Differences Seriously*, 190–91, contains many quotes from these and other books, including the following: "the most intolerable regret" and "angry that I was daft enough to believe female fulfillment came with a leather briefcase."

78 Sylvia Ann Hewlett, *Creating a Life: Professional Women and the Quest for Children* (New York: Talk Miramax Books, 2002).

79 Paul A. Rahe, *The Spartan Regime: Its Character, Origins, and Grand Strategy* (New Haven: Yale University Press, 2016), 26–29.

80 Okin, *Justice*, 122, 132, 171–75; Mary Lyndon Shanley, *Feminism, Marriage, and the Law in Victorian England* (Princeton: Princeton University Press, 1989), 66, 189–95.

81 Barash, *Out of Eden*, 81. Also Maccoby, *The Two Sexes*, 256: "in all known societies, women, whether they are working outside the home or not, assume most of the day-to-day responsibility for childcare."

82 Rhoads, *Taking Sex Differences Seriously*, 197–202.

83 See Diane Hales, *Just Like a Woman: How Gender Science Is Redefining What Makes Us Female* (New York: Bantam Books, 1999), 267; Wilson, *The Marriage Problem*, 188.

84 Maccoby, *The Two Sexes*, 266.

85 Maccoby, *The Two Sexes*, 269ff.

86 Maccoby, *The Two Sexes*, 266–68.

87 Maccoby, *The Two Sexes*, 277.

88 Several recent studies show how this general finding applies to science and math education in advanced countries. Consider Olga Khazan, "The More Gender Equality, the Fewer Women in STEM," *The Atlantic*, February 18, 2018, theatlantic.com.

Postscript to Chapter 5: On the Nature of Moderate Feminism

1 Friedan, "A Dialogue with Simone de Beauvoir," in Friedan, *"It Changed My Life,"* 304–5.
2 Friedan, *The Feminine Mystique*, 22, 31, 27.
3 Friedan, *The Feminine Mystique*, 336.
4 Friedan, *The Feminine Mystique*, 71, 77.
5 Friedan, *The Feminine Mystique*, 334.
6 Friedan, *The Feminine Mystique*, 316–17, 322, quoting Maslow's published and unpublished works.
7 Abraham H. Maslow, *Motivation and Personality* (New York: Harper & Row, 1954), 200.
8 Abraham H. Maslow, "Dominance, Personality and Social Behavior in Women," *Journal of Social Psychology* 10 (1939): 3.
9 Maslow, *Motivation and Personality*, xvii.
10 Maslow, *Motivation and Personality*, xii. See also 93: "What a man can be, he must be. This need we may call self-actualization. . . . It refers to the desire for self-fulfillment, namely, to the tendency for him to become actualized in what he is potentially. This tendency might be phrased as the desire to become more and more what one is, to become everything that one is capable of becoming."
11 Friedan, *The Feminine Mystique*, 322–26.
12 Some recent scientific evidence, cited by Friedan, seems to support such conclusions: some studies purport to show that autonomous or emancipated women (as opposed to those bewitched by the feminine mystique) are happier and experience more, and more profound, orgasms, while others purport to show that college-educated women have fewer unhappy marriages than those without advanced degrees. See Friedan, *The Feminine Mystique*, 319ff. (Maslow's study of 130 women), 327–29 (Kinsey's sex study), 329ff.
13 Friedan, *The Feminine Mystique*, 320.
14 Friedan, *The Feminine Mystique*, 334.
15 Friedan, *The Feminine Mystique*, 348.
16 Betty Friedan, *Life So Far: A Memoir* (New York: Simon & Schuster, 2000), 299.
17 Betty Friedan, "The Crises of Divorce," in *"It Changed My Life,"* 318, 321.
18 Friedan, *Life So Far*, 269.
19 Friedan, *Life So Far*, 215; see also 213.
20 Betty Friedan, "Abortion: A Woman's Civil Right," in Friedan, *"It Changed My Life,"* 126–27.
21 Betty Friedan, "The National Organization of Women: Statement of Purpose," in Friedan, *"It Changed My Life,"* 87.
22 Friedan, *Life So Far*, 205.

23 Friedan, *Life So Far*, 196, 205.

24 Betty Friedan, "Critique of Sexual Politics," in Friedan, *"It Changed My Life,"* 163–64.

25 Friedan, *Life So Far*, 223, 249.

26 Friedan, "A Dialogue with Simone de Beauvoir," in Friedan, *"It Changed My Life,"* 311–12.

27 Friedan, "A Dialogue with Simone de Beauvoir," in Friedan, *"It Changed My Life,"* 312.

28 Betty Friedan, "Tokenism and the Pseudo-Radical Cop-Out: Ideological Traps for New Feminists to Avoid," in Friedan, *"It Changed My Life,"* 115, 117 (emphasis in original).

29 Friedan, "Critique of Sexual Politics," in Friedan, *"It Changed My Life,"* 163.

30 Friedan, "Critique of Sexual Politics," in Friedan, *"It Changed My Life,"* 162–63. See also Friedan, "Tokenism and the Pseudo-Radical Cop-Out," in Friedan, *"It Changed My Life,"* 116.

31 Friedan, "A Dialogue with Simone de Beauvoir," in Friedan, *"It Changed My Life,"* 312, 314.

32 Kathleen Erickson, "Interview with Betty Friedan," Federal Reserve Bank of Minneapolis, September 1, 1994, minneapolisfed.org.

33 Friedan, "Tokenism and the Pseudo-Radical Cop-Out," in Friedan, *"It Changed My Life,"* 115.

34 Friedan, *Life So Far*, 132.

35 Friedan, *Life So Far*, 223, 231–32.

36 Friedan, "Critique of Sexual Politics," in Friedan, *"It Changed My Life,"* 164.

37 Friedan, "Tokenism and the Pseudo-Radical Cop-Out," in Friedan, *"It Changed My Life,"* 115.

38 Pinker, *The Sexual Paradox*, 59–61, 69–75, 81–82, 163–68, 180–82. This finding is consistent with other scientific findings wherein sex differences in personality are more pronounced in countries with greater sexual equality; see literature review and findings in Eric Mac Giolla and Petri J. Kajonius, "Sex Differences in Personality Are Larger in Gender Equal Countries: Replicating and Extending a Surprising Finding," *International Journal of Psychology* 54, no. 6 (2019); and Khazan, "Gender Equality."

6 The Problems of Contemporary Liberalism

1 Michael J. Sandel, *Liberalism and the Limits of Justice*, 2nd ed. (New York: Cambridge University Press, 1998); idem, *Democracy's Discontent: America in Search of a Public Philosophy* (Cambridge, Mass.: Belknap Press of Harvard University Press, 1998).

2 See Kautz, *Liberalism and Community*, 63–64.

3 See Clor, *Public Morality and Liberal Society*, 135–36, 149–65.

4 Lawrence M. Friedman, *The Republic of Choice: Law, Authority, and Culture* (Cambridge, Mass.: Harvard University Press, 1990), 3 (emphasis in the original).

5 Joseph Raz, *The Morality of Freedom* (Oxford: Clarendon Press, 1986), 162.

6 Tocqueville, *Democracy in America*, 47 (bk 1, part 1, chapter 3).

7 See John Locke, "First Treatise," in *Two Treatises of Government*, ed. Peter Laslett, 2nd ed. (1689; Cambridge: Cambridge University Press, 1988), 207–210; and esp. Thomas Jefferson, "Bill to Enable Tenants in Fee Tail to Convey their Lands in Fee Simple," in *The Papers of Thomas Jefferson*, vol. 1, *1760–1776*, ed. Julian P. Boyd (Princeton: Princeton University Press, 1950), 560–62; Tocqueville, *Democracy in America*, 49 (1.1.3): "English legislation on the transmission of goods was abolished in almost all the states in the period of the Revolution."

8 Tocqueville, *Democracy in America*, 49 (1.1.3).

9 Tocqueville's description is worth quoting in full:

> In peoples where estate law is founded on the right of primogeniture, territorial domains pass most often from generation to generation without being divided. The result is that family spirit is in a way materialized in the land. The family represents the land, the land represents the family; it perpetuates its name, its origin, its glory, its power, its virtues. It is an imperishable witness to the past and a precious pledge of existence to come.
>
> When estate law establishes equal partition, it destroys the intimate connection that exists between the spirit of the family and the preservation of the land; the land ceases to represent the family, for, since it cannot fail to be partitioned at the end of one or two generations, it is evident that it must constantly be diminished and in the end disappear entirely. . . .
>
> As family no longer presents itself to the mind as anything but vague, indeterminate, and uncertain, each concentrates on the comfort of the present: he dreams of establishment of the generation that is going to follow him, and nothing more.

Tocqueville, *Democracy in America*, 48–49 (1.1.3).

10 See Max Rheinstein, *Marriage Stability, Divorce, and the Law* (Chicago: University of Chicago Press, 1972), 51–105, 277–307, 311–316; Mary Ann Glendon, *The Transformation of Family Law: State, Law, and Family in the United States and Western Europe* (Chicago: University of Chicago Press, 1989), 188–96.

11 Barbara Dafoe Whitehead, *The Divorce Culture* (New York: Alfred A. Knopf, 1997).

12 JoAnne Sweeny, "Undead Statutes: The Rise, Fall, and Continuing Uses of Adultery and Fornication Criminal Laws," *Loyola University Chicago Law Journal* 46 (2014): 127–56.

13 See Mary Ann Glendon, *Abortion and Divorce in Western Law* (Cambridge, Mass.: Harvard University Press, 1987), 9, 139; Clor, *Public Morality and Liberal Society*, 76–86.

14 Clor, *Public Morality and Liberal Society*, 78 (emphasis added).

15 Even today many of those intellectually committed to privatization worry that old-world, patriarchal familial arrangements could take advantage of the space provided. See Susan Moller Okin, "Is Multiculturalism Bad for Women?" in *Is Multiculturalism Bad for Women?* ed. Joshua Cohen, Matthew Howard, and Martha C. Nussbaum (Princeton: Princeton University Press,

1999); Mark Twain, *A Connecticut Yankee in King Arthur's Court* (New York: Charles L. Webster, 1889).

16 Tocqueville, *Democracy in America*, 46 (1.1.3).

17 Jean-Jacques Rousseau, *On the Social Contract*, ed. Roger D. Masters, trans. Judith R. Masters (New York: St. Martin's, 1978), 124 (bk. 4, chap. 7).

18 Giddens, *The Transformation of Intimacy*, 58, 94–95, 146.

19 Thus the emphasis on abolishing marriage among autonomy advocates. Without a socially understood idea of marriage, individuals can choose for themselves the form, depth, and extent of their relationships. See Brake, *Minimizing Marriage*, 156–88; Metz, *Untying the Knot*, 113–51.

20 Giddens, *The Transformation of Intimacy*, 154.

21 Giddens, *The Transformation of Intimacy*, 142–44.

22 Giddens, *The Transformation of Intimacy*, 98, 104, 109.

23 Giddens, *The Transformation of Intimacy*, 62–63.

24 Giddens, *The Transformation of Intimacy*, 177–78, 180–81.

25 Claude Lefort, *The Political Forms of Modern Society: Bureaucracy, Democracy, Totalitarianism*, ed. John B. Thompson (Cambridge, Mass.: MIT Press, 1986), 303; Pierre Manent, *A World beyond Politics: A Defense of the Nation-State*, trans. Marc LePain (Princeton: Princeton University Press, 2006), 137–39.

26 Giddens, *The Transformation of Intimacy*, 49–64.

27 Tocqueville, *Democracy in America*, 358 (1.2.10); Aristotle, *The Politics*, 1261b10.

28 Aristotle, *The Politics*, 1263b32.

29 I cannot help but remember the line from Keanu Reeves in Ron Howard's movie *Parenthood*: "You need a license to buy a dog or drive a car. Hell, you need a license to catch a fish! But they'll let any butt-reaming a—hole be a father." *Parenthood*, written by Lowell Ganz and Babaloo Mandel, directed by Ron Howard (Universal City, Calif.: Universal Pictures Home Entertainment, 1989).

30 Hugh LaFollette, "Licensing Parents," in *Should Parents Be Licensed? Debating the Issues*, ed. Peg Tittle (Amherst, N.Y.: Prometheus Books, 2004), 57ff.; Jack C. Westman, *Licensing Parents: Can We Prevent Child Abuse and Neglect?* (New York: Insight Books, 1994), 245.

31 Westman, *Licensing Parents*, 245.

32 In fact, when licensing advocates describe the kind of "competent parenting" that they hope to promote through licensing, they often, unwittingly, it seems, describe something that resembles the effects of marriage on individual character. Consider Westman, *Licensing Parents*, 30, who describes competent parenting as "the abilities to tolerate frustration and to postpone gratifying immediate urges."

33 Westman, *Licensing Parents*, 3, 106–8, 110–11. Westman is almost completely silent on marriage, except to mention that we live in a postmarital culture that makes licensing necessary. Consider Westman, *Licensing Parents*, 110.

34 LaFollette, "Licensing Parents," in Tittle, *Should Parents Be Licensed?* 61. Westman, *Licensing Parents*, 210: "Because of the many problems involved in defining families, a more accurate and feasible approach would be to focus

on the parent-child relationship and design funding, services, and benefits around the goal of promoting competent parenting rather than around the ambiguous and controversial image of a family."

35 Westman, *Licensing Parents*, 210–12, 220–26.

36 Westman, *Licensing Parents*, 219.

37 LaFollette, "Licensing Parents," in Tittle, *Should Parents Be Licensed?* 59–61; Westman, *Licensing Parents*, 228–29.

38 Westman, *Licensing Parents*, 216.

39 Edgar Chasteen, "The Mythology of Family Planners," in Tittle, *Should Parents Be Licensed?* 286

40 See, for instance, William Blackstone, vol. 1 of *Commentaries on the Laws of England* (Chicago: University of Chicago Press, 1979), 434–40; Aristotle, *Nicomachean Ethics*, 1162a16–25.

41 Consider, in this context, the mixture of horror, ridicule, and disbelief with which Plato's proposals in his *Republic* for abolishing the family have been treated throughout the ages. It is enough to make one wonder whether Plato was completely serious in his suggestions—unlike Marx and Engels, who were serious about the postrevolutionary abolition of the family. See Yenor, *Family Politics*, 137–56.

42 Edmund Burke, "An Appeal from the New to the Old Whigs," in *Further Reflections on the Revolution in France*, ed. Daniel E. Ritchie (Indianapolis: Liberty Fund, 1992), 161.

43 Consider in this context C. S. Lewis, *The Abolition of Man* (1943; New York: Touchstone, 1996), chap. 2, appendix, 55–62.

7 The Problem with Ending Sexual Repression

1 Rosin, *The End of Men*, 21.

2 Yenor, *Family Politics*, 168–71; Ben B. Lindsey and Wainwright Evans, *The Companionate Marriage* (New York: Boni and Liveright, 1927).

3 Giddens, *The Transformation of Intimacy*, 49–64; Regnerus, *Cheap Sex*, 9.

4 Mansfield, *Manliness*, 144.

5 Giddens, *The Transformation of Intimacy*, 15: Sexuality is "something each of us has . . . no longer a natural condition which an individual accepts as a preordained state of affairs"; it is a "prime connecting point between body, self-identity, and social norms." See also Regnerus, *Cheap Sex*, 55, who relates an analysis from Jane Ward, a sociologist of queer politics: "We all know that sexual desire is deeply subject to social, cultural, and historical forces." Consider also a similar statement in Michel Houellebecq, *Atomised*, trans. Frank Wynne (1999; New York: Vintage, 2001), 292–93.

6 Jean-Jacques Rousseau, *The First and Second Discourses*, ed. Roger D. Masters, trans. Roger D. Masters and Judith R. Masters (New York: St. Martin's Press, 1978).

7 See Yenor, *Family Politics*, 157–68, for an extended treatment of Freud.

8 Consider Frederick Crews, *Freud: The Making of an Illusion* (New York: Metropolitan Books, 2017); Dorothy Rabinowitz, *No Crueler Tyrannies:*

Accusation, False Witness, and Other Terrors of Our Times (New York: Free Press, 2004).

9 See esp. James Miller, *The Passion of Michel Foucault* (New York: Anchor Books, 1994); Roger Kimball, "The Perversions of M. Foucault," *The New Criterion* 11, no. 7 (1993): 10ff.

10 Michel Foucault, *The Uses of Pleasure*, vol. 2 of *The History of Sexuality*, trans. Robert Hurley (New York: Vintage, 1985), 3–6.

11 Foucault, *The Uses of Pleasure*, 250.

12 Michel Foucault, *The Care of Self*, vol. 3 of *The History of Sexuality*, trans. Robert Hurley (New York: Vintage, 1988), 236, 238.

13 The Marquis de Sade, for instance, whom Foucault admires but worries that he had "not gone far enough," as related in Miller, *The Passion of Michel Foucault*, 278.

14 Robert J. Stoller, *Observing the Erotic Imagination* (New Haven: Yale University Press, 1985), 8, and generally chaps. 1–4, where he explores hostility involved in the viewing of pornography.

15 Giddens, *The Transformation of Intimacy*, 203.

16 Scruton, *Sexual Desire*, esp. 125–30.

17 Rhoads, *Taking Sex Differences Seriously*, 105, and generally 105–8, 128–31. See also Regnerus, *Cheap Sex*, 45–61, 77–80.

18 Symons, *The Evolution of Human Sexuality*, 292.

19 Phillip Blumstein and Pepper Schwartz, *American Couples: Money, Work, Sex* (New York: William Morrow, 1983). See Regnerus, *Cheap Sex*, 80–83; Symons, *The Evolution of Human Sexuality*, 298–99.

20 Symons, *The Evolution of Human Sexuality*, 293–94. See also Giddens, *The Transformation of Intimacy*, 144–47; Regnerus, *Cheap Sex*, 90–92.

21 Havelock Ellis, "The Evolution of Modesty," in *Studies in the Psychology of Sex*, vol. 1 (New York: Random House, 1936), 1–84.

22 See Yenor, *Family Politics*, 46; Jean-Jacques Rousseau, *Emile, or On Education*, trans. Allan Bloom (New York: Basic Books, 1979), 357ff.

23 Tocqueville, *Democracy in America*, 574 (2.3.12).

24 But see the blushing reaction of Kitty to the examination a young, handsome doctor performs when she is taken ill after rejecting Levin and after being rejected by Vronsky in Tolstoy, *Anna Karenina*, part 2, chap. 1. Perhaps a lack of shame in this circumstance itself presumes a revolution in human affairs.

25 Regnerus and Uecker, *Premarital Sex in America*, 168; see also 243–44.

26 Thus critic David Edelstein lampoons the film: "'No Strings Attached': Corny, Contrived, Conservative," *NPR*, January 21, 2011, npr.org.

27 *Ice Storm*, directed by Ang Lee (Century City, Calif.: Fox Searchlight, 1997).

28 Michel Houellebecq, *Whatever*, trans. Paul Hammond (1994; London: Serpent's Tail, 1998), 99.

29 Houellebecq, *Atomised*, 243, 265–66, 294–97.

30 Houellebecq, *Atomised*, 284–85, 328–36.

31 Houellebecq, *Atomised*, 26–32, 302–15.

32 Houellebecq, *Atomised*, 292–93.

33 Houellebecq, *Atomised*, 185ff.

34 Aldous Huxley, *Brave New World* (1932; New York: Harper Perennial, 1986), 37, 39.
35 Another dystopian novel, *The Giver*, also depicts the erosion of the connections between sex and procreation, procreation and education, and love and sex as a means of taming human beings through protecting them from strong, tension-laden emotions and through protecting them from their past: Lois Lowry, *The Giver* (Boston, Mass.: Houghton Mifflin, 1993).
36 Tocqueville, *Democracy in America*, 663 (4.4.6).
37 Huxley, *Brave New World*, 220.
38 Giddens, *The Transformation of Intimacy*, 77ff.
39 Consider esp. Plato, *Phaedrus*, trans. James H. Nichols Jr. (Ithaca: Cornell University Press, 1998), 37d2, 251d4–e2.
40 Plato, *The Laws of Plato*, trans. Thomas L. Pangle (Chicago: University of Chicago Press, 1988), 643d, 711d, 782e, 783a, 823e, 831c, 870a.
41 Plato, *Plato's Symposium*, trans. Seth Benardete (Chicago: University of Chicago Press, 2001), 205d1–2.
42 See James R. Stoner Jr. and Donna M. Hughes, eds., *The Social Costs of Pornography: A Collection of Papers* (Princeton: Witherspoon Institute, 2010).

8 A Sketch of a Better Family Policy

1 John Adams, *Autobiography, 1777–1780, Index*, vol. 4 of *Diary and Autobiography of John Adams*, ed. L. H. Butterfield (Cambridge, Mass.: Belknap Press of Harvard University Press, 1961), 123.
2 *Loving v. Virginia*, 388 U.S. 1 (1967).
3 *Zablocki v. Redhail*, 434 U.S. 374 (1978).
4 *Skinner v. Oklahoma ex rel. Williamson*, 316 U.S. 535 (1942).
5 James Madison, "Federalist 10," in *The Federalist*, ed. George W. Carey and James McClellan (1787; Indianapolis: Liberty Fund, 2001), 43.
6 The abandonment of Madison's indirect approach is a hallmark of Progressive political thinkers. Consider John Dewey, *Liberalism and Social Action* (Amherst, N.Y.: Prometheus Books, 1991), 46–48, for his criticisms of early liberals who thought individuals were "ready-made" instead of socially constructed.
7 See Tocqueville, *Democracy in America*, 275–88.
8 Horwitz, *Hayek's Modern Family*, 193–96.
9 See George Washington, "Farewell Address," in *George Washington: A Collection*, ed. William B. Allen (Indianapolis: Liberty Fund, 1988); Thomas Jefferson, "Jefferson to George Wythe, August 13, 1786," *The Papers of Thomas Jefferson*, vol. 10, *22 June–31 December 1786*, ed. Julian P. Boyd (Princeton: Princeton University Press, 1954), 243–45; Lorraine Smith Pangle and Thomas L. Pangle, *The Learning of Liberty: The Educational Ideas of the American Founders* (Lawrence: University Press of Kansas, 1993).
10 *Meyer v. Nebraska*, 262 U.S. 390, 399, 401 (1923).
11 See "Father Blakely States the Issue: Unsigned Editorial in *The New Republic*," in *American Progressivism: A Reader*, ed. Ronald J. Pestritto and William J. Atto (Lanham, Md.: Lexington Books, 2008), 136–37: "Twentieth-century

democracy believes that the community has certain positive ends to achieve, and if they are to be achieved the community must control the education of the young. . . . It insists that the plasticity of the child shall not be artificially and prematurely hardened into a philosophy of life, but that experimental naturalistic aptitudes shall constitute the true education." See also Paula Abrams, *Cross Purposes:* Pierce v. Society of Sisters *and the Struggle over Compulsory Public Education* (Ann Arbor: University of Michigan Press, 2009), 40–41, 95–96, 167–68, 191, 227, who shows that nativists such as the Ku Klux Klan and Progressives promoted the compulsory public education in the Oregon contexts and throughout the nation.

12 *Pierce v. Society of Sisters,* 268 U.S. 510, 534–35 (1925) (emphasis added).

13 A limiting case is *Prince v. Massachusetts,* 321 U.S. 158, 170 (1944), where the Supreme Court denied a parent's right to accompany her nine-year-old daughter while selling religious magazines. Selling literature, the Court held, would expose the child to "psychological and physical injury" and the parent's supervision cannot "entirely eliminate" these possible harms.

14 It is not as easy as I imply here, since civilized countries favor consensual sex and must put forward a complex of laws, manners, and expectations to encourage only consensual sex to arise. Chapter 10 considers this issue in depth.

15 Rhoads, *Taking Sex Differences Seriously,* 190–92. Cf. Firestone, *Dialectic of Sex,* 222–28, 259–60, where she asserts that parenting instincts are natural and deserve public support instead of public scorn.

16 See Rhoads, *Taking Sex Differences Seriously,* chaps. 4 and 8.

17 Larry Arnhart, *Darwinian Natural Right: The Biological Ethics of Human Nature* (Albany: SUNY Press, 1998), 101–16, 124–32.

18 Wilson, *The Marriage Problem,* 23–32, 41.

19 John Locke, *Essay Concerning Human Understanding,* ed. Peter Nidditch (1689; Oxford, Clarendon Press, 1979), 1.3.9; Locke, *First Treatise,* paras. 54–56.

20 See Orlando Patterson, "The Social and Cultural Matrix of Black Youth," in *The Cultural Matrix: Understanding Black Youth,* ed. Orlando Patterson (Cambridge, Mass.: Harvard University Press, 2015), 59–60, 69–74, 80–86, for difficulties of hypermasculinity.

21 In this regard, consider Arnhart, *Darwinian Natural Right,* 29ff., who lists twenty natural desires that "manifest themselves in some manner across history in every human society."

22 Wilson, *The Marriage Problem,* 219: "Marriage is a cultural response to a deep-seated desire for companionship, affection, and child rearing, desires so deep seated that surely they are largely the product of our evolutionary history."

23 W. Bradford Wilcox, *Soft Patriarchs, New Men: How Christianity Shapes Fathers and Husbands* (Chicago: University of Chicago Press, 2004).

9 Toward a New, New Sexual Regime

1 United States Commission on Civil Rights, *Statement on Affirmative Action* (Washington, D.C.: U.S. Government Printing Office, 1977), 2.

2 Ibram X. Kendi, *Stamped from the Beginning: The Definitive History of Racist Ideas in America* (New York: Nation Books, 2016), 10.

3 Let my treatment of them stand in for a similar treatment of all: the same mode of argument is applicable to each.

4 For literature reviews of such disparities consider esp. M. Ryan Barker, "Gay and Lesbian Health Disparities: Evidence and Recommendations for Elimination," *Journal of Health Disparities, Research and Practice* 2, no. 2 (2008): 91–120; James. E. Phelan, Neil Whitehead, and Philip M. Sutton, "What Research Shows: NARTH's Response to the APA Claims on Homosexuality. A Report of the Scientific Advisory Committee of the National Association for Research and Therapy of Homosexuality," *Journal of Human Sexuality* 1 (2009): 74–81; Matthew Todd, *Straight Jacket: How to Be Gay and Happy* (London: Bantam Press, 2016); Jeffrey Satinover, *Homosexuality and the Politics of Truth* (Ada, Mich.: Baker Books, 1996); Thomas E. Schmidt, *Straight and Narrow? Compassion and Clarity in the Homosexual Debate* (Downers Grove, Ill.: InterVarsity Press, 1995). Interestingly, those who emphasize the prevalence of homophobia (Barker; Phelan, Whitehead, and Sutton; Todd) and those who emphasize the intrinsic problems within homosexual behavior or the homosexual subculture (Satinover; Schmidt) cite many of the same studies and findings.

5 See, for example, Steven T. Russell and Kara Joyner, "Adolescent Sexual Orientation and Suicide Risk: Evidence from a National Study," *American Journal of Public Health* 91, no. 8 (2001): 1276–81.

6 Barker, "Gay and Lesbian Health Disparities," 95–102.

7 Mark L. Hatzenbuehler et al., "Structural Stigma and All-Cause Mortality in Sexual Minority Populations," *Social Science & Medicine* 103 (2014): 33–41, cautiously suggesting a twelve-year difference in mortality but the peer-reviewed article was later retracted because it seems to have overstated its case; Evan Wood et al., "Modern Antiretroviral Therapy Improves Life Expectancy of Gay and Bisexual Males in Vancouver's West End," *Canadian Journal of Public Health* 91, no. 2 (2000): 125–28, suggesting an eight- to twenty-year difference depending on how much of the population is actually homosexual; and Morten Frisch and Henrik Brønnum-Hansen, "Morality among Men and Women in Same-Sex Marriage: A National Cohort Study of 8333 Danes," *American Journal of Public Health* 99, no. 1 (2009): 133–37, suggesting a 4- to 12-year difference among those in same-sex marriages.

8 George Weinberg, *Society and the Healthy Homosexual* (New York: St. Martin's Press, 1972), ii.

9 Weinberg, *Society and the Healthy Homosexual*, 121 (emphasis added).

10 Barker, "Gay and Lesbian Health Disparities," 92.

11 Sejal Singh and Laura E. Durso, "Widespread Discrimination Continues to Shape LGBT People's Lives in Both Subtle and Significant Ways," *Center for American Progress* (blog), May 2, 2017, americanprogress.org.

12 "Gay and Bisexual Men's Health," Centers for Disease Control and Preven-
    tion, last modified February 29, 2016, cdc.gov.
13 Typical of such a formulation is the following from a literature review on
    elevated suicide rates among homosexuals: "Over the past decade, consensus
    has grown among researches that *at least part of* the explanation for elevated
    rates of suicide attempts and mental disorders found in LGB people is the
    social stigma, prejudice and discrimination associated with minority sexual
    orientation." See, for instance, Ann P. Haas et al., "Suicide and Suicide Risk
    in Lesbian, Gay, Bisexual, and Transgender Populations: Review and Recom-
    mendations," *Journal of Homosexuality* 58, no. 1 (2011): 20 (emphasis added).
    Though maintaining a studied openness on the extent to which homophobia
    causes disparities (the statement is consistent with homophobia being more
    than 0% of the cause and less than 100% of the cause), the article posits no
    other potential causes of health disparities or suicide; its authors make clear
    that this statement is potentially an understatement.
14 Perry N. Halkitis, "Discrimination and Homophobia Fuel the HIV Epidemic
    in Gay and Bisexual Men," *Psychology and AIDS Exchange Newsletter*, April
    2012, apa.org.
15 Barker, "Gay and Lesbian Health Disparities," 94–96.
16 As, for instance, the finding that gay men earn more money than straight
    (though that was not always the case). Consider Kitt Carpenter, "Gay Men
    Used to Earn Less than Straight Men; Now They Earn More," *Harvard Busi-
    ness Review*, December 4, 2017, hbr.org.
17 See, for instance, Haas et al., "Suicide and Suicide Risk," 10–51; Barker, "Gay
    and Lesbian Health Disparities," 96.
18 Haas et al., "Suicide and Suicide Risk," 21–22, 42. See countless such sur-
    veys and studies for exactly the same attribution of suicide to homophobia
    and the same recommendations. Steven A. Safren and Richard G. Heim-
    berg, "Depression, Hopelessness, Suicidality, and Related Factors in Sexual
    Minority and Heterosexual Adolescents," *Journal of Consulting and Clini-
    cal Psychology* 67, no. 6 (1999): 859–66; Jay P. Paul et al., "Suicide Attempts
    among Gay and Bisexual Men: Lifetime Prevalence and Antecedents," *Amer-
    ican Journal of Public Health* 92, no. 8 (2002): 1338–45.
19 Haas et al., "Suicide and Suicide Risk," 14–15. Consider also the Centers for
    Disease Control's study of suicide in Utah between 2011–2015 (when 150
    youth between 10–17 died by their own hand), which concludes that suicide
    among youth is not related strongly to the state's acceptance of alternative
    lifestyles, see Francis Annor, Amanda Wilkinson, and Marissa Zwald, *Unde-
    termined Risk Factors for Suicide among Youth Aged 10–17 Years* (Salt Lake
    City: Utah Department of Health, 2017), health.utah.gov.
20 See Charlotte Björkenstam et al., "Suicide in Married Couples in Sweden: Is
    the Risk Greater in Same-Sex Couples?" *European Journal of Epidemiology*
    31, no. 7 (2016): 685–90, which states that married homosexuals are three
    times more likely to commit suicide than married nonhomosexuals. See
    similarly for the Netherlands, Sanjay Aggarwal and Rene Gerrets, "Explor-
    ing a Dutch Paradox: An Ethnographic Investigation of Gay Men's Mental
    Health," *Culture, Health & Sexuality* 16, no. 2 (2014): 105–19; and Diana D.

van Bergen et al., "Victimization and Suicidality among Dutch Lesbian, Gay, and Bisexual Youths," *American Journal of Public Health* 103, no. 1 (2013): 70–72, which posits a four to six times greater rate of suicide attempts among Dutch homosexuals than heterosexuals. In Denmark, it seems, men married to men have a suicide rate eight times those of men married to women: see Robin M. Mathy et al., "The Association between Relationship Markers of Sexual Orientation and Suicide: Denmark, 1990–2001," *Social Psychiatry and Psychiatric Epidemiology* 46, no. 2 (2011): 111–17; Christian Graugaard et al., "Self-Reported Sexual and Psychosocial Health among Non-Heterosexual Danes," *Scandinavian Journal of Public Health* 43, no. 3 (2015): 309–14 (suicide attempt rates of same-sexers three times the rate of opposite sexers). I have been unable to find one country where the suicide rates or suicide attempt rates among homosexuals are the same as or lower than similar rates among those who are not homosexuals, and the extent and depth of alleged homophobia has little effect, or so it would seem.

21 See Richard Herrell et al., "Sexual Orientation and Suicidality: A Co-Twin Control Study in Adult Men," *Archives of General Psychiatry* 56, no. 10 (1999): 867–74, esp. 873 (showing a consistent suicidality rate across forty years); D. M. Lawrence et al., "Is Sexual Orientation Related to Mental Health Problems and Suicidality in Young People?" *Archives of General Psychiatry* 56, no. 10 (1999): 876–80.

22 See Barker, "Gay and Lesbian Health Disparities," 91–92.

23 "Suicide Statistics," American Foundation for Suicide Prevention, accessed November 5, 2019, afsp.org. Perhaps suicide is an indicator of oppression in some cases but not in others. Suicide could be an expression of "white privilege" and "male privilege." The violence that whites and males use to keep blacks and women down might occasionally, out of guilt or excess, be turned against themselves. If this is so, why then would same-sexers have higher suicide rates due to depression and rejection? Is suicide caused through an excess of power and a proud self-image or a poverty of power and a poor self-image?

24 Barker, "Gay and Lesbian Health Disparities," 99.

25 Barker, "Gay and Lesbian Health Disparities," 98. See also Michael E. Newcomb, Adrienne J. Heinz, and Brian Mustanski, "Examining Risk and Protective Factors for Alcohol Use in Lesbian, Gay, Bisexual, and Transgender Youth: A Longitudinal Multilevel Analysis," *Journal of Studies on Alcohol and Drugs* 73, no. 5 (2012): 783–93.

26 Edmund White, *States of Desire: Travels in Gay America* (New York: E. P. Dutton, 1980), 39; see also 8, 37, 60, 335–36.

27 Life may be too short to read all such books, but consider, for instance, Winston Gieseke, ed., *Team Players: Gay Erotic Stories* (Berlin: Bruno Gmünder, 2013); and the classic Andrew Holleran, *Dancer from the Dance* (1978; New York: Harper Perennial, 2001).

28 Barker, "Gay and Lesbian Health Disparities," 98.

29 The causes of alcohol abuse, drug use, smoking, and other risky behaviors may be tested through an experiment. If homophobia causes them, one would expect that they would be lower in San Francisco, the "mecca" and

"refuge" for homosexual men from America (or rather Amerika). If they are intrinsic to or celebrated in the homosexual subculture, they would be higher in San Francisco. Men who have sex with men in San Francisco seem have higher uses on these scores than in the city's population of men who do not have sex with other men. See Ron Stall and James Wiley, "A Comparison of Alcohol and Drug Use Patterns of Homosexual and Heterosexual Men: The San Francisco Men's Health Study," *Drug and Alcohol Dependence* 22, nos. 1–2 (1988): 63–73.

30 Only a cynic might wonder if these victims are capable of self-government or agency if they are so controlled by malignant external forces.

31 Ryszard Legutko, *The Demon in Democracy: Totalitarian Temptations in Free Societies*, trans. Teresa Adelson (New York: Encounter Books, 2016), 136–38; Tocqueville, *Democracy in America*, 412–15 (2.1.3).

32 Heresy and magic derive from comprehensive religious doctrines—and perhaps does sodomy as well. Perhaps Montesquieu is also interested in undermining such doctrines and hence would remove legal penalties enforcing them.

33 Forced sodomy, rape, and statutory rape are other things entirely, because they violate the idea of consent (and the state as an accuser must prove that) and in part the lasting harms of these acts are a matter of grave public concern.

34 Thus the direction pointed to in the American Founding, where laws against sodomy and bestiality included the death penalty before the revolution, but where the founding brought reduced sentences and lax enforcement. See Thomas G. West, *The Political Theory of the American Founding: Natural Rights, Public Policy, and the Moral Conditions of Freedom* (New York: Cambridge University Press, 2017), 230–32.

35 Montesquieu, *The Spirit of the Laws*, ed. and trans. Anne M. Cohler, Basia C. Miller, and Harold S. Stone (1748; New York: Cambridge University Press, 1989), 193 (12.6).

36 Montesquieu, *The Spirit of the Laws*, 194 (12.6). See also 41 (4.8): "We blush to read in Plutarch that the Thebans, in order to soften the mores of their young people, established by their laws a love that ought to be proscribed by all nations in the world."

37 See Montesquieu, *The Spirit of the Laws*, 104–5 (7.9), 120–21 (8.11); Diana J. Schaub, *Erotic Liberalism: Women and Revolution in Montesquieu's Persian Letters* (Lanham, Md.: Rowman & Littlefield, 1995), 141–42.

38 See also Kathryn M. Daynes, *More Wives than One: Transformation of the Mormon Marriage System, 1840–1910* (Chicago: University of Illinois Press, 2001), esp. 110–13, for a treatment of the same phenomenon among Mormons.

39 Montesquieu, *The Spirit of the Laws*, 331–32 (19.27).

40 Montesquieu, *The Spirit of the Laws*, 438 (23.17), referring to Aristotle, *The Politics*, 1272a24–26: "With a view to segregating the women, so as to prevent them having many children, [the Cretan lawgiver] has provided for relations between men." As the Cretan laws imitate the Spartan laws, the famed Spartan encouragement of same-sex relations, is related, as Aristotle writes

earlier, to the fact that Sparta "was ruined through its lack of manpower." Aristotle, *The Politics*, 1270a34.

41 See Xenophon, "*The Constitution of Sparta*," in *The Shorter Writings*, ed. Greg McBrayer, trans. Catherine S. Kuiper and Susan Collins (Ithaca, N.Y.: Agora Press, 2018), 1.5; Plutarch, "Life of Lycurgus," in *The Lives of the Noble Grecians and Romans*, trans. John Dryden (New York: The Modern Library, n.d.), 60–62; Rahe, *The Spartan Regime*, 26–28.

42 Montesquieu, *The Spirit of the Laws*, 450 (23.21).

43 See Regnerus, *Cheap Sex.*

44 Carl Wittman, *Refugees from Amerika: The Gay Manifesto* (New York: Red Butterfly, 1970).

45 Edward O. Laumann et al., *The Social Organization of Sexuality: Sexual Practices in the United States* (Chicago: University of Chicago Press, 1994), 208, table 5.9A; Dan Black et al., "Demographics of the Gay and Lesbian Population in the United States: Evidence from Available Systematic Data Sources," *Demography* 37, no. 2 (2000): 139–54.

46 See Gary J. Gates, *How Many People Are Lesbian, Gay, Bisexual, and Transgender?* (Los Angeles: Williams Institute, 2011), williamsinstitute.law.ucla.edu; "Relationships in America Survey," Austin Institute for the Study of Family and Culture, 2014, relationshipsinamerica.com. If the standard is "identify as same-sex or bisexual," the numbers are 5.6 (men) and 3.9 (women) according to the Austin report and 3.5 (total) according to the Gates compilation of research from the first decade of the 2000s.

47 Montesquieu, *The Spirit of the Laws*, 193 (12.6). See also 121 (8.11): "In Plutarch's time, the parks, where one fought naked and the wrestling matches, made the young people cowardly, inclined them to an infamous love and made only dancers of them."

48 Symons, *The Evolution of Human Sexuality*, 292. See also Regnerus, *Cheap Sex*, 80–83.

49 Symons, *The Evolution of Human Sexuality*, 292–97.

50 Midge Decter, "The Boys on the Beach," *Commentary*, September 1980, commentarymagazine.com, dramatizes the scientific description from Symons' book. Gore Vidal, a great critic of Decter, writes that Decter presents "every known prejudice and superstition about same-sexers but also [makes] up some brand-new ones," since, as Vidal claims, Decter went further in her slurs against gays than the *Protocols of the Elders of Zion* went against the Jews. Gore Vidal, "Some Jews and the Gays," *The Nation*, November 14, 1981, thenation.com. Critics agree that Decter's is a treasure of Old Wisdom on homosexuality, from a perhaps homophobic time when such matters were discussed openly. "The Boys on the Beach" gives an account of life at the Fire Island Pines, a fashionable locale off the coast of Long Island that was, in the early 1950s, mostly inhabited by men who have sex with men but came to be a world-famous mecca. Decter charts things at Fire Island from the relative innocence of the late 1950s to the celebrations of emancipation in the later years.

51 Symons, *The Evolution of Human Sexuality*, 298–303.

52 Manent, *A World beyond Politics*, 193–96.

53 Wittman, *Refugees from Amerika*, 2.

54 Must political communities have a soft preference for opposite-sex sex identity in order to have sufficient strength to favor natality and marital relations? If so, the accusing culture of homophobia and the affirming culture of sexual liberation are inimical to healthy politics and, perhaps, human happiness. Self-control and modesty are not enough—and a healthy public opinion must be reconstructed toward a soft preference for opposite-sex sexual identity. Nature can assist in this.

55 One might ask a statesmanlike question in this context: what is a bigger threat to healthy political communities at this time and place, population decline or homophobia?

56 Phillip Longman, *The Empty Cradle: How Falling Birthrates Threaten World Prosperity and What to Do about It* (New York: Basic Books, 2004); Nicholas Eberstadt, "The Demographic Future: What Population Growth—and Decline—Means for the Global Economy," *Foreign Affairs* 89, no. 6 (2010): 54–64; David P. Goldman, *How Civilizations Die (and Why Islam Is Dying Too)*, (Washington, D.C.: Regnery, 2011), esp. 1–26; Jonathan V. Last, *What to Expect When No One's Expecting: America's Coming Demographic Disaster* (New York: Encounter Books, 2013). See also more academic treatments such as Ann Buchanan and Anna Rotkirch, eds., *Fertility Rates and Population Decline: No Time for Children?* (New York: Palgrave Macmillan, 2013); and Noriyuki Takayama and Martin Werding, eds., *Fertility and Public Policy: How to Reverse the Trend of Declining Birth Rates* (Cambridge, Mass.: MIT Press, 2011).

57 Consider the following from Immanuel Kant, "Idea for a Universal History with a Cosmopolitan Intent," in *Perpetual Peace and Other Essays*, trans. Ted Humphrey (Indianapolis: Hackett, 1983), 29: "Since the free wills of men seem to have so great an influence on marriage, the births consequent to it, and death, it appears that they are not subject to any rule by which one can in advance determine their number; and yet the annual charts that large countries make of them show that they occur in conformity with natural laws as invariable as those governing the unpredictable weather, whose particular changes we cannot determine in advance, but which in the large do not fail to support a uniform and uninterrupted pattern in the growth of plants, in the flow of rivers, and in other natural events."

58 Longman, *The Empty Cradle*, 48–57. Consider this: In Japan, only 9% of mothers of children under 14 say they derive pleasure from child-rearing (compared to 40%–70% in the rest of the modern world); and only 12% of Japanese women would agree with the statement that marriage is for everyone, while 78% of American women think so. Its birth rate is well below 1.5. See also Rosin, *The End of Men*, 231ff.

59 Petula Dvorak, "The Child-Free Life: Why So Many American Women Are Deciding Not to Have Kids," *Washington Post*, May 31, 2018, washingtonpost .com.

60 Immanuel Kant, "On the Proverb: That May Be True in Theory but Is of No Practical Use," in *Perpetual Peace and Other Essays*, 67–68.

61 See Fyodor Dostoevsky, *Notes from Underground*, trans. Richard Pevear and Larissa Volokhonsky (1864; New York: Vintage Classics, 1994), 26–29, 32–35.

62 See Manent, *A World beyond Politics.*

63 See Last, *What to Expect*, 170, where he argues that "America's fertility problem is a result of an enormous, interconnected web of factors that constitute something like the entire framework of modern life." See also Last, *What to Expect*, 84, 87; Longman, *The Empty Cradle*, 32–34; Goldman, *How Civilizations Die*, 16, 19–21.

64 Nathan D. Grawe, *Demographics and the Demand for Higher Education* (Baltimore: Johns Hopkins University Press, 2017).

65 See David S. Reher, "Demographic Transitions and Familial Change: Comparative International Perspectives," in Buchanan and Rotkirch, *Fertility Rates and Population Decline*, 24–28; and Last, *What to Expect*, 90–94, for a review of this literature.

66 Reher, "Demographic Transitions," in Buchanan and Rotkirch, *Fertility Rates and Population Decline*, 27–28, 35–37.

67 Reher, "Demographic Transitions," in Buchanan and Rotkirch, *Fertility Rates and Population Decline*, 35.

68 See Moya Sarner, "We're Heading for a Male Fertility Crisis and We're Not Prepared," *New Scientist* (blog), November 15, 2017, newscientist.com.

69 Last, *What to Expect*, 162–69, 170, suggests Social Security reforms to reward parents, decreasing the need for personal outlays for colleges, and reducing costs associated with housing, though he acknowledges that these incentive programs will "probably not" have any effect. See also Last, *What to Expect*, 140–42, 144, 146, 149–150, 152, 154, for policies that did not make a difference or where efforts met with "total and unremitting failure."

70 Last, *What to Expect*, 160.

71 Lyman Stone, "No Ring, No Baby: How Marriage Trends Impact Fertility," *Institute for Family Studies* (blog), March 19, 2018, ifstudies.org.

72 Last, *What to Expect*, 158, 94.

73 Longman, *The Empty Cradle*, 1–5, 33–36.

74 For the regulations see Alison Lefkovitz, *Strange Bedfellows: Marriage in the Age of Women's Liberation* (Philadelphia: University of Pennsylvania Press, 2018), 39–74, 102–29.

75 "Increased Aid for Mothers and Children and Changes in Divorce Law," *American Review on the Soviet Union* 6 (1944): 69–76.

76 See Walter Laqueur, *Putinism: Russia and Its Future with the West* (New York: Thomas Dunne Books, 2015), 69–102, 118–21, 135–41.

77 Last, *What to Expect*, 140.

78 Longman, *The Empty Cradle*, 51; Rosin, *The End of Men*, 231ff.; Last, *What to Expect*, 144–47.

79 Rosin, *The End of Men*, 253.

80 Helen M. Alvaré, *Putting Children's Interests First in U.S. Family Law and Policy: With Power Comes Responsibility* (Cambridge: Cambridge University Press, 2017), 91–94, 99–101.

81 See Yenor, *Family Politics*, 183–86.

82 Beauvoir, *The Second Sex*, 698–99.

83 What follows is drawn from Tolstoy, *Anna Karenina*, 713ff. (part 6, chaps. 16–24).

84 Tolstoy, *Anna Karenina*, 751 (part 6, chap. 23).

85 Kim Parker and Wendy Wang, "Changing Views about Work," in *Modern Parenthood: Roles of Moms and Dads Converge as They Balance Work and Family* (Washington, D.C.: Pew Research Center, 2013), 9–18, pewsocialtrends.org; Elizabeth Becker and Cotton M. Lindsay, "Assortative Mating or Glass Ceiling: Under-Representation of Female Workers among Top Earners," in *Accounting for Worker Well-Being*, ed. Solomon W. Polachek (Bingley, UK: Emerald, 2004), 235–67; Linda Hirshman, "Homeward Bound," *American Prospect*, November 21, 2005, prospect.org; Vanderbilt University, "Women with Elite Education Opting Out of Full-Time Careers: Women with MBA's [*sic*] Are Most Likely to Work Less," *ScienceDaily* (blog), April 8, 2013, sciencedaily.com; Steven E. Rhoads, "Lean In's Biggest Hurdle: What Most Moms Want," *Institute for Family Studies* (blog), March 16, 2017, ifstudies.org; Pinker, *The Sexual Paradox*, esp. 70–75, 163–68, 176–80, and passim.

86 Betsey Stevenson and Justin Wolfers, "The Paradox of Declining Female Happiness," *American Economic Journal: Economic Policy* 1, no. 2 (2009): 190–225; Pinker, *The Sexual Paradox*, 159–68, 180–82.

10 Choosing One's Choice

1 All these paradoxes are given fuller treatment in Yenor, *Family Politics*, 259–61.

2 Stephen J. Schulhofer, *Unwanted Sex: The Culture of Intimidation and the Failure of Law* (Cambridge, Mass.: Harvard University Press, 1998), 39; see also 17–18, 266.

3 Catharine A. MacKinnon, *Toward a Feminist Theory of the State* (Cambridge, Mass.: Harvard University Press, 1989), 174.

4 See, for instance, MacKinnon, *Toward a Feminist Theory*, 177–78; Charlene Muehlenhard and Jennifer Schrag, "Nonviolent Sexual Coercion," in *Acquaintance Rape: The Hidden Crime*, ed. Andrea Parrot and Laurie Bechhofer (New York: Wiley, 1991), 115, 119–20, 122. See also Susan Brownmiller, *Against Our Will: Men, Women and Rape* (New York: Simon & Schuster, 1975), 11: rape is "a conscious process of intimidation by which *all* men keep *all* women in a state of fear" (emphasis in original).

5 Andrea Dworkin, *Intercourse*, rev. ed. (New York: Basic Books, 2006), 124–26, 137 (emphasis in original).

6 Schulhofer, *Unwanted Sex*, 81, 56, 57, 108–9 (emphasis added).

7 Schulhofer, *Unwanted Sex*, 56, 81.

8 Schulhofer, *Unwanted Sex*, 106; see also 107 ("judgements about autonomy always involve questions of degree").

9 Schulhofer, *Unwanted Sex*, 60–65.

10 Schulhofer, *Unwanted Sex*, 23, 59–67, 255–57, 260.

11 Schulhofer, *Unwanted Sex*, 111.

12 Susan Schwartz, "An Argument for the Elimination of the Resistance Requirement from the Definition of Forcible Rape," *Loyola of Los Angeles Law Review* 16 (1983): 567–72.

13 Schulhofer, *Unwanted Sex*, 283, 271–73.

14 Schulhofer, *Unwanted Sex*, 264–73. Thus the "Yes Means Yes" laws and regulations passed in various states and locales. See, e.g., Christine Helwick, "Affirmative Consent, the New Standard," *Inside Higher Ed* (blog), October 23, 2014, insidehighered.com. The issue of what constitutes affirmative consent is separable from the standard used to determine affirmative consent (preponderance of the evidence or beyond a reasonable doubt). California made this education code in 2014 with a "Yes Means Yes" law: "SB 967 Senate Bill—Amended," Official California Legislative Information, accessed November 6, 2019, leginfo.ca.gov.

15 Schulhofer, *Unwanted Sex*, 266 (emphasis in original). These statements appear in a section entitled "A Hidden Choice."

16 Ezra Klein, "'Yes Means Yes' Is a Terrible Law, and I Completely Support It," *Vox*, October 13, 2014, vox.com.

17 Catharine A. MacKinnon, *Sexual Harassment of Working Women: A Case of Sex Discrimination* (New Haven: Yale University Press, 1979), 221 (emphasis in original); see also 1–3, 6, 220.

18 See Daphne Patai, *Heterophobia: Sexual Harassment and the Future of Feminism* (Lanham, Md.: Rowman & Littlefield, 1998), 124–25; see also chap. 2.

19 See MacKinnon, *Sexual Harassment*, 220–21; Sheila Jeffreys, *Anticlimax: A Feminist Perspective on the Sexual Revolution* (London: Women's Press, 1990), 299–301: Heterosexual desire "originates in the power relationship between men and women" and leads to an ideology of difference, where "men need to be able to desire the powerless creatures they marry. So heterosexual desire for men is based upon the eroticizing the otherness of women, an otherness which is based upon a difference in power."

20 Patai, *Heterophobia*, 33–55, sure makes one think about a broader strategy, shared among those taken with our reigning civil rights ideology, where claims of victimhood expand without much limit and public authorities must correspondingly rise to the occasion. She argues that the sexual harassment industry manufactures and expands the crisis that sustains its existence: "sexual shakedowns" can be handled with contracts and torts, but "soft" sexual harassment demands special training to identify and a reconstruction of the environment to prevent. Properly trained people identify elements of a hostile environment including "unwanted sexual attention," "any questionable behavior on the basis of gender," jokes with a sexual connotation, knowing looks or looks thought to be knowing, and, perhaps, unauthorized thoughts (if we could but see them). Victims, suffering trauma, must be implicitly believed, both to minimize their trauma and because to disbelieve may deter future victims from coming forward. Crises are invented with legerdemain: while the most objectionable form of harassment is rare, "some form of" or "equally damaging" discomfort are very widespread—indeed have reached a crisis of epidemic proportions! Concepts are stretched. Once one agrees that the higher extremes are a problem for the reason that the sexual harassment

industry says, it is difficult to stop applying them to the lower, less objectionable words and actions. What is to be done about the epidemic? More
sensitivity training and greater encouragement to accuse.

21 Heather Mac Donald, *The Diversity Delusion: How Race and Gender Pandering Corrupt the University and Undermine Our Culture* (New York: St. Martin's Press, 2018), 123ff.

22 William Blackstone, vol. 2 of *Commentaries on the Laws of England* (Chicago:
University of Chicago Press, 1979), 210.

23 Blackstone, *Commentaries*, vol. 2, 211–12.

24 Firestone, *Dialectic of Sex*, esp. 88, 187.

25 See Regnerus and Uecker, *Premarital Sex in America*, 26; Regnerus, *Cheap
Sex*, 204; Laumann et al., *The Social Organization of Sexuality*, 324–29; Joseph
J. Fischel, "Per Se or Power? Age and Sexual Consent," *Yale Journal of Law &
Feminism* 22, no. 2 (2010): 279–341.

26 As Giddens, *The Transformation of Intimacy*, 98, writes, "It would certainly
not be right to suppose that childhood has remained unaffected by the world
of pure relationships."

27 Mary Eberstadt, "What Is the Sexual Revolution Doing to Children? The
'Pedophilia Chic,' Then and Now," in *Adam and Eve after the Pill: Paradoxes
of the Sexual Revolution* (San Francisco: Ignatius Press, 2012), 66–77.

28 See Blackstone, *Commentaries*, vol. 2, 212.

29 Carolyn E. Cocca, *Jailbait: The Politics of Statutory Rape Laws in the United
States* (Albany: SUNY Press, 2004), 11, 15.

30 Cocca, *Jailbait*, 23–24.

31 Cocca, *Jailbait*, 16–21, 36–39, 73–75, 129–33.

32 See, perhaps, Regnerus, *Cheap Sex*, 4–5, 89.

33 Norman Doidge, *The Brain That Changes Itself: Stories of Personal Triumph
from the Frontiers of Brain Science* (New York: Viking, 2007), 171; Mary Anne
Layden, "Pornography and Violence: A New Look at the Research," in Stoner
and Hughes, *The Social Costs of Pornography*, 63; and Jill C. Manning, "The
Impact of Pornography on Women: Social Science Findings and Clinical
Observations," in Stoner and Hughes, *The Social Costs of Pornography*, 76–79.

34 See esp. Rheinstein, *Marriage, Stability, Divorce*, chap. 2, entitled "From Free
to Indissoluble to Terminable Marriage," and his surveys of divorce evolution in Japan, Sweden, Italy, France, the USSR and the United States later in
the book; Mintz and Kellogg, *Domestic Revolutions*, 7, 60–62, 107–9, 228–31;
Glendon, *The Transformation of Family Law*, chap. 4, who treats the last stage
of this transformation in England, France, West Germany, Sweden, and the
United States, picking up the story where Rheinstein, to whom Glendon dedicates the book, left off in the early 1970s; and Cott, *Public Vows*, 46–53, 106–
9, 202–9.

35 See Rheinstein, *Marriage, Stability, Divorce*, 41–43; Hume, "Of Polygamy and
Divorces," in Miller, *Essays Moral, Political and Literary*, 189–90.

36 Hume, "Of Polygamy and Divorces," in Miller, *Essays Moral, Political and
Literary*, 188–89.

37 Rheinstein, *Marriage, Stability, Divorce*, 43; Hume, "Of Polygamy and
Divorces," in Miller, *Essays Moral, Political and Literary*, 188.

38 Rheinstein, *Marriage, Stability, Divorce*, 43–44.

39 Cf. Rheinstein, *Marriage, Stability, Divorce*, 157, with Frederick Engels, *The Origin of the Family, Private Property and the State*, ed. Eleanor Burke Leacock (1884; New York: International Publishers, 1972), 139–44.

40 Hume, "Of Polygamy and Divorces," in Miller, *Essays Moral, Political and Literary*, 189.

41 See Betsey Stevenson, "The Impact of Divorce Laws on Marriage-Specific Capital," *Journal of Labor Economics* 25, no. 1 (2007).

42 Wilson, *The Marriage Problem*, 162, catalogs the decreasing support for staying together for the children under America's no-fault divorce regime. In 1962 less than half of women agreed that divorce is permissible when children are present; in 1977 more than half agreed; in 1985, 82% agreed.

43 Margaret F. Brinig and Douglas W. Allen, "'These Boots Are Made for Walking': Why Most Divorce Filers Are Women," *American Law and Economics Review* 2, no. 1 (2000).

44 See Whitehead, *The Divorce Culture*, 54–65.

45 See Jennifer Roff, "Cleaning in the Shadow of the Law? Bargaining, Marital Investment, and the Impact of Divorce Law on Husbands' Intra-Household Work" (IZA Discussion Paper Series No. 10527, Institute of Labor Economics, Bonn, Germany, January 2017).

46 The following is drawn from Rheinstein, *Marriage, Stability, Divorce*, 195–214.

47 Rheinstein, *Marriage, Stability, Divorce*, 207.

48 Louis de Bonald, *On Divorce*, trans. and ed. Nicholas Davidson (1801; New York: Routledge, 2017), 110–11.

49 Bonald, *On Divorce*, 119, chap. 12.

50 Bonald, *On Divorce*, 136, 139–40, 141–42, contrasts between early, ruder times and modern cosmopolitanism.

51 Bonald, *On Divorce*, 120–21.

52 Bonald, *On Divorce*, 142, 140.

53 Bonald, *On Divorce*, 118, 145

54 Bonald, *On Divorce*, 148

55 Cf. Jesus, who explains that the Jews of Moses' time were granted the freedom to divorce because of the hardness of their hearts while asserting for a more demanding standard for Pharisees.

56 Bonald, *On Divorce*, 129. Consider also Denis de Rougemont, *Love in the Western World*, trans. Montgomery Belgion, rev. ed. (Princeton: Princeton University Press, 1956), 288–91, where he treats of the Soviet and Nazi attempts to reintroduce strong marital regimes under genuinely tyrannical conditions.

57 Bonald, *On Divorce*, 145.

58 Rheinstein, *Marriage, Stability, Divorce*, 207.

59 William Bacon Bailey, *Modern Social Conditions: A Statistical Study of Birth, Marriage, and Divorce* (New York: Century Company, 1906), 205–6.

60 https://www.cdc.gov/nchs/fastats/marriage-divorce.htm.

61 Consider also Rheinstein, *Marriage, Stability, Divorce*, 288–307, where he reports on studies of regional differences in countries with uniform codes

that purport to show the "overwhelming preponderance of mores over official law" in explaining divorce and marriage rates.

62 Wilson, *The Marriage Problem*, 161.

63 Or perhaps Bonald's law was evaded as couples simply split (without availing
themselves of the judicial separation that Bonald's law allowed) or couples
continued to live together but as strangers more than spouses, as those favoring the liberal arc story seem to suggest. See Rheinstein, *Marriage, Stability, Divorce*, 214, who sees "prostitution, the mistress system, and irregular
unions" multiplying in the period after Bonald's reforms.

64 For the framing of such a question, see Rougemont, *Love in the Western
World*, 288.

65 Such, at least, is a trajectory suggested by Wilson, *The Marriage Problem*, 198.

66 This language is borrowed from James Madison, "Federalist 10," in Carey and
McClellan, *The Federalist*, 43.

67 Whitehead, *The Divorce Culture*, 190.

68 Elizabeth Marquardt, *Between Two Worlds: The Inner Lives of Children of
Divorce* (New York: Three Rivers Press, 2006), 187–88.

69 Jennifer Roback Morse, "Why Unilateral Divorce Has No Place in a Free
Society," in George and Elshtain, *The Meaning of Marriage*, 94, citing several
studies in different times and places.

70 Could the rise of female-initiated divorce be a reason men are less interested
in entering marriage and hence less likely to manifest the character necessary
for marriage?

71 Morse, "Unilateral Divorce," 96–97.

72 Elizabeth Gilbert, *Eat, Pray, Love: One Woman's Search for Everything across
Italy, India and Indonesia* (New York: Riverhead Books, 2006); Cheryl
Strayed, *Wild: From Lost to Found on the Pacific Crest Trail* (New York: Vin-
tage, 2013). Strayed is an evangelist of this position, as she closes her second
book with poetry for this moral enrichment. See her *Tiny Beautiful Things:
Advice on Love and Life from Dear Sugar* (New York: Vintage, 2012):

> Go, even though you love him.
> Go, even though he is kind and faithful and dear to you.
> Go, even though he's your best friend and you're his.
> Go, even though you can't imagine your life without him.
> Go, even though he adores you and your leaving will devastate him.
> Go, even though your friends will be disappointed or surprised or
>   pissed off or all three.
> Go, even though you once said you would stay.
> Go, even though you're afraid of being alone.
> Go, even though you're sure no one will ever love you as well as he
>   does.
> Go, even though there is nowhere to go.
> Go, even though you don't know exactly why you can't stay.
> Go, because you want to.
> Because wanting to leave is enough.

11 The New Problem with No Name

1 Such are among the factors identified by Charles Murray, *Coming Apart: The State of White America, 1960–2010* (New York: Crown Forum, 2012), 168–225.

2 See Theodore Dalrymple, *Life at the Bottom: The Worldview That Makes the Underclass* (Chicago: Ivan R. Dee, 2001).

3 Wilson, *The Marriage Problem*, 2. See also Murray, *Coming Apart*, 144–48, and esp. the account of divergences in marriage between the upper 20% of the population and the lower 30%, 149–67.

4 Michael Harrington, *The Other America: Poverty in the United States* (New York: Penguin, 1962), 11, 17, 140–42; see also 143, 177. Ken Auletta, writing after opponents of the Moynihan Report poisoned the environment for such analyses, sees many of the same character traits including "present-time" orientation and fatalism in the new poor among people who are "rarely married." Ken Auletta, *The Underclass* (New York: Vintage, 1982), 34–35, 37; see also 17, 40, 43, 47–48, 165, 171–72, 242–43.

5 See, for instance, Harry Benson and Stephen MacKay, "The Marriage Gap: The Rich Get Married (and Stay Together). The Poor Don't," Marriage Foundation, Romford, UK, August 2015, marriagefoundation.org.uk.

6 Dalrymple, *Life at the Bottom*, 5, 10.

7 Dalrymple, *Life at the Bottom*, 140–43.

8 Patterson estimates about 25% of African Americans and 33% of African Americans between 18 and 24 years of age in major metropolitan areas are *disconnected* and disadvantaged, though the percentages are on the rise. See also Jason L. Riley, *Please Stop Helping Us: How Liberals Make It Harder for Blacks to Succeed* (New York: Encounter Books, 2016) on the pathologies of the streets, very much consistent with Patterson's summation.

9 Patterson, "The Social and Cultural Matrix," in Patterson, *The Cultural Matrix*, 81.

10 Patterson, "The Social and Cultural Matrix," in Patterson, *The Cultural Matrix*, 81; see also 73, 91–92, 100–101.

11 Patterson, "The Social and Cultural Matrix," in Patterson, *The Cultural Matrix*, 73–74.

12 Patterson, "The Social and Cultural Matrix," in Patterson, *The Cultural Matrix*, 80–82.

13 Patterson, "The Social and Cultural Matrix," in Patterson, *The Cultural Matrix*, 82.

14 Patterson, "The Social and Cultural Matrix," in Patterson, *The Cultural Matrix*, 55–56.

15 Patterson, "The Social and Cultural Matrix," in Patterson, *The Cultural Matrix*, 55–56.

16 Patterson, "The Social and Cultural Matrix," in Patterson, *The Cultural Matrix*, 70, 123–24, notes that many of these trends antedate the sexual revolution of the 1970s, but that they accelerated with the decline of "old cultural practice[s]" traceable to attempts to maintain the traditional bourgeois family norm. Cornel West calls this new cause nihilism, "the lived experience of coping with a life of horrifying meaninglessness, hopelessness, and (most

important) lovelessness." Cornel West, *Race Matters* (New York: Vintage, 1994), 14.

17 J. D. Vance, *Hillbilly Elegy: A Memoir of a Family and Culture in Crisis* (New York: Harper, 2016), 148.

18 Vance, *Hillbilly Elegy*, 228.

19 Stephanie Coontz, *Marriage, a History: From Obedience to Intimacy, or How Love Conquered Marriage* (New York: Viking, 2005), 289, 301, 308.

20 Coontz, *Marriage, a History*, 306, 308.

21 Tocqueville, *Democracy in America*, 669 (2.4.7).

22 See Murray, *Coming Apart*, 285–95.

23 Barbara Dafoe Whitehead, *Why There Are No Good Men Left: The Romantic Plight of the New Single Woman* (New York: Broadway Books, 2003), 76–77. These three goals are the topics of chaps. 3, 2, and 4, respectively. See also Rosin, *The End of Men*, on how "feminist progress is largely dependent on [the sexually promiscuous] hook-up culture" (21); "erotic capital" moves women ahead in the workplace (30); women are "less restricted by sexual taboos than at any other time in history," as evidenced by the New Woman's revolutionary openness to anal sex (37, 42); and most developments in the modern economy feminize the workplace and increase chances women achieve economic independence (106–9, 117–23, 135–36).

24 Whitehead, *Why There Are No Good Men Left*, 63.

25 Kay S. Hymowitz, *Manning Up: How the Rise of Women Has Turned Men into Boys* (New York: Basic Books, 2011), 49ff.

26 Whitehead, *Why There Are No Good Men Left*, 23–27, 78.

27 Whitehead, *Why There Are No Good Men Left*, 25.

28 See DiPrete and Buchmann, *The Rise of Women*, 27–52 and passim.

29 Whitehead, *Why There Are No Good Men Left*, 65–73. See also Hymowitz, *Manning Up*, 50–59; Rosin, *The End of Men*, 160–67; DiPrete and Buchmann, *The Rise of Women*, 180–99.

30 Whitehead, *Why There Are No Good Men Left*, 78–79.

31 Whitehead, *Why There Are No Good Men Left*, 58–60, 79–81.

32 Whitehead, *Why There Are No Good Men Left*, 79.

33 Jessie Bernard, *The Future of Marriage* (New York: Bantam Books, 1972).

34 Whitehead, *Why There Are No Good Men Left*, 100–101.

35 Rosin, *The End of Men*, 67.

36 Beauvoir, *The Second Sex*, 472.

37 Rosin, *The End of Men*, cf. 45 with 253.

38 See, for instance, Yanna J. Weisberg, Colin G. DeYoung, and Jacob B. Hirsh, "Gender Differences in Personality across the Ten Aspects of the Big Five," *Frontiers in Psychology* 2 (2011): https://doi.org/10.3389/fpsyg.2011.00178; Susan C. South, Amber M. Jarnecke, and Colin E. Vize, "Sex Differences in the Big Five Model Personality Traits: A Behavior Genetics Exploration," *Journal of Research in Personality* 74 (2018).

39 Stevenson and Wolfers, "The Paradox of Declining Female Happiness"; Pinker, *The Sexual Paradox*, 180–82.

40 Paul R. Albert, "Why Is Depression More Prevalent in Women?" *Journal of Psychiatry & Neuroscience* 40, no. 4 (2015): 219–21; Benedict Carey and

Robert Gebeloff, "Many People Taking Antidepressants Discover They Cannot Quit," *New York Times*, April 7, 2018.

41 The education of the New Man is presaged as Aristodemus, a dictator, ascended to power in Cumae and proceeded to provide an education that protected his rule. See Dionysius of Halicarnassus, *Books 6.49–7*, vol. 4 of *Roman Antiquities*, trans. Ernst Cary (Cambridge, Mass.: Harvard University Press, 1943), 7.9.

42 Jessie Bernard, "The Good-Provider Role: Its Rise and Fall," *American Psychologist* 36, no. 1 (1981), 1.

43 Hymowitz, *Manning Up*, 111.

44 For a popular summary of the literature, see Warren Farrell and John Gray, *The Boy Crisis: Why Our Boys Are Struggling and What We Can Do about It* (Dallas: BenBella Books, 2019).

45 Farrell, *The Myth of Male Power*, endorses this view as well, suggesting that male emotionalism, sensitivity, and communion can remedy the problem of increasing female demands on and declining appreciation for what men have to offer.

46 See the studies cited in Regnerus, *Cheap Sex*, 149: "Nowadays young men can skip the wearying detour of getting education and career prospects to qualify for sex. Nor does he have to get married and accept all those costs, including promising to share his lifetime earnings and forgo other women forever. Female sex partners are available without all that. . . . Sex has become free and easy. This is today's version of the opiate for the (male) masses. . . . Climbing the corporate ladder for its own sake may still hold some appeal, but undoubtedly it was more compelling when it was vital for obtaining sex" or, I would add, providing for a family.

47 George F. Gilder, *Sexual Suicide* (New York: Quadrangle, 1973), 40.

12 Dilemmas of Indirection

1 Jacob Joshua Ross, *The Virtues of the Family* (New York: Free Press, 1994), 158. Consider also 158–159: "Parents have the right to a reasonable measure of latitude in providing the welfare benefits owed to their children and to the maximum amount of freedom in fulfilling their duty to educate their children in accordance with their own moral and religious beliefs, provided only that this does not seriously hinder the provision of welfare benefits for their children or prejudice their acceptance of the minimal standards of social morality and good citizenship their society demands." Ross is responding to Jeffrey Blustein, who practically sees the family as an administrative unit of the state and does not see many reasons to respect the integrity of the family. Cf. Ross, *The Virtues of the Family*, 137–60, with Jeffrey Blustein, *Parents and Children: The Ethics of the Family* (New York: Oxford University Press, 1982), 139–61.

2 Much in this celebrated Soviet story is false. Apparently, the boy informed on his father at the behest of his mother, who was upset at the father's adultery and abandonment of the family, and the murder was not at the behest of the

broader family. See Yuri Druzhnikov, *Informer 001: The Myth of Pavlik Moro-zov* (New Brunswick, N.J.: Transaction, 1997).

3 Urie Bronfenbrenner, *Two Worlds of Childhood: U.S. and U.S.S.R.* (New York: Russell Sage Foundation, 1970).

4 See Aristotle, *The Politics* 1313a34–1314a29.

5 Cf. Phillip Kraft, "The Parent-Child Testimonial Privilege: Who's Minding the Kids?" *Family Law Quarterly* 18, no. 4 (1985): 505–43, for conventional liberal treatment of why children should mostly be made to testify against their parents or other family members in court proceedings.

6 Ladislav Holy, *Kinship, Honour and Solidarity: Cousin Marriage in the Middle East* (Manchester: Manchester University Press, 1989).

7 See Hegel, *Philosophy of Right*, paras. 168, 168A; Yenor, *Family Politics*, 76; Scruton, *Sexual Desire*, 311–15.

8 Consistent with feminism, it teaches the equal value boys and girls place on achieving pleasure within their sexual relations and hence the impor-tance of consent. Consistent with the principles of contemporary liberalism, the public teaching on sex education appears to be value free or reflect a state neutrality—concerned only with the supposedly value-neutral goal of promoting health, but it really ratchets sex out of the context where many citizens would have it understood (in light of the holy or the virtuous). Con-sistent with sexual liberation, it teaches that people and sexual acts are all equally valid and permissible, as long as they are consistent with consent and make people happy.

9 Certainly limiting such parental rights in the name of such harms would not survive the liberal wringer.

10 Consider esp. Richard A. Epstein, *How Progressives Rewrote the Constitu-tion* (Washington, D.C.: Cato Institute, 2007), 59–63, who shows that rates of child labor declined before states or congress passed laws proscribing child labor on the voluntary choices of parents.

11 See John Locke, "Some Thoughts Concerning Education," in *Some Thoughts Concerning Education and of the Conduct of the Understanding*, ed. Ruth W. Grant and Nathan Tarcov (Indianapolis: Hackett, 1996), cf. paras. 44–52 with para. 78.

12 Consider the meta-analysis Elizabeth T. Gershoff and Andrew Grogan-Kaylor, "Spanking and Child Outcomes: Old Controversies and New Meta-Analyses," *Journal of Family Psychology* 30, no. 4 (2017): 453–69, who find a link between spanking and adverse child outcomes such as aggressive behav-ior; and Robert E. Larzelere and Den A. Trumbull, "Research on Disciplinary Spanking Is Misleading," American College of Pediatricians, January 2017, acpeds.org.

13 For deep sympathetic defenses of "old obscenity," consider Walter Berns, "Beyond the (Garbage) Pale, or Democracy, Censorship, and the Arts," in *Censorship and Freedom of Expression: Essays on Obscenity and the Law*, ed. Harry M. Clor (Chicago: Rand McNally, 1971), 55–63; Harry M. Clor, *Obscen-ity and Public Morality: Censorship in a Liberal Society* (Chicago: University of Chicago Press, 1969), 224–45.

14 The *Hicklin* standard is related in *Butler v. Michigan*, 352 U.S. 380, 381 (1957).

15 Thus, the oft-noted, exaggerated claim that great works of old obscenity were banned in certain jurisdictions. See Clor, *Obscenity and Public Morality*, 115–16, for a treatment of what had been challenged and why. There have no doubt been overzealous prosecutions based on isolated lines but the general problem is a confusion of obscenity and sin. The wonder is that so few of the great works had been subject to prosecution.

16 No scholars contributed to making these arguments more than Berns, "Beyond the (Garbage) Pale," in Clor, *Censorship and Freedom of Expression*, 57–60; Clor, *Obscenity and Public Morality*, 16–23, 289, n. 53; and David Lowenthal, *No Liberty for License: The Forgotten Logic of the First Amendment* (Dallas: Spence, 1997), 97–99.

17 *Roth v. United States*, 354 U.S. 476 (1957). Much debate may exist about whether the Roth standard differs from the standard put forward in *Miller v. California*, 413 U.S. 15, 24 (1973): works are obscene, "which, taken as a whole appeal to the prurient interest in sex, which portray sexual conduct in a patently offensive way and which, taken, as a whole, do not have serious literary, artistic, political or scientific value." It appears much the same to me. See Clor, *Obscenity and Public Morality*, 44–89, for a profound treatment of the devolution of the *Roth* standards toward greater libertarianism.

18 See Alan Petigny, *The Permissive Society: America, 1941–1965* (New York: Cambridge University Press, 2009), 100–33, to show that the sexual revolution antedates, in part, the final deregulation of obscenity and pornography.

19 Later obscenity cases testify to these truths. Congress sought to protect minors from exposure to pornography in the Communications Decency Act of 1996. Pornographers who allowed 18-year-olds access to obscene material (defined in the vein of *Roth*) would be subject to civil penalties. The Court threw out the law in *Reno v. American Civil Liberties Union*, 521 U.S. 844 (1997) as being vague and overbroad, among other things. This has left pornography for the most part unregulated on the internet. All Americans now have a pornography shop in the form of a cell phone, with a corresponding change in public standards. More tellingly, child pornography is still banned, since its production involves rape and child abuse. (This may change somewhat with proposed liberalizing changes in the age of consent.) However, technology has found, and the Supreme Court has blessed, a loophole: virtual or digitized child pornography, not involving actual children, must not be regulated or prohibited, no matter its alleged effects on public morality. See James R. Stoner Jr., "Freedom, Virtue, and the Politics of Regulating Pornography," in Stoner and Hughes, *The Social Costs of Pornography*, 170–71. See esp. *Osborne v. Ohio*, 495 U.S. 103, 109 (1990); *Ashcroft v. Free Speech Coalition*, 535 U.S. 234 (2002); *United States v. Williams*, 553 U.S. 285 (2008).

20 These arguments are distilled from Charles Rembar, *The End of Obscenity: The Trials of* Lady Chatterley, Tropic of Cancer *and* Fanny Hill *by the Lawyer Who Defended Them* (New York: Bantam Books, 1969); Eberhard Kronhausen and Phyllis Kronhausen, *Pornography and the Law* (New York: Ballantine Books, 1959), 249–76; Albert Ellis, *The American Sexual Tragedy* (New York: Twayne, 1959), 293–302; and Paul Goodman, "Pornography and the Sexual Revolution," in *Utopian Essays and Practical Proposals* (New York: Vintage,

1962), 49ff.; and discussed by those interviewed in Pamela Paul, *Pornified: How Pornography Is Damaging Our Lives, Our Relationships, and Our Families* (New York: Times Books, 2005), 73 and passim.

21 Lowenthal, *No Liberty for License*, 166–67.

22 Richard F. Hettlinger, "Sex, Religion, and Censorship," in Clor, *Censorship and Freedom of Expression*, 89–90.

23 See broadly Rembar, *The End of Obscenity*; and William O. Douglas' dissent in *Roth v. United States*, 354 U.S. at 508–14.

24 See Paul, *Pornified*, 24–25, 58–60, 212–18.

25 See esp. Doidge, *The Brain That Changes Itself*, 93–131, on how pornography creates new, addictive neuroplastic changes as "sexually explicit pictures trigger instinctual responses" but that change over time and can only be triggered by increasingly graphic, novel experiences.

26 Thus the works of Berns, "Beyond the (Garbage) Pale," in Clor, *Censorship and Freedom of Expression*, 60–63; and Clor, *Obscenity and Public Morality*, 163–74, 187–201.

27 Harry M. Clor, "Obscenity and Freedom of Expression," in Clor, *Censorship and Freedom of Expression*, 99–100.

28 This is an interesting spin on the forbidden fruit claim of the sexual liberationists. Obscenity seems to require that there be forbidden fruit and that its viewers sense the naughtiness of the performance. This sets in motion the need to cross ever more boundaries, in ever more perverted ways. Those who consume pornography, for instance, make precisely this claim. See Paul, *Pornified*, 70, 80–88, 91, 178–79, 220–22; and also Tom Wolfe, *I Am Charlotte Simmons* (New York: Farrar, Straus and Giroux, 2004), 92–93, where Ivy Peters asks for porn from his fellow classmates, and when told that the "one-hand magazines" are upstairs claims that he had "built up a tolerance to magazines" and that he now "need[s] videos."

29 Regnerus, *Cheap Sex*, 125–26. Consider also the descriptions in Paul, *Pornified*, passim.

30 Data are drawn from K. Doran, "Industry Size, Measurement, and Social Costs," in Stoner and Hughes, *The Social Costs of Pornography*, 191. Laumann et al., *The Social Organization of Sexuality*, 135, show that 23% of men watch X-rated movies and 16% look at sexually explicit books or magazines in the early 1990s, just before the dawn of the internet. See also Paul, *Pornified*, 53–56, 58–65.

31 Regnerus, *Cheap Sex*, 114–15. See also the surveys treated in Paul, *Pornified*, 15, 116, 174–75.

32 See Regnerus, *Cheap Sex*, 241, n. 26.

33 Pamela Paul, "From Pornography to Porno to Porn: How Porn Became the Norm," in Stoner and Hughes, *The Social Costs of Pornography*, 3.

34 Doidge, *The Brain That Changes Itself*, 93–131; the review of the literature by Todd Love et al., "Neuroscience of Internet Pornography Addiction: A Review and Update," *Behavioral Sciences* 5, no. 3 (2015): 388–433. See also Paul, *Pornified*, 118–19, 218–20.

35 Ana J. Bridges, "Pornography's Effects on Interpersonal Relationships," in Stoner and Hughes, *The Social Costs of Pornography*, 99–105. See also Paul,

Pornified, passim; Manning, "The Impact of Pornography on Women," in Stoner and Hughes, *The Social Costs of Pornography*, 82, who sees relationships with "increased isolation" and greater "risk of sexual and physical abuse," among other things; Dolf Zillmann, "Influence of Unrestrained Access to Erotica on Adolescents' and Young Adults' Dispositions toward Sexuality," *Journal of Adolescent Health* 27, no. 2, supplement 1 (2000): 41–44.

36　See Regnerus and Uecker, *Premarital Sex in America*, 38–39. A corresponding increase in anal and oral sex and in favorable attitudes toward each is seen in the generation before the effective legalization of pornography (1960) and the generation afterward. See Laumann et al., *The Social Organization of Sexuality*, 98–99, 103–8, 157.

37　Paul, *Pornified*, 112–19, 131–33.

38　Clor, *Obscenity and Public Morality*, 170: "People are influenced by what they think others believe and particularly what they think are the common standards of the community. There are few among us whose basic moral beliefs are the result of their own reasoning and whose moral opinions do not require the support from some stable public opinion. The free circulation of obscenity can, in time, lead many to the conclusion that there is nothing wrong with the values implicit in it—since their open promulgation is tolerated by the public. They will come to the conclusion that public standards have changed—or that there are no public standards. Private standards are hard put to withstand the effects of such an opinion."

39　Regnerus, *Cheap Sex*, 123–26; Paul J. Wright and Ashley K. Randall, "Pornography Consumption, Education, and Support for Same-Sex Marriage among Adult U.S. Males," *Communication Research* 41, no. 5 (2014): 665–89.

40　Regnerus and Uecker, *Premarital Sex in America*, 32–33, 39; Paula Kamen, *Her Way: Young Women Remake the Sexual Revolution* (New York: New York University Press, 2000), 74–77, 184–87; Paul, *Pornified*, esp. 77–78, 95–98, 131–33, 150–56, 166–68.

41　While one could claim that liberal advocates of deregulating pornography generally call scientific studies into question when they counter their positions and embrace them when they do not, it is more charitable to claim, on the basis of history, that scientific studies are never finally convincing *to anyone* on these matters. Controversy over the status of scientific claims is coeval with the government studies recommending a repeal of all laws regulating obscene material. The Commission on Obscenity and Pornography (1970) released a report, based on supposedly sound science, that exposure to erotic material did not produce any significant changes in sexual behavior, sexual or nonsexual deviancy, or moral attitudes, while several reputed scholars and several dissenting members called the report into question, including James Q. Wilson, "Violence, Pornography, and Social Science," *The Public Interest* 22 (1971): 45–55; and Clor, "Obscenity and Freedom of Expression," in Clor, *Censorship and Freedom of Expression*, 119–29. Essentially the long-range implications of living in a society more accepting of pornography are difficult, if not impossible, to measure and isolate. From this the advocates of deregulation conclude that no study has ever demonstrated the negative effects of such deregulation; such a truth is hardly exhaustive, since none has demonstrated anything with scientific certainty.

42 Giddens, *The Transformation of Intimacy*, 180.

43 See Regnerus, *Cheap Sex*, 121–23; Giddens, *The Transformation of Intimacy*, 119–21, 178–81, 187–90. The one boundary that remains is violence against women—something that has been generally on the wane during the period of internet pornography. See Gilder, *Sexual Suicide*, 105. Such violence is inconsistent with the theory of the pure relationship, despite the increasing prevalence of such violence in hard-core internet pornography.

44 Stoner, "Regulating Pornography," in Stoner and Hughes, *The Social Costs of Pornography*, 183.

45 Gerard V. Bradley, "The Moral Bases for the Legal Regulation of Pornography," in Stoner and Hughes, *The Social Costs of Pornography*, 215–17.

46 See Andrew Ferguson, "Where the Rubber Meets the Road," *Weekly Standard*, October 28, 2016, washingtonexaminer.com.

47 See *Ginsberg v. United States*, 390 U.S. 629 (1968); Clor, *Obscenity and Public Morality*, 80–84.

48 Bradley, "The Moral Bases," in Stoner and Hughes, *The Social Costs of Pornography*, 216.

49 See *Ginsberg v. United States*, 390 U.S. 629, 639; Clor, *Obscenity and Public Morality*, 80–82, 125.

BIBLIOGRAPHY

Abrams, Paula. *Cross Purposes:* Pierce v. Society of Sisters *and the Struggle over Compulsory Public Education*. Ann Arbor: University of Michigan Press, 2009.

Adams, John. *Autobiography, 1777–1780, Index*. Volume 4 of *Diary and Autobiography of John Adams*. Edited by L. H. Butterfield. Cambridge, Mass.: Belknap Press of Harvard University Press, 1961.

Aggarwal, Sanjay, and Rene Gerrets. "Exploring a Dutch Paradox: An Ethnographic Investigation of Gay Men's Mental Health." *Culture, Health & Sexuality* 16, no. 2 (2014): 105–19.

Albert, Paul R.. "Why Is Depression More Prevalent in Women?" *Journal of Psychiatry & Neuroscience* 40, no. 4 (2015): 219–21.

Alvaré, Helen M. *Putting Children's Interests First in U.S. Family Law and Policy: With Power Comes Responsibility*. Cambridge: Cambridge University Press, 2017.

Annor, Francis, Amanda Wilkinson, and Marissa Zwald. *Undetermined Risk Factors for Suicide among Youth Aged 10–17 Years*. Salt Lake City: Utah Department of Health, 2017. https://health.utah.gov/wp-content/uploads/Final-Report-UtahEpiAid.pdf.

Archer, John. "Sex Differences in Aggression in Real-World Settings: A Meta-Analytic Review." *Review of General Psychology* 8, no. 4 (2004): 291–322.

Aries, Phillippe. *Centuries of Childhood: A Social History of Family Life*. Translated by Robert Baldick. New York: Vintage, 1962.

Aristotle. *Nicomachean Ethics*. Translated by Robert C. Bartlett and Susan D. Collins. Chicago: University of Chicago Press, 2011.

———. *The Politics*. Translated and edited by Carnes Lord. Chicago: University of Chicago Press, 1984.

Arkes, Hadley. "The Family and the Laws." In George and Elshtain, *The Meaning of Marriage*, 116–41.

Arnhart, Larry. *Darwinian Natural Right: The Biological Ethics of Human Nature*. Albany: SUNY Press, 1998.

Augustine. *The City of God*. Translated by Marcus Dods. New York: Modern Library, 1993.

Auletta, Ken. *The Underclass*. New York: Vintage, 1982.

Bailey, William Bacon. *Modern Social Conditions: A Statistical Study of Birth, Marriage, and Divorce*. New York: Century Company, 1906.

Barash, David P. *Out of Eden: The Surprising Consequences of Polygamy*. Oxford: Oxford University Press, 2016.

Barker, M. Ryan. "Gay and Lesbian Health Disparities: Evidence and Recommendations for Elimination." *Journal of Health Disparities, Research and Practice* 2, no. 2 (2008): 91–120.

Beauvoir, Simone de. *The Second Sex*. Translated by H. M. Parshley. New York: Vintage, 1989. First published 1949.

Becker, Elizabeth, and Cotton M. Lindsay. "Assortative Mating or Glass Ceiling: Under-Representation of Female Workers among Top Earners." In *Accounting for Worker Well-Being*, edited by Solomon W. Polachek, 235–67. Bingley, UK: Emerald, 2004.

Belloc, Hilaire. *The Great Heresies*. Rockford, Ill.: Tan Books, 1938.

Benson, Harry, and Stephen MacKay. "The Marriage Gap: The Rich Get Married (and Stay Together). The Poor Don't." Marriage Foundation, Romford, UK, August 2015. https://marriagefoundation.org.uk/wp-content/uploads/2016/06/pdf-07.pdf.

Bernard, Jessie. *The Future of Marriage*. New York: Bantam Books, 1972.

———. "The Good-Provider Role: Its Rise and Fall." *American Psychologist* 36, no. 1 (1981): 1–12.

Berns, Walter. "Beyond the (Garbage) Pale, or Democracy, Censorship, and the Arts." In Clor, *Censorship and Freedom of Expression*, 49–72.

———. "Pornography versus Democracy." *Society* 36, no. 6 (1999): 16–25.

Björkenstam, Charlotte, Gunnar Andersson, Christina Dalman, Susan Cochran, and Kyriaki Kosidou. "Suicide in Married Couples in Sweden: Is the Risk Greater in Same-Sex Couples?" *European Journal of Epidemiology* 31, no. 7 (2016): 685–90.

Black, Dan, Gary Cates, Seth Sanders, and Lowell Taylor. "Demographics of the Gay and Lesbian Population in the United States: Evidence from Available Systematic Data Sources." *Demography* 37, no. 2 (2000): 139–54.

Blackstone, William. *Commentaries on the Laws of England*. Facsimile of the first edition, with an introduction by A. W. Brian Simpson. 2 vols. Chicago: University of Chicago Press, 1979. First published 1765–1769.

Blankenhorn, David. *The Future of Marriage*. New York: Encounter Books, 2007.

Blumstein, Phillip, and Pepper Schwartz. *American Couples: Money, Work, Sex*. New York: William Morrow, 1983.

Blustein, Jeffrey. *Parents and Children: The Ethics of the Family*. New York: Oxford University Press, 1982.

Boaz, David. "Privatize Marriage." *Cato Institute*. April 25, 1997. https://www.cato.org/publications/commentary/privatize-marriage.

Bonald, Louis de. *On Divorce*. Translated and edited by Nicholas Davidson. New York: Routledge, 2017. First published 1801.

Bradley, Gerard V. "The Moral Bases for the Legal Regulation of Pornography." In Stoner and Hughes, *The Social Costs of Pornography*, 199–217.

Brague, Rémi. *The Kingdom of Man: Genesis and Failure of the Modern Project*. Translated by Paul Seaton. Notre Dame: University of Notre Dame Press, 2018.

Brake, Elizabeth. *Minimizing Marriage: Marriage, Morality, and the Law*. New York: Oxford University Press, 2012.

Brandon, Mark E. *States of Union: Family and Change in the American Constitutional Order*. Lawrence: University Press of Kansas, 2013.

Bridges, Ana J. "Pornography's Effects on Interpersonal Relationships." In Stoner and Hughes, *The Social Costs of Pornography*, 89–110.

Brinig, Margaret F., and Douglas W. Allen. "'These Boots Are Made for Walking': Why Most Divorce Filers Are Women." *American Law and Economics Review* 2, no. 1 (2000): 126–69.

Bronfenbrenner, Urie. *Two Worlds of Childhood: U.S. and U.S.S.R.* New York: Russell Sage Foundation, 1970.

Brown, Norman O. *Life against Death: The Psychoanalytical Meaning of History*. Middletown, Conn.: Wesleyan University Press, 1959.

Brownmiller, Susan. *Against Our Will: Men, Women and Rape*. New York: Simon & Schuster, 1975.

Buchanan, Ann, and Anna Rotkirch, eds. *Fertility Rates and Population Decline: No Time for Children?* New York: Palgrave Macmillan, 2013.

Burke, Edmund. "An Appeal from the New to the Old Whigs." In *Further Reflections on the Revolution in France*, edited by Daniel E. Ritchie, 75–201. Indianapolis: Liberty Fund, 1992.

Butler, Judith. *Bodies That Matter: On the Discursive Limits of "Sex."* New York: Routledge, 1993.

———. *Gender Trouble: Feminism and the Subversion of Identity*. 2nd ed. New York: Routledge, 2006.

———. *Undoing Gender*. New York: Routledge, 2004.

Calhoun, Cheshire. "Who's Afraid of Polygamous Marriage? Lessons for Same-Sex Advocacy from the History of Polygamy." *San Diego Law Review* 42, no. 3 (2005): 1023–42.

Carey, Benedict, and Robert Gebeloff. "Many People Taking Antidepressants Discover They Cannot Quit." *New York Times*, April 7, 2018.

Carpenter, Kitt. "Gay Men Used to Earn Less than Straight Men; Now They Earn More." *Harvard Business Review*, December 4, 2017. https://hbr.org/2017/12/gay-men-used-to-earn-less-than-straight-men-now-they-earn-more.

Chasteen, Edgar. "The Mythology of Family Planners." In *Should Parents Be Licensed? Debating the Issues*, edited by Peg Tittle, 281–99. Amherst, N.Y.: Prometheus Books, 2004.

Clor, Harry M., ed. *Censorship and Freedom of Expression: Essays on Obscenity and the Law*. Chicago: Rand McNally, 1971.

———. "Obscenity and Freedom of Expression." In Clor, *Censorship and Freedom of Expression*, 97–129.

———. *Obscenity and Public Morality: Censorship in a Liberal Society*. Chicago: University of Chicago Press, 1969.

———. *Public Morality and Liberal Society: Essays on Decency, Law, and Pornography*. Notre Dame: University of Notre Dame Press, 1996.

Cocca, Carolyn E. *Jailbait: The Politics of Statutory Rape Laws in the United States*. Albany: SUNY Press, 2004.

Cohen, Jacqueline N., and E. Sandra Byers. "Beyond Lesbian Bed Death: Enhancing Our Understanding of the Sexuality of Sexual-Minority Women in Relationships." *Journal of Sex Research* 51, no. 8 (2014): 893–903.

Coontz, Stephanie. *Marriage, a History: From Obedience to Intimacy, or How Love Conquered Marriage*. New York: Viking, 2005.

Costa, Paul T., Jr., Antonio Terracciano, and Robert R. McRae. "Gender Differences in Personality Traits across Cultures: Robust and Surprising Findings." *Journal of Personality and Social Psychology* 81, no. 2 (2001): 322–31.

Cott, Nancy F. *Public Vows: A History of Marriage and the Nation*. Cambridge, Mass.: Harvard University Press, 2000.

Crews, Frederick. *Freud: The Making of an Illusion*. New York: Metropolitan Books, 2017.

Dalrymple, Theodore. *Life at the Bottom: The Worldview That Makes the Underclass*. Chicago: Ivan R. Dee, 2001.

Daly, Martin, and Margo Wilson. *Homicide*. Chicago: AldineTransaction, 1988.

Daynes, Kathryn M. *More Wives than One: Transformation of the Mormon Marriage System, 1840–1910*. Chicago: University of Illinois Press, 2001.

Decter, Midge. "The Boys on the Beach." *Commentary*, September 1980. https://www.commentarymagazine.com/articles/the-boys-on-the-beach/.

Den Otter, Ronald C. *In Defense of Plural Marriage*. New York: Cambridge University Press, 2015.

Dewey, John. *Liberalism and Social Action*. Amherst, N.Y.: Prometheus Books, 1991.

Dionysius of Halicarnassus. *Books 6.49–7*. Volume 4 of *Roman Antiquities*. Translated by Ernst Cary. Cambridge, Mass.: Harvard University Press, 1943.

DiPrete, Thomas A., and Claudia Buchmann. *The Rise of Women: The Growing Gender Gap in Education and What It Means for American Schools*. New York: Russell Sage Foundation, 2013.

Doidge, Norman. *The Brain That Changes Itself: Stories of Personal Triumph from the Frontiers of Brain Science*. New York: Viking, 2007.

Doran, K. "Industry Size, Measurement, and Social Costs." In Stoner and Hughes, *The Social Costs of Pornography*, 185–98.

Dostoevsky, Fyodor. *Notes from Underground*. Translated by Richard Pevear and Larissa Volokhonsky. New York: Vintage Classics, 1994. First published 1864.

Dowling, Colette. *The Frailty Myth: Women Approaching Physical Equality*. New York: Random House, 2000.

Druzhnikov, Yuri. *Informer 001: The Myth of Pavlik Morozov*. New Brunswick, N.J.: Transaction, 1997.

Dvorak, Petula. "The Child-Free Life: Why So Many American Women Are Deciding Not to Have Kids." *Washington Post*. May 31, 2018. https://www.washingtonpost.com/local/the-child-free-life-why-so-many-american-women-are-deciding-not-to-have-kids/2018/05/31/89793784-64de-11e8-a768-ed043e33f1dc_story.html.

Dworkin, Andrea. *Intercourse*. Rev. ed. New York: Basic Books, 2006.

Dworkin, Ronald. *A Matter of Principle*. Cambridge, Mass.: Harvard University Press, 1985.

———. *Taking Rights Seriously*. Cambridge, Mass.: Harvard University Press, 1977.

Eberstadt, Mary. "What Is the Sexual Revolution Doing to Children? The 'Pedophilia Chic,' Then and Now." In *Adam and Eve after the Pill: Paradoxes of the Sexual Revolution*, 66–77. San Francisco: Ignatius Press, 2012.

Eberstadt, Nicholas. "The Demographic Future: What Population Growth—and Decline—Means for the Global Economy." *Foreign Affairs* 89, no. 6 (2010): 54–64.

Edelstein, David. "'No Strings Attached': Corny, Contrived, Conservative." *NPR*. January 21, 2011. https://www.npr.org/2011/01/21/133091157/no-strings-attached-corny-contrived-conservative.

Ehrenreich, Barbara, Elizabeth Hess, and Gloria Jacobs. *Re-Making Love: The Feminization of Sex*. Garden City, N.Y.: Anchor, 1987.

Ellis, Albert. *The American Sexual Tragedy*. New York: Twayne, 1959.

Ellis, Havelock. "The Evolution of Modesty." In Volume 1 of *Studies in the Psychology of Sex*, 1–84. New York: Random House, 1936.

———. "Sex in Relation to Society." In Volume 2 of *Studies in the Psychology of Sex*, part 3. New York: Random House, 1936.

Engels, Frederick. *The Origin of the Family, Private Property and the State*. Edited by Eleanor Burke Leacock. New York: International Publishers, 1972. First published 1884.

Epstein, Richard A. *How Progressives Rewrote the Constitution*. Washington, D.C.: Cato Institute, 2007.

Erickson, Kathleen. "Interview with Betty Friedan." Federal Reserve Bank of Minneapolis. September 1, 1994. https://www.minneapolisfed.org/article/1994/interview-with-betty-friedan.

Falk, Armin, and Johannes Hermle. "Relationship of Gender Differences in Preferences to Economic Development and Gender Equality." IZA Discussion Paper Series No. 12059, Institute of Labor Economics, Bonn, Germany, December 2018.

Faludi, Susan. *Backlash: The Undeclared War against American Women*. Reprint. New York: Broadway, 2006.

———. "Death of a Revolutionary." *New Yorker*. April 15, 2013. https://www.newyorker.com/magazine/2013/04/15/death-of-a-revolutionary.

Farrell, Warren. *The Myth of Male Power: Why Men Are the Disposable Sex*. New York: Simon & Schuster, 1993.

Farrell, Warren, and John Gray. *The Boy Crisis: Why Our Boys Are Struggling and What We Can Do about It*. Dallas: BenBella Books, 2019.

"Father Blakely States the Issue: Unsigned Editorial in *The New Republic*." In *American Progressivism: A Reader*, edited by Ronald J. Pestritto and William J. Atto, 135–37. . Lanham, Md.: Lexington Books, 2008.

Feinberg, Leslie. *Transgender Liberation: A Movement Whose Time Has Come*. New York: World View Forum, 1992.

Feingold, Alan. "Gender Differences in Personality: A Meta-Analysis." *Psychological Bulletin* 116, no. 3 (1994): 429–56.

Ferguson, Andrew. "Where the Rubber Meets the Road." *Weekly Standard*. October 28, 2016. https://www.washingtonexaminer.com/weekly-standard/where-the-rubber-meets-the-road.

Ferguson, Ann. "Gay Marriage: An American and Feminist Dilemma." *Hypatia* 22, no. 1 (2007): 39–57.

Fine, Cordelia. *Delusions of Gender: How Our Minds, Society, and Neurosexism Create Difference*. New York: W. W. Norton, 2010.

Fineman, Martha Albertson. *The Autonomy Myth: A Theory of Dependency.* London: New Press, 2005.

Firestone, Shulamith. *Dialectic of Sex: The Case for Feminist Revolution.* New York: Bantam Books, 1970.

Fischel, Joseph J. "Per Se or Power? Age and Sexual Consent." *Yale Journal of Law & Feminism* 22, no. 2 (2010): 279–341.

Foucault, Michel. *An Introduction.* Volume 1 of *The History of Sexuality.* Translated by Robert Hurley. New York: Vintage, 1978.

———. *The Care of Self.* Volume 3 of *The History of Sexuality.* Translated by Robert Hurley. New York: Vintage, 1988.

———. *The Uses of Pleasure.* Volume 2 of *The History of Sexuality.* Translated by Robert Hurley. New York: Vintage, 1985.

Freud, Sigmund. *Civilization and Its Discontents.* Translated by James Strachey. New York: W. W. Norton, 2005. First published 1930.

Friedan, Betty. *The Feminine Mystique.* New York: W. W. Norton, 1997.

———. *"It Changed My Life": Writings on the Women's Movement.* Cambridge, Mass.: Harvard University Press, 1998.

———. *Life So Far: A Memoir.* New York: Simon & Schuster, 2000.

Friedman, Lawrence M. *The Republic of Choice: Law, Authority, and Culture.* Cambridge, Mass.: Harvard University Press, 1990.

Friedman, Milton. *Capitalism and Freedom.* Chicago: University of Chicago Press, 1962.

Frisch, Morten, and Henrik Brønnum-Hansen. "Mortality among Men and Women in Same-Sex Marriage: A National Cohort Study of 8333 Danes." *American Journal of Public Health* 99, no. 1 (2009): 133–37.

Ganz, Lowell, and Babaloo Mandel, writers. *Parenthood.* Directed by Ron Howard. Universal City, Calif.: Universal Pictures Home Entertainment, 1989

Gates, Gary J. *How Many People Are Lesbian, Gay, Bisexual, and Transgender?* Los Angeles: Williams Institute, 2011. https://williamsinstitute.law.ucla.edu/wp-content/uploads/Gates-How-Many-People-LGBT-Apr-2011.pdf.

"Gender Dysphoria." In *Diagnostic and Statistical Manual of Mental Disorders.* 5th ed. Arlington, Va.: American Psychiatric Association, 2013.

George, Robert P., and Jean Bethke Elshtain, eds. *The Meaning of Marriage: Family, State, Market and Morals.* Dallas: Spence, 2006.

Gershoff, Elizabeth T., and Andrew Grogan-Kaylor. "Spanking and Child Outcomes: Old Controversies and New Meta-Analyses." *Journal of Family Psychology* 30, no. 4 (2017): 453–69.

Giddens, Anthony. *The Transformation of Intimacy: Sexuality, Love and Eroticism in Modern Societies.* Stanford: Stanford University Press, 1992.

Gieseke, Winston, ed. *Team Players: Gay Erotic Stories*. Berlin: Bruno Gmünder, 2013.

Gilbert, Elizabeth. *Eat, Pray, Love: One Woman's Search for Everything across Italy, India and Indonesia*. New York: Riverhead Books, 2006.

Gilder, George F. *Sexual Suicide*. New York: Quadrangle, 1973.

Gilligan, Carol. *In a Different Voice: Psychological Theory and Women's Development*. Cambridge, Mass.: Harvard University Press, 1993.

Giolla, Erik Mac, and Petri J. Kajonius. "Sex Differences in Personality Are Larger in Gender Equal Countries: Replicating and Extending a Surprising Finding." *International Journal of Psychology* 54, no. 6 (2019): 705–11.

Glendon, Mary Ann. *Abortion and Divorce in Western Law*. Cambridge, Mass.: Harvard University Press, 1987.

———. *The Transformation of Family Law: State, Law, and Family in the United States and Western Europe*. Chicago: University of Chicago Press, 1989.

Goldberg, Steven. *The Inevitability of Patriarchy*. New York: William Morrow, 1973.

Goldman, David P. *How Civilizations Die (and Why Islam Is Dying Too)*. Washington, D.C.: Regnery, 2011.

Goodman, Paul. "Pornography and the Sexual Revolution." In *Utopian Essays and Practical Proposals*, 69–96. New York: Vintage, 1962.

Graugaard, Christian, Annamaria Giraldi, Morten Frisch, Lene Eplov Falgaard, and Michael Davidson. "Self-Reported Sexual and Psychosocial Health among Non-Heterosexual Danes." *Scandinavian Journal of Public Health* 43, no. 3 (2015): 309–14.

Grawe, Nathan D. *Demographics and the Demand for Higher Education*. Baltimore: Johns Hopkins University Press, 2017.

Greer, Germaine. *The Female Eunuch*. London: Book Club Associates, 1970.

———. *Sex and Destiny: The Politics of Human Fertility*. New York: Harper & Row, 1984.

Guimond, Serge, Nyla R. Branscombe, Sophie Brunot, Abraham P. Buunk, Armand Chatard, Michel Désert, Donna M. Garcia, Shamsul Haque, Delphine Martinot, and Vincent Yzerbyt. "Culture, Gender, and the Self: Variations and Impact of Social Comparison Processes." *Journal of Personality and Social Psychology* 92, no. 6 (2007): 118–34.

Gurstein, Rochelle. *The Repeal of Reticence: A History of America's Cultural and Legal Struggles over Free Speech, Obscenity, Sexual Liberation, and Modern Art*. New York: Hill and Wang, 1998.

Haas, Ann P., Mickey Eliason, Vickie M. Mays, Robin M. Mathy, Susan D. Cochran, Anthony R. D'Augelli, Morton M. Silverman, et al. "Suicide and Suicide Risk in Lesbian, Gay, Bisexual, and Transgender Populations: Review and Recommendations." *Journal of Homosexuality* 58, no. 1 (2011): 10–51.

Hakim, Catherine. "Economies of Desire: Sexuality and the Sex Industry in the 21st Century." *Institute for Economic Affairs* 35, no. 3 (2015): 329–48.

———. "The Male Sexual Deficit: A Social Fact of the 21st Century." *International Sociology* 30, no. 3 (2015): 314–35.

Hales, Diane. *Just Like a Woman: How Gender Science Is Redefining What Makes Us Female*. New York: Bantam Books, 1999.

Halkitis, Perry N. "Discrimination and Homophobia Fuel the HIV Epidemic in Gay and Bisexual Men." *Psychology and AIDS Exchange Newsletter*, April 2012. https://www.apa.org/pi/aids/resources/exchange/2012/04/discrimination-homophobia.

Halperin, David M. *Saint Foucault: Towards a Gay Hagiography*. New York: Oxford University Press, 1995.

Harrington, Michael. *The Other America: Poverty in the United States*. New York: Penguin, 1962.

Hartog, Hendrik. *Man and Wife in America: A History*. Cambridge, Mass.: Harvard University Press, 2000.

Hatzenbuehler, Mark L., Anna Bellatorre, Yeonjin Lee, Brian K. Finch, Peter Muenning, and Kevin Fiscella. "Structural Stigma and All-Cause Mortality in Sexual Minority Populations." *Social Science & Medicine* 103 (2014): 33–41.

Hawthorne, Nathaniel. *The Blithedale Romance*. New York: Penguin, 1983. First published 1852.

Hegel, G. W. F. *Elements of the Philosophy of Right*. Edited by Allen W. Wood. Translated by H. B. Nisbet. Cambridge: Cambridge University Press, 1991.

Hendel, Charles William. *Citizen of Geneva: Selections from the Letters of Jean-Jacques Rousseau*. Oxford: Oxford University Press, 1937.

Herrell, Richard, Jack Goldberg, William R. True, Visvanathan Ramakrishnan, Michael Lyons, Seth Eisen, and Ming T. Tsuang. "Sexual Orientation and Suicidality: A Co-Twin Control Study in Adult Men." *Archives of General Psychiatry* 56, no. 10 (1999): 867–74.

Hettlinger, Richard F. "Sex, Religion, and Censorship." In Clor, *Censorship and Freedom of Expression*, 73–96.

Hewlett, Sylvia Ann. *Creating a Life: Professional Women and the Quest for Children*. New York: Talk Miramax Books, 2002.

Hirshman, Linda. "Homeward Bound." *American Prospect*, November 21, 2005. https://prospect.org/article/homeward-bound-d2.

Hitchens, Peter. *The Abolition of Britain: From Winston Churchill to Lady Diana*. San Francisco: Encounter Books, 2000.

Holleran, Andrew. *Dancer from the Dance*. New York: Harper Perennial, 2001. First published 1978.

Holy, Ladislav. *Kinship, Honour and Solidarity: Cousin Marriage in the Middle East*. Manchester: Manchester University Press, 1989.

Horwitz, Steven. *Hayek's Modern Family: Classical Liberalism and the Evolution of Social Institutions.* New York: Palgrave Macmillan, 2015.

Houellebecq, Michel. *Atomised.* Translated by Frank Wynne. New York: Vintage, 2001. First published 1999.

———. *Whatever.* Translated by Paul Hammond. London: Serpent's Tail, 1998. First published 1994.

Hume, David. "Of Polygamy and Divorces." In *Essays Moral, Political and Literary,* edited by Eugene F. Miller, 181–190. Rev. ed. Indianapolis: Liberty Fund, 1987.

Hunter, Nan D. "Marriage, Law, and Gender: A Feminist Inquiry." *Law & Sexuality: A Review of Lesbian and Gay Legal Issues* 1 (1991): 9–30.

Huxley, Aldous. *Brave New World.* New York: Harper Perennial, 1986. First published 1932.

Hyde, Janet Shibley. "Gender Similarities and Differences." *Annual Review of Psychology* 65 (2014): 373–98.

Hymowitz, Kay S. *Manning Up: How the Rise of Women Has Turned Men into Boys.* New York: Basic Books, 2011.

"Increased Aid for Mothers and Children and Changes in Divorce Law." *American Review on the Soviet Union* 6 (1944): 69–76.

Jefferson, Thomas. "Bill to Enable Tenants in Fee Tail to Convey their Lands in Fee Simple." In *The Papers of Thomas Jefferson,* vol. 1, *1760–1776,* edited by Julian P. Boyd, 560–62. Princeton: Princeton University Press, 1950.

———. "Jefferson to George Wythe, August 13, 1786." in *The Papers of Thomas Jefferson,* vol. 10, *22 June–31 December 1786,* edited by Julian P. Boyd, 243–45. Princeton: Princeton University Press, 1954.

Jeffreys, Sheila. *Anticlimax: A Feminist Perspective on the Sexual Revolution.* London: Women's Press, 1990.

———. *Gender Hurts: A Feminist Analysis of the Politics of Transgenderism.* London: Routledge, 2014.

Kamen, Paula. *Her Way: Young Women Remake the Sexual Revolution.* New York: New York University Press, 2000.

Kant, Immanuel. *Perpetual Peace and Other Essays.* Translated by Ted Humphrey. Indianapolis: Hackett, 1983.

Kautz, Steven. *Liberalism and Community.* Ithaca: Cornell University Press, 1995.

Kendi, Ibram X. *Stamped from the Beginning: The Definitive History of Racist Ideas in America.* New York: Nation Books, 2016.

Kersten, Katherine. "Transgender Conformity." *First Things,* December 2016. https://www.firstthings.com/article/2016/12/transgender-conformity.

Khazan, Olga. "The More Gender Equality, the Fewer Women in STEM." *The Atlantic,* February 18, 2018. https://www.theatlantic.com/science/archive/2018/02/the-more-gender-equality-the-fewer-women-in-stem/553592/.

Kimball, Roger. "The Perversions of M. Foucault." *The New Criterion* 11, no. 7 (1993): 10.

Kinsey, Alfred C., Wardell B. Pomeroy, and Clyde E. Martin. *Sexual Behavior in the Human Male*. Philadelphia: W. B. Saunders, 1948.

Kinsey, Alfred C., Wardell B. Pomeroy, Clyde E. Martin, and Paul H. Gebhard. *Sexual Behavior in the Human Female*. Philadelphia: W. B. Saunders, 1953.

Klein, Ezra. "'Yes Means Yes' Is a Terrible Law, and I Completely Support It." *Vox*, October 13, 2014. https://www.vox.com/2014/10/13/6966847/yes-means-yes-is-a-terrible-bill-and-i-completely-support-it.

Koppelman, Andrew. *The Gay Rights Question in Contemporary American Law*. Chicago: University of Chicago Press, 2002.

Kraft, Phillip. "The Parent-Child Testimonial Privilege: Who's Minding the Kids?" *Family Law Quarterly* 18, no. 4 (1985): 505–43.

Kronhausen, Eberhard, and Phyllis Kronhausen. *Pornography and the Law*. New York: Ballantine Books, 1959.

LaFollette, Hugh. "Licensing Parents." In *Should Parents Be Licensed? Debating the Issues*, edited by Peg Tittle, 51–63. Amherst, N.Y.: Prometheus Books, 2004.

Lakoff, Robin Tolmach. *Language and Woman's Place: Text and Commentaries*. Edited by Mary Bucholtz. Rev. ed. New York: Oxford University Press, 2004.

Laqueur, Walter. *Putinism: Russia and Its Future with the West*. New York: Thomas Dunne Books, 2015.

Lasch, Christopher. *Haven in a Heartless World: The Family Besieged*. New York: W. W. Norton, 1995.

Last, Jonathan V. *What to Expect When No One's Expecting: America's Coming Demographic Disaster*. New York: Encounter Books, 2013.

Laumann, Edward O., John H. Gagnon, Robert T. Michael, and Stuart Michaels. *The Social Organization of Sexuality: Sexual Practices in the United States*. Chicago: University of Chicago Press, 1994.

Lawrence, D. M., David M. Fergusson, L. John Horwood, and Annette L. Beautrais. "Is Sexual Orientation Related to Mental Health Problems and Suicidality in Young People?" *Archives of General Psychiatry* 56, no. 10 (1999): 876–80.

Layden, Mary Anne. "Pornography and Violence: A New Look at the Research." In Stoner and Hughes, *The Social Costs of Pornography*, 57–68.

Lee, Ang, dir. *Ice Storm*. Century City, Calif.: Fox Searchlight, 1997.

Lefkovitz, Alison. *Strange Bedfellows: Marriage in the Age of Women's Liberation*. Philadelphia: University of Pennsylvania Press, 2018.

Lefort, Claude. *The Political Forms of Modern Society: Bureaucracy, Democracy, Totalitarianism*. Edited by John B. Thompson. Cambridge, Mass.: MIT Press, 1986.

Legato, Marianne J. *Why Men Never Remember and Women Never Forget*. New York: Rodale, 2005.

Legutko, Ryszard. *The Demon in Democracy: Totalitarian Temptations in Free Societies*. Translated by Teresa Adelson. New York: Encounter Books, 2016.

Levy, David. *Love and Sex with Robots: The Evolution of Human-Robot Relationships*. New York: Harper Perennial, 2008.

Lewis, C. S. *The Abolition of Man*. New York: Touchstone, 1996. First published 1943.

Lindsey, Ben B., and Wainwright Evans. *The Companionate Marriage*. New York: Boni and Liveright, 1927.

Lippa, Richard A. "Sex Differences in Personality Traits and Gender-Related Occupational Preferences across 53 Nations: Testing Evolutionary and Social-Environmental Theories." *Archives of Sexual Behavior* 39, no. 3 (2010): 619–36.

———. "Sex Differences in Sex Drive, Sociosexuality, and Height across 53 Nations: Testing Evolutionary and Social Structural Theories." *Archives of Sexual Behavior* 38, no. 5 (2009): 631–51.

Locke, John. *Essay Concerning Human Understanding*. Edited by Peter Nidditch. Oxford: Clarendon Press, 1979. First published 1689.

———. "First Treatise." In *Two Treatises of Government*, edited by Peter Laslett, 141–264. 2nd ed. Cambridge: Cambridge University Press, 1988. First published 1689.

———. "Some Thoughts Concerning Education." In *Some Thoughts Concerning Education and of the Conduct of the Understanding*, edited by Ruth W. Grant and Nathan Tarcov, 7–161. Indianapolis: Hackett, 1996. First published 1693.

Longman, Phillip. *The Empty Cradle: How Falling Birthrates Threaten World Prosperity and What to Do about It*. New York: Basic Books, 2004.

Love, Todd, Christian Laier, Matthias Brand, Linda Hatch, and Raju Hajela. "Neuroscience of Internet Pornography Addiction: A Review and Update." *Behavioral Sciences* 5, no. 3 (2015): 388–433.

Lowenthal, David. *No Liberty for License: The Forgotten Logic of the First Amendment*. Dallas: Spence, 1997.

Lowry, Lois. *The Giver*. Boston, Mass.: Houghton Mifflin, 1993.

Lukianoff, Greg, and Jonathan Haidt. *The Coddling of the American Mind: How Good Intentions and Bad Ideas Are Setting Up a Generation for Failure*. New York: Penguin, 2019.

Lundberg, Ferdinand, and Marynia F. Farnham. *Modern Woman: The Lost Sex*. New York: Harper, 1947.

Maccoby, Eleanor E. *The Two Sexes: Growing Up Apart, Coming Together*. Cambridge, Mass.: Belknap Press of Harvard University Press, 1998.

Mac Donald, Heather. *The Diversity Delusion: How Race and Gender Pandering Corrupt the University and Undermine Our Culture*. New York: St. Martin's Press, 2018.

Macedo, Stephen. "Homosexuality and the Conservative Mind." *Georgetown Law Journal* 84 (1995–1996): 261–300.

MacKinnon, Catharine A. *Sexual Harassment of Working Women: A Case of Sex Discrimination*. New Haven: Yale University Press, 1979.

———. *Toward a Feminist Theory of the State*. Cambridge, Mass.: Harvard University Press, 1989.

Madison, James. "Federalist 10." In *The Federalist*, edited by George W. Carey and James McClellan, 42–49. Indianapolis: Liberty Fund, 2001. First published 1787.

Maillard, Kevin Noble. "Beyond Marriage, Blood or Adoption." *New York Times*, June 7, 2012. https://www.nytimes.com/roomfordebate/2012/02/13/family-ties-without-tying-the-knot/beyond-marriage-blood-or-adoption.

Manent, Pierre. *A World beyond Politics: A Defense of the Nation-State*. Translated by Marc LePain. Princeton: Princeton University Press, 2006.

Manning, Jill C. "The Impact of Pornography on Women: Social Science Findings and Clinical Observations." In Stoner and Hughes, *The Social Costs of Pornography*, 69–88.

Mansfield, Harvey C. *Manliness*. New Haven: Yale University Press, 2006.

Marcuse, Herbert. *Eros and Civilization: A Philosophical Inquiry into Freud*. Boston: Beacon, 1966.

———. *One-Dimensional Man: Studies in the Ideology of Advanced Industrial Society*. Boston: Beacon, 1964.

Marquardt, Elizabeth. *Between Two Worlds: The Inner Lives of Children of Divorce*. New York: Three Rivers Press, 2006.

Maslow, Abraham H. "Dominance, Personality and Social Behavior in Women." *Journal of Social Psychology* 10 (1939): 3–39.

———. *Motivation and Personality*. New York: Harper & Row, 1954.

Mathy, Robin M., Susan D. Cochran, Jorn Olsen, and Vickie M. Mays. "The Association between Relationship Markers of Sexual Orientation and Suicide: Denmark, 1990–2001." *Social Psychiatry and Psychiatric Epidemiology* 46, no. 2 (2011): 111–17.

McClain, Linda C. *The Place of Families: Fostering Capacity, Equality, and Responsibility*. Cambridge, Mass.: Harvard University Press, 2006.

McDonagh, Eileen, and Laura Pappano. *Playing with the Boys: Why Separate Is Not Equal in Sports*. New York: Oxford University Press, 2008.

Metz, Tamara. *Untying the Knot: Marriage, the State, and the Case for Their Divorce*. Princeton: Princeton University Press, 2010.

Meyer, Robinson. "We Thought Female Athletes Were Catching Up to Men, but They're Not." *The Atlantic*, August 9, 2012. https://www.theatlantic .com/technology/archive/2012/08/we-thought-female-athletes-were -catching-up-to-men-but-theyre-not/260927/.

Mill, John Stuart. "The Subjection of Women." In *Essays on Equality, Law, and Education*, edited by John M. Robson, 259–340. Volume 21 of *The Collected Works of John Stuart Mill*. Edited by John M. Robson. Toronto: University of Toronto Press, 1984.

Miller, James. *The Passion of Michel Foucault*. New York: Anchor Books, 1994.

Millett, Kate. *Sexual Politics*. Garden City, N.Y.: Doubleday, 1970.

Mintz, Steven, and Susan Kellogg. *Domestic Revolutions: A Social History of American Family Life*. New York: Free Press, 1988.

Mohr, Richard D. *The Long Arc of Justice: Lesbian and Gay Marriage, Equality, and Rights*. New York: Columbia University Press, 2005.

Money, John. *Gendermaps: Social Constructionism, Feminism, and Sexosophical History*. New York: Continuum, 1995.

Montesquieu. *The Spirit of the Laws*. Edited and translated by Anne M. Cohler, Basia C. Miller, and Harold S. Stone. New York: Cambridge University Press, 1989. First published 1748.

Morgan, Catharine, Roger T. Webb, Matthew J. Carr, Evangelos Kontop-antelis, Jonathan Green, Carolyn A. Chew-Graham, Nav Kapur, and Darren M. Ashcroft. "Incidence, Clinical Management, and Mortality Risk Following Self Harm among Children and Adolescents: Cohort Study in Primary Care." *BMJ* 359 (2017), https://doi.org/10 .1136/bmj.j4351.

Morse, Jennifer Roback. "Why Unilateral Divorce Has No Place in a Free Society." In George and Elshtain, *The Meaning of Marriage*, 74–99.

Muehlenhard, Charlene, and Jennifer Schrag. "Nonviolent Sexual Coercion." In *Acquaintance Rape: The Hidden Crime*, edited by Andrea Parrot and Laurie Bechhofer, 115–28. New York: Wiley, 1991.

Muñoz, Vincent Phillip. *God and the Founders: Madison, Washington, and Jefferson*. New York: Cambridge University Press, 2009.

Murray, Charles. *Coming Apart: The State of White America, 1960–2010*. New York: Crown Forum, 2012.

Neal, Patrick. *Liberalism and Its Discontents*. New York: NYU Press, 1999.

Newcomb, Michael E., Adrienne J. Heinz, and Brian Mustanski. "Examining Risk and Protective Factors for Alcohol Use in Lesbian, Gay, Bisexual, and Transgender Youth: A Longitudinal Multilevel Analysis." *Journal of Studies on Alcohol and Drugs* 73, no. 5 (2012): 783–93.

Okin, Susan Moller. "Is Multiculturalism Bad for Women?" In *Is Multiculturalism Bad for Women?* edited by Joshua Cohen, Matthew Howard, and Martha C. Nussbaum, 7–26. Princeton: Princeton University Press, 1999.

———. *Justice, Gender, and the Family*. New York: Basic Books, 1989.

———. *Women in Western Political Thought*. Princeton: Princeton University Press, 1979.

Pangle, Lorraine Smith, and Thomas L. Pangle. *The Learning of Liberty: The Educational Ideas of the American Founders*. Lawrence: University Press of Kansas, 1993.

Parker, Kim, and Wendy Wang. *Modern Parenthood: Roles of Moms and Dads Converge as They Balance Work and Family*. Washington, D.C.: Pew Research Center, 2013. https://www.pewsocialtrends.org/2013/03/14/modern-parenthood-roles-of-moms-and-dads-converge-as-they-balance-work-and-family/.

Patai, Daphne. *Heterophobia: Sexual Harassment and the Future of Feminism*. Lanham, Md.: Rowman & Littlefield, 1998.

Pateman, Carole. *The Sexual Contract*. Stanford: Stanford University Press, 1988.

Patterson, Orlando. "The Social and Cultural Matrix of Black Youth." In *The Cultural Matrix: Understanding Black Youth*, edited by Orlando Patterson, 45–138. Cambridge, Mass.: Harvard University Press, 2015.

Paul, Jay P., Joseph Catania, Lance Pollack, Judith Moskowitz, Jesse Canchola, Thomas Mills, Diane Binson, and Ron Stall. "Suicide Attempts among Gay and Bisexual Men: Lifetime Prevalence and Antecedents." *American Journal of Public Health* 92, no. 8 (2002): 1338–45.

Paul, Pamela. "From Pornography to Porno to Porn: How Porn Became the Norm." In Stoner and Hughes, *The Social Costs of Pornography*, 3–20.

———. *Pornified: How Pornography Is Damaging Our Lives, Our Relationships, and Our Families*. New York: Times Books, 2005.

Petigny, Alan. *The Permissive Society: America, 1941–1965*. New York: Cambridge University Press, 2009.

Phelan, James E., Neil Whitehead, and Philip M. Sutton. "What Research Shows: NARTH's Response to the APA Claims on Homosexuality. A Report of the Scientific Advisory Committee of the National Association for Research and Therapy of Homosexuality." *Journal of Human Sexuality* 1 (2009): 1–121.

Pinker, Susan. *The Sexual Paradox*. New York: Scribner, 2008.

Plato. *The Laws of Plato*. Translated by Thomas L. Pangle. Chicago: University of Chicago Press, 1988.

———. *Phaedrus*. Translated by James H. Nichols Jr. Ithaca: Cornell University Press, 1998.

———. *Plato's Symposium*. Translated by Seth Benardete. Chicago: University of Chicago Press, 2001.

———. *The Republic of Plato*. Translated by Allan Bloom. New York: Basic Books, 1968.

Plutarch. "Life of Lycurgus." In *The Lives of the Noble Grecians and Romans*, translated by John Dryden, 49–73. New York: The Modern Library, n.d.

Popenoe, David. *Disturbing the Nest: Family Change and Decline in Modern Societies*. New Brunswick, N.J.: AldineTransaction, 1988.

Rabinowitz, Dorothy. *No Crueler Tyrannies: Accusation, False Witness, and Other Terrors of Our Times*. New York: Free Press, 2004.

Rahe, Paul A. *The Spartan Regime: Its Character, Origins, and Grand Strategy*. New Haven: Yale University Press, 2016.

Rawls, John. "The Idea of Public Reason Revisited." *University of Chicago Law Review* 64, no. 3 (1997): 765–807.

_____. *Justice as Fairness: A Restatement*. Cambridge: Belknap Press, 2001.

———. *Political Liberalism*. New York: Columbia University Press, 1993.

———. *A Theory of Justice*. Cambridge, Mass.: Belknap Press of Harvard University Press, 1971.

Raymond, Janice G. *The Transsexual Empire: The Making of the She-Male*. Boston: Beacon, 1979.

Raz, Joseph. *The Morality of Freedom*. Oxford: Clarendon Press, 1986.

Regnerus, Mark. *Cheap Sex: The Transformation of Men, Marriage, and Monogamy*. New York: Oxford University Press, 2017.

Regnerus, Mark, and Jeremy Uecker. *Premarital Sex in America: How Young Americans Meet, Mate, and Think about Marrying*. Oxford: Oxford University Press, 2011.

Reher, David S. "Demographic Transitions and Familial Change: Comparative International Perspectives." In Buchanan and Rotkirch, *Fertility Rates and Population Decline*, 22–43.

Reich, Wilhelm. *Listen, Little Man!* Translated by Theodore P. Wolfe. London: Souvenir, 1972. First published 1945.

———. *The Mass Psychology of Fascism*. Translated by Theodore P. Wolfe. New York: Orgone Institute, 1946. First published 1933.

———. *The Sexual Revolution*. Translated by Therese Pol. New York: Touchstone, 1974. First published 1945.

Rembar, Charles. *The End of Obscenity: The Trials of* Lady Chatterley, Tropic of Cancer *and* Fanny Hill *by the Lawyer Who Defended Them*. New York: Bantam Books, 1969.

Rheinstein, Max. *Marriage Stability, Divorce, and the Law*. Chicago: University of Chicago Press, 1972.

Rhoads, Steven E. *Taking Sex Differences Seriously*. New York: Encounter Books, 2004.

Riley, Jason L. *Please Stop Helping Us: How Liberals Make It Harder for Blacks to Succeed*. New York: Encounter Books, 2016.

Robinson, Paul. *The Modernization of Sex: Havelock Ellis, Alfred Kinsey, William Masters and Virginia Johnson*. New York: Harper & Row, 1976.

Roff, Jennifer. "Cleaning in the Shadow of the Law? Bargaining, Marital Investment, and the Impact of Divorce Law on Husbands' Intra-Household Work." IZA Discussion Paper Series No. 10527, Institute of Labor Economics, Bonn, Germany, January 2017.

Rosin, Hanna. *The End of Men and the Rise of Women*. New York: Viking, 2012.

Ross, Jacob Joshua. *The Virtues of the Family*. New York: Free Press, 1994.

Rothbard, Murray N. *The Ethics of Liberty*. New York: NYU Press, 1998.

Rougemont, Denis de. *Love in the Western World*. Translated by Montgomery Belgion. Rev. ed. Princeton: Princeton University Press, 1956.

Rousseau, Jean-Jacques. *Emile, or On Education*. Translated by Allan Bloom. New York: Basic Books, 1979.

———. *The First and Second Discourses*. Edited by Roger D. Masters. Translated by Roger D. Masters and Judith R. Masters. New York: St. Martin's Press, 1978.

———. *On the Social Contract*. Edited by Roger D. Masters. Translated by Judith R. Masters. New York: St. Martin's Press, 1978.

Rubin, Leslie G. *America, Aristotle, and the Politics of a Middle Class*. Waco, Tex.: Baylor University Press, 2018.

Russell, Stephen T., and Kara Joyner. "Adolescent Sexual Orientation and Suicide Risk: Evidence from a National Study." *American Journal of Public Health* 91, no. 8 (2001): 1276–81.

Ryan, Christopher, and Cacilda Jethá. *Sex at Dawn: How We Mate, Why We Stray, and What It Means for Modern Relationships*. New York: Harper, 2010.

Safren, Steven A., and Richard G. Heimberg. "Depression, Hopelessness, Suicidality, and Related Factors in Sexual Minority and Heterosexual Adolescents." *Journal of Consulting and Clinical Psychology* 67, no. 6 (1999): 859–66.

Sandberg, Sheryl. *Lean In: Women, Work, and the Will to Lead*. New York: Alfred A. Knopf, 2013.

Sandel, Michael J. *Democracy's Discontent: America in Search of a Public Philosophy*. Cambridge, Mass.: Belknap Press of Harvard University Press, 1998.

———. *Liberalism and the Limits of Justice*. 2nd ed. New York: Cambridge University Press, 1998.

Satinover, Jeffrey. *Homosexuality and the Politics of Truth*. Ada, Mich.: Baker Books, 1996.

Schaub, Diana J. *Erotic Liberalism: Women and Revolution in Montesquieu's Persian Letters*. Lanham, Md.: Rowman & Littlefield, 1995.

Schmidt, Thomas E. *Straight and Narrow? Compassion and Clarity in the Homosexual Debate*. Downers Grove, Ill.: InterVarsity Press, 1995.

Schmitt, David P. "The Evolution of Culturally-Variable Sex Differences: Men and Women Are Not Always Different, But When They Are . . . It Appears *Not* to Result from Patriarchy or Sex Role Socialization." In *The Evolution of Sexuality*, edited by Todd K. Shackelford and Ranald D. Hansen, 221–56. New York: Springer, 2014.

Schmitt, David P., Anu Realo, Martin Voracek, and Jüri Allik. "Why Can't a Man Be More Like a Woman? Sex Differences in Big Five Personality Traits across 55 Cultures." *Journal of Personality and Social Psychology* 94, no. 1 (2008): 168–82.

Schulhofer, Stephen J. *Unwanted Sex: The Culture of Intimidation and the Failure of Law*. Cambridge, Mass.: Harvard University Press, 1998.

Schwartz, Susan. "An Argument for the Elimination of the Resistance Requirement from the Definition of Forcible Rape." *Loyola of Los Angeles Law Review* 16 (1983): 567–99.

Schwarzer, Alice. *After the Second Sex: Conversations with Simone de Beauvoir*. Translated by Marianne Howarth. New York: Pantheon Books, 1984.

Scruton, Roger. *Sexual Desire: A Philosophical Investigation*. New York: Continuum, 2006.

Sedgwick, Eve Kosofsky. *Epistemology of the Closet*. Berkeley: University of California Press, 1990.

Shanley, Mary Lyndon. *Feminism, Marriage, and the Law in Victorian England*. Princeton: Princeton University Press, 1989.

South, Susan C., Amber M. Jarnecke, and Colin E. Vize. "Sex Differences in the Big Five Model Personality Traits: A Behavior Genetics Exploration." *Journal of Research in Personality* 74 (2018): 158–65.

Spaht, Katherine Shaw. "The Current Crisis in Marriage Laws, Its Origins, and Its Impact." In George and Elshtain, *The Meaning of Marriage*, 213–41.

Stall, Ron, and James Wiley. "A Comparison of Alcohol and Drug Use Patterns of Homosexual and Heterosexual Men: The San Francisco Men's Health Study." *Drug and Alcohol Dependence* 22, nos. 1–2 (1988): 63–73.

Stevenson, Betsey. "The Impact of Divorce Laws on Marriage-Specific Capital." *Journal of Labor Economics* 25, no. 1 (2007): 75–94.

Stevenson, Betsey, and Justin Wolfers. "The Paradox of Declining Female Happiness." *American Economic Journal: Economic Policy* 1, no. 2 (2009): 190–225.

Stoller, Robert J. *Observing the Erotic Imagination*. New Haven: Yale University Press, 1985.

Stoner, James R., Jr. "Freedom, Virtue, and the Politics of Regulating Pornography." In Stoner and Hughes, *The Social Costs of Pornography*, 165–84.

Stoner, James R., Jr., and Donna M. Hughes, eds. *The Social Costs of Pornography: A Collection of Papers*. Princeton: Witherspoon Institute, 2010.

Strassberg, Maura I. "Distinctions of Form or Substance: Monogamy, Polygamy and Same-Sex Marriage." *North Carolina Law Review* 75 (1997): 1501–624.

Strauss, Erwin W. *Phenomenological Psychology: Selected Papers*. New York: Basic Books, 1966.

Strayed, Cheryl. *Tiny Beautiful Things: Advice on Love and Life from Dear Sugar*. New York: Vintage, 2012.

———. *Wild: From Lost to Found on the Pacific Crest Trail*. New York: Vintage, 2013.

Stryker, Susan. "(De)Subjugated Knowledges: An Introduction to Transgender Studies." In *The Transgender Studies Reader*, edited by Susan Stryker and Stephen Whittle, 1–18. New York: Routledge, 2006.

Su, Rong, James Rounds, and Patrick Ian Armstrong. "Men and Things, Women and People: A Meta-Analysis of Sex Differences in Interests." *Psychological Bulletin* 135, no. 6 (2009): 859–84.

Sweeny, JoAnne. "Undead Statutes: The Rise, Fall, and Continuing Uses of Adultery and Fornication Criminal Laws." *Loyola University Chicago Law Journal* 46 (2014): 127–73.

Symons, Donald. *The Evolution of Human Sexuality*. Oxford: Oxford University Press, 1979.

Takayama, Noriyuki, and Martin Werding, eds. *Fertility and Public Policy: How to Reverse the Trend of Declining Birth Rates*. Cambridge, Mass.: MIT Press, 2011.

Tannen, Deborah. *You Just Don't Understand: Women and Men in Conversation*. New York: William Morrow, 1990.

Tavris, Carol. *The Mismeasure of Woman: Why Women Are Not the Better Sex, the Inferior Sex, or the Opposite Sex*. New York: Touchstone, 1992.

Tocqueville, Alexis de. *Democracy in America*. Translated and edited by Harvey C. Mansfield and Delba Winthrop. Chicago: University of Chicago Press, 2000.

Todd, Matthew. *Straight Jacket: How to Be Gay and Happy*. London: Bantam Press, 2016.

Tolstoy, Leo. *Anna Karenina*. Translated by Louise Maude and Aylmer Maude. New York: Everyman's Library, 1992. First published 1878.

Townsend, John Marshall. *What Women Want—What Men Want: Why the Sexes Still See Love and Commitment So Differently*. New York: Oxford University Press, 1998.

Twain, Mark. *A Connecticut Yankee in King Arthur's Court*. New York: Charles L. Webster, 1889.

United States Commission on Civil Rights. *Statement on Affirmative Action*. Washington, D.C.: U.S. Government Printing Office, 1977.

Van Bergen, Diana D., Henny M. W. Bos, Jantine van Lisdonk, Saskia Keuzen-kamp, and Theo G. M. Sandfort. "Victimization and Suicidality among Dutch Lesbian, Gay, and Bisexual Youths." *American Journal of Public Health* 103, no. 1 (2013): 70–72.

Vance, J. D. *Hillbilly Elegy: A Memoir of a Family and Culture in Crisis.* New York: Harper, 2016.

Van Creveld, Martin. "A Woman's Place: Reflections on the Origins of Violence." *Social Research* 67, no. 3 (2000): 825–47.

Vanderheiden, Steve. "Why the State Should Stay out of the Wedding Chapel." *Public Affairs Quarterly* 13, no. 2 (1999): 175–90.

Vidal, Gore. "Some Jews and the Gays." *The Nation*, November 14, 1981. https://www.thenation.com/article/some-jews-gays/.

Ward, Lester F. *Dynamic Sociology, or Applied Social Science.* 2 vols. New York: D. Appleton, 1897. First published 1883.

Washington, George. "Farewell Address." In *George Washington: A Collection*, edited by William B. Allen, 443–69. Indianapolis: Liberty Fund, 1988.

———. "George Washington to James Madison, 31 March 1787." In vol. 1 of *The Founders' Constitution*, 189. Chicago: University of Chicago Press.

Wedgwood, Ralph. "Fundamental Argument for Same-Sex Marriage." *Journal of Political Philosophy* 7, no. 3 (1999): 225–42.

Weinberg, George. *Society and the Healthy Homosexual.* New York: St. Martin's Press, 1972.

Weininger, Otto. *Sex and Character: An Investigation of Fundamental Principles.* Translated by Ladislaus Loeb. Bloomington: University of Indiana Press: 2005. First published in German in 1903 and translated into English in 1906.

Weisberg, Yanna J., Colin G. DeYoung, and Jacob B. Hirsh. "Gender Differences in Personality across the Ten Aspects of the Big Five." *Frontiers in Psychology* 2 (2011), https://doi.org/10.3389/fpsyg.2011.00178.

Wellington, Adrian Alex. "Why Liberals Should Support Same Sex Marriage." *Journal of Social Philosophy* 26, no. 3 (1995): 5–32.

West, Cornel. *Race Matters.* New York: Vintage, 1994.

West, Robin. "Integrity and Universality: A Comment on Ronald Dworkin's Freedom's Law." *Fordham Law Review* 65 (1997): 1313–34.

West, Thomas G. *The Political Theory of the American Founding: Natural Rights, Public Policy, and the Moral Conditions of Freedom.* New York: Cambridge University Press, 2017.

Westman, Jack C. *Licensing Parents: Can We Prevent Child Abuse and Neglect?* New York: Insight Books, 1994.

White, Edmund. *States of Desire: Travels in Gay America.* New York: E. P. Dutton, 1980.

Whitehead, Barbara Dafoe. *The Divorce Culture*. New York: Alfred A. Knopf, 1997.

———. *Why There Are No Good Men Left: The Romantic Plight of the New Single Woman*. New York: Broadway Books, 2003.

Wilcox, W. Bradford. *Soft Patriarchs, New Men: How Christianity Shapes Fathers and Husbands*. Chicago: University of Chicago Press, 2004.

Wilson, E. O. *On Human Nature*. Cambridge, Mass.: Harvard University Press, 1978.

———. *Sociobiology, the New Synthesis*. Cambridge, Mass.: Harvard University Press, 1975.

Wilson, James Q. *The Marriage Problem: How Our Culture Has Weakened Families*. New York: HarperCollins, 2002.

———. "Violence, Pornography, and Social Science." *The Public Interest* 22 (1971): 45–55.

Wittman, Carl. *Refugees from Amerika: The Gay Manifesto*. New York: Red Butterfly, 1970.

Wolf, Naomi. *The Beauty Myth: How Images of Beauty Are Used against Women*. New York: Harper Perennial, 2002.

Wolfe, Tom. *I Am Charlotte Simmons*. New York: Farrar, Straus and Giroux, 2004.

Wolfson, Evan. "Crossing the Threshold: Equal Marriage Rights for Lesbians and Gay Men and the Intra-Community Critique." *New York University Review of Law & Social Change* 21 (1994–1995): 568–615.

Wood, Evan, Sophie Low-Beer, Kim Bartholomew, Monica Landolt, Doug Oram, Michael V. O'Shaughnessy, and Robert S. Hogg. "Modern Antiretroviral Therapy Improves Life Expectancy of Gay and Bisexual Males in Vancouver's West End." *Canadian Journal of Public Health* 91, no. 2 (2000): 125–28.

Wright, Paul J., and Ashley K. Randall. "Pornography Consumption, Education, and Support for Same-Sex Marriage among Adult U.S. Males." *Communication Research* 41, no. 5 (2014): 665–89.

Xenophon. "*The Constitution of Sparta*." in *The Shorter Writings*, edited by Greg McBrayer, translated by Catherine S. Kuiper and Susan Collins, 107–125. Ithaca, N.Y.: Agora Press, 2018.

Yenor, Scott. *David Hume's Humanity: The Philosophy of Common Life and Its Limits*. New York: Palgrave Macmillan, 2016.

———. *Family Politics: The Idea of Marriage in Modern Political Thought*. Waco, Tex.: Baylor University Press, 2011.

———. "Toward Plural Marriage: Understanding and Countering the Liberal Wringer." *Public Discourse*, December 7, 2015. https://www.thepublicdiscourse.com/2015/12/15908/.

Zillmann, Dolf. "Influence of Unrestrained Access to Erotica on Adolescents'
    and Young Adults' Dispositions toward Sexuality." *Journal of Adolescent
    Health* 27, no. 2, supplement 1 (2000): 41–44.

INDEX

abolition of marriage or family: how contemporary liberalism points to, 41, 46, 47–50, 54–58; how feminism points to, 23, 28, 33–34, 106–7, 115–16, 211; how sexual liberationists point to, 73–76; how Sexual Revolution points to, x

abortion, 9; importance to feminism, 22–23, 112–13; *see also* contraception

Aristotle: on decline of regimes, 4, 133, 284n11; on the mixed regime, 4–5, 8; on the nature of social science, 296n14; on population decline, 184, 312–13n40; on regimes 2–3

Augustine, 3

Beauvoir, Simone de: on confrontation with Friedan's moderate feminism, 36–37, 114–18; on contraception, 22, 196; Founding Mother of second wave feminism, 19, 25–26, 35, 109–10, 267, 285n6; Firestone radicalizes, 28–31; on love, 235–36; scientific critique of, 87ff., 93, 99; on women being made the second sex, 17, 19–24

birth control: *see* contraception

Boland, Louis de, traditional argument against divorce 219–21; *see also* divorce

Burke, Edmund, 138–39

Butler, Judith: transgenderism and, 32–35, 286n24; truth unrelated to reality, 88–90

childhood sexuality: age of consent laws, 211–15; how feminism promotes, 27, 32, 114; sexual liberation promotes, 62

Clinton, Hillary, 234

Clor, Harry, 256; on pornography, 69, 257; on public morality, 128, 327n38

consent, 8, 12, 77–78, 171, 191; affirmative, 204–11; age of consent laws, 129, 211–15; contested nature of, 42, 132, 139, 201–3, 207–8, 216–17, 225; and divorce, 215–24; and sex, 65, 146, 206–8

liberalism, 47–50; on the fifty-fifty
society, 27, 83, 89, 93; as under-
laborer, 25
Old Wisdom: on divorce, 219; on
logic of sex, 210–11; Montesquieu's
speculations on crimes against nature,
185ff., 313n50; on need to unearth, x,
10, 244; on obscenity, 253ff.

parental licensing: *see* contemporary
liberalism, blind spots in
parental rights, 13; abuse and neglect,
246–47; center of indirect policy,
164–73, 244, 246–53; child informers,
248–49; relation to education, 166–68,
247–48; under threat by rolling
revolution, 36, 42
perversions: akin to heresy, 69; examples
of, 69–70, 274
Plato: import of cave image, 3, 84; and
abolition of family, 37; on *eros*, 158–59
plural marriage: arguments against,
278–79; how proscriptions on cannot
survive liberal wringer, 44–45, 52–53,
128
polygamy: *see* plural marriage
population decline, 103, 189–99, 244
pornography: effects of on character
and mind, 256–59; and children,
213–14, 261; liberal wringer, 71–72,
254–56; policies to regulate, 259–63;
public morality, 212, 253–63; sexual
liberation, 62, 69–70, 78, 100, 148,
236, 254; *see also* perversions
privatizing marriage: *see* libertarianism
prostitution, arguments against, 276–77;
how proscriptions on cannot survive
liberal wringer, 42–44; within sexual
liberation theory, 67, 73, 78
pure relationship, 11; defined, 130;
plastic sexuality, 154, 168; the secret
goal of contemporary liberalism,
130–32, 134, 142, 172, 216–18, 227,
235, 250–51, 256, 259, 263, 268

queer theory, 32–33, 35, 36; *see also*
Michel Foucault

rape: affirmative consent, 149, 203–11;
feminist view of, 204, 209, 211,
276; and the legislation of morality,
204–5, 208; promises from sexual
liberationists, 142–43; statutory, 20,
142, 213–14, 225, 262; "totality of
circumstances," 206–7, 208–10, 273–74
Rawls, John, 290n36–37; on family as
a fundamental institution, 47–48;
inadequacies in as seen by feminists,
55, 290n29
Reich, Wilhelm, 64; as sexual
liberationist, 73–75, 143
reigning civil rights ideology: defined,
12, 176, 202; arising from feminism,
116, 176–77, as applied to claims of
homophobia, 177–79, 188; problems
endemic to, 179–82, 184–85, 189,
276; *see also* Okin, Susan Moller, on
the fifty-fifty society
retail feminism, relation to radical
feminism, 17–18, 25, 27, 31, 36–37,
56–58, 94, 109, 245
rolling revolution: contemporary
liberalism and, 39–41, 43–47, 53, 59,
134; defined, x, 9, 15–16; exposing the
limits of, 12, 92, 106; feminism and,
17, 27–32, 35, 92, 112, 119; sexual
liberation, 62, 73–77; *see also* sexual
liberation
Rosin, Hannah: rise of women, 97, 141,
233–38; on sex differences, 100–101;
on sexual indifference, 195
Rousseau, Jean-Jacques, 25, 101, 129,
150–51, 236, 238

Schulhofer, Stephen J.: *see* rape,
affirmative consent
Scruton, Roger, 89; on perversion, 69
sex: limits to modernized view of,
143–58, 293n4; logic of, 151–52,
208–10, 212, 276; modernized view
of, 63–72, 78, 143
sex and gender: relationship as conceived
by evolutionists, 84–87; relationship
between, 83–84, 84–90; relationship
between as conceived by first-wave